And Jacob Digged a Well

Also by Theodore M. Snider

The Continuity of Salvation: A Study of Paul's Letter to the Romans
The Divine Activity: An Approach to Incarnational Theology

And Jacob Digged a Well

Faith in the Twenty-First Century

THEODORE M. SNIDER

iUniverse, Inc.
Bloomington

And Jacob Digged a Well
Faith in the Twenty-First Century

Copyright © 2012 by Theodore M. Snider.

All rights reserved. No part of this book may be used or reproduced by any means, graphic, electronic, or mechanical, including photocopying, recording, taping or by any information storage retrieval system without the written permission of the publisher except in the case of brief quotations embodied in critical articles and reviews.

iUniverse books may be ordered through booksellers or by contacting:

iUniverse
1663 Liberty Drive
Bloomington, IN 47403
www.iuniverse.com
1-800-Authors (1-800-288-4677)

Because of the dynamic nature of the Internet, any web addresses or links contained in this book may have changed since publication and may no longer be valid. The views expressed in this work are solely those of the author and do not necessarily reflect the views of the publisher, and the publisher hereby disclaims any responsibility for them.

Any people depicted in stock imagery provided by Thinkstock are models, and such images are being used for illustrative purposes only.
Certain stock imagery © Thinkstock.

ISBN: 978-1-4759-1697-3 (sc)
ISBN: 978-1-4759-1696-6 (hc)
ISBN: 978-1-4759-1695-9 (ebk)

Library of Congress Control Number: 2012907572

Printed in the United States of America

iUniverse rev. date: 04/27/2012

In memory of
my father, Earl Maurice Snider (1917-1962),
who taught me to ask questions
In honor of
all those who are not afraid to ask difficult questions

CONTENTS

CONTENTS

PREFACE

"All theology is biography, for it is in the context of one's life that we can truly understand the shaping of theologians and their thoughts."

—Luis G. Pedraja

My Struggles

The subject of christology has been a struggle for the church from the very beginning. It has resulted in divisions, crusades, inquisitions, persecutions, and a wide range of creeds. Governments have been involved in shaping the argument as they have sought to use the church to shape their own policies. From its very beginning, differences between Christians have created numerous denominations, with each group denying validity to the others. Each group claims that it possesses the truth—a truth revealed to them, a particular turn on belief that they alone rightly proclaim.

My personal struggles with christology have been paramount for about forty years, although many of the questions shaping this struggle were present even in my youth. After several years of study and wrestling with theological concepts, my dissatisfaction with the usual ways of thinking has not been abated. Through a lifetime of questioning, I have lived up to one of my father's aphorisms: "Don't believe anything you hear and only half of what you see." I have therefore been prone to ask, "How do you know?" In an article about her friend and fellow journalist David Halberstam, Anna Quindlen wrote, "His totem was the question mark."[1] The same can be said of me.

I was born into a Christian family. As an infant, I was dedicated to God's service, just as Samuel had been centuries before. I cannot remember a time when the church and its faith were not a part of my life. And, therefore, there can be no doubt that I have been deeply influenced by Christian thought and its particular contributions to understanding the world. As a child, I was always asking "religious" questions of my parents, grandparents, and teachers. Where did God come from? Did Cain and Abel marry their sisters? When the children of Adam and Eve went to a distant place to find mates, where did these other people come from? How could anyone live to be hundreds of years old? Since God confused the languages of people at the Tower of Babel, is God afraid that humans can *really* be like God? And very puzzling was the whole Noah thing. How did he build a boat big enough to get all those animals on it? How did he get animals from all over the world in such a short time? And how did he feed them? Of course, the New Testament stories were just as confusing. If Jesus was God, whom did he pray to? And why did he need to pray at all?

One of the stories I remember being told as a child was about the three blind men who were each touching an elephant. The first man was holding the elephant's leg. He said, "I think an elephant is like the trunk of a great tree." The second man disagreed. While holding the elephant's trunk he said, "I believe an elephant is like a large snake." The third man, touching the side of the elephant, said that they were both wrong. "An elephant is like a great wall," he exclaimed. In a certain sense, I learned, each blind man was both right and wrong—without ever realizing they were all touching the same elephant. I was taught that there is always more than one way of looking at things, and therefore I should be slow in judging others and their opinions. "Yes, but . . ." became my mantra.

As I grew older, I continued to ask questions. In reading the creation story, it is odd that after Adam and Eve have eaten from the forbidden fruit God cannot find them. How could that be true? Hearing a sermon on the destruction of Sodom and Gomorrah it sounded very "human" of God to be open to negotiating the terms of their salvation or destruction. That meant that God could change his mind. After the Israelites were delivered from Egyptian slavery, God became angry with them and was ready to destroy them because of their idolatry—but Moses talked God out of that decision. I could never understand—even at a much younger age—how God could order the wholesale slaughter of innocent men, women, children, and even animals when these were part of the opposition. Nor could I understand how a God that was in control of everything—and supposedly loved humanity—could be so jealous and vengeful. At worst, my questioning was answered with, "It's a mystery!" At a better level, I was told that these things needed interpretation. But, how could I be expected to accept the Bible as the literal word of God and at the same time be allowed to interpret despicable scenes away. To my young mind, this seemed dishonest.

By early grade school, I began questioning Christian theological arguments for the exclusivist particularity of Christian faith against all other faith stances. This questioning of such a key aspect of the faith has been true ever since—even when as a young pastor I proclaimed with evangelical fervor, "You must be born again!"

Having a favorite aunt and uncle who were devout Catholics, I questioned my childhood church's teaching that Catholics were not "true Christians" and would not be welcome in heaven. That seemed to me—at the very young age of seven or eight—to be a highly suspect conclusion and I rejected it. How could someone who was a second mother to me and someone I loved so much not be acceptable to God simply because of the church she attended? And how could God simply reject people who had never even heard about Jesus? That did not seem fair by any standard. My faith in God's love for all people grew largely out of my grandmother Snider's deep faith in God's gracious love—and her gracious love for others. She explained that God loved all of God's children, not just a few. When I think of God, I think of my grandmother.

My developing faith continued to be a source of questioning throughout grade school. I was moved more by "This Is My Father's World" than by "There is a Fountain Filled with Blood." The blood language of Temple sacrifices was difficult to understand. The language of nature and nature's awesome imagery were easier to see and understand. God's powerful presence within what I could experience was truly *incarnational* to me, even before I had ever heard the word. Experience always precedes abstract ideas.

By the age of 12, as a student at Chicago Christian Academy, I was wrestling with the moral question of why God didn't want me (or anyone) to read comic books or listen to popular music. Didn't God have bigger issues to deal with? Besides, music had been so much a part of my life that I couldn't see why all music wasn't acceptable to God—with the proper lyrics, of course. Why was God more concerned about my music than about the persons I met in the inner city missions where my father often preached? And what about the women and men in the nursing homes where our family went to sing and witness? Were not these street people and lonely aging persons more important to God than popular music? In my own youthful way, I questioned if the church had its priorities wrong—or if not, were *God's* priorities wrong? For most of its historical existence—and in my own experience—the Church seems to have focused more on sexuality, right belief, and maintaining the institution than on peace, mercy, and justice issues.

At about this time a nagging question began to find voice. How can a good and loving God allow evil and suffering? The church taught that God *could* prevent suffering, but chooses not to for reasons that our small minds cannot understand. It's a part of the mystery of God, they said. When the question was pushed further, the church's response explained that this was one of the purposes of heaven and hell—to deal out rewards for the good and punishment for the bad. And, of course, the Church hierarchy decided who was good or bad (somewhat like Santa Claus!). (There have always been dissenters and heresies in religion that resisted these pronouncements.) I could accept that to some degree, but it still did not answer the question: if God can make things better now, why not do it? And if the righteous are to be rewarded, why not do it now as well? Most of us have struggled with this in our spiritual journeys.

By the age of 14, I was forced to confront the issue of creation vs. evolution—a struggle that lasted for another five years. I did not do well at all in Mrs. Brown's high school biology class. I continually argued the issue of creationism versus evolution with her—sometimes disrupting the class with it. God could do *anything* that God wanted to do, including creating everything that exists in just six days—but I had trouble believing God could create through evolution over millions of years! And, of course, I argued that there has been nothing new created since then. Because of this conflict between faith and science, I did not take another science class in high school.

In the mid-1950s, I had a large map of the Middle East on my bedroom wall. I was only 15, but it was important for me to see what was taking place and why. Questions arose about why land could be so important to people, especially holy land to religious people. How could one group of people claim another people's property as their own—and defend their taking the land as a biblical promise, or as the result of religious prophecy? Later this question would also include how the land in the United States could be taken from the Native Americans as part of some "manifest destiny."

During my first year of college, my worldview was continually challenged. One day the college chaplain said in a sermon that if heaven was floating around on a cloud all day playing a harp and singing church hymns, he didn't want to go there. While that seems very tame today, it forced me to consider just what heaven might consist of. This would prove to be a meaningful question to discuss with my father over Christmas vacation—when I learned he had spinal cancer.

Despite that, the whole evolution/creation issue continued to challenge me. One day while in the college library, I stumbled onto a magazine article written by a Catholic scholar concerning the vastness of the universe—of God's amazingly complex creation. This was a breakthrough moment that opened a completely new world to me. It was another road on my search for meaning—not only in personal experience but also in how scientific discoveries could be a friend to faith.

From that point on, I tried to discover how these scientific discoveries impact the things we believe. And for the first time, I did not feel "unfaithful" by questioning the articles of traditional belief I had been taught from childhood. I experienced a freedom to nurture and strengthen my faith. As my worldview changed and encompassed a wider circle, so my faith changed and became more inclusive. Just as centuries earlier it was discovered that we do not live on a flat, three-story earth, or that the universe is not geocentric, changed the way we look at the world, it also changed the way we understand God and the God-human and God-nature relationships.

As a junior in college I was introduced to Zen Buddhism and was captivated by what I discovered—all that it had to offer Christians in better understanding our own faith. With that discovery, my world continued expanding. And in discovering truth in another faith tradition, I began to seriously question the infallibility of scripture. I had lived with its authority long enough to question it.

I began questioning the whole intermediary idea. Raised with an unconscious anti-Judaism bias, I was taught that before Jesus came, people did not have direct access to God; they had to go through the priest at the Temple. With the coming of Jesus, that had changed, and we now have direct access to God. I came to see, however, that this could not be the case, at least logically, since the only way to God was now through

Jesus—*another* intermediary. I began looking even more in earnest for a direct path that was also acceptable in the Christian tradition. I kept coming into the same roadblock at each turn.

The more I studied and struggled to understand the Christian tradition, the more I came to see its very human origins. It became apparent that Christianity—and all other religions as well—were cultural products. I could see how religion provides certain psychological and social functions for both the individuals and the larger society in which they participated. But I could no longer affirm with any sense of integrity that they were divinely ordained. Just *how* God was involved in any of the various religious structures remained an open question.

It seems that all previous experiences of struggling with christology came to a head in the issue of this thing called the "Trinity"—and the christology that accompanied it. I had never really understood this fourth-century concept, and the argument that it was a "mystery" was not a satisfactory explanation. When I asked Robert Guthrie, one of my professors at MacMurray College, about this, his response was: "When you understand it, you will understand it." That was not very satisfying, either! It sounded a lot like a Yogi Berra comment. How could I justify a Trinitarian stance over against radical monotheism? How could the Trinity possibly avoid becoming polytheistic?

I grew increasingly uncomfortable with the creeds and, like the moderate Arians of the third and fourth centuries—and countless others ever since—I found a way to recite the creeds by referring to my own meanings. While I tried to understand trinitarianism (and thereby tried to be a "good" Christian), it always seemed to lead to bitheism. Like the early Christians, the third "person" of the Trinity did not pose an issue since it only seemed natural that a "person"—even God—should have an emanating influence or spirit that works beyond the person and usually takes on a life—an identity—of its own in the process. After all these years of being a Christian pastor, I still twinge when we sing hymns and songs about "Jesus, my God," because Jesus is *not* my God. When asked to affirm that Jesus is "my all, my everything," I feel idolatrous.

During my seminary years, there were several times when I experienced the presence of the holy through nature. Walking down the wooded pathway from the library to the dormitory in the late evening, I was filled with what the Jewish theologian Abraham Heschel called "radical amazement." Being separated from my wife and children for three to four days a week left me with a deep loneliness for them. This loneliness was combined with head-swirling information that I was learning both in the classroom and on my own in the library. These two feelings of loneliness and a passion for learning were strangely mingled. Even now, it is difficult to put into words, but looking at the starry sky above and feeling the cool breeze on my face, I had the experience of not being alone. These experiences gave me a sense of being at one with the world and its creator. They were moments in which my personal sense of being and my place in the world were transforming. They were moments in which mystery could find no words, moments in which I was caught up is something greater than myself. Upon reflection, I considered these moments as an experience of the holy. I say "the holy" rather than God because "the holy" is a much broader concept.

In those seminary years, I continued my christological quest, writing my doctoral thesis on the subject of incarnation—of God's continuing activity in the world of persons and nature from the very beginning of creation to the present. I also began looking at how Christians in Marxist countries were struggling to understand and restate faith in that context. This led to an investigation of atheism: How do the conclusions of atheists really differ from that of Christians on moral and eschatological issues?

A few years ago, I led an all-day seminar at the Wesley Foundation on the campus of the University of Illinois. The seminar was "Theological Options" and included a dozen different approaches to Christian faith. At the end of the seminar, one of the U of I professors from the biology department, approached me and said, "I have always felt that I was on the fringe of acceptability since I could not accept a lot of what the tradition teaches. But when you described process theology, I felt that I had finally found a place in the church."

He was expressing what many people are experiencing. Many have moved to the edge and others have moved out of the church because of the church's refusal to deal honestly with the new worldview that years of scientific research has helped to unfold. Many say that they can no longer pretend to believe the strange miracle stories of the Bible. I am among those who find no problem affirming that Jesus had two human parents or that the risen presence of Jesus was, as the Apostle Paul argued, a spiritual experience. While affirming the importance of the biblical story and the gospel proclamation, I also affirm that persons in all places at all times have had some sense of transcending amazement. I have no problem in affirming that Jesus sinned, just like any other human being; and that his "sinlessness" was only in the sacrificial sense, as the writer of Hebrews affirms. I have no problem affirming that the universe has evolved over billions of years. Nor do I have problems affirming that humans may not be the highest form of intelligence in the universe. These things do not, or would not, change the focus of my faith.

Throughout my life, I have been fortunate to find persons who listened seriously to my questions and encouraged me to seek my own answers. Of course, there were those who parroted the standard answers, as well as those who cautioned that we should not doubt the Bible or question God. But those who were instrumental in my faith formation did not feel the need to protect God from my questions and doubts or to keep my faith in a securely tight box. In the questioning, there was the support of tradition even as I was stepping out of it. There were times when there was retreat into old and more secure patterns of thinking, but these times were, in the broader sense, resting periods during which new information was tested and processed. I must admit that it is easier not to question beliefs at a deep level. Surface questioning is not difficult, and is, in fact, generally expected. But to seriously question the foundational issues of belief—that is hard, and I fear that most people leave that kind of questioning to others.

I learned to live with a degree of doubt and uncertainty. Indeed, not knowing is a major impetus to all learning and growth. More than that, it is the lifeblood of a meaningful faith. As Emerson wrote more than a century-and-a-half ago, "foolish consistency is the hobgoblin of small minds." Doubt and uncertainty give us freedom to step into the waters of the unknown and to enter territories that were once forbidden. We were once taught to fear these things since God was threatened by our freedom and our questioning—although just why was never explained. But that fear was simply a way to control our thoughts and behaviors. We can be free, free even from "God"—free of God's wrath over Eve's and our inquiring minds, and of God's disapproval of Babel's search, and ours, for the mind of God.

My purpose in these pages is not to deny God, nor is it to affirm God, since neither statement can be fully demonstrated to be true. My purpose is rather to affirm with Lao Tzu: "the Tao that can be told is not the universal Tao."

Because of my questioning of the church's traditions, I have often found myself more comfortable among—and more challenged by—those who were outside of the church. Many seemed to sense this and were open to share their own questions and doubts, fears and hopes. Without all of the baggage of the institutional church, their nascent faith was refreshing. Not settling for simple religious jargon-encrusted answers, there was an attractive honesty in their struggles. Indeed, I often found more faith outside of the church than within its walls.

The changes taking place in my life have usually come slowly. They occurred as one way of understanding the world was replaced by another. Most of these changes introduced provisional or transitional stepping-stones. They did not offer complete answers, but they did provide what I considered as better answers than the ones I previously held. Over time, it became clear to me that asking about the *factuality* of biblical stories was meaningless. As a pastor, I used and interpreted these stories as stories that contained lessons for life. Over the years, I became less and less interested in formal religion and its cultic practices and more interested in discerning how the church could become a positive social force in breaking down the walls that divide and separate human beings from each other and from nature, and how it could become a life-changing instrument to heal the hurts and alienations of persons.

I confess to being a "believer in exile." Bishop John Shelby Spong describes such a believer as one who "wants to believe but who increasingly lives in exile from the traditional way in which Christianity has heretofore been proclaimed."[2]

In telling its stories, the early church used the images of a flat-earth, three-story universe, even though some of the Greek philosophers/scientists had already rejected such a worldview long before the time of Jesus. Because of its antiquated worldview, the church continues to talk about Christ's coming into the world from above, descending into hell upon his death, and ascending up into the heavens after the resurrection; and many Christians today continue to operate within that ancient worldview, expecting Jesus to return on the clouds from above.

Why should the church be held captive to a worldview that has been out-of-date for over 2,000 years? It is way past time for the church to get its head out of the sands of ancient images and begin to speak in a clear and intellectually honest language. The church must to throw off the restraints of intellectual dishonesty that it places on not only theologians and pastors, but the laity as well. It must take up a sense of wonder once again and realize that many are curious about how to understand God in this "new universe."

Such a change in understanding the world will not come about easily. Indeed, the stronger the commitment to defending the older worldview, the more aggressively the religious and political conflicts will be waged. One need only look at the Middle East conflicts to see how doctrines of Christian, Islamic, and Jewish radicalisms alike are being played out against each other. Biblical prophecies of Armageddon play a major role in the current war against terrorism. Both sides are supported by fundamentalist, literalistic interpretations of apocalyptic holy wars.

If the Church is to have a significant voice in this postmodern, post-Christian world, it will have to undergo a new Reformation far more radical than Christianity has ever experienced before. It will be more radical both because it must deal with the very foundations of its faith tradition, and because things move so much more swiftly today that the faithful will get lost in the sweeping changes.

Many writers have helped me along this journey of faith. These include especially: Leslie Weatherhead, *The Christian Agnostic*; J.B. Philips, *Your God Is Too Small*; J.A.T. Robinson, *Honest to God*; James Pike, *A Time for Christian Candor*; Martin Buber, *I and Thou*; Paul Tillich, *Systematic Theology*; Daniel Day Williams, *The Spirit and Form of Love*; David Ray Griffin, *A Process Christology*; Pierre Tielhard de Chardin, *The Phenomena of Man*; and Norman Pittinger, *Christian Faith and the Question of History*. In the field of science writers like Paul Davies, Brian Greene, Daniel Dennett, and Stephen Hawking have challenged me.

I have been fortunate to be challenged not only by professors like Robert Guthrie and Clark Williamson, my mentors, but also by the questioning members and staff in the churches I have served. These persons were not satisfied with the easy answers and pushed me to a level of honest inquiry that most pastors avoid and run away from.

In my earlier effort to address the issue of Incarnation, I wrote: "Incarnation stands as a witness to our belief that the presence of the Divine is deeply a part of the structures of our existence. This incarnating activity of the Divine in human life and in the physical and social structures of existence is at the very heart of the Christian faith."[3] If this incarnating activity is true beyond the metaphorical level, it is to be seen in every aspect of cosmic reality.

The conclusions I present here are the result of my search for a larger understanding of the world and how new worldviews create new Godviews.

CHAPTER 1

Imagining a World

"Taking evolution seriously forces theology and humankind in general to refrain from fixing truths in unchangeable doctrines."
—Karl Schmitz-Moorman

"The reality you observe depends on what questions you choose to ask."
—Sharon Begley

Transcending Concepts

Einstein once said, "Imagination is more important than knowledge." As the process of reflection produces more information, it also produces more questions. Imagination opens us to new perspectives on current knowledge and reveals new insights. The more I learn, the more I know that I do not know. Imagination is essential in our search for knowledge. Indeed, curiosity and inquiry is the essence of the intellectual life.

Most commonsense thinking is human-centered and earth-centered. Of course, nobody would deny the importance of human beings or the Earth we inhabit. But we tend to focus on a few *thousand* years of human culture rather than taking into account the fifteen *billion* years of the history of the universe. When we think of the world, we tend to focus on planet Earth rather than the billions of galaxies of the observable universe—not to mention the 140 billion or so galaxies in our multiverse. Again, since we are human and live on planet Earth, we are concerned about the things that affect us on a daily basis at the personal level. However, there is more to life than this.

As parents, some of us teach our children to think critically. Our child finds something of interest and we ask them to reflect on their observation. One day as our family was approaching a store, our younger son saw something moving on the sidewalk, and he went over to observe. We followed. It was a large locust struggling for life. As our family stood there looking at this locust through the wondering eyes of a three-year-old, others curiously came to see what we were seeing. "Oh, it's just a bug!" they said and walked off disappointed. But to our younger son, this was a learning moment and for the rest of us it was a teaching moment. Some see the wonder while others see only the mundane. We come to understand reality by means of observation, experience, reflection, interpretation, and response to the concepts and ideas that result. These concepts and ideas in turn become the basis for how we view the world around us—and within us. This is not a once-for-all phenomenon, but a process that continues occurring indefinitely.

Over time, transcending concepts develop out of common human experiences. These include theories, principles, laws, or dogmas that are considered true beyond the present moment. These become guiding rules or standards by which all other experience is measured. In the best of our conclusions, there remains an openness for further clarification or development—or, in cases where these are demonstrated to be no longer relevant or "true," they are reinterpreted, abandoned, or replaced. The longer these transcending concepts are embedded in our cultures and traditions, the more worth or value that is attributed to them. The more these are vested as "truth," the more they are considered to be worth living and dying for. This is true not only for religious transcending concepts, but for all other areas of knowledge.

The search for transcending concepts involves all human beings at some level of awareness. We want to know the best possible explanation for what we are experiencing and for the newness we are discovering. Therefore, transcending concepts exist to communicate *meaning*, not necessarily history or "fact." We cannot live in a world devoid of meaning. Whether that meaning comes from a divine, physical, or human source, it results in direction and purpose for life. There are many who maintain that the purpose of the cosmos is the human experience. It is not difficult to demonstrate how deeply this narcissism is embedded in our thinking. Nor is it difficult to show how this narcissism has negatively influenced existence.

Transcending concepts can be restrictive and destructive when they matter more than truth itself. The more these embedded concepts are believed to be unchangeable, the more resistance there is to changing them—even when new evidence demonstrates that they are inadequate or no longer true. From our youngest years, we are taught—in a variety of ways—to value "the traditions"—traditions found in the family, clan, region, nation, religion, science, etc. We normally learn to accept these honored truths without question. To question them, regardless of our age or other circumstance, brings down upon us, in one way or another, "the wrath of the Gods."

A major shift in the way we view the world and ourselves occurs when new knowledge radically changes our understandings. This is a constant process: we both make changes and are changed. We create and are created by the world. Thus, "our religious experiences and cultural biases, our upbringing, language, and socioeconomic status all affect the way we envision and express our faith."[4]

The search for truth never ends. This seems to be the only attitude that is sufficiently humble and therefore worthy of our allegiance. While it does not do this perfectly, science has a methodology that is error correcting, a "mechanism for keeping us honest in spite of our chronic tendencies to project, to misunderstand, to deceive ourselves and others."[5] For this reason, any honest search for truth will involve a healthy dose of skepticism.

Challenges to Old Truths

We live in a complex time during which our society is undergoing unprecedented change. To discover truth, we must be willing to question everything and to give a fair hearing to differing points of view. Those who are open-minded and asking questions are the clavigers who hold the keys to a positive future.

A problem arises when what is believed is so attached to a currently secure way of thinking that it is difficult, if not impossible, to accept new knowledge without it threatening to destroy an understanding of life as we have known it. New knowledge requires new ways of relating to the world. New information requires new transcending concepts or, at the very least, a new way of interpreting the older ones. That is not easy, since change brings confusion and usually results in fear. We are experiencing this today as our nation is being divided by a culture of fear. It is clear that we face tremendous challenges, but if we do not give in to these fears, we may discover even greater opportunities.

Another problem is that after several reinterpretations, usually over a long period, the original transcending concept is barely perceptible and its original meaning no longer valid. This is not a problem for most areas, especially in the past when changes usually evolved slowly over long periods. The problem arises when old ways of relating become so obsolete that radical changes must be made. We reject not only the current reinterpretations but also the foundational myths upon which they are based. However, resistance is strong, and it does not seem to matter to the "faithful" that the foundation of this belief is faulty and crumbling. This is as true, for instance, of the "true believer" who refuses to acknowledge the truths of evolutionary theory as it was for Einstein who could not embrace many of the implications of quantum theory.

An example of the failure to incorporate new information into old stories might be seen in the way the Christian holiday of Christmas is celebrated, especially in the United States. "New" information, such as the dating of the birth of Jesus—probably in August—creates initial concern, but is soon reinterpreted to say that since no one knows for certain what the actual date was, the traditional December date is still acceptable. We have known for centuries that Christmas in December *intentionally* coincides with the Roman birth of the Sun God and that it was accepted by the early Christians as a way of avoiding persecution in the Roman world. In 354 Liberius, Bishop of Rome, declared December 25 as the date of the nativity. First century Christian commentator Publilius Syrus wrote about the advantage of celebrating Christmas Day on this date:

> It was a custom of the pagans to celebrate on the same December 25 the birthday of the Sun, at which they kindled lights in token of festivity. In these solemnities and revelries the Christians also took part. Accordingly, when the Church authorities perceived that the Christians had a leaning to this festival, they took counsel and resolved that the true Nativity should be solemnized on that day.[6]

Not only did the church gradually absorb all other winter solstice rites in its Christmas celebrations, it also claimed the Roman solar imagery for its own. "Thus the solar disks that had once been depicted behind the heads of [pagan] rulers became the halos of Christian luminaries."[7]

As time went on, Christmas took on meanings that were more secular, so that even people who were not Christians celebrated this holiday. Today persons attend Christmas Eve services in great numbers, even though many of them do not believe in virgin births, wise men from the East, or divine incarnations. Christmas has evolved into a time for people to connect to a sense of the holy without actually believing the transcending stories surrounding the event. It is like a good story or film that touches our emotions deeply and affects us. This happens at Christmas—even though we know it is only a story—because it conveys a transcending truth, relating us to a sense of the holy and to the holy within others. Even a completely secularized Christmas has this power.

Religious concepts and doctrines are created in particular languages with their own distinctions of time, place, culture, prejudices, etc. Because of this, these notions are not understood in the same way as they were understood by our ancestors—or even as our neighbors did or do—nor will the generations yet to come understand in the same way as we do today. Thus, our transcending concepts are not unchanging or infallible truths. Indeed, even if we were "presented with unquestionable truths in angelic languages given to us by God, these truths once received are conditioned by human language and interpreted by us . . . [and] embodied in the particularities of human history, culture and society."[8] Such contextuality is a strength and not a weakness, since transcendent truth must be contextual in order to have any relevance to our lives.

Major change occurs when new knowledge asks us to go beyond our present way of understanding. For instance:

- When we look to the biblical stories, we discover that Abraham left his parents' home and their Gods, and embraced one God.
- The destruction of the Temples, especially the Second Temple, changed the way Jews understood worship and sacrifice.
- Constantine introduced radical changes in the church when he set in motion the process creating a powerful religious ally for the Roman Empire—complete with all the trappings of politics

and power—and when he accepted and then enforced a particular understanding of Christianity.

- Since it was clearly no longer the movement inaugurated by Jesus, the church continually redefined Jesus to reflect its structural developments—and the new understandings accompanying those developments—until finally there was no longer the need for Jesus. Only the Christ of the church was necessary.
- Gandhi and Martin Luther King, Jr. stood on the foundations others had built as they not only proclaimed but also demonstrated with their lives a new way for human beings to relate to one another.
- For many persons, the Shoah—or Holocaust—and the obliteration of Hiroshima and Nagasaki are pivotal events resulting in major shifts in understanding religious beliefs, changing not only foundational doctrines but also ways of thinking about other issues relating to what it means to be human.

These are just a sampling of the radical shifts in religious worldviews. Some of these changes took decades—even centuries—to be adopted. Some of these changes are centuries old and are still struggling to find a foothold. Regardless, when the old moorings become obsolete, anxiety sets in—anxiety over values and morality. If long-standing "truth" is no longer true, what can be trusted?

Prior to the eighteenth century, life was largely shaped by religious authority and its traditions. Any change, any new idea, had to run the religious gauntlet and few made it through unscathed. Persons were not free to explore new ideas. However, by the middle of the seventeenth century, cracks and fissures in this religious domination of thought were becoming apparent. The new scientists made discoveries that did not conform to the traditions, and they bravely proclaimed that the traditions of the past could be selectively followed or wholly rejected. Standing on the shoulders of great thinkers like Copernicus, Galileo, and Newton, countless others have opened to us new worlds.

The past 200 years have witnessed tremendous scientific changes and challenges to how we understand the world. These discoveries have invited religious communities to examine the manner in which they express their transcending concepts. A full decade before Darwin published his *On the Origin of Species*, Neanderthal fossils were discovered which challenged the creation theory that argued Earth was little more than five thousand years old. Richard Carrington (1826-1875) discovered solar flares on the sun, paving the way for the discovery of similar stellar flares on other stars more recently. He also observed sunspots that revealed the differential rotation of the sun. Gregor Mendel (1822-1884), an Augustinian monk from Austria, formulated the basis for genetics. In 1869, chemist Fredrich Meischer (1844-1895) isolated a substance from white blood cells he called "nuclein," which we today know as DNA.

The mid-1800s also experienced Karl Marx's critique of the social order that favored the wealthy at the expense of the poor. As a result of his study of history and society, he concluded that it is not enough to simply interpret social history but to change it.

In *The Essence of Christianity*, Ludwig Feuerbach (1804-1872) argued that God is really a human creation and that the characteristics attributed to God are simply human qualities. He argued it is the material world that is real, but religion in general has put forth specific ideologies that have prevented people from clearly seeing the material conditions of their lives. Reflecting on Feuerbach's writings, Marx assailed religion that promised a heaven and threatened a hell in order to lull the exploited and oppressed poor into accepting a wretched existence. We might wonder how different the world would be if, throughout history, religion had valued the human person as much as it has valued wealth and power!

The work of Charles Darwin (1809-1882) was one of those pregnant points of the mid-1800s. Although he was not the first to write about the evolution of life, his writing became a lightning rod for all future imagining. Many religious leaders of the time were able to accept his theory of natural selection by limiting his ideas to the material domain where logical analysis and scientific investigation were not seen as a threat. There are many who want to keep this dualism alive today. This simply keeps the psychological, anthropological, sociological, religious, and philosophical "worlds" divided from the "world" of the physical or hard sciences. The basis of this notion is that if evolution can be demonstrated to have *no* implications for human values, ideals, and behaviors, then scientific discoveries pose no threat to the rest of culture. That, of course, was—and is—a preposterous notion!

More recently, there are the sciences that have expanded our knowledge of the depth of the universe and the microscopic levels of protons. Albert Einstein's theory of relativity and general relativity opened new avenues for seeing the complexity of the universe. Neuroscientists have shown us how the brain works. Anthropologists have shown us the ages of biological life in Earth.

It should be unnecessary by now to say how much evolutionary theory has changed the way we view almost everything. While many in the Abrahamic faiths will continue to hold to the prescientific belief that everything is as God created it to be, a growing number of the faithful no longer believe the ancient creed. The evolutionary origin of life is as certain "as the roundness of the Earth, the motion of the planets, and the molecular composition of matter."[9] Over the past 150 years, evidence for evolution has increased a thousandfold, meaning that it is impossible to seriously refute it.

In passing, it is interesting to note that the creationist position that began to solidify largely in the 1920 has changed its face over the years and now includes what is called intelligent design. To the creationists, evolution is an evil that threatens all that is important to life. They refer to evolution as atheistic, materialistic, immoral, etc. When this is carried over into the political arena, this evil is equated with anarchy, liberalism, and communism, among other things. Evolution is considered atheistic since it does not require a God to bring about every change, and because it is able to create novelty. It also denies the literal "truth" of the Bible.

However, the theory of evolution is not atheistic but *secular*, and it is not necessarily in conflict with religious faith. In the 1950 encyclical, *Humani Generis*, Pope Pius XII (a "conservative's conservative") affirmed that "Catholics could believe whatever science determined about the evolution of the human body, so long as they accepted that, at some time of his choosing, God had infused the soul into such a creature . . . ." Like Stephen Jay Gould's NOMA, Pius "acknowledged and respected the separate domains of science and theology."[10]

In 1996, Pope John Paul II took the dictum of Pius and added to it. In the document "Truth Cannot Contradict Truth," John Paul "defended both the evidence for evolution and the consistency of the theory with Catholic religious doctrine." Pius had "forcefully proclaimed that while evolution might be legitimate in principle, the theory, in fact, had not been proven and might well be entirely wrong." John Paul took into account nearly 50 years of work on evolution and stated that "evolution can no longer be doubted . . . ."[11]

In the 1970s, creationists made a major shift in tactics. Instead of trying to make it illegal to teach evolution in schools, they demanded equal time in science classrooms for the notion of creation. When this was continually rebuffed by the courts, another shift occurred, this time turning the biblical story into "scientific creationism," an oxymoron. This was quickly changed to the intelligent design argument in which the proponents were instructed to avoid religious language in their debates. However, the courts correctly saw this as a shell game and rebuffed it as well. "Giving the 'theory' of intelligent design . . . equal status [with evolution] . . . is little different from giving equal status to the idea that the sun goes around Earth."[12]

It is interesting to note that even the leaders of the intelligent design movement "agree with evolutionists on the basic timeline of cosmic and biological emergence . . . . *Why* (and for some, exactly *how*) the living and non-living worlds have morphed over the eons is the focus of debate. But the *fact* that our Universe has been transforming along a discernable path for billions of years—the fact that creation was not a one-time event—is of little or no dispute."[13]

Although Darwin, Mendel, and Meischer were all contemporaries, the importance of their discoveries did not begin coming together until 1937 with the publication of *Genetics and the Origin of Species* by the Russian-born American naturalist and experimental geneticist Theodosius Dobzhansky, and until 1953 when James Watson and Francis Crick discovered what Meischer had stumbled onto nearly a hundred years earlier—the structure of SNA as the hereditary material contained in the chromosomes of every cell's nucleus. Each of these persons stood on the shoulders of others, and others today stand on their shoulders. And while creationists spend their time attacking Darwin's 150-year-old writings, biologists today have moved beyond that and instead deal with a modified and expanded version of Darwinism.

Language and Images

Language and images shape the ways we see and think about the world, as well as the way we live our lives. Lera Boroditsky and her colleagues at Stanford University collected data from around the world and have concluded, "People who speak different languages do indeed think differently and that even flukes of grammar can profoundly affect how we see the world."[14]

Illustrating how language shapes the way we see and think about our world, Richard Dawkins relates the following:

> I once read a science-fiction story in which astronauts voyaging to a distant star were waxing homesick: "Just to think that it's springtime back on Earth!" You may not immediately see what's wrong with that, so ingrained is our unconscious northern hemisphere chauvinism. "Unconscious" is exactly right. That is where consciousness-raising comes in.
>
> I suspect it is for a deeper reason than gimmicky fun that, in Australia and New Zealand, you can buy maps of the world with the south pole on top. Now, wouldn't that be an excellent thing to pin to our classroom walls? What a splendid consciousness-raiser. Day after day, the children would be reminded that north has no monopoly on up. The map would intrigue them as well as raise their consciousness. They'd go home and tell their parents.[15]

New York Times columnist Thomas L. Friedman points to one of the basic changes in worldview occurring today. Using the phrase "flat world," he explains:

> What I mean when I say that the world is flat is that sometime in the late 1990s a whole set of technologies and political events converged—including the fall of the Berlin Wall, the rise of the Internet, the diffusion of the Windows operating system, the creation of a global fiber-optic network, and the creation of interoperable software applications, which made it very easy for people all over the world to work together—that leveled the playing field. It created a global platform that allowed more people to plug and play, collaborate and compete, share knowledge and share work, than anything we have ever seen in the history of the world.[16]

His emphasis, unlike many futurists dealing with some of these issues, is that "the world isn't going to be flat, it *is* flat." For the world to be flat means that it is connected. The current worldwide economic crisis is an example of the effects of this globalization. But Friedman takes this a step further, arguing that "the lowering of trade and political barriers and the exponential technical advances of the digital revolution have made it possible to do business, or almost anything else, instantaneously with billions of other people across the planet." While this is not news to many people, Friedman's point is that "just when we stopped paying attention to these developments—when the dot-com bust turned interest away from the business and technology pages and when 9/11 and the Iraq War turned all eyes toward the Middle East—is when they actually began to accelerate." What he calls *Globalization 3.0* "is driven not by major corporations or giant trade organizations like the World Bank, but by individuals: desktop freelancers and innovative startups all over the world (but especially in India and China) who can compete—and win—not just for low-wage manufacturing and information labor but, increasingly, for the highest-end research and design work as well."[17]

The frightening thing is that almost all of our politicians still think of the world in terms of vertical thinking that places the US at the top of a world hierarchy—American domination. On the other hand, most of the leading U.S. companies get it and are responding to it in appropriate ways. "Because they're in the middle of it," Friedman said in an interview, "they could break the code for me." These business leaders cannot survive without being on the cutting edge and able to "connect the dots in larger ways."

The significance of Friedman's comments for our study here is to demonstrate that the world is experiencing a tremendous amount of change in our own day that will affect the way we interact with persons around the world and the way in which we value religious traditions. It changes the way we see the world as much as Marx, Darwin, Einstein, or Hawking. It is increasingly difficult to hold onto old worldviews. Religions that seek to do this through restoration and renewal efforts find little long term benefit from these efforts. The challenge for religion is to find ways to maintain the best of their traditions while letting go of that which is no longer useful in understanding and dealing with a changing world.

Another change taking place in the world today is the rise of religious fundamentalism. While it might be argued that this has been present for centuries, seen in the Christian crusades and inquisitions, religious fundamentalism seems to be rearing its head in new and ways that are more dangerous. In writing about Christian fundamentalism, H.L. Menchen stated: "No amount of proof of the falsity of their beliefs will have the slightest influence on them."[18] The same could be said of any form of extremism. Religious fundamentalism feeds the appetites of political fundamentalism. It claims that its ideology is commanded by God. The "war on terrorism" is in reality a war on jihadism, best understood as a radical fundamentalism within Islam that argues it is the duty of every true Muslim to do whatever is necessary by any means to bring the peoples of the world—including moderate Muslims—into submission to their particular understanding Islam. At the ideological level, an earlier incarnation of this was the anti-modernism battle of the Catholic Church around the turn of the last century. Religious fundamentalism is a fight against modernity, including freedom of expression, toleration, and the separation of church and state.[19] It is a fear that the threatening challenges will result in chaos and immorality.

Breeched Walls

We cannot ignore the fact that traditionalists question anyone's right to modify a long-standing, or "revealed," transcending concept. However, revelation is something that originates within human endeavor and cannot be understood as a stagnant, once-for-all event; rather, it is something that continues—and changes—throughout time. New revelations—or better, new insights—are no longer encased as the mystery of a special word from God. Today we may not be knocked off our donkeys, as St. Paul was on his way to Damascus, but that does not mean that new insights are any less valid. If we insist on keeping the word revelation—and that appears to be a dubious choice—it should be understood as continuous insights that are part of a normally gradual and cumulative process. It is a dynamic process that places us in tension between doubt and faith. We live in the gray areas, not in a black and white world. Rabbi Zalman M. Schachter Shalomi suggests that theologians drive by looking at the rearview mirror. Their traditions no longer have transformative power, he says, but they cannot understand why they are losing adherents.

In his speeches, the famous preacher Henry Ward Beecher (1813-1887) delighted in telling a story about his old dog Noble. Henry once saw

Noble chase a red squirrel into the crevice of a stone wall in Lenox. The squirrel never appeared there again, but the dog couldn't stop obsessing about that hole. "When there were no more chickens to harry, no pigs to bite, no cattle to chase, no children to romp with," said Beecher, "he would walk out of the yard, yawn, and stretch himself, and then look wistfully at the hole, as if thinking to himself: 'Well, as there is nothing else to do, I may as well try that hole again.'" Some people, he said, keep bring up old arguments and like old Noble, open "on this hole in the wall, and can never be done barking at it. Day after day it resorts to this empty hole."[20]

The past can teach us many things. Indeed, we create the future standing on the shoulders of giants of the past. There are also things that the past cannot teach because it has no frame of reference to understand the present. Seen from outer space, the Earth has no national boundaries. Rather, it possesses an organic wholeness. However, our traditions are filled with all kinds of boundaries—some to our benefit, but most are detrimental to human life and the survival of the Earth. The Beatles had a song called "Imagine" which challenged my generation to see the world from a unified point of view without boundaries.

The American philosopher John Dewey concluded more than seventy-five years ago that most of the problems in the past two centuries of Western culture stemmed from the failure of philosophy "to explain the findings of science as they came to light, and to provide leadership in the continuous forging of a world view compatible with those findings . . . ."[21] The result was, he argued, that the world was once again divided into two mutually-compatible worlds. As long as one did not encroach on the territory of the other, things worked well.

Stephen Jay Gould forcefully argued this idea in his 1999 book *Rocks of Ages*. Gould, who considers himself "a Jewish agnostic," writes:

> The lack of conflict between science and religion arises from a lack of overlap between their respective domains of professional expertise—science in the empirical constitution of the universe, and religion in the search for proper ethical values and the spiritual meaning of our lives. The attainment of wisdom in a full life requires extensive attention to both domains—for a great book tells us that the truth can make us free and that we

> will live in optimal harmony with our fellows when we learn to do justly, love mercy, and walk humbly."

He argues that his "Nonoverlapping Magisteria" (NOMA) is not "a mere diplomatic stance." Rather it represents a "mutual humility [that] has important practical consequences in a world of such diverse passions."[22]

With the dawning of Darwin's theory of natural selection, everyone's worldview was challenged. This theory produced some of the most far-reaching changes in recent centuries, affecting every area of knowledge. The idea of evolution had been around for a long time. The ancient Greek philosopher Anaximander [ca. 610—546 BCE] proposed that

> animals could be transformed from one kind into another, and Empedocles [ca. 490-430 BCE] speculated that they could be made up of various combinations of preexisting parts. Closer to modern evolutionary ideas were the proposals of early Church Fathers like Gregory of Nazianzus [c. 329—390] and Augustine [354-430], who maintained that not all species of plants and animals were created as such by God; rather some had developed in historical times from other of God's creations. Their motivation was not biological but religious. Some species must have come into existence only after the Noachian Flood because it would have been impossible to hold representatives of all species in a single vessel such as Noah's Ark.[23]

Alfred Russel Wallace (1823-1913) was a contemporary and friend of Darwin's. Wallace was a British naturalist who independently proposed a theory of natural selection. Wallace's work prompted Darwin to publish his *Origin of Species*. Unlike Darwin, Wallace argued for a non-material, spiritual origin for human mental faculties.

Darwin was grasped by the idea of natural selection through the influence of his grandfather. We might say that while he did not give birth to the idea, he was the midwife that gave it life. Despite the efforts to maintain the walls of separation between science and religion (and the social sciences as well), the walls became permanently breeched. Like the levies of New Orleans during and after Hurricane Katrina (2005), the religious walls were ill prepared for the onslaught.

Social Darwinism

A related theory, Social Darwinism, has a continuing influence on the current political and religious landscapes. While this theory has long been disproved, the English sociologist Herbert Spencer (1820-1903) took Darwin's biological theory of natural selection and applied it to ideas, beliefs, and behaviors of individuals and societies. While Darwin argued that natural selection showed the benefits of cooperation and community, Spencer's Social Darwinism argued in the opposite direction.

Spencer had considered the ideas of evolution prior to Darwin's *On the Origin of Species* (1859), and in 1857 published a paper in *The Westminster Review* on "Progress: Its Laws and Causes."[24] Progress, he wrote, is different from the evolution of the child into an adult. The evolution of intelligence "consist[s] in the produce of a greater quantity and variety of articles for the satisfaction of men's wants; in the increasing security of person and property; in the widening freedom of action enjoyed . . . ." What he was arguing for was social progress that "consists in those changes of structure in the social organism which have entailed these consequences." In order to understand progress, he wrote: "we must inquire what is the nature of these changes, considered apart from our interests." In this article, he argued against the Anthropic Principle that says the Earth was created specifically for human life.

Spencer coined the phrase "survival of the fittest." Although his theory quickly took on Darwin's name, Darwin did not agree with Spencer on what that might mean. Indeed, Darwin was well aware of the apparent paradox that many creatures make themselves *less fit* so that the group may survive. Spencer argued that society was evolving toward increased human freedom. Because of this, government in social and political life should be minimal at best. He argued that the role of government is "not to do anything to improve or alter" the relationship between the various classes in society. He argued further that the ultimate result of shielding persons from "the effect of their folly is to fill the world with fools."[25] Social Darwinism deplored a free public school system as "useless and destructive," and it rejected helping the poor and unemployed since "it would result in benefiting a selected few at the expense of the rest."[26] Leaders are born, not made, and those who are naturally most fit will find ways to make it on their own. Social Darwinism also opposed immigration as a threat to the "English" way, as well as being a sure way of watering-down the English gene pool that had guided America into prosperity.

Andrew Carnegie (1835-1919), a friend and supporter of Spencer, agreed that "people and societies grow and improve by weeding out the weak and reinforcing the fittest through the 'never-ceasing discipline of experience.'"[27] John D. Rockefeller (1839-1937), another supporter of Spencer, said in 1875: "The growth of a large business is merely a survival of the fittest, the working out of a law of nature and a law of God."[28]

Still another friend and supporter of Spencer was Yale sociologist William Graham Sumner (1840-1910). In Sumner, we see Social Darwinism taking another major step. He argued in 1874 that "capital is energy stored up for the future in the struggle for self-preservation, and thus the most important task for society is to promote capital accumulation, which is only 'rendered possible' by consistent renunciation of the present.'" Millionaires, he argued, "were a product of natural selection . . . . Capitalism ratified nature's and God's plan, and helter-skelter changes in government policy only eroded progress."[29]

Sumner was one of the strongest academic voices for Social Darwinism. He said in many different places: "If we do not believe in the survival of the fittest, we have only one possible alternative, and that is survival of the unfittest." Speaking of the suffering endured by so many in the 1873 Depression, he said that the "iron spur" of suffering "was necessitated by the progress of the race and the state had no place as mediator in that struggle."[30] Sumner's suggestion to Congress for the relief of those who had lost jobs and homes and savings as a result of the Depression was this: "The first thing is to give him the greatest possible measure of liberty in the directing of his own energies for his own development, and the second is to give him the greatest possible security in the possession and use of the products of his own industry." He went on to testify before Congress in 1878:

> Sir, the moment that government provided work for one, it would have to provide work for all, and there would be no end whatever possible. Society does not owe any man a living . . . . The fact that a man is here is no demand upon other people that they shall keep him alive and sustain him. He has got to fight the battle with nature as every other man has; and if he fights it with the same energy and enterprise and skill and

> industry as any other man, I cannot imagine him failing—that is, misfortune apart.[31]

For Social Darwinists, the expansion of government to meet the devastating needs of the weak and the unemployed—almost always understood as one and the same—produces a new tyranny that decreases the freedom of the rest of the citizens, *especially* the freedoms of society's strongest and best. As Spencer argued from his estate in England:

> The insidious growth of this organized and consolidated bureaucracy will go on . . . because the electorate cannot conceive the general but distant evils it entails, in contrast with the special and immediate advantages to be gained by its action. For the masses can appreciate nothing but material boon—better homes, shorter hours, higher wages, more regular work. Hence, they are in favor of those who vote for restricting time in mines, for forcing employers to contribute to men's insurance funds, for dictating railway fares and freights, for abolishing the so-called sweating system. It seems to them quite right that education, wholly paid for by rates [taxes], should be State-regulated; that the State should give technical instruction, that quarries should be inspected and regulated; that there should be sanitary registration of hotels.[32]

Social Darwinism is important to our discussion of religious faith since it taught—and still teaches under the cloak of conservatism—that its theory is a purification and exaltation of Christianity and morality. It is also important since its influence can be seen in the greed and resulting suffering in the current worldwide financial crisis. It also reveals the irony of those conservatives who vehemently argue against Darwin's evolutionary theory (which has been overwhelmingly accepted by scientists), and at the same time just as strongly support Social Darwinism (which has been overwhelmingly rejected). This inconsistency is especially surprising among poor and middle-class conservatives who seem to be afflicted by a sort of Stockholm syndrome. Fed on a diet of both fear and empty promises, they support the schemes of the wealthy in the effort of self-preservation. They are convinced of the rightness of their "captor's" actions—even though they will never enjoy the benefits that were held out before them. Religious conservatives have historically supported the wealthy against their own interests and the interests of their fellow citizens because they believe ala Calvin that what is, is right, because God had ordained it to be thus.

Another aspect of this changing worldview is the gender images of God. While the debate is important in correcting long-standing male domination, arguments on all sides of the debates about gender images of the divine are completely irrelevant since even scripture argues that God is spirit, not material, and the first commandment is a prohibition against creating an image of God as either male or female, or as animal or stone. Werth argues such images are simplistic ways of trying to personalize an abstraction.

- Language is far more than a means of expression and communication. It is the gateway to the mind. It organizes and provides access to the system of concepts used in thinking . . . .
- It does not merely express emotions, it can change them; not merely arouses or quell them, but change the role of emotion in one's life and the life of a nation.
- Language does not merely express identity; it can change identity. Narratives and melodramas are not mere words and images; they can enter our brains and provide models that we not merely live by, but that define who we are.
- Language is an instrument of creativity and power, a means of connecting with people or alienating them, and a force for social cohesion or separation.
- Language is sensual and aesthetic, with the power to woo and to repulse, to be beautiful or ugly, to be meaningful or banal.
- Language has moral force; it can bring out the best in people and the worst.[33]

Many of us learned in Religion 101 that our religious ancestors were at one time polytheistic and that monotheism arose over a long period. Rita Gross points to the exile in 586 BCE as a transition time when the ancient Israelite religion was transformed into early Judaism with a tendency towards a universalizing perspective, away from a strictly ethnic stance. An important aspect to this transformation involved a larger role for their deity. "The one deity was thought to be no longer merely the one deity properly worshipped by Israelites; it was also claimed to be *universally* the one deity, the deity who had allowed victory over Israelites and who meted out the destinies of all people, not merely the Israelites."[34]

Then along came the Christians. Rabbi Steiman, with whom I studied, used the American Western movie motif in talking about a Jewish response to the growing anti-Judaism in the early centuries of the Common Era: "Don't look back now. The SOB's are gaining on us." It wasn't long before Islam emerged into history, and the attitude that there is a universal deity to be worshipped and obeyed by all people of all cultures was unquestioned and unquestionable. "Muslims claimed only that Christian messages from that one universal deity had been superseded and made obsolete by the revelations given to Mohammed. Thus the only real question was who spoke for the universal deity, who, in fact, was the seal of the prophets."[35]

The Eastern religions—Hinduism, Buddhism, Confucianism, Taoism, and Shinto, to name the major ones—came at the deity issue from a completely different direction. For the most part, they have viewed religious diversity as "inevitable, beneficial, and necessary because of human diversity." When we look at the world scene, it is remarkable to us in the West that "the idea of exclusive loyalty to one religion is rather foreign and incomprehensible to most people."[36]

Summary

What we know is the result of measurement and analysis and ongoing study of human observation, experience, and imagination. We trust human insight and reason, but we also rely, to some extent, on what others in the past have learned and have passed on to us. What we think they got right we value and use to continue the development of knowledge. What we think they got wrong, we appreciate for its value in showing what paths we should avoid.

CHAPTER 2

Consciousness and Belief

"Science demonstrates that some events that occur in your world can never, even in principle, be known in mine, and vice versa."

—Clay Naff

We begin by looking at the brain and consciousness in order to explain why we value our various religious ideals and practices as important. For centuries, most philosophers and theologians contended that the human mind (or soul) was something immaterial and outside of the body. We now understand that the mind is not some immaterial thing outside of the body. Rather, "it *is* the brain, or, more specifically, a system or organization within the brain that has evolved in much the way our immune system or respiratory system or digestive system has evolved."[37]

This new understanding of the brain runs against the grain of centuries of Judeo-Christian tradition, which has taught:

- Humans are made in the image of God and are unrelated to animals.
- Women are derivative of men and destined to be ruled by them.
- The mind is an immaterial substance: it has powers possessed by no purely physical structure, and can continue to exist when the body dies.
- The mind is made up of several components, including a moral sense, an ability to love, a capacity for reason that recognizes whether an act conforms to ideals of goodness, and a decision faculty that chooses to behave.
- Although the decision faculty is not bound by the laws of cause and effect, it has an innate tendency to choose sin.

- Our cognitive and perceptual faculties work accurately because God implanted ideals in them that correspond to reality and because he coordinates their functioning with the outside world.
- Mental health comes from recognizing God's purpose, choosing good and repenting sin, and loving God and one's fellow humans for God's sake.[38]

These notions are based on a literal interpretation of the Bible and continue to be the most popular theory of human nature, especially in the United States. But the findings of science have made it impossible to continue to believe much of this. We now know that the brain is generally organized into three parts.

> Your most newly evolved brain tissues are wrapped around the outside. Further beneath the surface are the two vintage structures, the mammalian brain and then the reptilian brain. These older parts are generally the sites for brain functions—breathing, circulating blood, digesting food, and so on. They also operate undetected by conscious thought. They are constantly making rapid choices for you based on immediate sense impressions, like the features and expressions on faces of people you see. The newer, close-to-surface brain parts draw from all of the various brain regions, weigh different imparts, and then act like a slowly deliberating committee. The older regions act like an impulsive dictator, firing commands, unimpeded by the need to seek balance.[39]

The old view, which prevailed through the 1980s, was that the brain consists of many specialized modules that are hardwired from birth to perform specific jobs.

> But starting in the 1990s, this static view of the brain was steadily supplanted by a much more dynamic picture. The brain's so-called modules don't do their jobs in isolation; there is a great deal of back-and-forth interaction between them, far more than previously suspected. Changes in the operation of one module—say, from damage, or from maturation, or from learning and life experience—can lead to significant changes in

> the operations of many other modules to which it is connected. To a surprising extent, one module can even take over the functions of another. Far from being wired up according to rigid, prenatal genetic blueprints, the brain's wiring is highly malleable—and not just in infants and young children, but throughout every adult lifetime.

While other animals exhibit this plasticity, it seems that we are the only species whose brains "evolved the ability to exploit learning and culture to drive our mental phase transitions . . . ."[40]

It is interesting to note that vision does not occur in the eye. It occurs in the brain. We have as many as thirty visual areas in our brain. "Our perception of the world ordinarily seems so effortless that we tend to take it for granted. You look, you see, you understand—it seems as natural and inevitable as water flowing downhill . . . . Even though our picture of the world seems coherent and unified, it actually emerges from the activity of those thirty (or more) different visual areas in the cortex, each of which mediates multiple subtle functions."[41]

It is hard enough to understand that vision does not occur in the eye. That goes against commonsense to most people. But it is even more difficult to "get rid of the notion that the image at the back of your eye simply gets 'relayed' back to your brain to be displayed on a screen." Visual information is not an image. "We must think, instead, of symbolic descriptions that *represent* the scenes and objects that had been in the image." That is,

> The brain does not recreate the original image, but represents the various features and aspects of the image in totally new terms . . . in its own alphabet of nerve impulses. These symbolic encodings are created partly in your retina itself but mostly in your brain. Once there, they are parceled and transformed and combined in the extensive network of visual brain areas that eventually let you recognize objects. Of course, the vast majority of this processing goes on behind the scenes without entering your conscious awareness, which is why it feels effortless and obvious . . . .[42]

The thirty visual areas in our brain "are all specialized for different aspects of vision, such as color vision, seeing movement, seeing shapes, recognizing faces, and so on. The computational strategies for each of these might be sufficiently different that evolution developed for neural hardware separately."[43]

We seek to explain the universe and human existence through human observation, experience, experimentation, analysis, and imagination. Religion arises from our search for meaning, and is a cognitive and normative structure that helps persons "feel at home" in the universe. However, the experiences on which religion rely tend to be isolated and not universally "true."

Malcolm Jeeves reminds us that from the perspective of neuroscience, the role of consciousness is primary and "the cognitive agent in all that we do."[44] Consciousness is "an organism's awareness of its own self and surroundings." Its beginning is considered a major turning point in the evolutionary process since it was a development that opened the way for things we take for granted—things like conscience, religion, social and political organizations, the arts, the sciences, and technology. Perhaps even more compellingly, "consciousness is the critical function that allows us to know sorrow or know joy, to know suffering or know pleasure, to sense embarrassment or pride, to grieve for lost love or lost life."[45]

The discussion of consciousness combines two intimately related problems. The first is the problem of understanding how the human brain creates mental sensory patterns such as a sound image, a tactile image, or the image of a state of well-being. The second problem of consciousness is how the brain also creates a sense of self in the act of knowing.[46] While consciousness is an entirely private phenomenon, it is "closely tied to external behaviors that can be observed by third persons."[47] Although "consciousness and emotion are *not* separable . . . consciousness and wakefulness, as well as consciousness and low-level attention, can be separated."[48]

Core consciousness is a simple, biological phenomenon that is not exclusively human. It is not dependent on conventional memory, working memory, reasoning, or language. On the other hand, *extended consciousness* is a complex biological phenomenon with several levels of organization. It evolves across the lifetime of the organism. While extended consciousness is also present in some nonhumans, its highest realization is in humans. It depends on conventional memory and working memory, and is enhanced by language. Autobiographical memory is the organized record of the main aspects of an organism's biography.[49]

This means at the very least that other forms of animal life also have a core consciousness that allows basic organizing structures to operate. The degree of development of this consciousness varies. In humans this evolves to the degree that not only memory—which many other animals have—but also imagination, planning, analysis, and self-analysis takes place, thereby enabling the person to have considerable self-awareness and personal identity.

Role of Emotions

Again, consciousness and emotion are *not* separable. At one level, there is nothing distinctively human about emotions since many nonhuman creatures also have emotions. The distinction seems to be the complexity of those emotions that involves ideas, values, and complex planning. As Ramachandran says, "Any ape can reach for a banana, but only humans can reach for the stars."

> When pondering our uniqueness, it is natural to wonder how close other species before us might have come to achieving our cognitive state of grace. Anthropologists have found that the hominin family tree branched many times in the past several million years. At various times numerous protohuman and human-like ape species thrived and roamed the earth, but for some reason our line is the only one that 'made it.' What were the brains of those other hominins like? Just like us [*Homo neanderthalensis*] made art and jewelry, ate a rich and varied diet, and buried their dead. And evidence is mounting that their language was more complex than the stereotyped 'cave man talk' gives them credit for. Nevertheless, around thirty thousand years ago they vanished from the earth.[50]

Emotions are integral to the reasoning and decision-making processes. We are not conscious of *all* our feelings. Indeed, many judgments are made "automatically." It is believed that as much as 95 percent of our thinking occurs at the subconscious level.[51] Neuroscientist Michael Gazzaniga, director of the University of California-Santa Barbara's SAGE Center for the Study of the Mind, writes: "Some automatic pathways are learned over time (driving), and some are inherent (approach-avoidance with a negative bias). The latter can be affected by emotions, which also have been hardwired to varying degrees."[52]

Gazzaniga, who specializes in split-brain research, argues that the brain is lazy. "It will do the least amount of work it can. Because using intuitive modules is easy and fast and requires the least amount of work, that is the default mode of the brain."[53] This emotional default can sometimes be overridden by changing the way we think. It is like going into a computer program and making changes that will produce different results when utilized. Such a change or reappraisal changes the perception of the emotional data: Are the tears we observe in another's eyes tears of joy, sorrow, an allergy, or perhaps dry eye?

When input enters the brain, it is initially received as either positive or negative. It either feels right or wrong. We may act or refuse to act on the basis of this automatic categorizing of the input. Or we may bring it into consciousness for further reflection.

Michael Shermer talks about an episode of the television series *MythBusters*, in which Adam Savage was busted by the camera crew for forgetting his prediction about an axle being ripped out of a car, as supposedly occurred in the movie *American Graffiti*. Adam's response to the crew was: "I reject your reality and substitute my own." Shermer reminds us that "rejecting everyone else's reality and substituting your own almost always results in a failed belief system."[54]

Neuroscientists Sam Harris, Sameer Sheth, and Mark Cohen presented 14 adults with a series of statements that were designed to be plainly true, false, or undecidable. The subjects were to press a button indicating their belief, disbelief, or uncertainty. They were placed in a magnetic resonance imaging machine to capture their responses and to determine which part of the brain was doing the work. The most current research indicates that a stimulus induces an automatic process of approval or disapproval that may lead to a full-on emotional state. "The emotional state produces a moral intuition that may motivate an individual to action. Reasoning about the judgment or action comes afterward, as the brain seeks a rational explanation for an automatic reaction it has no clue about."[55]

This study is important to our current discussion. It appears, as Spinoza suggested in the 17th century, "most people have a low tolerance for ambiguity and that belief comes quickly and naturally, whereas skepticism is slow and unnatural. The scientific principle of the null hypothesis—that a claim is untrue unless proved otherwise—runs counter to our natural tendency to accept as true what we can comprehend quickly."[56]

This can be seen in the manner in which we receive our news today. TV commentators (not necessarily the reporters who do the hard work of searching for the facts) often plant the seeds of suspicion and mistrust in the minds of viewers—even while denying any validity to the statements they are about to make. They apparently do not have to have a valid reason for their wonderings. They just wonder—and wander! In this way, rather than commenting intelligently on the news, they *create* the news. This seems to occur for TV personalities in ways that do not occur—at least not to this extent—for the print journalist, who is quickly becoming an endangered species as newspapers merge or simply go out of business. TV journalists are more believable—or not—because their body movements, gestures, voice inflections, and facial expressions *add to* the event. In addition, an attractive male or female—and few on TV are not attractive—is usually more believable than one who is not.

We remember not only an event but also the emotions generated by that event. The event and the emotion are linked in the memory, so that when a similar event occurs, the emotions of the original event are recalled.

The simple exercise of walking might provide an example of how this works. A couple goes to the gym to walk a mile or two for cardiovascular benefit. As they begin walking, one experiences negative feelings about the exercise in this particular place because of negative experiences in high school gym several years before. The other person recalls energizing feelings that such exercise has produced in the past. A similar event with quite different emotions attached to it.

Fear continues to be one of the most popular forms of political manipulation. It is not only governmental leaders who have used this to political advantage; religious leaders have also used fear to further their own purposes. The title of a 2008 *Newsweek* article well states the point: "When It's Head versus Heart, the Heart Wins." Emotions all too often rule the day, a point also made by Dan Ariely's 2008 book, *Predictably Irrational: The Hidden Forces that Shape Our Decisions*.[57] In the *Newsweek* article, science editor Sharon Begley wrote: "The fact that people have what is euphemistically cognitive-processing limitations—most cannot or will not learn about and remember candidates' records or positions—means voters must substitute something else for that missing knowledge."[58]

That "something else" is often a political party, a religious or racial bias, a single issue, or how a candidate makes one feel. Voters often decide on the candidate with whom they most identify.

One implication of this is that religious persons also substitute something for their missing knowledge. Religious emotions are often connected with other emotions in the believer's background. They are often generated by how one relates to a pastor or teacher. A person might say: "I loved my grandmother very much. On Sundays, she took me to church with her, and after church we always stopped at the restaurant where we had happy and long talks. When I go to church now, I remember those good feelings." Once that person has accepted "grandma's religion," it will be hard for her to accept any idea that seems to go against it. Nostalgia is part of this process, and knowledge may have little to do with her belief. As GOP consultant Frank Luntz commented: "More important than what people think is how they feel."[59] This does not mean that people do not care about the issues—whether in politics or religion. Rather, it means that persons evaluate how a belief or political position makes them feel. "The strongest human emotions are fear and anxiety. Crucial to survival, they are programmed into the brain's most primitive regions, allowing them to trump rationality but not for rationality to override them."[60]

The same is true for other areas, including religion. Most people cannot or will not do the critical level of thinking necessary to fully appreciate or evaluate their beliefs. And so they unquestioningly accept the word of an authority figure or a holy book as a substitute. It is not that they do not care. Rather, they rely on the feelings of security they get from these authoritative voices.

The role of consciousness is important in understanding self and in determining life. The self is not static throughout time but rather is reconstructed moment by moment as new information is processed and internalized. Our sense of self results from our interaction with the physical world, especially from our interaction with other persons. And these interactions are always interpreted interactions, with their meanings and perceptions being subjective. Thus, there is no such thing as a *pure* perception of an object.

The role of consciousness is essential in understanding the importance of beliefs. According to psychologist Gregory W. Lester, "our brain's primary purpose is to keep us alive." While it certainly does more than that, he argues that survival is always its fundamental purpose, and survival always comes first. He illustrates this: "If we are injured to the point where our bodies only have enough energy to support consciousness or a heartbeat but not both, the brain has no problem choosing—it puts us into a coma (survival before consciousness), rather than an alert death-spiral (consciousness before survival)." Thus, "because every brain activity serves a fundamental survival purpose, the only way to accurately understand any brain function is to examine its value as a tool for survival." Our senses are a large part of this tool for survival. Lester writes:

> Obviously, we must be able to accurately perceive danger in order to take action designed to keep us safe. In order to survive we need to be able to see the lion charging us as we emerge from our cave or hear the intruder breaking into our house in the middle of the night. Senses alone, however, are inadequate as effective detectors of danger because they are severely limited in both range and scope. We can have direct sensory contact with only a small portion of the world at any one time. The brain considers this to be a significant problem because even normal, everyday living requires that we constantly move in and out of the range of our perceptions of the world as it is right now.[61]

Belief as a Survival Tool

This leads us to understand that belief is a survival tool of the brain designed to assist our other senses in identifying danger. "Beliefs extend the range of our senses so that we can better detect danger and thus improve our chances of survival as we move into and out of unfamiliar territory." Functionally, beliefs operate as "internal maps" providing assumptions for those parts of the world with which we do not have immediate sensory contact. Lester provides an illustration of this.

> As I sit in my living room I cannot see my car. Although I parked it in my driveway some time ago, using only immediate sensory data I do not know if it is still there. As a result, at this moment sensory data is of very little use to me regarding my car. In order to find my car with any degree of efficiency my brain

> must ignore the current sensory data (which, if relied on in a strictly literal sense, not only fails to help me in locating my car but actually indicates that it no longer exists) and turn instead to its internal map of the location of my car. This is my belief that my car is still in my driveway where I left it. By referring to my belief rather than to sensory data, my brain can "know" something about the world with which I have no immediate sensory contact. This "extends" my brain's knowledge of and contact with the world.[62]

(Of course, someone may have stolen the car, in which case his belief system would give him incorrect information.) In this sense, the brain has the ability to reach beyond the range of our immediate senses through beliefs and the assumptions that are based on these beliefs. This is a survival tool. Lester concludes:

> When data and belief come into conflict, the brain does not automatically give preference to data. This is why beliefs—even bad beliefs, irrational beliefs, silly beliefs, or crazy beliefs—often don't die in the face of contradictory evidence. The brain doesn't care whether or not the belief matches the data. It cares whether the belief is helpful for survival. Period. So while the scientific, rational part of our brains may think that data should supersede contradictory beliefs, on a more fundamental level of importance our brain has no such bias. It is extremely reticent to jettison its beliefs.[63]

This belief function applies not only to religious belief but also to beliefs of all sorts. Their survival function, when applied to spirituality, is associated with, but not limited to, the survival of the personality beyond death. As long as there is a possibility, even a remote possibility, of some sort of after-death continuation, the survival mode remains active. And since the afterlife is an area of inquiry with no available data, one cannot definitively prove the issue one way or the other. In such a situation, survivability plays the odds in favor of the possibility.

Beliefs of all sorts do not occur individually or in a vacuum. It is important to note that beliefs are related to one another in a tightly interlocking system that creates the brain's fundamental worldview. The brain relies on this system "in order to experience consistency, control, cohesion, and safety in the world. It must maintain this system intact in order to feel that survival is being successfully accomplished." This means that even seemingly *small* changes in what one believes can create an avalanche and cause the brain to move into a survival mode. In this sense, any change in belief, regardless of how insignificant or irrational it may seem, is a threat to survival. This is why, for instance, when confronted with tons of data indicating the proof of evolutionary theory, a creationist will refuse to give it credence. Anything challenging the truthfulness of the biblical text is seen as a threat to one's entire system of belief. But beyond this, it is experienced as a survival threat to the brain, and thus to the human organism.

Because of the survival value of beliefs, evidence that contradicts what one believes will rarely be sufficient to change beliefs, even in "otherwise intelligent" people. I have encountered this resistance as I have consulted with churches over the past few years. Many churches would rather close than make the changes necessary to regain strength and fulfill their stated purposes. In fact, the stated purposes that are publicly affirmed are at odds with their private and often unconscious goals. In other instances, one person's control and manipulation is the source of a group's unrest, but the group will not oppose the controlling person because of their fear that he or she is the only thing keeping their group going—despite their dislike of the state of things.

While data is always necessary, it is rarely sufficient to change one's beliefs, behavior, or intellectual orientation. If we are looking for some change to occur, we must go beyond specific data to explore the *implications* that changing the belief, behavior, or intellectual orientation will have on the person's or group's fundamental worldview. Since this process of change is experienced as a threat to the brain's sense of survival, one must introduce the change in a way that will meet the needs of the brain to maintain a sense of wholeness, consistency, and control in life. We must address the "existential anxiety that is stirred up any time beliefs are challenged. The task is every bit as much philosophical and psychological as it is scientific and data-based."[64]

This disconnect can be seen in the current, almost paranoid, atmosphere of US politics. Despite indisputable proof of President Obama's birth as an American citizen, the "birthers" belief cannot be changed by facts. Facts are irrelevant to closed minds. The same is true with other issues. The fear that one's way of life will be destroyed often overrides facts and rationality. In such situations, persons may reject and fight against the very thing that can save them. Such fear and the irrationality it produces contains the seeds of its own destruction.

This disconnect can also be seen in the fact that the US has an extremely high percentage of persons who do not trust the findings of science. This irrational anti-intellectual movement can only weaken the future of the nation.

Metaphor

Cognitive scientists George Lakoff and Mark Johnson have argued that all human thought is both propelled and constrained by metaphors originating from experience.[65] Accordingly, religious concepts and images are to be treated on par with all other concepts and images. There is no clear cut distinction between a religious imagination and other sorts of imagination. The religious imagination is triggered by and grows out of life experiences. Niels Gregersen writes that religious imaginations and concepts emerge in the creative zones and tensions of interaction. "Religious imagination, in this perspective, comes about by blending and combining templates of understanding used for other purposes as well."[66]

The findings of psychological research offer a good news/bad news message for religion. These findings will be welcome by those who wish to see religion as belonging to the human condition and not likely to ever die out. However, the same findings also suggest that religion is substantially a pre-rational phenomenon that we continue to use simply because it has worked so well in the past "and because it continues to enhance our personal well-being, our social commitments and our cognitive orientation."[67]

Religions evolve. They change over time. Many of these changes can be seen only from the perspective of history, while others are clearly evident in one's current experience. Lakoff and Johnson argue that language and theoretical concepts are built on primary metaphors that are learned through bodily experiences and practices from childhood onward. This is true with religion as well.

Far below the threshold of consciousness, metaphors from one source of experience (e.g. bodily location) are blended and conflated with metaphors from another source (e.g. visual sensation), and they end up forming complex networks of imageries. We can, for instance, be summoned to search for our "inner light." In addition, there is a constant flow back and forth between these spatial-bodily "source areas" and the "target areas" that one wants to address. As time goes on, metaphors and images, on the one hand, and the subject matters we want to talk about, on the other hand, are blended and combined in ever-new configurations. Consequently, we may end up understanding our inner life as a "journey," and talk about "reaching our goals" or "losing ourselves."[68]

Metaphors are mental structures independent of language, although we are normally conscious of them through language. "Metaphorical thought is ordinary, and mostly unconscious and automatic. Indeed, it is so unconscious and automatic that the basic way it works was discovered only" in the mid-1970s.[69] Metaphors, then, are not just words. In fact, "we think metaphorically, all thought is brain activity, and the neural theory of metaphor explains why we have the primary metaphors we do. Primary metaphor arises from embodied experience, from two experiences that regularly occur together. It should not be surprising then that metaphors can have behavioral effects."[70] They can create massive effects as they not only reflect but also create reality. This is why male-dominated language has been under fire, especially during the past 40 years.

An illustration of this might be seen in the metaphors associated with love. We might wonder what love has to do with destination. "In Western culture, people are supposed to have purposes in life—life goals, things you plan to achieve over a lifetime . . . . That is, life is supposed to be purposeful. Given the metaphor that Achieving Purpose is reaching a Destination, long-term life goals are metaphorically seen as destinations to be reached over the course of a lifetime." Persons in this culture are supposed to not only have life goals, but lovers are supposed to have compatible life goals, that is, "destinations they can reach together. The Love-is-a-Journey metaphor is about the difficulties in doing so: long, bumpy roads, dead-end streets, getting stuck, going in different directions, being at a crossroads, and so on."[71]

Metaphors and concepts, then, do not necessarily represent objective realities or phenomena "out there." This was a mistake Plato made. Rather, imagination mirrors the continuous and creative interactions with our environments. Imagination is not a separate mental faculty isolated from—or even overruled by—other mental capacities. Such separation is hardly tenable in light of current research. What is characteristic for the operation of the human mind is the constant coming together of metaphors.

A Pattern-Seeking Species

We humans are a species that invents symbols. We are pattern-seeking, storytelling, and mythmaking animals that invest our symbols with passion and authority, *and then forget that we were the ones who invented them.* Human experience is always conditioned by symbolic references. "The symbolic universe of human existence includes not only the discursive aspects of experience such as science, mathematics, and logic; it also includes those non-discursive aspects such as art, myth, and religion."[72] In his theory of symbolic reference, Whitehead argued that emotion is an essential element in experience and is therefore a source of knowledge. He illustrated this by using the example of burning incense during sacred rituals. "It is easier to smell incense than to produce certain religious emotions; so if the two can be correlated, incense is a suitable symbol for such emotions. Indeed, for many purposes, certain aesthetic experiences, which are easy to produce, make better symbols than do words, written or spoken."[73] Many other examples might be cited, including sounds, music, art, smells, glimpses, words, touch, location, etc.

Things are seen before they are spoken. Things are felt before they are drawn. Things are anticipated before they are perceived. Things are experienced as novel before they are described. Because of this, experience is primary as a source of knowledge. Experience is an internalizing of symbolic meaning. *Story always precedes text.*

The brain has very specialized systems that are organized to understand and interpret the world of experience. These problem-solving systems are the result of gradual adaptations of biological evolution. Since the world is complex and filled with missing information, we are constantly looking for patterns to fill in the gaps. In the process, we imagine hidden forces and causes. Thus, when something unusual or unexpected happens, we begin looking for causes. We seek to bring order out of chaos. It seems that we cannot accept that things happen randomly or by chance. We tend to see the world as orderly and organized, and therefore we often detect patterns that are not really present. We are, therefore, prone to explain the unusual or the mysterious to a supernatural source and largely ignore "the multitude of mundane events that do not fit this interpretation." Indeed, writes Hood, "Much of what controls the world is hidden from direct view, and so our minds have evolved to infer the existence of things we cannot see."[74]

While it is true that we can make causal connections and patterns that may not exist, our minds "take in information from the environment, combine it with aspects of memory, shape it to satisfy certain needs, and produce a belief that may or may not have anything to do with reality."[75] Because of this, we must always be suspicious, to some degree, of our own experience. Simple perceptions are anything but simple. What we see is not always the true nature of reality. Perception involves a combination of sensory input, including such things as memory, emotion, and our hopes and fears. Our perception is often expectation—the way we *think* things should be. My father taught me: "Don't believe anything you hear and only half of what you see." While he did not mean that literally, it was intended to provide a check on perceptions. Because we humans tend to read our own interpretations and expectations into all life experiences, including religious experiences, there is more than one way of seeing reality. We react to the world in terms of our perceptions and expectations.

When I was in the sixth grade, my father took me to the reference room in the old downtown Chicago Library to do some research. While we were there, a huge gust of wind shattered one of the windows and slammed closed the large wooden doors. People began noisily rushing to get the door open and to get out of the room. My father looked around the room, made sure I was ok, and continued his work. When I asked why we weren't hurrying out of the room like everyone else, he calmly said, "The damage has already been done. There is no need to leave now." Where almost everyone else in the room saw the event as a need to fear and escape, my father saw it with other, more rational eyes.

Perceptions can become misperceptions that are stored in our memories. And these, in turn, affect the way we see or experience new events. In the same way, each current time views the past with different eyes. Thus, when we see a person or object, we always see that person or object in relation to a cultural and even historical background. Therefore, in different periods of time people have different understandings about what is reasonable and possible. Susan Greenfield writes:

> Although you are born with pretty much all the brain cells (neurons) you will ever have, it is the connections between these

> brain cells that are forged, in many brain regions, after birth and which in turn can be affected very strongly by individual experiences. In extreme cases, for example, it has been shown that children born with congenital cataracts, which are then removed by surgery, nonetheless can have lasting impairments of vision because of the lack of a working eye during a critical period when the appropriate connections are established.[76]

In recent years, brain science has been revolutionized by "imaging" techniques. Technology allows us to "see" the brain at work. Read Montague writes, "I am stunned, myself, by how well we can eavesdrop and get practical measures of what's going on in people's heads. Today, we can tell whether or not you are thinking about yourself or somebody else. While this might sound crude, we previously had nothing like it. We wouldn't even have had this conversation ten years ago."[77] Perhaps the most exciting discovery from these imaging techniques is that far more brain regions seem to participate in functions than we ever thought possible. It used to be accepted that each region of the brain had a separated and isolated function. But that does not seem to be the case. Different regions of the brain work together for different aspects of a function. For example, there are at least 30 brain areas contributing to vision.

The issue of just how the mind works is one of the current challenges in brain research. "Just because we know how something works on one level, that of cells, it doesn't necessarily mean we know how things work at another, that of coordinated brain function." What we do know is that "it is experience that enables us to interpret the world around us in a relevant and highly individual way . . . . Every process, person or object one encounters will be interpreted in the light of prior experiences and neuronal connections, and will in turn lead to the modifications of those connections."[78]

The human impulse to interpret our lives in terms of purpose and meaning leads us to identify patterns of divine activity in nature that may or may not exist. This argument begins with the anthropological presupposition: human beings seek patterns. In fact, writes theologian Ted Peters, "pattern-seeking could be judged as essential to all that humans do—in science as well as religion." In their own ways, science and religion each search for patterns that provide predictability. "Laws of nature can be formulated and united with one another by the presumed pattern of all patterns, a universal mathematical structure. Science is the preeminent example of human pattern-seeking."[79] Michael Shermer agrees that as pattern-seeking animals it is virtually impossible for us not to see the pattern. "Our brains are hard-wired to seek and find patterns, whether or not the pattern is real . . . . We seek and find patterns because we prefer to view the world as orderly instead of chaotic, and it is orderly often enough that this strategy works . . . . Those patterns have to be given an identity, and for thousands of years many of those identities were called gods . . . . [80]

Immanuel Kant argued in his *Critique of Pure Reason* (1781) that all human knowledge begins at the intuitive level. Bruce Hood illustrates this in the way that children generate knowledge through their own intuitive reasoning about the world around them. Hood writes that the process of understanding the world for infants begins long before education has any role to play. "Children chop the world of experience up into different categories of things and events. To make sense of it all, they generate naïve theories that explain the physical world, the living world, and eventually the psychological world of other people. While children's naïve theories are often correct, they can be wrong because the causes and mechanisms they are trying to reason about are invisible." He points out that "children naturally categorize the world into different kinds of things. If the child is not certain about where to draw the boundaries or misattributes properties from one area to another, the child is going to be thinking supernaturally." For example, "if a child thinks that a toy (physical property) can come alive at night (biological property) and has feelings (psychological property), this would represent a violation of the natural order of things."[81] Swiss psychologist Jean Piaget (1896-1980) found the same sense of animism in his study of children, ages 4 to 12. They thought the inanimate world was alive.

Children tend to understand things in terms of how it relates to them. They attribute "purpose to everything in the world by assuming things were made for a reason. The sun was made for me." Thus, "young children do not readily make the distinction between things that have been created for a purpose and those that just happen to be useful for a purpose. For example, if I can use a stick for prodding, I may be inclined to see sticks as having a purpose. In other words, sticks exist as something for me to use."[82]

We adults encourage this type of thinking in children by emphasizing that magic and abnormal events (talking animals, walking trees, toys that come alive, etc.) are part of normal experience. Is this because our early childhood intuitive theories are not completely abandoned, even when we become adults? Does that, in turn, lead us as adults into irrationality? Does it lead us to see faces where there are none—like the face in the moon, animals in cloud formations, faces in the wood grain of a door, pictures of Mary and Jesus on oil stains and toast, etc.?

In his book *Faces in the Clouds*, Stewart Guthrie argues that our intuitive pattern-processing biases us toward seeing faces, which leads us to assume that hidden agents surround us.

> Our mind is predisposed to see and infer the presence of others, which explains why we are prone to see faces in ambiguous patterns. If you are in the woods and suddenly see what appears to be a face, it is better to assume that it is one rather than ignore it. It could be another person out to get you. Seeing faces leads to inferences of minds. Those minds may have maleviolent intentions against us. Why else would they be hiding in the shadows? Such a bias could be just one of the mechanisms that support a sense of supernatural agents in the world.[83]

Of course, our stories about talking animals, walking trees, and toys that come alive have a positive aspect, as it allows children to project themselves into another place or into the "life" of another, thereby encouraging them to understand themselves and others from a different, usually non-threatening, point of view. It helps them to make sense of their world. It helps them to feel their way into another's life.

Pattern seeking is a basic function of the brain. Once humankind in the evolutionary process became conscious of itself and the world around it, it was this attempt to put things together—to put ideas together—that helped it make sense of its experience. "What if" became a question necessary for not only problem-solving survival skills, but also for mental and social development.

SUMMARY

The issue of consciousness is a major question for brain researchers today, an issue that goes well beyond mere awareness or shifting attention. It is just the tip of the iceberg in trying to discover what goes on in the brain. When we look at something, we tend to see the whole summarized into a single point without much thinking about how the thing happened—although later we may well ask how this thing occurred.

It is easy to demonstrate that material reality differs for different observers. It is also clear that some events that occur in your world can never, even in principle, be known in mine, and vice versa. There is also good evidence that persons differ in the extent to which they experience order or chaos in the world around them. This should give us a humbling sense of reality.

Having briefly stated how the brain may process incoming data and some possible implications of this for religious belief, we need to look at the sources of that data and how persons come to form religious beliefs and concepts. If new transcending concepts can shake the established towers of knowledge to their foundations, how can we know what is true?

CHAPTER 3

A Quintrilateral Way of Discerning Truth

"You have to take care about what assumptions you make or you will just end up 'discovering' your hidden assumptions."

—William Calvin

There is more than one history of the world."

—John Crowley

I have spent a lifetime asking almost everyone I know the same question, "How do you know?" The purpose of questioning is not primarily to deepen existing belief, although that may certainly occur; rather it is to increase knowledge and understanding. That is, questioning does not stem from the desire to believe, but rather arises from the need to "find out" and to grow intellectually, morally, and ethically. This has led me to be skeptical about most things, including faith issues. How do we know what we know? How do we verify that something is "true"—especially in light of the fact that some events that occur in your experience can never occur in mine? Every assumption or hypothesis must be tested. The scientific test we have grown accustomed to is the repeatable experiment. But is this the only valid way?

For several centuries, scholars have used a method now called by some the "Quadrilateral." United Methodists have made this method a part of their formal statement of the "theological task." It consists of the following four parts: scripture, tradition, reason, and experience. Most Christians would agree with this prioritized listing. Scripture is listed first because it is believed that it is God's word—revealed, in some way and to some degree, by God to specially chosen human beings. This belief is also held by many other religious traditions concerning their sacred writings.

This order needs to be reversed since experience is always the beginning point, tested by reason, passed on by tradition (or history), and finally written down as scripture (or embedded tradition). The task of interpretation follows the same path. What is interesting is that inspiration as a source for knowledge is not listed as part of the Quadrilateral except in its reference to revelation whereby scriptures alone are believed to have been revealed or inspired. The Quadrilateral needs to become a *Quintrilateral* to include intuition (or inspiration) as a source of knowledge.

My long-time mentor and former professor, sociologist Robert V. Guthrie, has suggested his own formula for ascending intellectual growth: Empiricism, Introspection, Intuition, Traditional Transmitted Information, and Systematic Logic. He prefers to use Systematic Logic in place of reason since it is measured by consistent verifiable results and rational discrimination, and since reason can be wrong, especially when it becomes an intellectual straitjacket. As a sociologist, he argues, along with Durkheim and others, that humanity is a product of history and hence of becoming. Sociology applies the principle, "everything human has been made by humans," to reason. "All that constitutes reason, its principles and categories, has been made in the course of history."[84]

Experience

We discussed experience in the previous chapter. This can be summarized in the short sentence: *Story always precedes text.* What the church calls "revelation" always grows out of human experience. Revelation is not an event that somehow occurs between the holy and the human; nor is it a unique text or single moment or person. Rather, the whole of existence is equally valuable and persuasive. The term "revelation" is properly attributed to the transcending insights we glean from experience.

While all knowledge of what exists is rooted in experience, we know that experience, when taken alone, is fallible. This, of course, is not a new insight. In their scientific search for truth, the best thinkers of ancient Greece appreciated the critical importance of sight, "but distrusted the axiom that 'seeing is believing,' for they knew how readily the mind can be fooled by what the eye is shown."[85] The Greek "mythical imagination was beginning to be displaced by the imaginative power of science" as the scientists/natural philosophers began stripping the older mythological explanations of their power. For instance, it was generally believed that Echo was a nymph who was punished for her talkativeness. She was cursed and forbidden to speak her own thoughts. She could only "echo" the last words spoken by others. Thus, the popular mythical understanding was that when you heard an echo, it was Echo repeating other people's words.[86] The Greek fascination with abstraction led them to see the shape of the Earth as spherical rather than as a flat disk, the prevalent understanding in most of the world at that time. "The end of Greece's classical era and the emergence of an intellectually expansive Hellenistic world had strained the bonds between the Greeks and the old gods of Olympus." The new science affected other areas as well. These new ideas not only challenged the flat Earth belief, they also began "replacing traditional rituals and beliefs with novel, personal approaches to the search for spiritual fulfillment." The Epicureans "challenged the very notion of the gods ruling an orderly universe, arguing instead that in a random universe it was the individual's obligation to seek his or her own pleasure." We need to keep in mind, though, that "however rational Greek science might seem in its quest for truth, it did not entirely divorce itself from spirituality."[87]

"If there was any doubt at the turn of the twentieth century, by the turn of the twenty-first, it was a foregone conclusion: when it comes to revealing the true nature of reality, common experience is deceptive." For instance, "Through physical and mathematical rigor, guided and confirmed by experimentation and observation, we've established that space, time, matter, and energy engage a behavioral repertoire unlike anything any of us have ever directly witnessed." Now, after decades of penetrating analyses, scientific discoveries "are leading us to what may be the next upheaval in understanding: the possibility that our universe is not the only universe."[88]

What we used to understand as "universe" is changing with the theoretical notions of parallel worlds or multiple universes. Therefore, we are forced to ask, "What exactly constitutes a world or a universe? What criteria distinguish realms that are distinct parts of a single universe from those classified as universes of their own?"[89]

We can be mistaken about what our senses tell us. Eyewitness accounts of an event are often wrong, and as the childhood game demonstrates, as the account travels through the "grapevine," the content gets muddled. In a legal research paper, Ebbesen and Konecni reported that "factors such as stress, racial dissimilarity, weapon focus, confidence, selective attention, reconstructive memory, short exposure durations, suggestion, and unconscious transference detrimentally affect the accuracy of eyewitness identifications and testimony."[90] In a study using a mock trial, "two separate sets of the jurors heard evidence differing only by the presence or absence of an eyewitness. With no eyewitness, only 18% of jurors gave guilty verdicts. Addition of eyewitness identification increased the proportion of guilty verdicts to 72%. Moreover, even when the identification was impeached, the guilty rate was still 68%."[91]

Most belief is based on the actions and words of a trusted relative, friend, religious leader, political leader, or scientist who says something that we consider true or who acts in a way that we find desirable. This operates most of the time without much notice or consequence. However, without a healthy skepticism, we are apt to believe just about anything. The required question in science is, "What would make this statement false?" This is the falsification principle. It is not enough to claim that something is true because one has never experienced the opposite.

The now famous "black swan" example of Karl Popper (1902-1994) is a good illustration of this.[92] The term "black swan" comes from the ancient Western belief that all swans were white. Black Swan theory refers to events and ideas, "outliers," that lie "outside of regular expectations, because nothing in the past can convincingly point to its possibility. Second, it carries an extreme impact. Third, in spite of its outlier status, human nature makes us concoct explanations for its occurrence *after* the fact, making it explainable and predictable." Thus, Black Swans are characterized as "rarity, extreme impact, and retrospective (though not prospective) predictability."[93]

Taleb argues that "Black Swan logic makes *what you don't know* far more relevant than what you do know. Consider that many Black Swans can be caused and exacerbated by their being unexpected." Further, "*The inability to predict outliers implies the inability to predict the course of history*, given the share of these events in the dynamics of events." The importance of this is that "almost no discovery, no technologies of note, came from design and planning—they were just Black Swans."[94]

If every encounter with the holy always occurs within historical and cultural contexts, then incarnation is not a special enfleshing of the divine in one particular event or person, but rather the discovery of transcendence within the mundane. Christians speak of experiencing the divine in Jesus, but it is just as true that we experience the divine in other persons as well. If we speak of incarnation as discovering the divine in the awesomeness of creation, we also speak of discovering the divine in the mundaneness of creation as well. One person or one aspect of creation does not contain any more transcendence than any other. It is only that our experience in that moment or place or person is deeper and more meaningful *to us*—for whatever reason.

Persons have transcending experiences that can be described as awe and wonder. In this sense, transcendence is experienced only when we are caught up in the Other—any other—in such a way that we become part of it and it becomes part of us. An at-one-ment experience can only be described poetically or metaphorically. Thus, we choose to believe some things and reject others because those we choose to believe are the result of transcending experiences that challenge or call us to be part of something greater than ourselves.

Pedraja argues that in Latino/a theology, daily experience itself is revelatory. In this context, he writes of *lo cotidano*, the daily lived experience of women and men in their struggle, praxis, work, and care for the preservation and nurture of life. "Many spiritual traditions value the spirituality of the ordinary, of the daily activities, and experiences of life. Buddhism, for instance, values mindfulness, as awareness of what we do . . . . In all of these activities, there is a nourishment of life and a deep-seated spirituality that must be explored."[95]

Roger Stein proposes a simple definition of experience as "an event that one lives through . . . and of which one is conscious."[96] For Whitehead, experience was understood as immediate and uninterrupted and "the individualized basis for a complex of reality."[97] It is not just humans who enjoy this. "Experience shapes the very process of becoming that is enjoyed by all actual entities."[98] Experience does not occur in a vacuum. It is always filtered through a multicontext of culture, language, personal bias, physical and mental dispositions, among others.

Philosopher Daniel Dennett takes the extreme reductionist position that experience simply does not exist; what we call experience is simply the operation of the functions of brain. This position is somewhat like peeling an onion only to discover that it is a series of layers of certain chemical compositions. However, even an onion is more than the sum of its parts, and a part of that identity is the associations we bring to it. These associations are essential since all thought is dependent on communal experience in its process of discernment. We can only relate to our world through overlapping and contextually interpreted experience. Thus, even though there is a common experience, each of us nevertheless encounters it from a different perspective. There is enough that we hold in common to allow for dialogue and even to arrive at certain conclusions, although total agreement on a common viewpoint is not possible.

We relate to our world only through interpreted experience, and the basic way experience is interpreted is in terms of metaphor. Metaphor gives us a plethora of new insights into ideas and concepts that are used to explain and understand the world around and within us. Metaphors, approximations, or suggestive images are always deeper than their stated meanings.

It is not too much to say that we could not very well understand any aspect of experience without the language of comparison. Even the most exacting aspects of science rely on metaphor to express their truths. James Gleick, author of *Chaos* (1987), argued that chaos theory, a science of everyday things, offers a metaphorical understanding of reality. And Richard Dawkins points out that explaining technical literature in ways that a wider audience can understand "requires insightful new twists of language and revealing metaphors. If you push novelty of language and metaphor far enough, you can end up with a new way of seeing. And a new way of seeing . . . can in its own right make an original contribution to science."[99] Metaphors, then, have the power to open us to new ways of seeing, new ways of understanding. Whereas we once talked about "building blocks" of knowledge, the newer metaphors of "network" and "web" move our language from objects to relationships.

Decades ago, Martin Buber wrote of experiencing life in terms of relationship, moving from the objectifying I-It to the subjective I-Thou relationship. Beginning in the 1920s and onward, process theology and process philosophy have assisted us in seeing the world in terms of interconnectedness. In addition to that, the growing influence of Eastern thought in the West has contributed to a better appreciation of spiritual experience in the commonness of daily life.

Of course, much of the richness and uniqueness of life is captured in our reception and response to serendipitous experience. The beauty of a flower or the awe-inspiring vastness of the universe or the love that wells up within us for another person are experiences that cannot be quantified or measured. However, their importance is not thereby diminished.

Reason

The German poet Rainer Maria Rilke (1875-1926) advised: "You should learn to love the questions themselves like locked rooms, or like books written in a very foreign tongue."[100] Alan Lightman comments that Rilke's point was "you want the present to be unfinished. You want to be able to receive and be open." He compared it to the beginner's mind in Buddhism. The ideal is always to be a beginner at everything, because when you are a beginner, you're receiving the most. You're not coming in with preconceived notions."[101] Curiosity and questioning is essential for new insight.

The greatest enemy of truth is authoritarianism, regardless of whether it is a person, a book, or some divine entity. The discovery of truth can be an exhilarating, if not mystical, achievement. The human mind, while easily misled, is nevertheless the only instrument we possess that can accomplish this discovery. As Bertman writes: "Humanity can possess an experience no god could ever have: the thrill of victory won by risking everything against great odds." The Greeks understood this, believing that "such a thrill was reserved for mortals, precisely because their lives were inherently so fragile and their power so finite."[102] It is not surprising that the Greek Goddess of intelligence, Athena, gave the gift of wisdom to humankind. This is in considerable contrast to the biblical God who forbade Adam and Eve to eat from the Tree of Knowledge.

Religious leaders have rarely affirmed reason, and today it remains under a cloak of suspicion in many quarters of the church. Higher Criticism, a prime target of religious conservatives, is based on reason and is similar to the scientific method for biblical scholars. Early on, reason was condemned by the church as a mortal sin. God and reason were by definition one and the same. Therefore, any questioning of "revealed truth" was an opposition to God and his perfectly ordered creation. Indeed, for some, like Martin Luther, reason was to be distrusted and discarded by the common person. Luther, like many other leaders throughout the generations of the church, understood that reason is a major threat to belief. He frequently called reason "the damned whore."[103] Here are a few of the quotes and references to Luther's thought on the matter:

- "Reason is the greatest enemy that faith has; it never comes to the aid of spiritual things, but more frequently than not struggles against the divine Word, treating with contempt all that emanates from God."
- "Whoever wants to be a Christian should tear the eyes out of his reason."
- "Reason should be destroyed in all Christians."
- "Reason is the Devil's greatest whore; by nature and manner of being she is a noxious whore; she is a prostitute, the Devil's appointed whore; whore eaten by scab and leprosy who ought to be trodden under foot and destroyed, she and her wisdom . . . Throw dung in her face to make her ugly. She is and she ought to be drowned in baptism . . . She would deserve, the wretch, to be banished to the filthiest place in the house, to the closets."
- "Reason must be deluded, blinded, and destroyed. Faith must trample underfoot all reason, sense, and understanding, and whatever it sees must be put out of sight and . . . know nothing but the word of God."
- "People gave ear to an upstart astrologer [Copernicus] who strove to show that the earth revolves, not the heavens or the firmament, the sun and the moon. Whoever wishes to appear clever must devise some new system, which of all systems is of course the very best. This fool wishes to reverse the entire science of astronomy; but sacred scripture tells us [Joshua 10:13] that Joshua commanded the sun to stand still, and not the earth."
- "We know, on the authority of Moses, that longer than six thousand years the world did not exist."
- "All our experience with history should teach us, when we look back, how badly human wisdom is betrayed when it relies on itself."

We can assume that Luther protested against reason so vehemently because reason raised doubts in his mind about the truthfulness of a literal understanding of faith. He had, after all, converted Christians into a "people of the Book," something that would be undermined if reason were allowed to play a major role in interpreting that Book! Because of this anti-rational bias, Luther said of Copernicus' claim that the sun was the center or our universe: "This fool wishes to reverse the entire science of astronomy; but sacred Scripture tells is that Joshua commanded the Sun to stand still, and not the Earth."[104]

Despite this kind of opposition, reason is an essential element in determining what to believe. Reason is not something divorced from experience since experience has to be tested in terms of its practical application and repeatability. John Dewey argued that reason is "experiential intelligence." Pedraja describes reason as a way of grasping and interacting with the world around us, a way by which "we order reality, think about things, make judgments, and relate to our world." In many ways, he writes, reason can set us free.

> [But] reason can become an instrument of domination that establishes a totalitarian and monolithic understanding of truth through which we measure all things. In equating truth with reason and reason with reality, we make the quest of reason simply a question of determining what is "truly" real—that is, what actually exists or is the case. The result is the reduction of reason to a simple form that merely orders, clarifies, and qualifies "reality" without ever recognizing that there is also a dimension that must also qualify reality by exploring not merely what is the case, but also what ought to be the case.[105]

Reason becomes an instrument of oppression when it uncritically excludes the voices of those who present alternative interpretations or demand change. Thomas Aquinas argued the point by stating, "When reason dictates whether one chooses to say yes to God, there is a decrease in the value of faith."[106] Yet Aquinas used reason to establish his wide-ranging proofs for the existence of God! He took the "logic" of Aristotle and Christianized it. Aristotle "reasoned" that a ten pound ball would fall twice as fast as a five-pound ball. Newton and others, of course, disproved this. In the same way, Aquinas' proofs for the existence of God were "reasoned" arguments based on Aristotelian logic, arguments that could not be verified.[107]

In *The Political Mind*, George Lakoff, professor of Cognitive Linguistics at the University of California, Berkeley, argues that reason used to be understood as

- conscious (we know what we think)
- universal (truth or facts are the same for everyone everywhere)
- disembodied (free of the body and independent of perception and action)
- logical (consistent with the properties of classical logic) unemotional (free of passion)
- value-neutral (the same reason applies regardless of one's values)
- interest-based (serving one's purposes and interests)
- literal (able to fit an objective world precisely, with the logic of the mind able to fit the logic of the world).[108]

However, he demonstrates that this understanding of reason is not valid. A basic problem in continuing to use this older understanding of reason is that it leads us into fallacy of believing that if people are only made aware of the facts, they will certainly "reason" to the "right" conclusions. However, the tremendous amount of information that is produced and disseminated—both liberal and conservative—usually results, at best, in limited consequences. This fallacy is based on the belief that reason and emotions are separate. But this is not true. Indeed, as Damasio demonstrates in *Descartes' Error*, reason *requires* emotion.[109]

This new understanding of reason takes into consideration the notion that 98 percent of our thinking is unconscious; that is, it is reflexive—automatic and uncontrolled. Our brain processes make innumerable decisions of which we are not consciously aware. This new understanding also includes the fact that the brain "extends throughout the body via the nervous system, all meaningful perception and action is mediated by our brains, whether physical, social, emotional or interpersonal. However, brains alone without bodies and physical and social interactions do nothing. It is the brain connected to the body functioning in the physical and social world that gives meaning and grounds real reason."[110]

This means that reason is an *embodied* reason, "reason shaped by our bodies and brains and interactions, in the real world, reason incorporating emotions, structured by frames and metaphors and images and symbols, with conscious thought shaped by the vast and invisible realm of neural circuitry not accessible to consciousness."[111]

The process of reasoning requires the use of facts to verify or discredit some act, idea, or belief in order to understand the external world. It employs a set of criteria designed to describe, interpret, observe, evaluate, or otherwise act upon some phenomena. By using these criteria, a testable body of knowledge is assembled to test the veracity of the phenomena. The principle of rationality, then, is the basis for understanding all of existence.

In the past, emotion was usually viewed as an impediment to reason, but this need not be the case. Feelings and emotions are essential aspects of the human reasoning process. Together they serve a vital role in the survival of the species. In essence, writes George Ellis, they

> continuously evaluate our situation as being satisfactory or unsatisfactory, and signal both the conscious and unconscious brain when change is needed. Without emotion, intellect cannot function adequately because emotions underlie the development of rationality in neuro-scientific terms. They provide a value system that guides the development of the intellect in response to internal and external senses and experiences, as the individual interacts with family and society.[112]

The implication of this is that "the theoretical concept of pure rational brain activity is an illusion."[113]

Ellis is a cosmologist who fully believes in the scientific method, yet he sees its boundaries. He understands that physics and chemistry underlie our existence, although "they cannot explain the complexity of vibrant, living beings." He says that much of life boils down to the "struggle between emotion and rationality—the calm analyst deciding on a logical basis what we should do versus the emotional hothead who rushes into action and just does things." [114]

We see this struggle in the US as leaders, politicians, and citizens decide how to handle various catastrophes. The media, many politicians, and various citizen groups demand the President show more public display of emotions. In response to the 2010 oil disaster in the Gulf of Mexico,

> *New York Times* columnists want to see Obama angry; the filmmaker Spike Lee is demanding that the president "go off"; Democratic strategist James Carville wants "rage." Whole cable shows have been devoted to the question. One Fox anchorwoman complained about what Obama was wearing when he visited the Gulf coast. Reflecting the media frenzy, the *Today* show's Matt Lauer informed the president that his critics were saying, "This is not the time to meet with experts and advisers; this is the time to . . . kick some butt.[115]

Science editor Sharon Begley echo's Zakaria's frustration: "Scientists are always such spoilsports, always insisting on gathering data on the likely effects of a strategy, before implementing it. Politicians are more inclined just to go for it, especially when they're desperate."[116]

There are different types or levels of knowing. Part of this knowing is observed through the reasoning of the scientific method, while other knowledge is experienced in more emotive ways—including the spiritual or mystical. Reason can help us to discern the importance or helpfulness of these emotive ways.

Truth is found in the reasoning process of dialogue. While many theologians courageously and honestly engage the intellectual complexities of contemporary culture, there are far more who retreat into a religious ghetto where the preferred language is comfortably triumphal and saccharine. It is not that theology should abandon its specialized language and metaphors, but if it is to enter into a true dialogue with the world, it must be able to speak in a language that is able to interpret its specialized language and metaphors to a wider audience.

While social scientists and theologians might disagree, the assumptions of their disciplines are not as accurate as those of the physical sciences, although even the physical sciences operate within a given margin of error. It is important to acknowledge that science is fallible, but that fallibility need not be fatal, since there is built within the scientific method a self-correction. When mistakes are made, or hastily drawn conclusions are proven wrong, the mistakes will become known and be retracted. As Richard Feynman writes: "If you're doing an experiment, you should report everything that you think might make it invalid—not only what you think is right about it, other causes that could possibly explain your results."[117]

How would theologians fare if they were to report how a particular doctrine or practice or other conclusion could be falsified, or how this perceived result (as with "answered" prayer) could be attributed to something else? Of course, such a verification process works against the purposes of the theologian who, by definition, works with a body of divine certainties that do not require any human verification simply because *they are divinely given.* If prayer, for instances, works on one case but not on the next twenty or next hundred cases, the religious person will fall back on mystery and divine will. "God had his reasons for answering the one and not answering the other prayers." And, if we should suggest there was an alternative reason for the healing of the one, the religious trump card is that God was involved in the alternative options as well. Perhaps we just need to heed the advice of comedian Emo Philips who said, "When I was a child, I used to pray to God for a bicycle. But then I realized that God doesn't work that way—so I stole a bike and prayed for forgiveness!"

Religious persons are not alone in waving the magic wand to justify their conclusions. Physicians, historians, psychologists, lawyers, educators, sociologists, politicians, and theologians deal with the less precise knowledge gained from experience. These experiential thinkers "can work only on the basis of a knowledge which unites 'controlling and receiving elements.' The truth of their knowledge is verified partly by experimental test, partly by a participation in the individual life with which they deal."[118] Much of what they deal with is anecdotal evidence.

One basic difference between experiential thinkers and scientific thinkers is that for experiential thinkers their results are often "true" only in *particular* contexts, that is, the truth of their arguments are not required to be proven for all times and in all places. Verification for experiential thinkers is reached by stressing reason and logic, symbolic connections and intuition, or hands-on experiment. But even then, it is only when enough of the scientific community or the religious community or any other community "(particularly those in positions of power) are willing to abandon the old orthodoxy in favor of the (formerly) radical new theory, then, and only then can the paradigm shift occur."[119]

Any search for truth must be intimately linked with a critique of all assumptions. For the religious person, this means that all doctrine and dogma must endure the rigor of experiment and philosophical testing. Sometimes the truth of an assumption is discovered in interpretation.

At other times, interpretation is not enough, and the assertion must be replaced by that which *has* been tested and verified.

As we seek to determine how we know what we claim to know, it is important to recognize the role of human desire in the production of knowledge. We can only avoid the extremes by being honest about the motives and interests that inform the production of knowledge.

Tradition

Nearly five hundred years before Jesus, Lao Tzu questioned Confucius who was interested in studying the history of the Ancients. Lao Tzu said to him, "The men of whom you speak are long since dead and their bones are turned to ashes in their graves!"

We can learn from the dead, but they were not infallible. They spoke for and in terms of their own time, but their words do not necessarily apply to our time. As Lao Tzu implied, what the ancestors said may be exactly the opposite of what we need to hear today. When that is true, their words need to be rejected outright.

For many, holding onto tradition is like collecting antiques. We collect things because we believe they are somehow important, even though most of our personal possessions often have little financial value. They are extensions of how we view ourselves. Yet, when we die, most of our "valued" possessions will be sold or donated, or else they will end up in a garage sale or simply put out with the trash. As Bruce Hood writes: "It's sobering to see how pointless a lifetime of collecting of objects seems once the collection is gone." He goes on to argue that psychologically, "we treat them as if there were some invisible property in them that makes them what they are." It is as if they have some intangible essence.[120] We often collect things because of the memories they engender.

However, memories are never just stored. They are created anew and often changed—and sometimes *your* memories are unconsciously remembered by me as my own!

Despite its value, tradition can hold us back from seizing new opportunities. If we hold too tightly to tradition, we cannot learn from new experiences. However, the reality is that the more we learn, the more tradition becomes a history lesson rather than a bedrock of truth. Of course, many refuse to open themselves to new truth.

There is a relationship between tradition and power. According to Foucault, "it is precisely tradition, and the progressivist perspective of uninterrupted continuity we project onto it, that preserves the power relations that underlie all conventions and oppressions."[121] He sharply criticizes all thinking that situates itself in the context of an ongoing, continuous tradition. This is the postmodern crisis of continuity: it "disrupts the accepted relationship between an event and a tradition that gains its stability from that relationship."[122] It is clear to see that this view of tradition radically challenges religions such as Judaism, Christianity, or Islam—religions that try to live in continuity with an event, a person, the witness of sacred writings, and the tradition that encompasses and embeds this collection of experiences. Disrupting this relationship of continuity calls into question the very integrity of tradition.

We create tradition out of the phenomena of shared experience. It is the distillation of the wisdom of thousands of generations that is designed to ensure the survivability of the present and future generations. The problem is that the world is rapidly changing and survival demands we be able to change rapidly. In this kind of climate, the old answers of tradition are often inadequate or wrong. Tradition is created for very pragmatic purposes, and for it to remain relevant, it must embody a flexibility that allows it to change as the circumstances demand. That flexibility must include the probability that the truth maintained by the tradition may be invalidated in light of new evidence. Only then does tradition have a survival value that "creates, sustains, and recreates" social and individual cohesion.[123]

Religious traditions rely on the wisdom of ancient truths. Reflecting back to the beginning of the modern era in the mid-1600s, we see that Newton and his contemporaries "had boundless faith in what they called 'the wisdom of the ancients' . . . . God had revealed those truths long ago, but they had been lost."[124] Thus, the new scientists had to *rediscover* them. The ancient wisdom had decreed as a bedrock belief that "the universe had been arranged by an all-knowing, all-powerful creator. Every aspect of the world . . . represented an explicit decision by God." This meant that God was the author of all things and "used events great and small—earthquakes, fires, victories [or defeats] in war, illness, a stumble on the stairs—to demonstrate his wrath or his mercy. To imply that anything in the world happened by chance or accident was to malign Him."[125] Chance played no part in the world that was seen as rational and orderly. One could not say, as we might, "It just so happens that . . . ."

Nor was someone praised for having an original thought. Anything new was viewed with suspicion. A new idea was a dangerous idea! This being so, the great European universities were there "not to discover the new but to transmit a heritage."[126] The same is true of today's churches and most schools of theology. Skepticism then—and in many places today—is viewed as just one very short step away from heresy. According to Augustine,

> The believers' task . . . was to defer to authority and refrain from asking questions, literally to "take it on faith." Augustine railed against the sin of curiosity with a fury and revulsion that, to modern ears, sound almost unhinged. Curiosity was, he wrote, a form of lust as despicable as any lusting of the flesh. The "lust to find out and know" was a perversion born of the same evil impulse that leads some people to peek at mutilated corpses or sneak into sideshows and stare at freaks. God intended that some mysteries remain beyond the bounds of human insight. Did not the Bible warn that "what the Lord keeps secret is no concern of your; do not busy yourself with matters that are beyond you?" [Ecclesiastes 3:22-23][127]

Much like the controversy surrounding evolution for the past century, new discoveries have always enraged traditionalists. New discoveries challenge widely held understanding and commonsense views of the world. After all, what could be less disputable than that we live on a fixed and solid Earth? Then along came those with a new theory that began by flinging the Earth into space and sending it hurtling, undetectably, through the cosmos. If the world is careening through space like a rock shot from a catapult, why don't we feel it? Why don't we fall off? Further, if humans are in the same class as animals, as Georges-Louis Leclerc de Boffon (1707-1788) argued—and Julian Offray de LaMettrie (1709-1751) before him—then "far from being the crown of creation, humans are a part of nature, different from all other animals by degree, but not by kind . . . ."[128]

Writing at the close of the seventeenth century, Pierre Bayle (1647-1706) argued that too many historians wrote to support the wisdom of tradition, but their efforts were worthless. "If historians have no expertise on the subject, it does not matter how many of them have been of the same ignorant opinion. Moreover, the populace is no different. "The crowd will uncritically believe whatever others hold to be true and will be careful not to contradict received wisdom."[129] He wrote, "I say it once again: it is an illusion through and through to assume that a sentiment which has passed from century to century, could not be entirely false."[130] In former times, this radical statement would have gotten him burned at the stake or beheaded. In that time, "any argument about truth and history [was] necessarily about the truth of religion" and the authority of an ancient book, the Bible. It was a dangerous and heretical idea, "for if the ancients are not to be relied on, divine revelation itself becomes uncertain."[131]

Tradition had required all insights to begin from a biblical constant, such as the account of creation or of the flood, and then fit the data to that. This meant that if an idea does not accord with the biblical constant, it must be false.

All thought is dependent on one's understanding of the world, although few people are willing to admit this or to revise their belief systems in light of new discoveries. And so, most Christian and Islamic believers still formulate their doctrine and dogma in terms of a flat-earth three-story universe paradigm—even though such a worldview was challenged three-hundred and fifty years *before* the life of Jesus by Aristotle and many others (See Chapter 7). Many find comfort in a set of interpretative experiences that do not change—even in the face of contradiction. Because of this refusal to allow for change, religious language and practice may be seen as unreliable sources of knowledge. At the very least, they lie under a heavy cloud of suspicion. The same can be said of political and cultural belief systems.

Tradition can be defined in this way: "One can only transmit what one can conserve." Michael Cronin looks at monuments (of all kinds) and writes: "The standing stone links the past, present, and future. It reminds those who are of those who were before and indicates a future time when they will no longer be but others will be there in their place contemplating the same stone. In linking a tangible presence to an intelligible absence, the stone or tomb or reliquary is performing a primary symbolic operation." The monument allows the individual to transcend death through objectification and memory. The object "allows the subject to emerge and it is in and through objects that our subjectivity is constructed and endures."[132]

This is a good image for understanding tradition, for the best of tradition points us not simply to a dead past but also points us to a possible future. Looking at these stones, we are reminded not only of the great deeds of the past, but also reminded of the importance of those deeds in bringing its contemporaries to a new level of understanding, change or achievement. The continuing impact of the Vietnam War Memorial in Washington, DC is an excellent example of this. The memorial is a symbol reminding us not so much of a war but of the 58,249 individual lives lost in battle. Memorials, at their best, challenge us to use memory to press forward to adopt our own new levels of understanding, change, and achievement. The standing stone has two faces: one looks back and the other looks forward. That is a proper function of tradition. Indeed, we look backward only to discover signposts pointing us to the future. As Joshua reminded his people: in years to come, children will ask what these stones mean. And you are to tell them . . . . (Joshua 4:6-7)

Tradition, then, can be understood as a mythic way of interpreting experience, since myth is a narrative where the question is not so much "Is this factually true?" but more "What truth can be discerned from this story?" Dennis Ford writes that to the mythic mind any object can be the realm of the sacred. "By manifesting the sacred, any object can be transformed into something else, yet remain itself."[133] He was echoing Eliade, who wrote, "A *sacred* stone remains a *stone* . . . . Nothing distinguishes it from all other stones. But for those to whom a stone reveals itself as sacred, its immediate reality is transmuted into a supernatural reality. In other words," he writes, "all nature is capable of revealing itself as cosmic sacrality."[134]

Tradition is interpretative history. It involves sets of theories that we construct to make sense of the continuities and discontinuities of the past and present. Is it possible to do theology with a tradition whose continuity no longer has to be guaranteed by questionable history? If the answer is affirmative, then we have the power to criticize the tradition while standing within it.

As we noted, tradition does not always operate in a positive manner. Karl Marx noted this when he wrote in 1852: "Men make their own history, but they do not make it just as they please; they do not make it under circumstances chosen by themselves, but under circumstances directly encountered, given and transmitted from the past. The tradition of all the dead generations weighs like a nightmare on the brain of the living."[135]

Pedraja writes that when Latino/a theology utilizes tradition as a source for theology, "we give serious consideration to the way power, politics, and context play a role in the shaping of our faith. Even our culture and cultural memories affect our theological reflection and our understanding of tradition."[136] As Latina theologian Jeanette Rodríguez points out, tradition is not simply the *content* that is handed down but also the process of transmission. "This process involves people who live in a society and culture that carry memories, all occurring within political, historical, and social contexts. All of these processes involved in remembering and handing down tradition also carry and evolve the affections, images, ideals, hopes, and feelings of the people who inherit and pass on their traditions."[137]

Tradition, then, "is not a simple monolithic body of truth, but a multifaceted strand of intertwined threads that often bind together and that other times unravel. What we call tradition is merely the strands we choose or are told to follow."[138]

Our task is to examine the tradition, not to simply repeat or defend it. We are not only free to, but also required to, seek out its intent. Critical engagement with tradition never happens in isolation. Just the opposite. We enter this critical engagement with our own personal convictions. After all, we relate to the past and to our traditions through *interpreted* experience. The notion that the continuity of tradition rests on an unchanging premise from which we can deduce all other truths can no longer be maintained. There are several interpretations of the same tradition in this pluralist world.

At their best, beliefs are determined by living and evolving traditions that may be modified or replaced when such a change is meaningful and more compelling. All tradition is defined by the worldview of which it is a part.

Traditions are never completely isolated from one another. For instance, when we open the Tanakh, we find many different cultures and traditions influencing the Hebrew text. It is understood that the Christian texts are likewise a composite of different traditions. The same is true of the Qur'aan. (It is also true of our "sacred" political documents like the Declaration of Independence and the Constitution.) Despite the accepted notion that traditions provide unchanging continuity, because of their contextual nature, traditions—whether religious, political, etc.—do change and evolve. If they do not, they are lifeless and meaningless.

Broadly stated, our lives are defined and shaped by a complex variety of political, moral, and religious traditions. As we evaluate our beliefs, opinions, and viewpoints, "the movement thus goes from individual judgment to communal evaluation to intersubjective conversation." Every judgment and rhetorical argument "always takes place in some community, and each community has a particular tradition and history."[139]

Memes as Tradition?

Connie Barlow writes that "the capacity for religious experience and explanation is just that—a capacity. Genes do not tell us how the world came into being. Genes do not determine what we revere. These crucial details are, rather, the workings of the cultural counterpart of genes: memes."[140] Memes are cultural replicators, that is, information that is copied from person to person, or from person to artifact.

Does the debated notion of memes operate as a form of tradition? Evolutionary biologist Richard Dawkins coined the term meme (rhymes with "theme"). Examples of memes are "tunes, ideas, catchphrases, clothes, fashions, ways of making pots or of building arches." In *The Selfish Gene* (1976), he argues that "just as genes propagate themselves in the gene pool by leaping from body to body via sperms or eggs, so memes propagate themselves in the meme pool by leaping from brain to brain."[141] Memes, writes Barlow, "are what give substance to our inchoate capacities for religious feelings. Whether they enter our minds by thoughtful or thoughtless invitation or by indoctrination, particular memes are usually what we judge when we speak of religion in friendly or unfriendly ways."[142]

Susan Blackmore is a major voice in the current debate. Her views are perhaps the most controversial. One of her claims is that *imitation alone* supplies the means for replicating memes. She writes, "Memes are stories, songs, habits, skills, inventions, and ways of doing things that we copy from person to person by imitation."[143] Some memes exhibit a "viral structure," which includes a "copy me," instruction along with threats and promises which insure their reproductive survival. Blackmore sums up her perspective in this way: "We are neither the slaves of our genes nor rational free agents creating culture, art, science, and technology for our own happiness. Instead we are part of a vast evolutionary process in which memes are the evolving replicators and we are the meme machines."[144]

Thus, for Blackmore, memes explain our uniquely human mental attributes and the complexities of our cultures. She admits that "humans exhibit a discontinuity from other species, but only because two replicators, not one, have designed us. That is, genes generate peoples and memes make cultures through a dual form of evolutionary design."[145]

Religions qualify as memes since they are transmitted through culture. Blackmore suggests the "God-meme" arose perhaps to alleviate fear and provide comfort. Claiming that the God-meme endures only as a maladaptive fiction, she argues that God-memes survive not because they are true or correspond to metaphysical reality in any sense: "No—they have survived because they are selfish memes and are good at surviving—they need no other reason."[146] They are selfish because they influence their own survival independently of the human agents they inhabit.

Dawkins considers faith a kind of memetic sickness because "faith sufferers" believe not only without evidence—but also consider this lack of evidence to be a virtue. In this sense, Dawkins is not far from most theologians who would agree that faith without any rational foundation is unsound. The problem with these statements by Blackmore and Dawkins is that they lump all expressions of faith together.

This new field of memetics has been referred to as "Darwinizing culture."[147] It remains to be seen whether it is a sustainable theory or whether it is making mistakes similar to Spencer's Social Darwinism. Regardless, anthropologists and sociologists have been making similar arguments for decades. While it seeks to explain the complexities of culture and mind, memetics is still so new that it is struggling to find consensus at the theoretical level. One question is whether or not it can be scientifically demonstrated that imitation can truly account for the more complex processes of how concepts are transmitted *abstractly*, such as through recombination, deduction, induction, and abduction. The challenge is that in order for memetics to serve the science of culture, *there must be some observable and verifiable evidence.*

Tradition falls into the description of memes. Barlow suggests that "religious memes that can soothe the inevitable human-to-human, group-to-group, and nation-to-nation tensions in an increasingly crowded but interconnected world are surely worth every bit of support each and every human culture can muster." While human beings have been searching for ways to live together peacefully, the sad fact is that they have used their traditions to build dividing walls even higher. They have used their traditions to alienate their sisters and brothers from each other, and have devised all means of terror and destruction to protect themselves from outsiders and enemies. As Barlow summarizes the point, "Those that promote peace and harmony within the group may be bloody terrors without."[148]

Summary

Max Planck once wrote, "A new scientific truth does not triumph by convincing its opponents and making them see the light, but rather because its opponents eventually die, and a new generation grows up that is familiar with it."[149] We naturally begin by choosing criteria that are the most rationally compelling to us and those we believe will be able to help us adequately address the questions and goals we pursue. That means our criteria for judgment are always "a strategy of interpretation." By utilizing a cross-disciplinary method, rationality is not simply limited to one's own tradition, and we can begin the evaluation with as few presuppositions as possible. By approaching our search for knowledge through broader understandings of experience, reason, and the creative aspects of tradition, we are freed from the prison of our narrower concepts of faith. All of these things together can keep faith as a vital aspect of life. They also remind us that each generation defines the boundaries of what qualifies as "religious truth." Because the needs change, so the content changes. Of course, many will argue that this contaminates belief and therefore any changes are to be rejected. However, that view is so narrow that it must be rejected.

In the next chapter, we will examine the fourth aspect of the quintrilateral—embedded tradition.

CHAPTER 4

It Was Said of Old . . .
Embedded Tradition

> *"The group that emerged as victorious and declared itself orthodox determined the shape of Christianity for posterity—determining its internal structure, writing its creeds, and compiling its revered texts into a sacred canon of Scripture."*
>
> —*Bart Ehrman*

Psychologist William James was asked in a questionnaire, "Do you accept the Bible as authority in religious matters?" James replied, "No. No. No. It is so human a book that I don't see how belief in its divine authorship can survive the reading of it."[150] Another way to answer the question is, "The Bible is true—when it is true!"

The fourth aspect of the quintrilateral is embedded tradition. Scriptures (Tanakh, Bible, Qur'aan, Avesta, the Vedas, Guru Granth, the Sutras, I Ching, and others) do not, in and of themselves, have the ability to settle any issues. They can only give some wisdom that may then help the reader discern an answer. Some contemporary ethical issues have no literal scriptural solution since these sacred writings are grounded in pre-scientific beliefs and cultural assumptions that are no longer relevant today. And some of what they have to say is simply wrong—and dangerous!

All language, including that of scripture, is a human activity that necessarily reflects the cultural assumptions and biases of the writers. Those who have read any of these scriptures will know they are full of both scientific and historical errors as well as many contradictions. Because of this fact, it is a dead-end street to argue for the scriptures to be free of error and devoid of human involvement in their writing. It is meaningless to proclaim, "The Bible says . . ." since the Bible "says" many contradictory things. In this context, the Bible says whatever we want it to say! This is true of the embedded traditions of *all* religions. The truth of scripture is demonstrated in the lives of those who claim to live by it. For Christians, this is a Protestant principle. As United Methodist theologian Tyron Inbody writes, "The truth of an idea is not a stagnant property inherent in it. It becomes true, is made true, by events."[151]

The danger is always that these embedded traditions become fossilized beliefs that leave no room for new insights. It is simply ludicrous to assume that scriptures are divinely revealed, unadulterated truth untouched and unaffected by human actions and human input. Experience is essential to relationship, and to claim that scripture is unchangeable is a denial of an individual's current experiences of the divine.

While Protestants place religious authority in the Bible, their "paper Pope," it is not correct to say that they therefore do not rely on hierarchies or traditions to direct the faithful. The abortion debate in the US is a good example of this. Conservative Protestants do not simply agree with the Catholic arguments. They rely on the Roman Catholic Church for its pronouncements and their guidance. They are, of course, reluctant to admit this, since many conservatives still do not consider Catholics to be Christians; but one has only to compare their literature and arguments to see the truth of this.

The Protestant reliance on tradition rather than scripture is also clear in its acceptance of Nicene Trinitarianism. To prove its truth, the church refers back to the pronouncements of the Council of Nicaea, not to the Bible, since it is not found there. A church committed to *sola scriptura* would not make its appeals to church councils but to the scripture as its final authority.

In addition, the hierarchies of religious authority are as prevalent in Protestantism as it is in Catholicism. The Protestant teaching magisterium includes the strong voices of both past and current leaders, men such as Billy Graham, Bob Jones, Jerry Falwell, Benny Hinn, Bill Hybels, Bill McCartney, Jack Van Impe, John MacArthur, Robert Schuller, Pat Robertson, Max Lucado, T.D. Jakes, Charles Swindoll, and James Dobson, to mention just a few.

All sides in an argument—regardless of the religious expression we examine—appeal to an embedded tradition to establish their position. As Margaret Zulik has argued, the *sola scriptura* tradition, with its closed canon of revelation, experiences anxiety whenever a prophetic voice emerges, because the latter assumes God's continuing authoritative revelation with the world. "In a *sola scriptura* solution, there is no way to resolve arguments that arise over differing interpretations of Scripture or over apparent conflicts within the profoundly heterogeneous Scripture itself. Arguments cannot be resolved because assigning ultimate authority to Scripture alone leaves no existential standing point for revelation."[152]

The Bible is embedded tradition that records very human transcending stories, and its authority lies not in its recorded words, but in its relation to lived reality. As Pedraja argues, "the context, the way we use it, its location in language—all change its meaning. This fluidity of meaning is particularly true when we are speaking of a written language."[153]

It is an interesting fact that during the first three centuries of the nascent church, there were many writing considered sacred. Some that were lost were recovered from caves and monastic libraries in the latter half of the 20th century. Some we know only from references made to them from the early church leaders. Although Irenaeus created a list as early as 180 CE, an authorized list known as the canon was not made official until the Council of Hippo (393-397) and the Council of Carthage (397). It took nearly 400 years to get an authorized list mainly because up until that time it was not a burning issue. To complicate the matter, there is *still* not one list (canon) that is agreed on by all the major Christian bodies. On this issue as well, Protestants rely on church councils as their authority.

In the earliest period of the Christian movement, not only was the Old Testament the only accepted scripture, but since the followers expected the second coming of Jesus to occur at any moment, there was no need for anything else. As the distance between Jesus and thc Church widened, the letters and gospels of the earliest leaders became important interpretations of what they believed Jesus had taught. These writings were read along with the Old Testament in the worship services. However, it also took this long because there was no clear-cut, widely accepted theology. Baigent reminds us that until key decisions were made with regard to the person of Jesus, there simply was no "officially sanctioned criteria by which to choose" and reject texts.[154] Besides, it was not any easier to add new things to the Bible then than it would be today. After all, there were biblical warnings not to add anything to the accepted scriptures, in both the Tanakh and the new Christian writings.[155]

In 367 CE, Athanasius, Bishop of Alexandria, wrote an episcopal letter indicating the books that his churches were to accept as sacred scripture. He first listed the books of the Jewish scriptures, the Tanakh, that Christians called the "Old" Testament. He also included, for devotional purposes only, the Old Testament Apocrypha. Then he listed the 27 books that we now know as the New Testament. However, different Christian bodies held—and continue to hold—different books as sacred scripture. For instance, Syrian Christians do not accept 2 Peter, 2 and 3 John, Jude, and Revelation, giving them a New Testament of 22 books. The Ethiopian Church accepts the 27 books plus 4 others, giving them a New Testament of 31 books. Thus, "there never has been complete agreement on the canon throughout the Christian world."[156]

Of course, Jesus and his disciples already had a canon of scripture—the Tanakh. By the fourth century, establishing a new canon of scripture was seen as necessary to give boundaries to what was and was not acceptable belief. This was essential in order to counter the forces of heretical teachings.

Different viewpoints employed different criteria in determining the authenticity and applicability of the many diverse writings available to the church. As a result, "very human decisions were made, based upon very human priorities"—and as the structure of the church developed, most of these decisions were based on control and power.[157] Irenaeus argued that "the central unified organization of the Church was a measure of its universal appeal, nature, and truth. Thus, centralization and orthodoxy were established as proofs of validity and rectitude: *physical power was one of the proofs of God's support.*"[158]

Translation and Interpretation

The Gospels were written by individuals, relying on various sources. It is widely accepted that the authors to whom they are traditionally ascribed did not write them. (And, needless to say, they were obviously not dictated or even revealed by God, unless God was afflicted by dementia!) An important aspect of both tradition and its scripture is translation. There are numerous examples of *faux pas* where leaders have used an incorrect translation for a word or phrase and were embarrassed by saying something the original authors certainly did not intend. (In our own day, businesses have introduced products into other cultures where a seemingly positive name turned out to be an insult either to the product or to the intended consumers.) Even biblical translators have difficulty translating concepts from one era or one culture to another. Translation is extremely important—and exceedingly difficult. The purpose of translation is to universalize, "to take a text from one spatially-bound language and culture, and transplant it into a different language and culture."[159] Every translation introduces new ideas into the text.

Even then, tradition rules the day. In the early 1980s, I was working on a commentary of 1 Corinthians when I discovered that Paul was writing the entire letter in what I called a "dialogical" manner. He would quote portions of the reports he had received from Chloe and from others, and then he responded to them. When read in this manner, it challenged certain accepted interpretations. During one of my trips to Clermont School of Theology for meetings of the Faith and Process group, I stayed in the home of William Beardslee, one of the translators for the New Revised Standard Version of the Bible. I shared my research with him and suggested that the addition of quotation marks to differentiate between the reports and Paul's responses would be very helpful and important to our understanding. His response was that translators are bound to tradition (in order to sell Bibles!), and to add quotation marks would be too great a challenge to tradition. Tradition, then, rules the day in all translations.

As mentioned earlier, theologians and biblical scholars have for centuries used a four-fold path to religious knowledge: scripture, reason, tradition, and experience. They have stated this in different ways, but the method is similar. Scripture is the trusted writings of the past. For science, these trusted writings could be as old as Aristotle and Plato or as recent as Darwin or Einstein. They are held in high esteem because they have added significantly to what was known *up to that point*. For religious persons, embedded traditions are based on a similar trust level, except that in science, when something is later proven wrong, it is corrected. Religions rarely—if ever—correct their scriptures, although they may attempt to correct past interpretations. Most scholars simply try to explain away the error. For instance, when the Christian gospel of John was demonstrated to be clearly anti-Judaic, it was explained in such a way to remove or at least dull the sharp edges. The same can be said of the scriptures of other religions. Religious fundamentalists of all persuasions take some of the most negative or esoteric aspects of the scriptures and focus on them. Since scriptures are embedded traditions, they show us how we got to a particular point in time. (One problem is that these books are rarely printed in the chronological order of their writing. Rather, they are placed in theological order, thereby leading many to wrong conclusions.)

When scriptures become entombed, tradition loses its ability to continue the process of ongoing interpretation. It creates a dependence upon belief in traditions that are closed to any analysis of its truth. This dependence is established at the expense of knowledge. Indeed, no text can be entombed with any sense of unchanging truth without shutting off all rational inquiry. (As we saw with Luther, Augustine, and Aquinas, reason is the enemy of embedded truths.) However, we can recognize the finite and flawed nature of embedded traditions and still appreciate their efforts at expressing mythic truth.

Embedded traditions beg the question of whether it is ever possible to really know the meaning of a text. After all, embedded traditions were written and read in specific times and places, and with specific intentions for specific audiences that are now at considerable distance from us. What one hears or reads depends on one's own personal time, place, situation, and expectations. Hearing and reading are therefore *always* a matter of interpretation, translation, and transformation of the text. It is therefore impossible for us ever to capture a final truth—we can only know approximations. As Robert Stanton argues, we cannot even see our own immediate environments directly. Instead, we construct a mental image of it and "see" that mental construct. Our visual images are not like cameras. We do not see an image

> until our optic nerves have sent their individual little bits of data up to and through a series of centers in our brain that combine and interpret these bits with the aid of knowledge stored in our memories. Our feelings help us to construct the image, but also distort it. Our emotions and cultures make some things beautiful and important, other things ugly and trivial. We continually make mistakes.[160]

But we can improve our image of what is "really" out there. The corrections can come from what we learn by experience, from history, and the knowledge we get from others. None of us is always right, although some people are right more often than others, at least within their "fields of expertise." Our knowledge can be tested, especially with double-blind experiments and peer review.

Almost from the very beginning, religious people of many different persuasions have struggled with the insufficiency of their scriptures and have added to it—corrected, modified, altered, tweaked—and otherwise developed its meaning through tradition. They have done this because they realized that the scriptures cannot stand alone. Even admitting to this, many nevertheless remain troubled by the very need for such solutions, although this need not be seen as a negative. Rather, it might be seen as a conclusion of faith, based on loyalty to the inherited tradition *seen in its totality*.

Scripture did not stand alone in ecclesiastical authority until the Protestant Reformation. Even then, tradition was not abandoned but was relegated to a minor position, even as new traditions were begun. Standing alone as the final authority of belief and practice, it was easy for many to regard the Bible as a Book fallen from Heaven. The once mythical (symbolic and metaphorical) expressions of its creation became concretized, and the written words themselves took on the aura of verbal inspiration and infallibility. Sheppard reminds us that the Reformers did more than simply raise up a battle cry against the practices of the Roman Catholic Church. Their declaration of *sola scriptura* established biblically-based theology in place of philosophical theology. "In a more biblically based theology, the primary assumption is that faith in the truth of Holy Scripture is both necessary and sufficient for a believer to know the divine . . . . By contrast, while philosophical theology stresses the Bible as its foundation, it also tries to make good use of the natural human ability to reason . . . ."[161]

Rather than allowing embedded tradition to live and breathe new life into each future, it is usually treated as a dead instrument. Most believers paradoxically want a literal reading that will also apply to current situations. I have never met or even heard of a pure literalist. Many of those who insist on a fully literalistic reading use prophecy as a way around apparent contradictions. Of course, believers have often used this course to prove their rightness. Probably one of the clearest examples of this is in the proof-texting of the New Testament writers who took partial readings out of context in order to prove that Jesus was the answer to the hopes proclaimed by the prophets.

When the reformers spoke of the infallible word, they normally referred to its *unfailing message*. It was infallible in terms of its message of salvation. By the end of the nineteenth century, however, the emerging fundamentalist movement exalted the book to a position of worship. Having been absolved of any errors or discrepancies, scripture lost its role as a witness *to* revelation and was seen as the very revelation itself. While arguing against the Catholic dogma of transubstantiation—the literal changing of the wine and bread into the very blood and body of Christ—fundamentalists made the same argument for the words of the Bible.

Several years ago I asked a United Methodist professor at the very conservative Trinity-Evangelical Divinity School how he could sign the required faith statement that included among other things the belief that the scriptures are infallible in their original script. He responded, "No one has yet found the original scripts!" That's a little like crossing one's fingers when claiming to tell the truth. However, it also illustrates how persons find ways to get around the legalisms of religious faith.

Ehrman poses an interesting question: "How does it help us to say that the Bible is the inerrant word of God if in fact we don't have the words that God inerrantly inspired, but only the words copied by the scribes—sometimes correctly but sometimes (many times!) incorrectly?"[162] He tells us that we currently have access to nearly 5,400 Greek copies of all or part of the New Testament, ranging from scraps of a verse or two to bound copies of the complete 27 books. We know that the words have been changed because no two copies are exactly alike. While most of the differences are insignificant, there are others that are important. For instance, scribes who opposed adoptionistic views of Jesus modified the texts in order to stress their views that Jesus was not just human, but also divine.[163] Examples of this include:

1 Timothy 3:16
  Original: Christ "who was made manifest in the flesh"
  Changed: "God made manifest in the flesh"

Luke 2:53
  Original: "his father and mother"
  Changed: "Joseph and his mother"

In Luke 2:11 Jesus was born as the Christ, while Acts 2:28 affirms that Jesus became Christ at the resurrection (cf., Romans 1), and in Acts 10:37-38 Jesus became Christ at his baptism (cf. Mark 1). In the prologue of John (1:18) Jesus is not merely God's unique Son, as in the earlier witnesses, but becomes uniquely *God himself*!

Changes occur in the scriptures because scribes sometimes altered the text to make them say what the scribe thought they meant. While this is not necessarily a bad thing, once the texts were altered, "the words of the texts quite literally became different words, and these altered words necessarily affected the interpretations of the words by later readers." Sometimes these texts were changed because of theological disputes that were vying for attention. Other factors in the altering of texts had to do with the social conflicts of the day, "conflicts involving such things as the role of women in early Christian churches, the Christian opposition to Jews, and the Christian defense against attacks by pagan opponents."[164]

Ehrman grew up and was educated in fundamentalism but eventually concluded, "It would have been no more difficult for God to preserve the words of scripture than it would have been for him to inspire them in the first place . . . . And if he didn't perform that miracle, there seemed to be no reason to think that he performed the earlier miracle of inspiring those words."[165] The Bible is a very human document from beginning to end. Yet, many see no difference between saying "God says" and "the Bible says." If the Bible is a human book and not divinely or inerrantly inspired, what is the difference between "the Bible says" and "the Qur'aan says" or any other sacred writing of any other religion? "As Homer said in the *Iliad* . . . ."

Textual literalism is the bedrock of the chronic obscenity of religious and political fundamentalism. It arises from the need for something that will support and authorize the religious institution's survival from generation to generation. Nevertheless, textual literalism leads to fossilized belief, in which case there is no room for further transcending experiences or encounters with the divine. As Justo González points out in *Mañana*, "our idols not only lead us to a dead end and cold god of rigid concepts and ideas, but they can also become instruments of socioeconomic oppression by protecting the cherished notions and ideals of a given culture."[166]

Religions create ways to monitor both internal and external threats, and seek to deal with these threats in order to maintain the community's welfare and to preserve stability through rewards and punishments. Because of the security function of literalism, religion is prone to seek absolutes, to the point of suppressing the prophetic/critical element.

Fundamentalism as Self-Deception

Fundamentalism is "an adaptive act of self-deception" in the face of rapid social, scientific, and cultural change. Self-deception and the deception of others seem to be a part of our survival tool kit.

Primatologist Frans De Waal documents how prevalent deception is among our closest relatives, the primates. Among other behaviors, he notes that chimps feign injury, signal reconciliation in order to get advantage in an attack, pretend ignorance of hidden food items, and manipulate humans in order to get their help in escaping captivity.[167] This is significant because "the capacity to mislead in children is one of the more important indicators of cognitive development. In children younger than seven or eight, spontaneous changes of truth are common and relatively unconscious. At roughly eight years of age, intentional manipulation of others through lying begins, and by ten consciousness of others' potential manipulations is well established.[168] By the time humans reach adulthood, they are fully involved in a complex web of deceptions. In short, "duplicity is part and parcel of the human condition." Duplicity, it seems, is so vital to the functioning of human interactions that cognitive psychologist David Smith argues our society "would collapse under the weight of too much honesty." Being neither immoral nor pathological in and of itself, "the capacity for deception is a central component in human functioning."[169]

Braxton tells us "from an evolutionary vantage point, it appears the mind evolved the capacity to bias its perceptions because this confers advantage to the self thus deceived." Therefore, "we process information about our life experiences in manners that are systematically advantageous to us." We do this in order to see ourselves as masters of our world. We need to feel that we are somehow in control. "Whether we create the illusion of control because of deep psychological needs, or for other reasons we do not as yet understand, empirical studies over and over again report that we overestimate our personal control."[170] This relates to the religious question by suggesting that the subjective experience of certainty may be just such an adaptive self-deception.

Revelation

While I would prefer not to continue using the term, revelation is not data or information that God or the Gods give to some chosen human beings. It is not an unchanging truth, one that is untouched and unaffected by the environment of the human writers. It is a very human process of gleaning transcending insight for living from the world around us. Thus, the narrative of the Garden of Eden, the lost paradise, is not a historical event, but a story whose purpose was to help persons understand the human predicament. Why is there sin? The premise of the story is that at the "beginning," everything was perfect, but humanity fell from that perfection through the disobedience of the first parents. At the end of the fourth century, Augustine developed this story into the doctrine of original sin. The Eden story no longer satisfies its original purpose, since we no longer accept its worldview. We know that there was no original state of perfection and therefore no fall from perfection or grace. What we have gleaned from observing the world requires us not simply to reinterpret the ancient story, but to reject it.

The issue of revelation was a major problem for the early church since the anticipated second coming of Jesus did not occur. Noting that the prophecies of the second coming and the coming of the Kingdom did not materialize, Ehrman asks these questions for us:

> How can we imagine that God has spoken to his prophets, even his theologically correct prophets, if their predictions do not come true? Moreover, how can divine teaching be controlled if it is a matter of personal inspiration? What prevents one person, even if well intentioned and completely orthodox, from claiming a divine revelation that stands completely at odds with someone else's divine revelation? Or worse yet, what should be done with a direct personal revelation that contradicts the written revelation of Scripture? And what kind of tactical handles can be applied to heretics who claim revelation, direct from God? The Gnostics, of course, claimed secret knowledge. Why were their claims any less plausible than those of the proto-orthodox? In short, how can one determine whether a "prophecy" is from God or not? If it agrees with Scripture? But if Scripture is the key to everything, why does one need prophecy at all?[171]

These questions certainly add up to an argument for the rejection of revelation from a deity altogether. After all, the measure of prophetic authenticity is that what is said really comes true.

The church was not open to continuous revelation for obvious reasons. The Catholic Church hedged this by allowing God to talk to the pope, but Protestants have largely opted to limit revelation to the biblical period. But even this is fuzzy since despite their claims of biblical primacy, conservative Protestants have argued that the time of revelation ended only *after* the Council of Nicaea (325). Why stop there? Why not earlier, or later?

The bottom line is that what we understand as "revelation" arose out of the imagination, experience, and reasoning processes of ancient religious leaders. We now know that what we call revelation was influenced by other cultures. Their stories were "borrowed" and became our stories. Thus, the flood story of Gilgamesh became the flood story of Noah, the Babylonian story of the righteous sufferer Eukidu became the story of the righteous sufferer Job, the virgin birth stories of the Greek and Roman Gods became the virgin birth story of the Christian God Jesus, and so on. Revelation is not concerned with literal truth or historical fact. It is only concerned with theology.

Appeals to revelation can be seen as lazy excuses to avoid the hard tasks of reflection and serious intellectual thought. Or, as William Placher has said, the phrase "Thus saith the Lord" sounds a lot like, "Shut up and do as you're told." Revelation can be seen as a means of control and manipulation.

Process theologians generally understand revelation as a special experience of insight whereby unification between the divine initial aim and the human subjective aim is experienced to such a particularly high degree that this occasion becomes decisive and informative to all other experiences. Even then, the revelatory experience is received and interpreted through the faculties of human reason.

All thought involves value judgments by which some aspect of reality is taken as an important clue to the understanding of the rest of reality. As such, revelation is not a series of definitive pronouncements from on high that ends all future conversation or development. It is not something infallible and applicable for all people at all times. When it is seen as infallible, revelation is simply an excuse for lazy thought as it urges an escape into "mystery." At its best, revelation is a way of talking about transcendence in ways that have been discerned by human beings and the trustworthiness of which is tested in every time.

If one is forced to use the term "revelation" at all, it is to be understood as any event that enables us to see with particular clarity how we are constantly surrounded by transcendence through which we can understand, at least in principle, the rest of reality. A revelatory event is not necessarily distinguishable from any other event. Because revelation is a perceptual insight enabling one to see a larger picture or meaning, it is important to realize that there is a distinction between the facts as perceived and the facts as they are in themselves. This distinction implies that although our perceptual insights may structure our experience, they do not constitute the reality of that which is experienced. The facts of any experience have their reality prior to, and therefore are independent of, that experience.

As I have written elsewhere,[172] the question about why persons choose certain occasions as revelatory when others do not raises a complex issue. An occasion of insight provides one with a coherent and convincing understanding into the nature of reality as seen from that particular vantage point. Because different persons are open to new insight at different stages of readiness and from different worldviews, what one considers revelatory will vary with the particular histories, traditions, and the cultures. Therefore, one form of understanding will appear more appropriate, illumining, and convincing than another. In this sense, French Catholic priest and paleontologist Pierre Teilhard de Chardin wrote: "It is much better to present 'tentatively' a mixture of truth and error than to mutilate reality in trying to separate before the proper time the wheat from the chaff."[173]

Summary

There are few, if any, who follow their sacred texts completely. Indeed, this would be impossible since the texts often contradict themselves. The truth is that believers pick and choose passages they wish to follow while also choosing which not to follow. Whether they admit it or not, even the most ardent fundamentalist acts on the principle that not all things were written for all people in all circumstances in all times. These sacred writings may contain "truths" that are worthwhile and contribute to personal growth and "salvation." But they also contain teachings that are no longer relevant and even dangerous to the survival of humanity. They are limited to time, place, circumstance, and cultural development. Shermer states the case well against the church's inconsistent use of its sacred texts:

> If you are going to claim the Bible as your primary (or only) code of ethics and proclaim (say) that homosexuality is sinful and wrong because the Bible says so, then to be consistent you

> should kill rebellious youth, nonvirginal premarried women, and adulterous men and women. Since most today would not endorse that level of consistency, why pick on gays and lesbians but cut some slack for disobedient children, promiscuous women, and adulterous men and women? And why aren't promiscuous men subject to the same punishment as women? The answer is that in that culture, at that time, men legislated and women obeyed. Thankfully, we have moved beyond that culture. But what this means is that we need a new set of morals and an ethical system designed for our time and place, not one scripted for a pastoral/agricultural people who lived 4,000 years ago. The Bible and other sacred texts have wonderfully edifying and sometimes transcendent passages, but we can do better.[174]

It is hard to dispute Sam Harris when he writes: "If our species ever eradicates itself through war, it will not be because it was written in the stars but because it was written in our books; it is what we do with words like 'God' and 'paradise' and 'sin' in the present that will determine our future." He goes on to state that "our technical advances in the art of war have finally rendered our religious differences . . . antithetical to our survival."[175] Pointing to this anti-survival orientation, he writes:

> Tell a devout Christian that his wife is cheating on him, or that frozen yogurt can make a man invisible, and he is likely to require as much evidence as anyone else, and to be persuaded only to the extent that you give it. Tell him that the book he keeps by his bed was written by an invisible deity who will punish him with fire for eternity if he fails to accept its every incredible claim about the universe, and he seems to require no evidence whatsoever.

Again:

> Our world is fast succumbing to the activities of men and women who would stake the future of our species on beliefs that should not survive an elementary school education. That so many of us are still dying on account of ancient myths is as bewildering as it is horrible, and our own attachment to these

> myths, whether moderate or extreme, has kept us silent in the face of developments that could ultimately destroy us.[176]

It is hard to argue with Harris that our embedded traditions continue to create religious identities that often perpetuate conflict; and we need not go back to the Crusades or the Inquisitions to see this.

It normally takes a long time for new worldviews to be widely accepted. One result of the Enlightenment was a secularization in which religion has "little or no function in determining what is to be discovered and communicated by physicists, astronomers, biologists and historians, how markets work, how governments are structured, what course of study organizes public schools and universities, and what entertainments and uses of leisure time take place." Fundamentalists in all religions feel powerless before such openness. But the reality is that "each religion must find a way to survive not just as a specific community or people but as a faith amidst institutions, world views, and everyday life practices utterly empty of divine import."[177]

This is the stage on which responses to a new worldview are played out.

CHAPTER 5

Intuition as a Source of Knowledge

"No statement, theological or otherwise, should be made that would not be credible in the presence of burning children."

—Rabbi Irving Greenberg

There are different ways of coming to reliable knowledge about the world. Intuition, or what the church refers to as inspiration, is one of them. In this discussion, I will use these terms interchangeably. Intuition has been defined as "our capacity for direct knowledge, for immediate insight without observation or reason." Intuitions—whether social, psychological or moral—operate "at a level so fast and subtle that they cannot be considered a product of rational thought."[178] In this manner of knowing, one cannot fully explain, at least immediately, why she or he came to a particular view.

This discussion of intuition begins by looking at the psychological research. Inspiration/intuition is found under many different headings including: automaticity, automatic processing, subliminal priming, implicit memory, heuristics, spontaneous trait inference, right-brain processing, instant emotions, nonverbal communication, and creativity. All of these point to that which deals with our intuitive capacities. Thinking, memory, and attitude all operate on two levels—conscious/deliberate and unconscious/automatic. Some researchers today call this "dual processing."[179] Malcolm Gladwell prefers to use the description "rapid cognition."

Generally speaking, "researchers are finding that unconscious thought processes powerfully determine many aspects of our life, from how we perceive and react to other people to how we make moral decisions."[180] Intuition/inspiration is not resource free. It operates within broadly defined cultures of influence from which it draws or creates new insights. This unconscious thought process does not operate in a vacuum. For instance, a person who is totally unaware of, and not influenced by polytheism, would never conceive of the Christian doctrine of the Trinity.

Intuition's retrieval is so rapid that all we are aware of is a general feeling that something is right or wrong. As occupational psychologist and professor Gerard Hodgkinson of Leeds University Business School points out, "People usually experience true intuition when they are under severe time pressure or in a situation of information overload or acute danger, where conscious analysis of the situation may be difficult or impossible."[181]

John A. Bargh takes evidence from several different subdisciplines and argues that consciousness—that thing which gives us our experience of deliberate control—exists exactly to make automatic behaviors possible. He writes that in a very real sense, intuition evolved "for the assemblage of complex nonconscious skills." As William James argued in 1890, these unconscious processes operate on a level where consciousness is not required and frees consciousness for other things. "Intriguingly, then, one of the primary objectives of conscious processing may be to eliminate the need for itself in the future by making learned skills as automatic as possible. It would be ironic indeed if, given the current juxtaposition of automatic and conscious mental processes in the field of psychology, the evolved purpose of consciousness turns out to be the creation of ever more complex nonconscious processes."[182]

Bargh, a leading investigator of what he calls "the automaticity of being," understands that our unconscious mental influences are, for the most part, in our best interests as they orchestrate behaviors ingrained over a long period of time. "They are, if anything, 'mental butlers,' who know our tendencies and preferences so well that they anticipate and take care of them for us, without having to be asked. Conscious direction of behavior is important, but it takes place a small minority of the time."[183] In fact, social psychologists studying the phenomenon of automaticity have concluded that, in our daily lives, our conscious will "plays a causal role only [five percent] or so of the time."[184]

Some would suggest that intuition/inspiration points to something mystical. That may or may not be true, but the fact of the matter is that intuition is not something that occurs to just a select few. "Everyone makes use of information that seems to bubble up from the subconscious . . . ."[185]

Intuition's Survival Value

From an evolutionary perspective, "the subcortical areas of the brain evolved first and would have had to help individuals fight, flee and scavenge well before conscious, distinctly human layers were added later in evolutionary history." In this sense, intuition operates as an open-ended, adaptive agent acting on behalf of the broad, genetically encoded aims—automatic survival systems.[186]

Intuition occurs in a blink, seeming to appear instantaneously. Interestingly, when psychologist John Bargh flashed an image of an object or face for just two-tenths of a second, his New York University students evaluated it instantly. "We're finding that everything is evaluated as good or bad within a quarter-second," he reports. Before engaging in rational analysis, we may find ourselves mildly loathing or loving someone. This biological wisdom linking perception and emotion has a survival value. "When confronting someone or something in the wilderness, one needed instantly to decide: Is this a threat? Those who could read facial expressions quickly and accurately were more likely to survive and leave descendants (us). And that helps explain our intuitive prowess at instantly distinguishing among expressions of anger, sadness, fear, and pleasure."[187]

In the 1970s, University of Massachusetts psychologist Seymour Epstein developed the "cognitive experiential self theory." In it, he pointed out that human beings process information through two systems: "Just as we learn things consciously all the time—the cognitive part of the theory—we also learn things experientially, without realizing we've learned them." Intuition, he wrote, "is just the things we've learned without realizing we've learned them. And sometimes they're useful. Sometimes they're maladaptive."[188]

Thinking without awareness is also referred to as "automatic processing." Researchers have confirmed that most of our everyday thinking, feeling, and acting operate outside conscious awareness, and these things are often "primed" by subtle influences. This idea is not easy for most people to accept because we believe that our intentions and choices are freely made and rule our lives. This is understandably, "since tip-of-the-iceberg consciousness is aware only of itself." However this sense of free will is often overrated. "In reality, we operate like jumbo jets, flying through life mostly on intuitive autopilot."[189]

We are reliant on automatic processing as we read faces, experience sudden creative insights, even as we perceive the everyday world. From each of our two eyes our brain receives slightly differing images of an object, and in a microsecond, it analyzes the difference and infers the object's distance.[190] University of Durham psychologist David Milner describes the brain's two visual systems as "one that gives us our conscious perceptions, and one that guides our actions."[191] He calls this second one "the zombie within." He describes "a woman with brain damage who can see fine details—the hairs on the back of a hand—without being able to recognize the hand. Asked to use her thumb and forefinger to estimate an object's size, she can't do it. Yet when reaching for the object, her thumb and forefinger are appropriately placed."[192]

Studies now show that as we gain expertise, even reasoned judgments often become automatic. Intuition, in these instances, is learned expertise that is instantly accessible. However, learned expertise is quite different from novice intuition. Psychologist Herbert Simon notes:

> In everyday speech, we use the word *intuition* to describe a problem-solving or question-answering performance that is speedy and for which the expert is unable to describe in detail the reasoning or other process that produced the answer. The situation has provided a cue; this cue has given the expert access to information stored in memory, and the information provides the answer. *Intuition is nothing more and nothing less than recognition.*[193]

However, intuition can be wrong as well as being right. Hundreds of experiments have shown that people greatly overestimate "their lie-detection accuracy, their eyewitness recollections, their interviewee assessments, their psychic powers, and their stock-picking talents. It's humbling to realize how often, relying on our own gut instincts, we misjudge and mispredict reality, and then display 'belief perseverance' when facing disconfirming information."[194]

Suspicion as Reality Check

We should always check our intuitions/inspirations against available evidence. This questioning and testing of the knowledge we receive through the intuitive process is not an attempt to deny or destroy it.

Without a doubt, intuition—a "below-the-radar" source of thought—is definitely one way of knowing. Suspicion is a reality check. Can this new insight hold its own against other ways of knowing? The quintrilateral being proposed in these opening chapters functions as one way to check our intuitions against the facts. So, we welcome "the creative whispers of the unseen mind." But then we must follow that up with a critical examination of our assumptions, evaluate the evidence for and against, invite critique from others, and test our conclusions.

While we clearly need both conscious and nonconscious thought processes, neither is intrinsically better than the other. Both share common sources that interact with the others and even govern much of our daily experiences. This way of coming to knowledge is at least as important as analytic logic. Although we need to be aware of the perils of relying too much on intuition or inspiration, we need to understand that intuition and studied analysis are complementary, not necessarily competitive. "Without intellect our intuition may drive us unchecked into emotional chaos. Without intuition we risk failing to resolve complex social dynamics and moral dilemmas . . . ."[195]

When we move into the area of "thinking without awareness," we are entering the field of subjectivity. Just because experiments cannot be made on them, at least initially, does not rule out their contribution to our search for knowledge. While inspiration is subjective, it is not totally so. It is a definite way of knowing also referred to as "aesthetic reason" or the *eureka* moment "in which we not only grasp an idea, but we are also drawn to it in such a way that the idea takes hold of us."[196]

Transcending Experiences

Moving from the more analytical level to the experiential level, we affirm that intuition/inspiration is not only a source of knowledge but can also be a source of motivation to move beyond a thought to an action. It is a transcending experience that may at times call us to participate in something that is greater than ourselves.

Inspiration literally means, "filled with spirit." When someone is inspired, something happens to make that person not only feel that they *want* to do something, but also that they *can* do it. Inspiration is normally a sudden experience that results in a new idea or a new perspective on an old issue, or an unexpected activity, although, as we demonstrated above, it certainly grows out of the unconscious dimension of our thought processes. For instance, a writer is blocked and cannot proceed. Given some distance from the project, an idea suddenly comes that allows the writer to move through and beyond the mental blockage. When this happens, the writer usually experiences time stopping and is, for moments and even hours, "in another dimension." Time seems infinite.

More often than not, these "flashpoints" come during times of boredom or times when the brain is freed from "overload." This allows us to reach beyond the mundane and capture the essence of the moment's experience. Sometimes the source of inspiration is unknown to us, leading religious persons to attribute it to divine sources. While the content of intuitive thinking seems to come all at once, it has existed as the germ of an idea that has been fermenting at an unconscious level for some time. It is an experience of intense focus, an intensity that fills everything around us with meaning.

The church (and other religious traditions as well) does not trust intuition/inspiration as a source of knowledge. There is a fear that a whole host of new religious leaders would arise, running the range from Joseph Smith on one end to Jim Jones on the other.[197] That objection is duly noted, but it does not apply any criteria concerning an evaluation of the inspiration. The quintrilateral and the scientific method provide this reality check. Another objection is that any new religious knowledge must conform to what has already been "revealed" in the canon of embedded tradition. So, for instance, on the issues of homosexuality, women, war, or care of creation, there can be no change from that original two thousand year old "revelation" and the traditions that have interpreted it. There can be no new word on the matter. New information gleaned through scientific discovery, including the social sciences, is rejected when it does not agree with that tradition—tradition based on the sociopolitical context and limited understandings of ancient times. The attitude is that old is good and the older the better.

But intuition or inspiration need not be threatening to either religion or science. How inspiration comes about is less of a mystery than it was in former times, thanks to the cognitive sciences that are helping to unravel it. But does knowing the source of the inspired moment make a difference in its importance or significance? If it changes the way we were thinking before, or it causes us to act in a way that is perceived as more caring or more responsible or more ethical, does it matter whether it comes as a consequence of normal reasoning or whether it comes from a transcendent source? That, it seems, is a matter of perspective.

Einstein's theory of special relativity grew out of a fantasy thought of riding a light beam. When he was sixteen years old, he imagined trying to run fast enough alongside a light beam so that it would appear to stop. He wondered what it would look like.

> He realized that no one had ever seen such a thing, and that led him to the idea that maybe it was impossible to run alongside a light beam—that no matter how fast you were running, it would always be faster. And that, I think, was part of the thinking that led him to his main postulate of relativity theory. A light beam always passes any observer at the same speed, no matter how fast that observer is running. That violates all common sense, because common sense tells us that if you run toward an oncoming car, it's going faster than if you run away from it. But Einstein says if that oncoming car is a light beam, it will come at you at the same speed whether you are running toward it or away from it, which is a pretty outrageous idea. Yet from that postulate came all of the theory of relativity.[198]

In her recent research, Angela Dimoka, director of the Center for Neural Decision Making at Temple University, found that "with too much information, people's decisions make less and less sense." With a glut of information crowding out due diligence, the way we think is changing, and not always for the better. The booming science of decision making has shown that "an unconscious system guides many of our decisions, and that it can be sidelined by too much information. And it has shown that decisions requiring creativity benefit from letting the problem incubate below the level of awareness—something that becomes ever-more difficult when information never stops arriving."[199]

> A key reason for information's diminishing or even negative returns is the limited capacity of the brain's working memory. It can hold roughly seven items . . . anything more must be processed into long-term memory. That takes conscious effort, as when you study for an exam. When more than seven units

> of information land in our brain's inbox, argues psychologist Joanne Cantor . . . the brain struggles to figure out what to keep and what to disregard.[200]

The more information there is to process, the harder the task or sorting and deleting.

The point here is that "creative decisions are more likely to bubble up from a brain that applies unconscious thought to a problem, rather than going at it full-frontal, analytical assault." Cantor argues, "If you let things come at you all the time, you can't use additional information to make a creative leap or a wise judgment. You need to pull back from the constant influx and take a break."[201] Taking a break, writes Begley, "allows the brain to subconsciously integrate new information with existing knowledge and thereby make novel connections and see hidden patterns." While it has been the experience of many throughout the centuries, it came as a genuine surprise to decision making scientists "that some of our best decisions are made through unconscious processes."[202]

As we have mentioned, intuition/inspiration is not limited to the realm of the religious. Scientists, writers, speakers, great leaders, as well as common ordinary people are among the many who claim such experiences without necessarily grounding that experience in the divine.

Einstein, for instance, spoke of a "cosmic religious feeling" that inspired his reflections on the order and harmony of nature. Physicists Brian Josephson and David Bohm believe that regular mystical insights achieved by quiet meditative practices can be a useful guide in the formulation of scientific theories. Roger Penrose describes mathematical inspirations as a sudden 'breaking through' into a Platonic realm. Kurt Gödel spoke of the "other relation to reality," by which he could directly perceive mathematical objects, such as infinity. Gödel was apparently able to achieve this by adopting meditative practices, such as closing off the other senses and lying down in a quiet place. For still other scientists the experience happens spontaneously, in the midst of the daily clamor. Russell Stannard writes of the impression of facing an overpowering force of some kind, "of a nature to command respect and awe . . . . There is a sense of urgency about it; the power is volcanic, pent up, ready to be unleashed."[203] And philosopher Daniel Dennett addresses the question "Is nothing sacred?" by replying: "Is something sacred? Yes, I say with Nietzsche. I could not pray to it, but I can stand in affirmation of its magnificence. This world is sacred."[204]

Fred Hoyle told Paul Davies about an incident that occurred to him while he was driving through the North of England. "Rather as the revelation occurred to Paul on the Road to Damascus, mine occurred on the road over Bowes Moor." Hoyle and his collaborator Jayant Narlikar had, in the late 1960s, been working on a cosmological theory of electromagnetism that involved some daunting mathematics. One day as they were struggling over a particularly complicated integral, Hoyle decided to take a vacation from Cambridge to join some colleagues hiking in the Scottish Highlands.

> As the miles slipped by I turned the quantum mechanical problem . . . over in my mind, in the hazy way I normally have in thinking mathematics in my head. Normally, I have to write things down on paper, and then fiddle with the equations and integrals as best I can. But somewhere on Bowes Moor my awareness of the mathematics clarified, not a little, not even a lot, but as if a huge brilliant had suddenly been switched on. How long did it take to become totally convinced that the problem was solved? Less than five seconds. It only remained to make sure that before the clarity faded I had enough of the essential steps stored safely in my recallable memory. It is indicative of the measure of certainty I felt that in the ensuing days I didn't trouble to commit anything to paper. When ten days or so later I returned to Cambridge I found it possible to write out the thing without difficulty.[205]

Davies tells about a conversation he had with Richard Feynman describing what a moment of inspiration feels like, and of it being followed by an enormous sense of euphoria, lasting for maybe two or three days. "I asked how often had it happened, to which Feynman replied 'four,' at which we both agreed that twelve days of euphoria was not a great reward for a lifetime's work."[206]

Accepting a level of mystery, accepting the existence of the unexplainable or at least that which we cannot yet explain, does not mean a repudiation of science. Indeed, faith and science come into contact with each other when human wisdom reaches the frontiers of intuition.

Mysticism as a Way toward Intuition

Mysticism may be seen as a structural method to encourage (and force in some instances) moments of inspiration and unification of self with transcendence. Scientist Paul Davies views mysticism as a route to knowledge that lies alongside rational scientific inquiry and logical reasoning. Bernard of Clairvaux (1090-1153) also saw mysticism as a way of knowing. Mysticism in a religious context is the idea that the soul of the believer can make contact with God in a direct manner. This way of knowing, however, "contained a seed that eventually weakened the authority of the church hierarchy and helped pave the way for the Reformation."[207] While mysticism has normally meant that a sense of transcendence is found in contemplation rather than in argument and axiom, it need not exclude them.

Sam Harris, coming from an atheistic point of view, writes, "while Eastern mysticism has its fair share of unjustified belief, it undoubtedly represents humankind's best attempt at fashioning a spiritual science. The methods of introspection one finds in Buddhism, for instance, have no genuine equivalents in the West." He goes on to affirm that "mysticism, shorn of religious dogmatism, is an empirical and highly rational enterprise." He defines spirituality or mysticism—"both words are pretty terrible, but there are no good alternatives in English"—as "any process of introspection by which a person comes to realize that the feeling he calls 'I' is a cognitive illusion. The core truth of mysticism is this: it is possible to experience the world without feeling like a separate 'self' in the usual sense."[208]

The language used to describe mystical experiences reflects the culture of the individual concerned. "Western mystics tend to emphasize the personal quality of the presence, often describing themselves as being with someone, usually God, who is different from themselves but with whom a deep bond is felt." Eastern mystics, on the other hand, "emphasize the wholeness of existence and tend to identify themselves more closely with the presence."[209]

In Eastern mysticism, reality is apprehended directly and immediately, meaning "without any mediation, any symbolic elaboration, any conceptualization, or any abstractions; subject and object become one in a timeless and spaceless act that is beyond any and all forms of mediation." Mystics universally speak of contacting reality in its essence, without any intermediaries. The unifying experience is beyond words, symbols, names, thoughts, or images. Reality becomes one. "The essence of the mystical experience, then, is a type of shortcut to truth, a direct and unmediated contact with a perceived ultimate reality."[210] Among other names, this ultimate reality is called the One, the Good, Reality, God, the Cosmos, the Mind, the Void, and the Absolute. "Western religions have a long tradition of identifying God with the Infinite, whereas Eastern philosophy seeks to eliminate the differences between the One and the Many, and to identify the Void and the Infinite—zero and infinity."[211]

In his book, *The Problem of the Soul*, Owen Flanagan, while resisting the notion of mysticism, argues that the scientific pursuit to understand our world and ourselves and our various relationships generates an awe and reverence that was previously associated with religion. "There is benevolence and compassion expressed by a feeling of connection to all creatures, indeed even to the awesome inanimate cosmos."[212] This sense of transcendence for Flanagan comes not from the *answers* that science discovers but in the *quest* for those answers.

Personal Integration

Mysticism is a method of spirituality that is not necessarily grounded in institutionalized religion. Peter Van Ness has argued that a growing number of North Americans have concluded that spirituality is not necessarily dependent on adherence to religious beliefs or even participation in religious practices. "Being spiritual is an attribute of the way one experiences the world and lives one's life."[213] Therefore, spiritual meaning can be discovered in non-religious events. John Macquarrie (1919-2007) seemed to give credence to this when he wrote that spirituality simply means "becoming a person in the fullest sense."[214]

Spirituality, then, can be understood as a quest for personal integration. Sandra Schneiders concluded that all the various definitions of the concept suggest that it "has something to do with the unification of life by reference to something beyond the individual person." Thus, in the broadest sense, spirituality refers to "the experience of consciously striving to integrate one's life in terms not of isolation and self-absorption but of self-transcendence toward the ultimate value one perceives."[215]

Baptist theologian Stanley Grenz writes that the search for the spiritual "is born out of the attempt to discover some semblance of personal identity in the form of a unified sense of selfhood. Viewing the matter from this perspective suggests why spirituality so readily becomes a watchword in the postmodern context, for one crucial characteristic of the postmodern condition is the loss of the centered self." He bases his argument on the fact that in the ancient world, one's sense of identity was closely linked to the place of humans in the cosmos. Thus, in looking at the vastness and majesty of the universe, the psalmist declared: "What are mere mortals that you are mindful of them, human beings that you care for them?" (Psalm 8) The psalmist continued in amazement by placing humans in the context of creation and by speaking about the human responsibility of exercising dominion over other living creatures. In the modern era, however, we humans have been dissociated from creation. "In contrast to the psalmist who thought of humans in terms of being at 'home' within the created order, the modern response to the quest for an understanding of true humanness, and hence the sense of personal identity, came in the form of the construction of the self."[216]

While the seeds of this construction of the self might be found in Augustine's emphasis on the inner self, the full impetus of discovering personal identity through the sense of selfhood emerged in the wake of the Enlightenment. Here "philosophers declared that lying at the core of what it means to be human is reason or rationality, which was now understood as the ability to disengage from one's natural environment and social context so as to be able to objectify the world."[217] Such disengagement from nature became the foundation for the notion of individual autonomy and the freedom to choose one's own purposes apart from the controlling influence of natural and social forces. In this way, humans had dominion not only of other living things but also over their own lives.

Today this view is largely rejected, and is replaced by the social self that is constituted by a myriad of social relationships. One implication of this is the fluidity of the self that is not only impermanent but also highly unstable. The social self is derived from one's primary social group. Thus, "who I am" is determined to a great extent by the group of which I am a member. And mysticism provides a response to this in terms of transcendence, in terms of that which is more that one's self in isolation.

Summary

Intuition is known by many names, most of them nonreligious. The experience is found to some degree in all of us. It is grounded in our psychological processes. While intuition tends to be more biologically based, and inspiration is more psychologically based, the two are in practical terms so closely linked that they can be interchangeable. They are the result of the way our brains store, process, and retrieve information at an unconscious level.

Mysticism is a method used by both religious and nonreligious persons to seek moments of lucidity and the unification of the self with transcendence. Mysticism deals with that which is by definition nebulous—whether it is attributed to the divine or to the human subconscious. Those moments of lucidity are sometimes referred to as moments of inspiration or revelation, or new insight. The reality we experience is filled with far more than we can ever know, and if quantum physicists are correct, it may contain dimensions of which we have not even begun to understand.

Each of us is a story within stories. A child's story is part of both her mother's and her father's stories. Their story is part of the larger family's story, the neighbor's story, the state's story, etc.

> Those stories, in turn, are [part of] the story of a religious tradition, a civilization, [culture], humanity as a whole, and then beyond to the story of our planet, our star system, the Milky Way, Galaxy, and, finally, to the story of the Universe itself. Each of us is thus a story within a story within stories within stories. Each of us will have a felt relationship with the larger contexts of our existence only to the extent that we are given . . . stories for these larger wholes that we find meaningful.[218]

CHAPTER 6

And Jacob Digged a Well

"One should accept the truth from whatever source it proceeds."
—Moses Maimonides (1135-1204) Jewish philosopher

"The religion that fears science, insults God and commits suicide."
Ralph Waldo Emerson

". . . People once worried about the boundary between the living and the nonliving. Today, the boundary seems meaningless."
—William Calvin

The human obsession with meaning grows out of the belief that data must be interpreted, and that data must be configured in such a way as to make sense to one's time and circumstance. It appears that humans are the only animals that question why things are as they are and how they affect us individually and communally. When something seems not to fit into the scheme of our current understanding, we consider it meaningless and try to dismiss it.

Framing and Neural Binding

George Lakoff writes in *The Political Mind* that there are two competing modes of thought that lead to contradictory ways of governing our country, one fundamentally democratic and one fundamentally antidemocratic. The same is true for religion. It is not simply that one is right and the other wrong. In fact, these two competing modes of thought are both located in each of our brains. One aspect might be stronger than the other, but they are both present.

To understand this, it is useful to see another way the brain works. The new math that began in the early 1960s emphasized mathematical structure, especially set theory. The concept of sets provides a common example to explain recent brain research. Neuroscientists now assert that the mind works by thinking with frames. Linguist Charles Fillmore discovered that "words are all defined relative to conceptual frames." Following his lead, scientists began discovering that the same was true for groups of related words and forms of reasoning about some subject matter. This led them to conclude: "Frames are among the cognitive structures we think with . . . . The neural circuitry needed to create frame structures is relatively simple, and so frames tend to structure a huge amount of our thought. Each frame has roles (like a cast of characters), relations between the roles, and scenarios carried out by those playing the roles."[219]

Lakoff gives this illustration. Think of the concepts and frames necessary for a child to understand the simple sentence: Jill bought the car from Harry. The concept of "buy" relates to a commercial frame that is composed of buyers, sellers, goods, and money. It relates to a related relationship frame of buyer and seller. It involves the concept of exchange of value. Because of the word order, Jill the Buyer is the protagonist. It refers to an action frame—something is happening. For an older child the questions might arise: Can she afford the car? Will the car run? What does it look like? When did the transaction occur? Where did she get the money? How much did it cost? And so forth.

A similar scenario could be taken from a religious context. The process would be the same. For instance, consider the simple assertion: Jesus rose from the dead. Assuming some understanding of the man Jesus, Christians begin with the frame of "dead." That frame relates to the distinctions between life and death, and then to the various memories of persons who have died. In this example, the thought process is a little more complex with the concept of coming back to life. Who else have I known or heard of who has been resurrected? Who saw it? Why did it happen to one and not to others? And so on.

It is instructive to note, "Most of what we understand in public discourse is not in the words themselves, but in the unconscious understanding that we bring to the words." This means that each word "is defined relative to at least one conceptual frame. Those frames evoke other frames in the system. Understanding involves drawing out the logic of the frames. In a great many cases, metaphorical thinking is used as well."[220]

Religion is also about the worldviews that culture and circumstances make available, understandings that define our possibilities, challenges, and actual lives. Lakoff states that when one accepts a particular way of understanding the world around them, they "ignore or hide realities that contradict it."[221] Thus, when scientific discovery calls into question something we believe—for instance, a literal biblical view of creation or the possibility of the sun remaining stationary in the sky for Joshua's battle—our strongest urge is first to deny the new evidence and then to disregard it by making an even stronger defense of the belief.

A number of deep frames of thought can be activated together, producing a base of meaning. They are essential since we cannot understand either other persons or ourselves without recognizing and seeing how we fit into the rest of the world. The synapses of the neural circuits in these joint activations are so strong that the highly general, deep ways of understanding are permanently part of our brains.[222] Neural bindings allow us to bring together neural activity in different parts of the brain to form a single integrated whole. For instance, when we see a blue square, "it appears as a single object. Yet the color and shape are registered in different parts of the brain."[223] "Neural binding allows these permanent general narratives [rescue, redemption, women's lot, etc.] to be applied to ever-new cases. That's why the same narrative structures keep recurring, from war to war, from celebrity to celebrity, from one political figure to another,"[224] and from one religious scandal to the next.

In prior ways of thinking, we used to take language and concepts at face value. This led to the fallacy of believing that one's own conclusions are the only right way. Language and concepts were understood to be literal and universal. This also led to the conclusion that those who disagree are either mistaken and in need of further information, irrational and need to have their reasoning corrected, downright immoral and in need of correction, or simply ignorant and unable to learn the truth.[225] This, of course, has been true for both liberals and conservatives.

There are two opposite modes of thought in each person's brain—conservative and progressive, or maybe better, strict and nuturant. This means, "people can simultaneously have two inconsistent worldviews and use them in different areas of life without even noticing."[226] For this reason, what we often refer to as hypocrisy may not always be perceived as such by the "hypocrite." Hypocrisy "is defined relative to what we will call a value-consistency frame, in which values are supposed to be consistent and all encompassing, the same ones used in all cases." However, as we have just seen, the two-world concept is simply a fact about brains. "The 'hypocrite' may not even notice the 'hypocrisy' if his brain automatically and unconsciously switches back and forth depending on context."[227]

It is interesting to note in this context that for the Victorian frame of mind during the 19th century, "hypocrisy served as a safety valve against the constant robust pressure to behave faultlessly. Victorians were at severe pains to seem forever courteous, honorable, and altruistic, and to maintain a sterling reputation; to appear always to be better than they were." One of the most famous preachers of the 19th century was Henry Ward Beecher. He was accused—rightly—of adultery and a large public scandal developed, although the case was not proven when it eventually went to court. It is said that as Beecher was preaching one Sunday during this public embarrassment, he "seemed to be winking at his audience that hypocrisy might in fact *develop* from morality, and that the more moral we become, the more it becomes necessary to distance words from deeds."[228]

While it might seem obvious, conservative thought has a very different moral basis than progressive thought. "It begins with the notion that morality is obedience to an authority—assumed to be a legitimate authority who is inherently good, knows right from wrong, functions to protect us from evil in the world, and has both the right and duty to use force to command obedience and fight evil."[229] When this authority is understood as God who has revealed his absolute will in an infallible Bible, that authority cannot be rejected or ignored without some sort of punishment. And when any earthly authority is empowered by divine authority to carry out its demands, we get an unbending fundamentalism. A foundational character of conservative thought is that people are born bad and from their birth are in need of redemption.

A practical way in which the conservative or "strict" reasons is that it sees the market as a legitimate authority that makes rational decisions. This is based on the principles of Social Darwinism that were discussed in a previous chapter.

> Prosperity is seen as a mark of discipline, which is in turn, seen as moral, since discipline is required to obey moral laws and whatever is required by those in authority. By the logic of

> this system of thought, if you are not prosperous, you are not disciplined, and therefore cannot be moral, and so deserve your poverty. It follows that of people are given things they have not earned, they become dependant and lose their discipline, and with it their capacity to obey moral laws and legitimate authority . . . . To maximize their self-interest, they need to learn discipline, to follow the rules and obey the laws, and to see wealth rationally.[230]

Again, we all have within us versions of both modes of thoughts—both conservative and progressive (or strict and nuturant). These two modes of thought are ways of reasoning. Sometimes this is conscious, but it is more often unconscious. They are general, and exist across all issues. The truth is that we use both of these modes of thought differently at different times in our lives. Normally we do not use both at the same time. The brain is designed so that they are mutually inhibited—the activation of one mode of thought naturally inhibits the other. "Each is a coherent system of concepts in itself, and they coexist happily if they can be kept apart."[231]

Through neural binding, a general mode of thought can be applied to a special case, such as applying general conservatism to health care, or applying general progressivism to global warming. Therefore, it is possible to have an authoritarian progressive or a flexible conservative. "One reason is that means and ends can function as different domains of experience. Thus one can have progressive ends but authoritarian conservative means"[232] and vice versa.

Wise persons have known for centuries that getting a person to think and talk about those issuc areas where there is already some degree of agreement can change another's worldview. This sounds easier than it really is. Cognitive research tells us "when people define their very identity by a worldview, or a narrative, or a mode of thought, they are unlikely to change—for the simple reason that it is physically part of their brain, and so many other aspects of their brain structure would also have to change; that change is highly unlikely."[233] Since ideas are "physically instantiated as part of our brains and that changes occur at the synapses," synaptic changes occur under two conditions—trauma (where there is especially strong neural firing) and repetition (where neural firing recurs)." That is, if you tell a lie often enough, people will believe it, especially if they are already leaning slightly in that direction.

Neuroscience also tells us that you cannot simply erase such changes. Like every stroke on your computer, they remain there even when you think they have been erased. They may be difficult to recall, but they are there. "You can add a structure that might bypass the 'war on terror' idea, or perhaps inhibit its activation, or add a modifying structure—perhaps even one that delegitimates it. But you can't just get rid of it at will." Moreover, when an expression like "war on terror" or "Jesus Saves" becomes a fixed part of your brain, "you tend to use it *reflexively*, not *reflectively*."[234] A large part of the effectiveness of political and religious language is that the ideas expressed are processed reflexively, and that means most of the time *you don't even know what you are thinking!*

What is true?

How, then, do we define the terms real and true? This question is compounded when a new discovery violates our common sense. For instance, "Electrons can disappear and reappear elsewhere, and electrons can be at many places at the same time." With the development of quantum physics, "chance and probability were . . . introduced right into the heart of physics which previously had given us precise predictions and detailed trajectories of particles, from planets to comets to cannon balls."[235]

The Newtonian worldview was purely deterministic with no room for chance or randomness. For that worldview, probability was simply the consequence of human ignorance that would be explained when more was learned and when better technology was developed. Determinism is bound by an umbilical cord to causality—the notion that every effect has a cause. However, in quantum theory, probability is not an ignorance that can be eliminated. Rather, it is an inherent feature of atomic reality.[236] Thus, "even when we have all information about a system, the outcome is still probabilistic."[237]

We cannot simply rely on common sense in the more complex arenas of thought. Another illustration is the concept of quantum entanglement that affirms: "Particles vibrating in coherence have some kind of deep connection linking them together." This deep connection can be extremely deep. When two electrons are "entangled," it means that "their wave functions beat in unison" and that their wave functions are connected, as it were, "by an invisible 'thread' or umbilical cord." This means that "whatever happens to one automatically has an effect on the other." It further means that in some sense "what happens to us automatically affects things instantaneously in distant corners of the universe, since our wave functions were probably entangled at the beginning of time."[238] Thus, all things are not only in process, but also are interrelated at the basic level of physics, although the relationship may be random and inconsequential at a macro level.

The inclusion of chance and randomness in our understanding of the development of the world challenges our religious sense of certainty. In earlier times, there was no way of even *suspecting* that some event was utterly random; everything was presumed to mean something, if only we knew what. It was important to believe that things were orderly and predictable. This led Einstein to exclaim as he confronted the randomness found in quantum physics, "God does not play dice." In the past, doubt and questioning were considered wrong and sinful. Today we understand that faith is not only compatible with doubt, but also that a real and growing faith *requires* it. "Truth" is not something fixed and definitive.

Each new scientific discovery challenges our worldviews and our Godviews. And this can be disconcerting, to say the least.

> In times of uncertainty, fear becomes the overwhelming faculty. People seek out quick and easy answers and comfort, and religion offers both. It is soothing to think that when the ground shakes—killing two hundred thousand people in an already destitute nation—there is a grander purpose to it all, an underlying beneficent plan. Much less comforting is the objective explanation: that the Earth's tectonic plates constantly move and grind against one another, so there is compression and subduction, and the occasional violent rupture—a terrifying, but ultimately random and meaningless event.[239]

A discovery as seemingly simple as spots on the sun can challenge religious assumptions in unexpected ways. As astronomer John Eddy wrote:

> We have always wanted the Sun to be better than the other stars and better than it really is. We wanted it to be perfect, and when the telescope came along and showed us that it wasn't, we said, "At least it's constant." When we found it inconsistent,

> we said, "At least it's regular." It now seems to be none of these; why we thought it should be when other stars are not says more about us than it does about the Sun.[240]

When that which we consider to be perfect, or constant, or regular proves not to be any of these, the metaphors and myths we have built around those former truths are weakened and eventually become useless in our storytelling. Most creation stories declare that the Sun is supreme over the Moon and the stars (cf., Genesis 1). Religious metaphors compared God with the supreme, permanent, and unchanging nature of the Sun, and Christian hymns compare the Son with the Sun. Science has demonstrated that our Sun is but one of numerous other suns in the multiverse, and not even the largest in the observable universe. Not only is the Sun demoted, so are the stories that had elevated it to supreme status. However, this desacralization of the Sun and the universe need not diminish our sense of awe and wonder. Indeed, it can heighten it.

Complexity Theory

Complexity research has implications for our current inquiry. As computers have encountered complex systems, it has become clear that it is difficult, if not impossible, to plan their outcomes centrally.

> John Holland, the pioneering University of Michigan mathematician, built the first computerized "complex adaptive system" by mimicking the free market. Looking for a way to model the human brain, Holland found that efforts to create a "command-and-control" model had already failed at MIT. So he solved the problem by making each digital "synapse" into an economic unit. Individual synapses were paid off for solving problems, with a "bucket brigade" to distribute the rewards to participating units. Economic reinforcement via the profit motive was an enormously powerful organizing force . . . .

Tucker tells us that computer experts at the Palo Alto Research Center discovered the same principle in 1988 when Xerox tried setting up a system to maximize use of its computers. Its engineers also discovered that a "command-and-control" system was unworkable since the information needed to coordinate decisions quickly overwhelmed the central processor. "So Xerox researchers invented SPAWN, a system in which individual computers are given 'money' and instructed to maximize their bank accounts by taking on tasks and trading computer downtime among themselves. Without any external direction or control, the computers quickly optimize their own use by trading on this internally created market."[241] Tad Hogue, a member of the research staff at Xerox PARC, explained that all complex biological and economic systems work this way.

> If every human cell's protein production had to be processed through the brain, the costs of coordination would quickly overwhelm the nerve cells' capacities. Consequently, most decisions are made within the cell, or by the internal communications of the endocrinal system, which bypasses most brain functions. Although we tend to think of ourselves being in complete command of our bodies, most of life's choices are made within the individual cells.[242]

Stuart Kauffman advanced the "patches" principle for solving problems in large organizations. Trying to find the best way for a large entity to solve a complex mathematical problem, Kauffman shows that if the entity is broken up into a grid of small "patches" and each patch is allowed to solve its own small portion of the problem, an optimal solution emerges. This sounds a lot like framing in the human brain. "When the system is broken into well-chosen patches, each adapts for its own selfish benefit, yet the joint effect is to achieve very good [solutions] for the whole lattice of patches. No central administrator coordinates behavior. Properly chosen patches, each acting selfishly, achieve the coordination."[243] Kauffman suggests that these findings have enormous implications for federalism and for decentralizing large corporate units.

The essential ingredient of the brain, then, is not the physical processes that it employs, but rather the organization of information. The brain is a machine, and neurons fire purely for electrical reasons. There are no *mental* causes of physical processes. In this understanding, thought processes are not uniquely human—with the implication that at least in principle, machines may, at some point in the future, think *and feel*. It is hard to reconcile this fact with the traditional notion of the human soul—and the implications of this for most religious thought are unsettling.

Artificial Intelligence

We are notoriously shortsighted beings who view life in relatively small segments. This problem includes a rather meager sense of history, and that problem is compounded as the attention spans of persons decrease. Not only does the average person have little appreciation or knowledge of history; they do not even make correct connections between current events. As Arthur Schopenhauer once wrote: "Everyone takes the limits of his own vision for the limits of our world."

A challenge that the future holds is artificial intelligence. As cybergenetics and artificial intelligence research continue to move forward into new areas of "thinking machines," how will one be able to tell the difference between human and non-human? And just as important, should knowing that make a difference?

When the question arises whether robots could ever achieve consciousness—able to make complex decisions and be responsible for those decisions—the short-term answer is probably not. However, when we look at the fact that it took millions of years for humans to develop to their current level, why should we doubt that given a thousand or more years that a similar development could take place for robots? Such technological growth would probably not take such a vast amount of time since this level of evolution is more conscious. The point is, given enough time it is at least conceivable.

The question then becomes, do these conscious robots have the same rights and freedoms as humans? And how, at that point, do we distinguish between the two? Will religion grant these robots souls that need to be saved, or will it declare them as soulless creatures?

It is interesting how the dreams and thoughts of the great minds of former centuries have a way of being fulfilled years later. Italian philosopher and former Dominican monk Giordano Bruno (1548-1600) was imprisoned by the Catholic Church and after five years was declared a heretic, taken to the place of execution with his tongue gagged, stripped naked, hung upside down on a stake, and burned alive. He was killed because of his agreement with Galileo and for speculations that there were innumerable suns and innumerable earths revolving around those suns—and that there could be intelligent creatures like us living out there. His speculations are now commonly understood and accepted, and he is regularly vindicated as new extrasolar planets are discovered orbiting distant stars.

The great Italian painter, sculptor (really, a "jack-of-all-trades") Michelangelo (1475-1564) made sketches of a flying apparatus that would carry persons into the sky for travel. A century later English mathematician John Wilkins (1614-1672) wrote about how someday people would journey to the moon in a flying chariot. And in the 1880s, Samuel Butler wrote in his *Unconscious Memory*:

> I first asked myself whether life might not, after all, resolve itself into the complexity of arrangement of an inconceivably intricate mechanism . . . . If, then, men were not really alive after all, but were only machines of so complicated a make that it was less trouble to us to cut the difficulty and say that that kind of mechanism was "being alive," why should not machines ultimately become as complicated as we are, or at any rate, complicated enough to be called living, and to be indeed as living as it was in the nature of anything at all to be? If it was only a case of their becoming more complicated, we were certainly doing our best to make them so.[244]

That was in the 1880s!

There have been numerous science fiction movies about artificial life forms, including *D.A.R.Y.L.* (1985), *The Bicentennial Man* (1999), *AI: Artificial Intelligence* (2001), *I, Robot* (2004), *Stealth* (2005), *The Island* (2005), and *Surrogates* (2009), to mention just a few. They all deal with how the development of artificial life leads these forms to become more and more human. Today these forms are still primarily in the realm of science fiction. However, researchers are contemplating how to create computers that can think for themselves, heal themselves of viruses, and make relatively informed decisions based on what the computer has learned from past experience.

"Although physicists have a good understanding of Newtonian mechanics, Maxwell's theory of light, relativity, and the quantum theory of atoms and molecules, the basic laws of intelligence are still shrouded in mystery. The Newton of AI probably has not yet been born." Currently, there are at least two major problems holding back the efforts to create intelligent robots: pattern recognition and common sense. "Robots can see much better that we can, but they don't understand what they see. Robots can also hear much better than we can, but they don't understand what they have." For example, writes Kaku, "When we enter a room, we immediately recognize the floor, chairs, furniture, tables, and so forth. But when a robot scans a room it sees nothing but a vast collection of straight and curved lines, which it converts to pixels." The difference is that our brain unconsciously recognizes objects "by performing trillions upon trillions of calculations when we walk into a room—an activity that we are blissfully unaware of. The reason that we are unaware of all our brain is doing is evolution . . . ."[245]

From the time of our birth, we are constantly learning by "bumping into reality." This process means that we learn tons of common sense laws without being aware that we are learning them. At this point in time, computers are not able to program all the laws of common sense into a single computer. More than this, researchers have not yet discovered a single paradigm that explains consciousness—a paradigm, he argues, that may not exist.

Will computers eventually surpass us in intelligence? Kaku believes that may be possible since there is nothing in the laws of physics to prevent it. "If robots are neural networks capable of learning, and they develop to the point where they can learn faster and more efficiently than we can, then it's logical that they might eventually surpass us in reasoning."[246]

The latest experiment in artificial intelligence is IBM's DeepQA project called Watson, named after IBM's first president. It is the combined efforts of IBM's own team, along with the faculty and students of seven universities. Watson achieved fame in early 2011 by competing on the TV quiz show, *Jeopardy!* "Watson consistently outperformed its human opponents on the game's signaling device, but had trouble responding to a few categories, notably those having short clues containing only a few words." Watson's advantage was that it had access to "200 million pages of structured and unstructured content consuming four terabytes of disk storage," but it was not connected to the Internet during the game.[247] Watson can also process 500 gigabytes, the equivalent of a million books, per second.

According to IBM, "The goal is to have computers start to interact in natural human terms across a range of applications and processes, understanding the questions that humans ask and providing answers that humans can understand and justify."[248] The hope is that the project will develop into a commercial produce within the next two years that will be able to aid in the diagnosis and treatment of patients. Another application is legal research.

In 2008, David Levy, artificial-intelligence researcher at the Museum of Sex in New York City, predicted that in the future, marriages will be legalized between human and robots, and he is *not* a fan of science fiction. "If the alternative is that you are lonely and sad and miserable, is it not better to find a robot that claims to love you and acts like it loves you? . . . Does it really matter, if you're a happier person?"[249]

Levy is not new to the discussion of humanizing artificial intelligence. Beginning with writing programs for chess to "stimulate human thought processes," he moved on to writing programs "to carry on intelligent conversations with people, and then explored the way humans interact with computers." Over the decades of study, Levy noted that "interactions between humans and robots have become increasingly personal," especially robots that can adopt decidedly humanoid features and functions, like the robot Repliee from Japan.[250]

Programmers can already create machines "to match a person's interests or render them somewhat disagreeable to create a desirable level of friction in a relationship."[251] Levy says, "People will fall in love with a convincing simulation of a human being, and convincing simulations can have a remarkable effect on people." A 2007 study from the University of California at San Diego, reported that toddlers grew to accept a two-foot-tall humanoid robot named QRIO that responded to the children. The children even covered it with a blanket and said "night, night" to it when its batteries ran down. Pointing to this study, Levy believes that "people who grow up with all sorts of electronic gizmos will find android robots to be fairly normal as friends, partners, lovers." He also points to the fact that modern communication allows persons to fall in love without ever having met face-to-face. "So many people nowadays are developing strong emotional attachments across the Internet, even agreeing to marry, that I think it doesn't matter what's on the other end of the line . . . . It just matters what you experience and perceive." Nevertheless, most people will continue to have sex, love, and marriage in the old-fashion way. However, Levy points out, "I think there are people who feel a void in their emotional and sex lives for any number of reasons who could benefit from robots."[252]

Whether such a human-android relationship would be emotionally healthy is debated—and largely dismissed by most. Sherry Turkle writes in her book *The Second Self*: "If you are lonely but afraid of intimacy, relationships with machines can enable you to be a loner yet never alone, give you the illusion of companionship without the demands of friendship. There is nothing to celebrate here. To me, the seductiveness of relationships with robots speaks to what we are not getting from people." She feels that humans should be able to fulfill this role and increase the lonely person's "repertoire for dealing with the complexity and challenges of relationships with people."[253] Is the church prepared to deal with this? Undoubtedly not.

Nevertheless, the issue will certainly surface within the next twenty-five years. And this will likely raise the related question of what constitutes the human person to a new level. In his book, *What about the Soul?* Joel Green writes about the perennial struggle of Data, the android bridge officer from television's *Star Trek: The Next Generation*. Data is a robot that can outperform all humans in strength and intelligence, and yet yearns to become human.

> If the voyages of the *Star Ship Enterprise NCC-1701-D* are famous for going boldly "where no one has gone before," Data's own journey is concerned by his yearning to become human. However, this begs the question, what does it mean to be human? In the episode, "The Measure of a Man," Captain Picard persuades a court of law of Data's right to self-determination. In "The Offspring," Data creates a "daughter" by mapping his own neural nets onto an android body he has fashioned, thus proving himself proficient in a form of procreation. Eventually the recipient of an "emotion chip," he is capable of affective response and in the movie *Star Trek: First Contact* is given, however temporarily, patches of human skin. Finally, in *Star Trek: Nemesis*, Data sacrifices himself for the sake of his friend. Do such attributes as these move Data closer to being "human?"[254]

Dennett argues that conscious machines apparently do not contradict any fundamental laws of nature. Frank Tipler argues that if a computer was "powerful enough to simulate consciousness—and, by extension, a whole community of conscious beings—from the viewpoint of the beings *within* the computer the simulated world would be real." He then asks a key question:

> Do the simulated people exist? As far as the simulated people can tell, they do. By assumption, any action which real people can and do carry out to determine if they exist—reflecting on the fact that they think, interacting with the environment—the simulated people also can do, and in fact do. There is simply no way for the simulated people to tell that they are "really" inside the computer, that they are merely simulated, and not real. They can't get at the real substance, the physical computer, from where they are, inside the program . . . . There is no way for the people inside this simulated universe to tell that they are merely simulated, that they are only a sequence of numbers being tossed around inside a computer, and are in fact not real.[255]

Do these simulated people need a God? Did Jesus die for their sins, too? When they come to the questions of origins, what kind of answers will they devise?

A further category, which I will not deal with here, is dreams. At the time of its occurrence, the dream is reality. If this is so, "can we be absolutely sure that the 'dream world' is illusory and the 'awake world' real? Could it be the other way about, or that both are real, [or] neither? What criteria of reality can we employ to decide the matter?"[256] This might seem like chasing rabbits, but they all relate to the issue of determining what we accept as reality. For the ancient mind, dreams were real and a time when the spirit traveled to other places. For many religious persons even today dreams are real in the sense that God is present in them and relates directly to humans through them.

As I think about the controversies surrounding artificial intelligence and cloning, I am reminded of the story that Harry Emerson Fosdick told in his autobiography about the opposition to the construction of the Erie Canal that opened in 1825 after Buffalo was destroyed in the War of 1812. "To be sure, the canal had been stoutly opposed, even on religious grounds. In one Quaker meeting a solemn voice had said: 'If the Lord wanted a river to flow through the state of New York, he would have put one there.' Then, after a profound silence, another member rose and said simply: '*And Jacob digged a well.*'" Fosdick went on to comment: "I have often wished, in facing similar situations, that so brief and crushing a retort could be found to religious reactionaries."[257]

Many, who today greatly fear a future where cybergenetics and cloning might play a greater role, fear what they cannot understand and, as a result, argue against them. They are afraid of creating something that humans may not be able to control—either those doing the creating, or even the creation itself. Others claim that we are creating life in order to prolong life—doing what only *God* is supposed to do. After all, isn't God the source and ending of all life—the creator who alone holds the right over life and death? This kind of argument is called the "naturalistic fallacy." It makes little if any sense to argue that a thing is good simply *because* it is natural or bad *because* it is unnatural. Indeed, the Hoover Dam is no less "natural" than a beaver's dam. Both are built in places where once there were no dams!

There is no credible evidence for any special divine quality in human beings, and "no fundamental reason is apparent why an advanced electronic machine should not, in principle, enjoy similar feelings of consciousness as ourselves." This is not, of course, to argue that computers do or do not have souls, although as artificial intelligence continues to advance, the argument will be made that concerning the soul, there is no difference between the thinking and feeling machine and the human being in this respect.

Scientific advances and technological hopes raise questions that former generations could not even conceive. Recently, surgeons have been able to do face transplants, just as they have been able to do organ, limb, and skin transplants. Will we ever be able to transplant a brain? (I cannot help but remember Steve Martin's 1983 film, *The Man with Two Brains.*)

> What would happen if your brain could be removed and placed in a "brain support system," remaining coupled to your body via some sort of radio communication network . . . . Your eyes, ears and other senses remain functioning as usual. Your body can operate without impediment. In fact, nothing would seem any different (perhaps a feeling of light headedness!), except that you could look down upon your own brain. The question is, "where would *you* be?"[258]

With the transplanting of body parts, skin, and even complete faces, we can see that the question becomes even more perplexing if we image that one's brain is transplanted into another body. Would it be correct to say that you had a new body, or that the other body had a new brain? "Could you regard yourself as the same person, with a different body? Perhaps you could. But suppose the body were of the opposite sex, or that of an animal? Much of what makes *you*, your personality, capabilities and so forth, is tied to chemical and physical conditions of the body." To complicate the matter further, what seems science fiction today may become the scientific practice of tomorrow. So what happens when one speculates about *duplication* of the self? "Suppose the entire information content of your brain were put on a giant computer somewhere, and your original body and brain died. Would *you* still survive—in the computer?"[259]

The question of personal identity becomes of greater importance as the reengineering and rebuilding of the systems and subsystems of our bodies and brains occur. And if this seems impossible, it is only because we see life in such short segments. However, when we realize that it took millions of years for humans to develop to their current level—not to mention the billions of years of Earth's evolution—why should we doubt that in the future, perhaps over hundreds or even several thousand years, a similar development might take place in AI and cybertronics? Such technological growth would probably not take such a vast amount of time, but regardless, the point remains that given sufficient time it could be possible.

If this does occur in the future, then, the question will revolve around the rights and freedom of conscious robots. For religions of all sorts, the basic question will be: Are these theological issues or simply technological questions? When conscious robotic "life" does occur, how do we distinguish between it and human life, or will this be another area of discrimination that societies will have to overcome?

These issues are still largely far in the future. But the day may come when that which we can now only speak about theoretically may become a reality. The day will come, perhaps sooner than later, when various transplants will raise the question, "Who am I *now*?"

Co-Creators

Today, the question is no longer, "Shall we play God?" but "How can we be ethically and morally informed creators?" Scientists today are able to do things that just a few decades ago many thought only God could do. It is obvious that we cannot avoid influencing the future. "Like a gardener in an established garden, whether we ignore it, weed it, or cultivate it further, what we decide will have an effect."[260] In many places of religious thought, it is almost commonplace to say that humans are co-creators with God.

"We are co-creators of a universe, biosphere, and culture of endlessly novel creativity," writes Stuart Kauffman. We are agents; "we act on our own behalf; we do things . . . . Agency has emerged in evolution and cannot be deduced by physics. With agency comes meaning and value." He goes on to write: "My claim is not simply that we lack sufficient knowledge or wisdom to predict the future evolution of the biosphere, economy, or human culture. It is [the radical notion] that these things are inherently beyond prediction."[261]

At least on the intellectual level, the question is no longer *if* humans will influence the future but *how* human creativity should be directed. However, on the more general level, many persons of faith are still caught up in unreliable ways of addressing this issue. Their thinking is still controlled by the thought that if God intended something to be so, it would be that way. But they have already rejected their own defenses by accepting the fact that it is ok to change certain things when it comes to *their own* survival.

Taking this responsibility seriously means that we understand our relatedness with all life forms. Theologically, we are as much creator as created. We are "co-creators with the evolutionary process that engendered us."[262] This should not be surprising. After all, ask Kauffman:

> Is it, then, more amazing to think than an Abrahamic transcendent, omnipotent, omniscient God created everything around us, all that we participate in, in six days, or that it arose with no transcendent Creator God, all on its own? I believe the latter is so stunning, so overwhelming, so worthy of awe, gratitude, and respect, that it is God enough for many of us. God, a fully natural God, is the very creativity in the universe . . . . This view of God can be a shared religious and spiritual space for us all.[263]

But even if one insists that God is responsible for initiating creation, humans are nevertheless co-creators. The task of assuming responsibility for life is neither simple nor easy, as Philip Hefner explains. "Sometime within the last fifty years or so, we reached the point where the domination of natural systems by human cultural systems became a necessity for human survival. For decades, our technological interweavings enabled a decline in the mortality rate and the lengthening of human life that enabled populations to increase." Now, humanity is dependent upon technology for its survival. We do not have the option of pulling back and removing our technological interface with the rest of nature. If we did, millions, even billions, of people would perish." Such is the world in which we live.

Hefner asks us to pause and consider how our culture-technology works. "Technology requires continuous conscious awareness, knowledge, planning, competent operation, monitoring, and evaluation. It requires constant accountability. Technology does not just happen and go its way on its own . . . . Technology must interface with the millions of other systems in the natural world." This interfacing with the environment is inescapable. We create the meanings of our experience almost instinctively. The task of being creators is complicated by the fact of our competency.

> We are not fully competent to maintain our secondary cultural environment, nor are we able to interweave adequately with the other systems of nature . . . . This inability to manage our culture adequately . . . is not just a case of how we use tools . . . . Since technology is the work of our cultured brains . . . [it] comes naturally to us, imagining alternative worlds and acting on that imagination. In this respect, *technology is natural and not "artificial."* (Italics added)

Humans are out of sync with other systems of nature, writes Hefner, and because of this, there is the angst of wondering where we fit in. In this crisis of being out of sync with other systems of nature, the crisis itself can be revelatory. "In our struggle with crisis and loss, we discover our identity."[264]

Moltmann put it this way: "The gaze into the infinite stellar spaces and the age-old times from which background radiation reaches us awakens in modern people nihilistic feelings of lostness and a transcendent homelessness."[265] He suggests that our desire for space travel and the search for extraterrestrial life not only grows out of this lostness but also from a desire for a "do over"—an escape from the Earth we are destroying in the hope that we will have a chance to start over and the hope that this time we will do it right. It also grows out of our fear or the "end of the earth" as we know it, and therefore escaping Earth becomes our chance to survive as a species.

It is clear that our self-understandings are different from our ancestors of even a few generations ago. We now realize that the notion we humans are superior beings sharply differentiated from other animals is no longer viable, theoretically or practically. We also realize that human culture, including technology, is not something separate from nature. This in turn has forced many of us reluctantly to concede that the rest of nature does not exist for our exploitation—something most former generations believed to be their right. And, as Hefner rightly points out, the notion that human nature possesses an essence that is stable, perennially enduring, and static can no longer be accepted as true.

If these older self-images no longer work to sustain wholesome life, what new identity is emerging for us? Just the opposite of conventional wisdom is true. Because we prefer that which is stable and unchanging, many are ambivalent about the idea of "human becoming." However, "stable and unchanging" does not reflect our current understanding of the self.

In his book *Our Posthuman Future*, Francis Fukuyama argues, "that biotechnology is dangerous because it threatens to alter human nature, with the loss of human dignity. Many people would rather not struggle with the new values of life that are engendered by current options in reproductive technology, because they prefer to think of sexuality and procreation as if those technologies had never emerged."[266] However, as Hefner points out, "science is a fundamental element of our situation today, and religion is challenged to tell a story that will make sense of that situation. There is more to our situation than science, but there is very little in our situation today that does not have a thread of connection to science and its consequences."[267]

Neuroscientist Terrence Deacon writes that we are always in the situation of "surplus of meaning" (Paul Ricoeur). "This is the seedbed in which our lives emerge. This is the refining fire in which the days of our lives are forged." Deacon calls it "a world full of abstraction, impossibilities, and paradoxes," "a shared virtual world." It seems likely that we are the only species that "has ever wondered about its place in the world, because only one evolved the ability to do so." No other species on earth—as far as we can discern—seems able to follow us into this virtual world of ideas.[268]

We are meaning-seeking animals. We take for granted what Deacon calls the "evolutionary anomaly." That is, we ask about our place in this world and seek the meaning of this virtual world. William James wrote that "experience is not given to us as orderly and meaningful;" rather the human mind is essentially a purpose creating mechanism that brings order to our experience of the world. "The world's contents are given to each of us in an order so foreign to our subjective interests that we can hardly by an effort of our imagination picture to ourselves what it is like. We have to break that order altogether . . . . We break it into histories, and we break it into arts, and we break it into sciences; and then we begin to feel at home."[269]

Summary

In a world where everything involves "life" or "feeling," the boundaries begin to fade rapidly. As William Calvin reminds us, the boundary between the living and the nonliving is increasingly meaningless as our knowledge increases.

The existence of conscious organisms is a fundamental feature of our world. Today we realize that this consciousness applies not simply to human beings. Other animals are aware of the physical world to some degree and respond to it. However, we humans claim to have a more developed sense of consciousness and therefore possess a deeper understanding and appreciation of the world and our place in it.

Returning to our opening image of "thinking machines," what if a machine could be made to respond in the same way as a human being? Since there would be no observable grounds for claiming that the machine did not think, would that machine also have a consciousness? It would seem that there would be no difference.

SECTION TWO

PREFACE

Faith is to be understood in its multi-dimensional expressions without confusing faith and the expression of any particular religion. This means that in making a case for one's particular faith claim, the particulars will necessarily remain somewhat ambiguous. In its multi-cultural expression, faith does not necessarily involve theism. An example might be to compare Chinese folk religion that is theistic, and Confucianism, which is not. It is certainly possible to have religion without theism. Religion is whatever puts one "in accord" with the universe. Religion is that which provides a meaning to existence.

During my years as a pastor, I was confronted by several who claimed they did not believe in God. I would normally ask them why and just what it was they did not believe in. Somewhere in the conversation, I almost always said that I did not believe in that God either. And I wondered if the traditional God ever existed anywhere except in the minds of persons who held onto those views in order to get something out of their belief—especially good harvest, fertility, and heaven.

Once a child's faith in the existence of Santa Claus, the Tooth Fairy, and the Easter Bunny gets debunked, skepticism begins to set in. At least it did for me. What we were told as children about God sounded an awfully lot like Santa: he had a long flowing beard and heavy royal robes, and he was omniscient, omnipresent, and omnipotent. "He knows when you've been bad or good, so be good for goodness sake." In order to know that, Santa had to be everywhere at all times—just like God!

The unsettling news that the poor children around the world "would have no Christmas" unless we put our pennies in the mission jar only complicated the matter. Did Santa really need us to buy the gifts? And if so, who bought ours? Was the ability to pay really the criteria and not just the goodness or badness recorded in Santa's Book of Life? Both God and Santa could make miracles happen, both knew if you'd been bad or good, both could give you good things, withhold necessary things, or even deliver bad things. Then came the fateful day when we learned that Santa was really our parent(s), and we may have wondered if God our Father was perhaps really our father who would always love us, take care of our needs, and make us happy—unless, of course, we were bad or simply didn't like him—or even worse, he didn't like us. As we grew older, we became aware of atrocities throughout the world in papers, magazines, and on TV, and we wondered where God was. Didn't God care about these people? Were *all* of the people killed in the crash of an airliner or who died in a horrible theater fire really bad people? How could *all* of the people killed in the German concentration camps be bad people?

Slowly but surely we began to question what we had been told. But we were assured that God was in control and everything would turn out all right—if not here then in heaven. We just needed to accept things the way they were. In our questioning we began to look more closely at the Bible. It was said that the Bible was divinely inspired—some even said that God dictated it word-for-word and that it was therefore without error—at least the 17th century King James Bible. The Bible said that we were created in God's image—but only white Christian folk—as even the Declaration of Independence implies. Oh, the Civil Rights movements began to change that significantly, but then our fathers and brothers went off to wars in which they were taught that the enemy was less than human. After all, you cannot easily kill someone you think is a child of God just like you—or a sensitive human being like you.

When we began to read our Bibles and looking at the God portrayed in its pages, we discovered a powerful male God who sounded at times like a drunken father who comes home late at night and wreaks havoc on his household. This God was angry, jealous, cruel, played favorites, and was even at times sadistic. This God created confusion between people, like when the citizens of Babel wanted to build a tower to reach into heaven where God lived. Later the anger of this God was so intense that he destroyed everything on the earth that lived, with the exception of those people and animals on the ark with Noah. And even when people wanted to do the right thing—like the Egyptian Pharaoh—God hardened their hearts to prevent them from doing it. And the Apostle Paul claimed that God hardened the hearts of Jews against Jesus so that Gentiles could be delivered and brought into the promises of the covenant. What kind of God was that?

In the biblical story of the "Tower of Babel" (Genesis 11:1-9), we discovered the insecurity of a deity who, like an earthly king, was jealously guarding his power. This God punished (and still punishes) self-reliance, human initiative, and the desire for self-determination. Living into the image of the God that is pervasive in the scriptures of the Abrahamic faiths, we were taught that it was all right to jealously guard whatever power we could accumulate, with the result that we learned divisive ways of relating to others. Rather than allowing humans to come together in an effort to avoid chaos and strife, divine intervention took place to keep humans separated. That was the conflicting message we received in Sunday School. On the one hand there was this God who divides, and on the other hand, there was the God who loved us all—"red and yellow, black and white, all are precious in his sight."

The story continued to be confusing. The desire of people to build a unified nation built on peace and security was punished by God. This divine punitive action may have been to teach that it is in *God's* power that we find unity and peace, rather than in our own efforts. But what we learned was that human beings are helpless children who live under strong parental control. The story *intensified* the alienation of humans from God, from others, and even from our own selves. The answer to such alienation—an alienation *created by God*—must be a reconciliation between us and that same God. We were made sinful in order that we might be saved. We were made sick in order to be healed. This is manipulation at its worst by a sadistic God!

God was a deity that forced psychological torture on the most faithful of believers, like Job and Abraham. I always had trouble with the story of Abraham and the sacrifice of his son Isaac. What kind of God would ask a father to do something like this? And what kind of father would follow through with such a request? For Abraham this would result in the worst kind of parental abuse of a child—although God stepped in and stopped Abraham from following through with the sacrifice. Nevertheless, Abraham would follow through with another divine directive by sending his first son Ishmael and Hagar, Ishmael's mother, out into the desert to live or die. Abraham played favoritism—*just like his God*! And what did God get out of both the Job and Abraham "testings?" God could mark up another manipulative victory over the weak and helpless. And these men would praise him!

From our daily newspapers and other media, we learned that war was brutal and that soldiers died—but that was ok since they did this so we could have the freedom to worship God. But we were appalled to learn from the Bible that God told his favorites to go in and take the property that already belonged to someone else. More than this, God told them to kill everyone there—men, women, *children*, and animals. Indeed, they were to swing babies by their feet and bash their tiny little brains out against a stone wall. We would learn that following this notion of divine gifting, our own country's founders did the same thing to the Native Americans in the name of God.

Even as a child, I could never feel comfortable with a God that seemed not only dishonest, but also extremely cruel. Our Sunday school teachers would defend God by saying that this God of the Old Testament was somehow different from the God of the New Testament. That in itself was confusing since we were also taught that there was only one God. Then we read in Revelation about God's bloodbath against most people (even more violent than the Flood story). All the while we were told to repent of our sins and be good so that we would not go to hell where the bad would be eternally tortured by the fires of hell. But, as an adult friend once reminded me, in the Old Testament God killed people or ordered them to be killed, whereas the New Testament God was sadistic since his anger could never be relieved as people burned forever and ever in hell. Wouldn't it be more "loving" just to kill them once and for all? I decided very early that I could not believe in a God that was like that. And who would want to spend eternity—whatever that is—singing endless praises to a deity that acted so despicably (let alone the boredom of "being in endless church" and perpetually doing the same thing over and over again—forever!)?

If God caused the flood to kill all those people in Noah's day, then God must also be responsible for the natural catastrophes that we experience. When I was in the fourth grade a tornado came down near where we lived, and a man just a couple blocks away was killed when a tree crashed into his house. I remember wondering if God did that and what the man had done to deserve that early death. "Only God knows," I was told. It is interesting that we have never outgrown that infantile kind of thinking as we still commonly refer to natural events such as tornados, earthquakes, floods, or droughts as "acts of God." Normal insurance doesn't even cover these things! I suppose to do so would somehow go against the purposes of the Gods and bring even greater destruction!

As a pastor, I admit that since I was so repulsed by this kind of a God, that I often avoided dealing seriously with the sadism of hell and the reality that God possessed all of our negative human characteristics. When I did confront them, at least early on, I made all of the defenses of God I could. However, that was not easy. I came to see that the Bible had limited authority, since there were some things that it just couldn't be trusted to be truthful about. God is a loving and good God, I believed, and these negative characteristics were simply human projections written into the stories to justify human actions. I came to the conclusion that bad things happen to good people and good things happen to not-so-good people for a whole host of reasons—but the favoritism or anger of the divine was not among them.

It did not take the Death-of-God controversy in the 1960s to convince me that God as traditionally understood had died—if in fact that traditional God had ever existed except in the minds of those who never took the time to think seriously about the matter. I came to realize that the death-of-God message was a *positive* voice in theology. Rather than causing a massive loss of meaning and value, it made everything holy.

The death-of-God message was more about the experience that the certainties of traditional religion were no longer tenable. There was no longer a divine authority to which one could appeal and on which one could rely to provide a meaning of life. It declared not simply the end of a certain way of thinking about God but was a detachment from the entire God-question. Holding onto the traditional absolutes is like possessing a key to a lock that can no longer be found. Purpose does not come from a supernatural source. We are not born with a pre-established purpose. Purpose is developed in the course of living, and it comes from many quarters.

The question "Does God exist?" is the wrong question since the question itself predetermines God in an object-like form. Therefore, theologians should not begin with God, but rather with human existence since it deals with our existential awareness of and concern about our place in the world and our own mortality. Martin Heidegger (1889-1976) taught that this awareness leads to *anxiety*, the dread of nothingness and meaninglessness. However, our anxiety actually can help us discover the range of possibilities available to us. We learn to cope with our "groundless situation through *understanding*—the ability to creatively use things and to function productively in society." But we also cope by absorbing ourselves in shallow, mundane concerns. We help to make athletes and entertainers into godlike multi-millionaires while we ignore the millions of persons around the world who die of starvation—as well as the 25% of children in the United States who currently live in poverty. We make offerings to the Gods in control of oil and energy who live in profound luxury at the expense of those who must choose between food and medicine and heat in the winter. We make offerings to the political priests who serve these Gods and who at the same time rob the poorest among us of life, liberty, and the pursuit of happiness.

We were confused by the church's professed concern for the sick, the poor, the homeless, the unemployed and the underemployed was largely empty. Then we understood that it was only following the example of the biblical God whose love and compassion was sporadic at best and a form of favoritism at worst. Of course, we have concern because it is humanly the right thing to do. However, concern without in some way implementing the desired change is useless. And often we do not implement the needed changes not because we are powerless but because we believe that we will someday be lucky enough to reach the point where we will be among the fortunate. When we reach those golden streets, we want to make sure that the benefits enjoyed now by the fortunate will still be there for us—even though we outwardly deplore it while we secretly desire it. The truth of the matter is that very few of us will ever arrive to walk on those golden streets of prosperity. But in the meantime, we make the prescribed offerings and sacrifices to the Gods who we pray will make our dreams come true.

We minister in spirit rather than in person, so that all our talk about social justice is just that—talk. Our concerns are not relevant to the world of those who are hurting and dying. For all the good religious institutions do, it is a mere pittance compared to what it does for itself. Paradoxically, religious persons across the board tend to be so focused at being at one with the divine that they fail to be at one with the rest of humanity. If we believe the Tower of Babel story to be for our instruction, perhaps our focus only reflects the self-interest of God at Babel.

If one assumes the existence of Gods or God, one must then define or describe what that might be. Renouncing the existence of the traditional God of faith is necessary when we realize how inappropriate this understanding of God is to the human situation. We do not need to deny the existence of God. Rather we need to deny that God exists as we normally understand existence.

Since my days at MacMurray College, I have been influenced by Taoism. Lao Tzu wrote: "I know not its name so I style it 'the way' (Tao)." And what is Tao? It is "the way (Tao) of that which is naturally so." He went on to affirm: "The name that can be named is not the enduring Tao."

In this section, the discussion will center on what we can and cannot say metaphorically and confidently about God.

CHAPTER 7

What Color Is An Invisible Dog?

If, as some say, God spanked the town
For being overly frisky,
Why did He burn the churches down
And save Hotaling's whiskey?[270]

"A God that exists only for a group, even if it is an oppressed group, would be a tribal God."

— *Anselm Kyongsuk Min*

The one question that every pastor has encountered from children—and a few courageous adults—is this: "Where did God come from?" Perhaps the best answer of how the idea of a deity arose comes from William Swatos who deftly writes, "Rain dances come first. Theologies of the rain god later."[271]

The biblical view is that God makes the sun shine, the moon glow, and all the weather events we can possible experience. The biblical view is that the Earth is a flat disk with the domed sky above supported by pillars. Through small openings in this dome come rain, snow, hail, etc. Above the Earth is heaven where God lives. Below the Earth are the threatening waters of the deep and the fires of hell. (Why the waters do not put out the fires, or why the fires do not dry up the waters, is never considered.) This view of the world was out-of-date even in biblical times, although the "science" opposing it was not widely accepted. Even though the biblical worldview has been proven wrong, its supernaturalism actually desacralized and depersonalized nature, eventually paving the way for the later emergence of science as we know it.

Flat Earth Worldview

The idea of a flat earth went out of "scientific" fashion by the fifth century BCE. By the fourth century BCE, the scientific question was no longer whether the earth was flat—it was not—but the size of the globe on which we live. Eratosthenes (c. 276-194 BCE) had estimated that the earth's circumference was about 29,000 miles—relatively close to the 24,860 miles we know today.

Eratosthenes followed in a long line of thinkers. A full 300 years before him, Pythagoras (c. 580-500 BCE) argued that the Earth was a perfectly spherical globe that was not necessarily the center of the cosmos.

Two hundred years before Eratosthenes, Leucippus (c. 480-420 BCE) was the first to argue that the universe is made up of tiny, invisible particles (atoms). He also argued that a flat visible portion of the Earth rested on a round base, like a covered bowl or drum. His student, Democritus of Abdera (c. 450-370 BCE), agreed that everything in the universe consisted of atoms and added that since there is an infinity of atoms, there must also be an infinity of worlds. Carrying his idea a step forward, Democritus argued that the Gods were also composed of atoms and that they lived in the spaces between the worlds. He went further off-script in heretically arguing that the Gods could not interact with any of these worlds. This created a crisis of faith for some of the Greeks in his day.

Hicetas of Syracuse (c. 400-335 BCE) was a Pythagorean who not only argued against a static geocentric cosmos, but also taught that *only* the earth moved. Aristarchus of Samos (c. 310-230 BCE) argued that the Sun was the center of the universe, and he was the first to calculate the size of a heavenly body. Seleucus of Seleusia (born c. 190 BCE) agreed with Aristarchus and went on to prove through logic that the sun is the center of the universe, that the tides are due to the attraction of the Moon, and that the height of the tides depends on the Moon's position relative to the Sun.

> It is easy to see that Eratosthenes was heir to a rich heritage of several possible universes. His earth could have been a flat disk (Thales), disk-like with a raised rim (Anaximenes), a cylinder (Anaximander), an object shaped like a snare drum (Leucippus), a body extending infinitely downward (Xenophanes), a shallow funnel (Democritus), or a sphere (Pythagoras). His sun could have been located just beyond the moon (Pythagoras, Anaxagoras, et

> al.), or farther away than Saturn (Leucippus); it could have been a nearby object just one foot across (Heraclitus), or a distant window on a vast wheel of fire (Anaximander). Eratosthenes' cosmos could have been geocentric (Thales and others), heliocentric (Aristarches), centered on "pure fire" (Pythagoras), floating on air (Anaxinenes), formed from a set of nested spheres (Eudoxus), characterized by epicycles (Apollonius), or something else that has not come down to us.[272]

While these thinkers had various proposals about the Earth's place in the universe, "the notion of the earth whirling and hurtling through the cosmos was, in the end, fatally counterintuitive to the ancient world." By the time of Eratosthenes, "most of those who thought seriously about such questions believed in the sphericity of the earth."[273] As with the ideas of global warming or evolution in our own time, serious people did not dominated public discussion. As Max Planck wrote: "A new scientific truth does not triumph by convincing its opponents and making them see the light, but rather because its opponents eventually die, and a new generation grows up that is familiar with it."[274] Since the Church was still resisting this truth about the Earth revolving around the Sun as late as the 18th century, it often takes more than the death of one generation!

By the late sixth century BCE, both Xenophanes (c. 570-c. 475 BCE) and Heraclitus (c. 535-c. 475 BCE) found seashells on the hilltops in the areas around Ephesus. They hypothesized that this high area had at one time been covered by the Mediterranean Sea. In the fourth century BCE, Aristotle argued that earthquakes were caused by forces of nature, not by the acts of the Gods.

Other discoveries were being made that called old assumptions into question. Some of the natural philosophers believed "that all substances share one and only one fundamental ingredient, such as water, air, or fire—or, according to Anaximander, a mysterious and imperishable element call 'the infinite,' from which all things arise." Other philosophers argued that all things are made from a variety of elements. For Empedocles (c. 495-435 BCE), these elements were earth or solids, water or liquids, air or gases, and fire or energy. He called these "reality's four roots." Anaxagoras (c. 500-c. 428 BCE) added to these four the ingredient of mind or intelligence. Democritus took another route, arguing instead, "at its most basic level matter consisted of a multiplicity of individual particles called 'atoms' (from the Greek word *atomos*, 'indivisible'). Plato added to the elements ether.[275]

In the area of biology, Herophilus (c. 330-c. 260 BCE) identified the brain—not the heart—as "the operational center of the human nervous system."[276] This was in opposition to Aristotle, Judaism and, later, Christianity, all of whom identified this center in the heart.

It is not surprising, then, that by the fourth century BCE, the Greeks were experiencing a crisis of belief. "To many thinking Greeks, the Olympian gods came to seem remote or irrelevant, and the myths nothing more than childish stories."[277] As Sophocles (c. 496-406 BCE) wrote in *Oedipus Tyrannus*, "The old prophecies concerning Laius [the father of Oedipus] are fading; already men are setting them at naught, and nowhere is Apollo glorified with honors; the worship of the gods is perishing . . . ."[278]

The response to such crises is usually an attempt to reestablish the roots of one's tradition. The same was true in ancient Greece as "the root stories that define Greekness had to be excavated and purified of corruption," in a manner comparable to the Christian reformulations beginning earnestly in the eighteenth century with biblical criticism. "The project of fixing the great heritage of Homeric epics in written form—and removing the anachronisms, errata, and interpolations that had infected the text over hundreds of years of oral transmission—consumed a vast amount of time and energy"[279] and produced even more unrest.

Eratosthenes emphasized nonmythological sources in developing a system of scientific chronology, a practice that ran counter to ancient instinct. To him, "the *Odyssey* was best taken as entertainment, not as a textbook on geography. To take the Homeric epic as the wellspring of scientific knowledge, as many of his colleagues did, was to fundamentally misunderstand the nature of poetry, which was actually more about seducing the ear than informing the mind."[280]

This attitude toward history and scientific discovery had not changed much when three centuries later Tertullian (c. 150-230 CE) confidently wrote:

> What then has Athens to do with Jerusalem, the Academy with the Church, the heretic with the Christian? Our instruction comes from the Porch of Solomon who himself taught us that the Lord is to be sought in the simplicity of one's heart . . . .

> We have no need of curiosity after Jesus Christ, nor of research after the gospel. When we believe, we desire to believe nothing more.[281]

A hundred and fifty years later, Augustine (354-430) called curiosity about the natural world nothing more than a "disease which can avail us nothing and which man should not wish to learn." Yet, curiosity is necessary for growth, whether in the small child or the old man. "Any system in which, by definition, there are no loose ends can only stifle enquiry, for it can never be confronted either by its own defects or by the way the world is. But for some people (then as now), ordered and meaningful wholeness is preferable to loose ends and open questions."[282]

As the church turned its back on the legacy of Greek rationalism, the Islamic world—the Arabs, Babylonians, Persians, and Indians—not only preserved it but they also refined and enlarged it. Then, when Islam began to turn its back on what they had received, the Christian West awoke from about a thousand-year sleep. Until quite recently in history, astrology was extremely important to the Church for a variety of reasons. Suffice it to say that by the tenth century, the Vatican launched a program of subsidizing astronomical research, not for its "science" but for what the stars could forecast. While this was "one of history's great about-faces, the Church . . . found itself sponsoring the revival of wisdom its founders had once disdained."[283] This revival would become the seeds of controversy that would sprout up again in the late 18th century and continuing into the 21st century.

Some early Christian theologians fought the idea of a round earth as well as a sun-centered universe not only based on biblical literalism, but also as a means of resisting pagan culture and its teachings. Christians, along with most others, could not understand how anything could exist upside-down on the other side of the earth. This was the "fable of the Antipodes." There was the added problem with Antipodes since the idea "conflicted with Christian belief in the unity of the human race, descended from Adam and Eve, and the consequent universality of original sin and redemption to be resolved on Judgment Day. If there was another race living in the Antipodes, how had they got there, how could they have received the Word of God . . . and why did the Bible not mention them?"[284]

There were major theologians who accepted a spherical earth, including Augustine (354-430 CE). He argued that scripture was to be understood allegorically and that the flat-earth depictions were simply metaphors. But he was convinced that people "could not live on the other side of the globe because the Bible 'speaks of no such descendents of Adam', does not mention any preaching of the gospel in that region, and Antipodeans would not be able to see Christ come down to earth when he returned on Judgment Day."[285] Many Christians today continue to base their belief systems on a flat-earth worldview.

Theologians of all religions tend to drive by constantly looking in the rearview mirror for direction. While we may receive value from the past, we cannot move forward toward a community of all humanity until we begin looking forward rather than backward.

Looking Up for Answers

Why are our spiritual instincts directed at the heavens "above"? When asking this question I cannot help but imagine various scenes from the movie *The Gods Must be Crazy*. Someone flying in a small plane throws a Coke bottle out of the window. It lands on the head of a primitive tribesman who sees it as a gift from heaven. Whether it is a gift or not is debated throughout the story since it seems to bring only pain and hostility. It is a strange mixture of good news/bad news!

William Calvin suggests that human fascination with the heavens above may have originated with the interaction of our hunter/gatherer ancestors with the phases of the moon. The workday was longer or shorter depending on the fullness of the moon. Once our ancestors began to understand the regularity of these moon phases, they could risk staying out later. They were at least psychologically emboldened. Because they assumed that for every action there was an actor, there was obviously someone or something—some God or Gods—up there moving the sun, moon and stars. It probably seemed natural for our primitive ancestors to assume that when a lunar eclipse occurred something up there was eating the moon. In social relationships, persons learned early that others could be influenced by pleading, flattery, and gifts. If there were actors in the heavens, then perhaps they too could be influenced by prayer, praise, and pay. In addition, if there are Gods up there, there must be Gods down here. As the known world grew in size, so did the Gods and their servants.

Those who had intimate contact with the Gods, the shaman and other holy persons, grew in importance and power because of their abilities of prediction and their powers of intercession with these Gods. The shaman was perhaps the first scientist, "having backed into doing science without really understanding very much beyond a simple correlation."

> The shaman's everyday activities surely involved producing placebo effects via authoritative reassurance. And who would doubt the shaman's "Take this and you'll feel better" after such a demonstration of being well connected? Since at least a third of modern pain patients respond temporarily to a placebo drug, we might expect that, after an eclipse, the shaman's treatments became even more effective at relieving pain and anxiety. I also imagine this protoscientific shaman as advancing to become the first full-time priest, supported by the community and no longer having to hunt, gather, and prepare food in the manner of a part-time shaman. The society likely came to rely upon warnings so as to conduct appropriate rituals beforehand.[286]

This lunar influence illustration is inadequate. There is probably a more primitive undercurrent of expecting Gods to be running things from a distance, somewhere up there. But it does suggest that our constant search for meaning stems from the desire to understand our surroundings. Our search for meaning is intertwined with most sensory input. As was pointed out earlier, our brains run ahead of the evidence, filling in the gaps of inadequate information. In our search for meaning, "what we see resonates in the memory of what we have seen; new experience always percolates through old, leaving a hint of its flavor as it passes. We live, in this sense, in a 'remembered present.'"[287]

Again, the view of the world in the great civilizations was that of the three-story universe. Riley writes that beginning in the sixth century BCE, Greek mathematicians and astronomers discovered that the five visible planets, the five "wandering stars," moved in regular patterns independent of the dome of the "fixed stars." To understand this movement, new models of the universe were required, and the older three-story universe had to be discarded. It is interesting to note that although the science of these centuries before the Common Era began to see the world in a completely different way, Christians continued to hold to the three-story model for the universe. Even today most Christian language, if not all religious language, employs the three-story universe and the flat Earth notion on which it was built. Scriptures that are believed to the inspired words of God fail to mention that the Earth is round, the Sun is the center of our universe, and the universe is infinite.

Pythagoras spent some time with the Egyptians at Memphis where he probably learned from their Memphis Theology about "divine creativity that provided an agent through which an idea in the mind of the creator became a physical reality. In many early cultures, a spoken or written word was understood to have creative power." Thus, in the book of Genesis, God speaks the world into existence, and centuries later in the Gospel of John the word, the logos, provided the bridge between the divine and the human. "The theology of the priests at Memphis divided that creative 'word' into two different roles. A link was required, a divine intermediary between an idea in the mind of the creator and the actual physical creation." Just as Christians viewed Jesus as that link, Ptah was the God in Memphis Theology who provided the link, "enabling an idea in the human mind (a craftsman or artist) to become a real-world product . . . . Pythagoras and his followers would later assign that creative role to numbers . . . ."[288]

The Pythagoreans were far ahead of others in their time. They discovered that not only was the Earth *not* the center of the cosmos, neither was it a disk as was generally supposed. According to Philolaus, a disciple of Pythagoras, "the Earth could not be the center of the cosmos, nor, for that matter, could the Sun. The center had to be a 'central fire,' a fiery 'hearth of the universe' around which the Earth, the Moon, the Sun, the five planets, and the stars revolve." The second-century CE scholar Aëtius wrote that "unlike other philosophers, who say that the Earth is at rest, Philolaus the Pythagorean said that it revolves about the fire in an inclined circle like the sun and moon." With the exception of Aristarchus of Samos (310-ca. 230 BCE) who proposed a sun-centered cosmos, no one in antiquity "was willing to consider a moving Earth that was not the center of the cosmos," and "scholar after scholar tried to show, or simply assumed, that the Pythagoreans could not really have meant this."[289]

Pythagoras' argument that the Earth was a sphere was simply that "if the planets move independent of the fixed stars, then the hemispherical 'dome' of the fixed stars must be an entire sphere surrounding us." Out of his reasoning came an entirely new understanding of the world. "The earth was a sphere at the center surrounded by eight concentric spheres—seven crystalline and invisible spheres to which the moon, sun, and five planets were attached, with an outer limit of the eighth on which were the fixed stars."[290]

Much like the discoveries of Newton, Galileo, and Darwin, this discovery by Pythagoras had a fundamental impact on religious thought. One implication of this discovery was that the universe was much larger than previously imagined. "The distance to the dome of the sky, once thought to be just a few thousand feet, was increased enormously." For the religious person, the question arose concerning God's location. This new discovery moved God far beyond any previous position or conception. "God could no longer be a humanlike being who could eat with Abraham and show his back to Moses. God had to be something else, entirely different, qualitatively different, from previous conceptions: God could no longer have a body."[291]

Evolution of Egyptian Divinity

God had usually been identified with, or compared to, the sun, the source of light and warmth. However, with the expansion of the universe, God as the source of light had to be situated beyond the eighth sphere. But more than this, God could not be identified as the sun, as the Egyptians had thought, since "the sun was itself a celestial object, another servant of God like the other planets." The new cosmology required God to be spiritual and made of light or fire or ether. "God was enormous beyond human comprehension, hidden and infinite behind the veil of the vastly distinct eighth sphere."[292]

The Egyptians reached their understanding of an invisible God during the Fifth Dynasty (2498-2345 BCE). Religious belief and political thought have always had some sort of connection, and this can be clearly seen in Egypt. Referring to the death of a pharaoh, the question arose:

> Assuming that the kings reached the next life on the other side of the horizon, what were they going to do there? Possibly, the pharaoh would continue his royal role . . . . If the early pharaohs were believed to continue their kingly functions in the afterworld, the sacrificial burials made a kind of sense. After all, if a king's power only lasts until his death, he must be obeyed

> during his life, but there is no good reason to follow him into death. If, on the other hand, he's still going to be waiting for you on the other side, his power becomes all-encompassing. The passage to the undiscovered country is simply a journey from one stage of loyalty to the next.[293]

The early pharaohs claimed to be the earthly embodiment of the God Horus, "carrying with them that power which does not 'vanish at night time,' or with death." However, the pharaohs did die, and so the Memphis Theology adapted.

> When the pharaoh died, he was no longer considered the incarnation of Horus. He became instead the embodiment of Osiris, who was both king of the underworld and the father of Horus, king of the living realm. The earthly son of the dead pharaoh now took on the role of the incarnate Horus, which demonstrates the practical uses of such a system . . . . the new king wasn't just the son of the old king. He was, in a sense, his father's reincarnation.[294]

By the mid—to late 2400s BCE, the limits of this theology were reached. During the Fifth Dynasty, as "power was shifting from the palace towards the temples," the pharaoh also became more closely identified with the sun-God. "He had Horus and Osiris; now he was the son of Ra. This likely brought him further under the control of the sun-god's high priests, who could convey to him his father's words." Instead of the earthly incarnation of God, the king was now the son of God, a subtle but meaningful demotion of the king. "The rings of divine power had rippled outwards, and the pharaoh was no longer the central and unquestioned conduit of it. And the idea of the pharaoh's continuing presence on earth after death also began to fade."[295] It was at this time that Amenhotep IV came to the throne, and the Fifth Dynasty experienced a surge in power. The priests of Ra (the God of the sun) began losing power to the priests of Amun, the ancient "father God." "Amun had always been a rather amorphous deity; in fact, one of his appearances was a non-appearance, as an invisible presence. He was nicknamed 'The Hidden One,' and was prone to borrow identities, temporarily claiming the powers of some other deity to mask his mysterious true nature. This gave his priests plenty of flexibility."[296] Amenhotep IV was on his way to becoming a monotheist as he started an entirely new religion. He saw the other Gods—Osiris, Horus, and Ra—as only representations of the true God, Aten.

> The disk of the sun itself was called "the Aten," and had not gone unrecognized in the past; it was simply one aspect of the sun-god Ra. But in the hands of Amenhotep IV, the sun-disk became something new. Rather than a god shaped like a mortal being, as Osiris and Horus and Ra himself were, the sun-disk was an abstract representation of the divine itself: the manifestation of a single power. In its glare, the other gods of the pantheon vanished. The sun was not merely the chief power; it was the only power. In its glare, the other gods of the pantheon vanished. The gods of the Egyptian pantheon had wives and consorts; Aten was alone and self-sufficient . . . . Aten had no form. The gods of the Egyptian pantheon had stories; Aten had no story at all.[297]

Not only this, but Aten had no need for priests or for religious bureaucracy. There was no God beside Aten. The political implication to this understanding of the invisible and indivisible God was that neither Aten nor Aten's representative on earth, the pharaoh, would tolerate shared power.[298] This Egyptian idea on God undoubtedly influenced the later Jewish religion's adoption of monotheism.

Implications of God's Location

The question of God's location was connected to another question about the definition of the universe. "If God was outside and infinite, then the cosmos must be inside God." This led to the idea that God contained the cosmos but was himself contained by nothing. "God was not in a place, but was the place in which all else was."[299]

This also led to the question of whether the cosmos was infinitely large. Archytas of Tarentum (428-347 BCE) was a Greek mathematician and philosopher, and the last prominent Pythagorean thinker. We have no written information about his cosmology, "but he developed the most famous argument for the infinity of the universe in antiquity."[300]

Archytas, and later the Christian theologian Origen, asked: "If I come to the limit of the heavens, can I extend my arm or my staff outside, or not?" This question continues to puzzle many today. Archytas decided that however the question was answered, "if he were out there performing the experiment, he could not extend his arm or staff farther, something beyond the supposed limit had to be stopping him."[301]

Nicholas of Cusa (1401-1464) also concluded that the universe had to be infinite since it had no limit but God who was infinite. Contrary to what most people of his day believed (they followed Aristotle's thinking on the matter), Nicholas "insisted that the universe was not made of different types of substance at different levels, such as the impure region near Earth and the pure region of the celestial spheres. The universe was homogeneous. The stars were 'each like the world we live in, each a particular area in one universe, which contains as many such areas as there are uncountable stars.'"[302] He was certain that "Earth was a star like the Sun and the other stars, and it moved. This was not the orthodox, Ptolemaic/Aristotelian stationary-Earth-centered astronomy that was being taught in the universities! Nicholas worked his ideas up in a highly original, mathematics-based system." Although "he apparently never worried whether his ideas about the arrangement of the cosmos might conflict with church doctrine," his suggestion was a definite challenge to the Earth-centered notion upon which much of the church's theology was based. Interestingly, the church never condemned or criticized him. [303]

As the implications of this notion that God was "the place in which all else was" continued to spread, even ethics took on a different meaning as humans came to be seen as "made up of two essentially different parts, body and soul. Passions and appetites, quite obviously, belong to bodies."[304] In place of the old anthropomorphic terminology, philosophers developed a negative theology that explained God by saying what God was *not*. Accordingly, God was described negatively: infinite, immaterial, unknowable, invisible, immeasurable, ineffable, immortal, unbegotten, incomprehensible, imperishable, unnamable, unchanging, and so forth.

With the split of body and soul, the material body came to be identified as sinful. "In Persian Zoroastrianism, inherited by Christianity, the world was created good and was then defiled by the Devil; its destiny was that it would be destroyed and replaced with a new world."[305] The soul was identified with the upper world and needed to escape the material world and the body in which it existed.

This produced another challenge to religion. In the past God (s) had been worshipped by offerings of food, incense, and various kinds of sacrifices. Established priesthoods had considerable investment in the old views of the Gods. The ancient views of the divine had to be protected or the priests would be out of a job. Scientific discoveries have never ceased being problems for the priesthood!

God as Creative Activity

There is nothing that we can know directly about God, and most of the traditional arguments for God do not hold up under scrutiny. The questions we raise about God are similar, if not the same, as those we raise about the universe. As Carl Sagan stated in his 1985 Gifford Lectures on Natural Theology at the University of Glasgow:

> God can have always existed but will not exist for all future time. God might have no beginning but might have an end. God might have a beginning but no end. God might have no beginning and no end. Likewise for the universe. The universe might be infinitely old but it will end. The universe might have begun a finite time ago but will go on forever, or it might have always existed and will never end.[306]

I do not doubt the experiences of transcendence I have had. In the past, I have normally associated these with God. I find that after years of wrestling, I am compelled to believe that transcendent reality exists, although I have no confidence about just what that is. I find it difficult, if not impossible, to convincingly argue otherwise. I reject the characteristics traditionally attributed to God. In the end, perhaps the notion of "God" is best lost in mystery and experienced in inexplicable momentary flashes of mystical flight.

Is understanding this transcendent reality as creative energy simply another form of the ancient doctrine of vitalism—a theory that was largely abandoned in the early 19th century—or another way of saying that all life is divine? Does the notion of creative energy end up being just another dualism? Is it a reflection of the Star War's philosophy of "The Force is with you?" I do not believe that these are necessary conclusions.

Creativity is essential for life since life requires progress, not stasis. Creativity—including reproduction—is part of everything, but creativity itself is not necessarily more than the sum of all things, nor does it necessarily exist apart from material reality. Davies corrects the popular notion that living things require energy. In a technical sense, energy that is released in the body as food is metabolized and that energy is dissipated into the environment as heat—as work or activity. "The total energy content of a person's body remains more or less unchanged. What happens is that there is a *flow* of energy through the body. This flow is driven by the orderliness, or negative entropy, of the energy consumed. The critical ingredient for maintaining life, then, is negative entropy."[307] This, in itself, does not negate understanding transcendence as the creative energy that results in elegance, awe, wonder and mystery—as well as chaos, change, and extinction.

Since creativity is at work at every level of existence, we see the evidence of it absolutely everywhere. To align creativity with traditional notions of God, though, is to invoke a "God-of-the-gaps" kind of argument that leaves us open to the need to retreat later in the face of new scientific information.

The notion of creativity existing apart from being and substance is the Taoist concept of *wu*. This is commonly translated as "void," but it is not simply nothingness, but rather "the indeterminate and formless creative ground which gives rise to the formation and determination of things."[308] Like the Tao, God is unknowable except as a hypothesis. Even if one poses God as the creator of the universe—the source of creativity itself—it is not difficult to argue that once the laws were conceived, the universe then became self-creating and self-sustaining. While we may affirm that the source is "God," it is nevertheless impossible to speak of this God in any definitive manner, and certainly not in traditional religious images and language. For a growing number of persons, there is no need for a deity of any kind in this process unless that deity is identified as the very laws of the process itself—in which case it is no longer divine but natural. A recent survey of American religious beliefs indicates that 44 percent of Americans do not believe in a God who acts in the world or in their personal lives. Christians answering in this manner might be considered "deist" Christians.

On the other side of the issue, a 2005 Pew Trust poll found that 42% of Americans reject the scientific explanation and believe that humans and other animals have existed in their present form since the beginning of time. According to Bloom and Weisberg, this makes these persons more reactionary than "Intelligent Design" proponents, "who deny only that natural selection can explain complex design."[309]

At this moment, we do not know whether Earth is the only place in the vastness of the universe (or the multiverse) that is inhabited by conscious life forms. The current evidence is that we are probably *not* alone. To speak of Earth as the *only* place of conscious life is like speaking in terms of the biblical story of Isaac being Abraham's *only* son or of Jesus as being the *only* son or child of God. The term *only* cannot indicate quantity since Abraham had another son Ishmael and the Bible speaks of others as being sons of God. The term in this sense must refer to quality, thereby reflecting a value of priority.

I remember the tremendous impact of reading J. B. Phillips' *Your God Is Too Small.* I was a young college student struggling with questions about the whole religious enterprise. That little book was a "faithquake" to me, causing me to question certain assumptions about God. It helped to prepare the way for changes in my thinking, changes I could never have imagined prior to its reading. My youthful assumptions had seen God in very small and limited ways. Now four decades later, after looking at the world in a much deeper and broader context, I have come to suspect that even the notion of transcendence as creativity is still remarkably small and hemmed in.

I am most often like the biblical Thomas confessing, "I believe. Help my unbelief. Give me understanding." With all of the intricacies of the quantum world and the unimaginable vastness of a universe of universes, I cannot but believe in creativity and process. On the other hand, looking at randomness and chance in the universe and the agonizing poverty plaguing most of humanity, I can only affirm that the God (s) of traditional thought are far too tribal, far too robotic to be the source or locus of creativity—or even creativity itself.

I am inclined to believe that if the notion of God is to be maintained, it will be as the creativity that ignites imagination, casts a vision, devises the laws of nature, inciting and imbuing all that was, is, and ever shall be. To understand that Earth is but a grain of sand on an infinite beach or that our galaxy is but one of billions to populate the multiverse, is inconceivable even for those who try to describe such vastness. Strictly speaking, creativity is not personal, judging, knowing everything, and so on. Creativity is simply the natural process of change, growth, experimentation, chance, randomness, dead-ends, disorder, and order. Creativity is without form or substance.

Creativity gives rise to the new and novel in the never-ending process of change. To speak of creative energy or creativity in reference to transcendence avoids calling forth the traditional image of the "cosmic person" standing outside of the world. Rather than speaking of divine purpose, this also allows us to speak of "directional movements or trajectories that emerge spontaneously in the course of evolutionary and historical developments."[310]

We are not the first to grapple with a growing sense of wonder at the vastness of the world. In the biblical world, the writer of Psalm 8 wondered about human significance in this awe-inspiring enormity. The prophet Isaiah wrote of God whose thoughts are not at all like human thoughts and whose ways of acting are as incomprehensible as the world is big. How much *more* do we, centuries later with a quantum worldview and an infinite cosmology, wrestle with these questions.

While natural catastrophes—like tsunamis, hurricanes, earthquakes, droughts and floods that kill and displace thousands of persons—raise questions for traditional understandings concerning God, the issue is not new, nor do these catastrophes necessarily force us to redefine our faith stance to the extent that the Holocaust did. Indeed, while theologians are still debating traditional understandings of God, much of the recent work began in earnest almost 300 years ago with scholars like Hermann Reimarus (1694-1768), and later by persons such as F. C. Baur (1792-1860), Ludwig Feuerbach (1804-1872), David F. Strauss (1808-1874), Walter Bauer (1877-1960), Albert Schweitzer (1875-1965), and scores of others. The search for the historical Jesus, the history of early Christianity, the development of the institutional church, and the impact of scientific discoveries on religious belief all began and resulted in a questioning of and restating of doctrine and ecclesial authority.

Traditional understandings continue to hang on long after they have been rendered untenable, especially in the United States. Europe is a somewhat different story. At best, the security of religious myth offers comfort; at its worst, it results in religious imperialism and acts of terror and destruction. Keeping these traditional understandings alive makes no sense. As Spong argues, "Divine artificial respiration is a waste of time."[311]

And yet, the hard work of making sense of this notion called God has to be done—and the results will not be popularly accepted. Since the doctrine of God is fundamental to all other doctrines of the church, conclusions made about it will affect everything else. The disconcerting fact is that, as Robert Scharlemann suggests, the issue will never be even temporarily answered.

God is a symbol of creativity of which we can speak only in metaphor. Certainly, we understand more about how creation unfolds—theoretically, back to within seconds of its beginning. However, it seems that we cannot get beyond that boundary. As David Toolan writes, to continue to use literalistic and descriptive terms about God "is to lose our way." God is not a static thing with being—that is, God does not exist as we exist. God is better understood as "limitlessly charged energy, bonding force, vibrant field, and creative chaos . . . ."[312] These metaphors suggest that transcendence cannot be defined or described in absolute terms.

To speak of divine transcendence as creativity—*not* as an agent that is the *source* of creativity—is to contemplate the empowering idea, the energy field that brings into being things that did not exist, the bonding force that brings together, or the expanding force that pulls apart. Creativity can be described much as time is described in Ecclesiastes. There are times that are appropriate for all things. Just as there are times that are appropriate for a variety of often competing or opposing actions, so there is an appropriate action to all aspects of creativity. This notion is also found in Taoism. That which is random creates order, so that that which is ordered includes that which is not ordered, and vice versa. Creativity operates in terms of disrupting order. It looks at peace and brings disorder. It looks at disorder and creates peace. We are not creativity; we are the result of it and made creative by it.

To speak of transcendence cannot mean that creativity exists outside of time and space. Rather it is found only within time and space. It is the process in which all things come to be.

The notion of "nothingness" outside of the universe introduces an invisible border at the place where space ends and the nothing begins. But what would it mean for the universe to exist within nothingness? Logically, by definition, the universe cannot exist in nothingness and therefore exists only in time and space. As mind boggling as it may be, it seems that the universe of universes is infinite, without beginning or end. Now, if it is true that something can exist only in space and time, then all that is exists in space and time, regardless of how far in or out we may reach. In this universe of universes, new worlds are continuously being born while others are dying.

The focus on a traditional creative agent within the universe is to argue that in some manner all of creation has a predetermined direction or purpose. But direction or purpose as commonly understood is not apparent when we look at the past several billion years. Regardless of how direction or purpose is experienced, it seems that purpose and direction are created within the process of creativity. Otherwise, it would be difficult to explain the dead-ends of the evolutionary process as well as the worlds that are constantly being created and destroyed in the development of the multiverse. Whatever purpose or direction we see in the evolutionary processes that have formed the universe or multiverse and all that is within it, is well illustrated in an example given by Nobel laureate physicist Philip W. Anderson. The example is based on his concept of symmetry breaking.

> Consider, for example, a vertical pole on a flat surface—say a pencil miraculously balanced on its eraser. Before it falls, physicists speak of the pencil as having full 360-degree symmetry. After it falls in some direction, say to the north, it has broken that full 360-degree symmetry on the plane surface. A specific direction has emerged. This is a simple example of symmetry breaking, in which the underlying physical symmetry of the plane is not violated, but the broken symmetry creates a new macroscopic condition; a pencil pointing north, from which other specific broken symmetries may follow.[313]

This is the nature of creativity: We cannot say ahead of time what novelty will arise.

It has been argued that the norms and values that give direction to a community or wider culture are related to the way in which the world is conceived. In the past century, the physical sciences began discovering new and interesting, even bizarre, knowledge about the world. New ideas were formulated about space and time, the relation of mind and body, the solar system and multiverses. These new insights resulted in significant and radical reformulations of how reality is to be understood. Physicists and cosmologists talk in almost mystical ways about a self-creating universe, a universe of universes, spontaneous creation, possible parallel universes, and much, much more.

Carl Sagan wrote eloquently in the Introduction to Stephen Hawking's *A Brief History of Time*:

> We go about our daily lives understanding almost nothing of the world. We give little thought to the machinery that generates the sunlight that makes life possible, to the gravity that glues us to an Earth that would otherwise send us spinning off into space, or to the atoms of which we are made and on whose stability we fundamentally depend. Except for children (who don't know enough not to ask the important questions), few of us spend much time wondering why nature is the way it is; where the cosmos came from, or whether it was always here; if time will one day flow backward and effects precede causes; or whether there are ultimate limits to what humans can know.[314]

Hawking's book was about God, or as Sagan suggested, about the absence of God. It is his quest to "know the mind of God." Hawking gives us a picture of a universe without beginning or ending, a universe with no edge in space, and "nothing for a Creator to do." But eventually, as Davies reminds us, "we all have to accept something as given, whether it is God, or logic, or a set of laws, or some other foundation for existence."[315] We will always reach the point of mystery beyond which we cannot advance, although that point moves with every increase in knowledge. The question concerning God can be argued theologically, philosophically, scientifically, and logically, but cannot finally be either proved or disproved. What we can do is to disprove certain aspects that have been attributed to God.

The question for most religious people is not so much about the existence of God but the *kind* of God that is being promulgated or defended. Trying to answer the question of what God is like is comparable to trying to answer the question, "What color is an invisible dog?" or "What does air look like?" We can describe air, even though we cannot see it. We can list its characteristics, we can experience its effects, we can measure its compounds, but we cannot see it, and yet we cannot live without it. All of life depends on it. Religious persons are called to rethink their conceptions of the divine by allowing new knowledge of the world to inform them. Scientific discovery does not determine belief, but it should certainly inform it. Not surprisingly, in many places the Bible speaks of God in the invisible terms of spirit, breath, or wind/air. Because of this understanding, the Ten Commandments affirm that God cannot be captured in *any* form.

Hawking retells the story of when Bertrand Russell (others say it was some other scientist) was giving a public lecture on astronomy.

> He described how the earth orbits around the sun and how the sun, in turn, orbits around the center of a vast collection of stars called our galaxy. At the end of the lecture, a little old lady at the back of the room got up and said: "What you have told us is rubbish. The world is really a flat plate supported on the back of a giant tortoise." The scientist gave a superior smile before replying, "What is the tortoise standing on?" "You're very clever, young man, very clever," said the old lady. "But it's turtles all the way down!"[316]

We all approach the subject of transcendence with our own defining stories and images, some of which state that "God simply is and that is all there is to it." Others affirm God while at the same time wrestle with what this concept means. Still others push God language and images to the edge or abandon the concept altogether. Karl Marx wisely came to a point in his life when he refused to speak about God, even to deny God, saying that in order to deny God, one had to first postulate the existence of God. Sounds like a catch-22.

All speech about God is expressed in human terms and familiar images, and it is therefore metaphorical and not literal. Indeed, all that theologians claim to understand about God is derived from human experiences and reflections on those experiences. Because of this, it is extremely difficult—if not impossible—*not* to invent images of the divine that simple reflect our own needs and desires. As David Pailin writes, any suggested understanding of divine reality "must be shown to be consonant with what common experience discloses as the actual character of reality. Otherwise, that understanding may be attractive to believers because it tells them what they want to hear but be as unrealistic and untrue as many of the other tales that are told to give people a false sense of security."[317]

We have given the name "God" (and similar names in other traditions) to the process of creativity, since creativity determines everything and in return is influenced by everything. Carl Stecher, part-time English professor at Salem State College in Salem, Massachusetts, argues that this is both bad science and bad theology because it is not in line with the theist view. However, he should certainly know that there are more options in theology than the supernatural theistic one. He writes, "The energy that is the cosmos itself is completely amoral, entirely apart from any human concept of good and evil, and unresponsive to prayer. This 'God' is embodied equally and indifferently in flowers and fungi; in saints and slugs; in a grain of dust, a cancer cell, a turd. But this 'God' at least lacks the appalling malice of the Christian God."[318] We might respond, "So what is the problem?"

Stecher has the terms reversed. It is not that God is amoral energy—although that is not denied—but that amoral energy is given the tag of God. *Creative* energy generates possibilities and enables potentiality from which the world may choose. Part of this "choice" is determinate while other aspects of it are indeterminate. This is true of every aspect of reality. In terms of humanity, we see that human freedom, while limited by various determining factors, is the act of consciously choosing and implementing a course of action or thought. In this sense, freedom is not a "gift" that is granted or allowed by some divine being, but rather the natural result of the creative process itself. Claiming in each particular moment the best option from the many possible choices contributes to the success of creation in all its aspects.

Can the divine, understood as creativity, be seen as caring? The creation of new possibilities in each and every moment and the lure to fulfill the greatest good in our choices, the enabling of potentiality to implement this good, and the rewarding of the whole of creation when this occurs is certainly not uncaring *in its effects*. Creativity moves the world into greater complexity and greater interdependence and is neither personal nor impersonal. Its lure into fulfillment of life and potential is not caring in the individualistic classical sense, but it may be seen as caring nonetheless.

The problem remains that too often what is defined as personal really means "my own best interest" regardless of the interests of others or the larger interest of the rest of creation. In that sense, a personal deity does not exist. Creativity does not distinguish between the splitting of an atom and the splitting of a cell and therefore does not put my interest above the interests of any other aspect of the world. Nor does it put human interests above the interest of the molecules in a rock. This desire for a personal care-for-me God who will meet my needs is little more than selfish interest—what tradition has called idolatry.

It is creativity, then, that operates in the entire universe throughout the span of time and space—in the novelty occurring in a moment of individual experience as well as in the creation of new universes and the destruction of dying ones. Understood as creativity, transcendence cannot be understood as a substantive being but is rather an action. As my friend and theological mentor Clark Williamson would say, "God is a verb." In the fourth century, Origen wrote that "if God were creative, there must have always been some form of ongoing creation. Otherwise, God's nature would have changed"—something that Origen's acceptance of divine immutability inherited from Greek philosophy would not allow.[319] We might agree with Origen that creativity means that there has always been some form of ongoing creation, however, creativity means that there is always change.

It is obvious that life *and* death are normal parts of all existence. New possibilities for life in some form occur in spite of, or as the result of, death and destruction. How can "caring" as normally understood be interpreted in the process of species and worlds coming into being and then fading into extinction? Is the normal cycle of life and death itself part of divine "caring?" Is it necessary to invoke some sort of existence after death—whether resurrection or reincarnation—in order to make this caring ring true? And if so, is "life after death" true of all creation and not simply human beings? If so, what does that look like for a dying star?

We know that intelligent life on Earth was almost extinguished in the past. Kaku writes:

> About a hundred thousand years ago, there were probably only a few hundred to a few thousand humans, based on the latest DNA evidence. Unlike most animals within a given species, which are separated by large genetic differences, humans are all nearly alike genetically. Compared to the animal kingdom, we are almost like clones of each other. This phenomenon can only be explained if there were "bottlenecks" in our history in which most of the human race was nearly wiped out. For example, a large volcanic eruption might have caused the weather to suddenly get cold, nearly killing off the entire human race.[320]

One of the extinct species of humans seems to be the recently discovered—and controversial—"Hobbits" discovered on the Indonesian island of Flores. The remains of a thirty-year-old female—*Homo floresiensis*—had a brain smaller than most chimpanzees and the height of a three-year-old child. It was determined that this human species lived from about 95,000 to 12,000 years ago. "We have known for many years that different species of prehumans and early humans may have coexisted, particularly in Africa prior to 2 million years ago," said paleontologist Chris Stringer who heads the human origins department at the Natural History Museum in London. "But the Flores find raises the possibility that as recently as 50,000 years ago, there could still have been at least four species of humans on Earth: *Homo sapiens* spreading from Africa; *Homo neanderthalensis* in western Eurasia; *Homo erectus* surviving in Java; and now *Homo floresiensis*, perhaps surviving as late as 12,000 years ago in Flores."[321] Heather Wax comments on this discovery: "We are left to reset our perspective and reshape the story of evolution. A human species with half our body size and less than one-third our brain size, recently lived alongside us. It appears they hunted, began using fire, and made sophisticated tools; they may have crafted boats."[322] And Mike Morwood, an archaeologist from the University of New England who led the excavation team commented: "The clear implication is that, despite tiny brains, these little humans were intelligent."[323]

We know that, like we *homo sapiens*, *Homo neanderthalensis* "made art and jewelry, ate a rich and varied diet, and buried their dead. And evidence is mounting that their language was more complex than the stereotyped 'cave man talk' gives them credit for. Nevertheless, around thirty thousand years ago they vanished from the earth." When we look at *Homo floresiensis*, the Hobbits, we have to wonder, "If the hobbits had had the resources of the Eurasian continent at their disposal, might they have invented agriculture, civilization, the wheel, writing? Were they self-conscious? Did they have a moral sense? Were they aware of their mortality? Did they sing and dance?"[324]

How does the extinction of these *human* species fit in as part of a divine purpose? And if these species became extinct over tens and hundreds of thousands of years, it seems possible that our human species will also become extinct, only to be replaced by another. Would that devalue our degree of humanness, or would it help us to see ourselves in a much broader evolutionary light? If this *is* a possibility, what impact would it have upon our understanding of traditional religious categories?

Power

The church and all other institutions of control have understood power as coercion and force, however benign the intent. The doctrine of infallibility—of God, Jesus, scriptures, or religious dogma—is the foundation of religion's power and its rejection of anything that would challenge its authority. Traditional religions of almost every kind argue for power defined in terms of a force that causes things to occur, so that, for instance, miracles are brought about by a divine force that interrupts natural laws and processes in order to produce a result that would otherwise have been impossible. Thus, for success in a battle led by Joshua, God caused the sun to stand still in the sky—thereby disrupting literally everything in this universe of universes. A few years ago, fundamentalist Pat Robertson claimed a miracle as a result of his prayers. (This was not unusual since he claims to witnessing miracles and hearing God personally speak to him on a regular basis.) There was a tornado headed straight for his TV studio. He prayed that the studio would be spared. Sure enough, it was—except that there were some nearby homes that were now in the new path of the storm, and they were destroyed in the process. He claimed a miracle from God, despite the havoc it brought to others. What kind of miracle is that? What kind of God is that? In the natural world, something one person experiences as a miracle is often a tragedy for another.

Jesus dealt with this issue. One day someone in the group gathered around him told him about some Galileans whose blood Pilate had mingled with their sacrifice. It was not because of their sin that this happened, Jesus responded. Nor was it because of anyone's sin that eighteen persons were killed when the tower in Siloam fell on them. They were at the wrong place at the wrong time. In the same way, he said to another group, God makes the sun to rise and the rain to fall on the evil and the good alike.[325] In the words of Rabbi Kushner, bad things happen to good people, and good things happen to bad people. There is no difference.

When we speak of creativity, it is better to avoid the term "power" and instead refer to creative influence that operates through possibilities. It makes no sense to speak of a divine power that interrupts natural laws.

Indeed, any interruption in natural law, such as Joshua's miracle of the sun standing still in the sky, not only interrupts things in one place but the entire universe! Of course, when the story was first told, it was believed that this would be possible without any problems. To repeat the story as factual today is an exercise in perpetuating ignorance.

It obviously places major responsibility on humans to be more aware of the interdependence that exists between all things and for humans to respond in ways that contribute to the highest good possible. This requires humans to live in harmony with nature. It further requires humans to understand that "subduing the earth" is an act of forceful power that in the long run cannot be to anyone's or anything's benefit. It requires us to take the long view—something that we seem increasingly unable to do.

There are those who claim that God has freely constricted divine power in order to make room for natural selection and free will among the resulting creatures. The argument that "God could do *whatever* but chooses not to," is an inadequate and capricious God. This divine compromise of integrity arises from a "God-of-the-gaps" mentality.

When we speak of freedom and natural selection, we acknowledge that the future is truly open and results from a combination of trial-and-error. Only a few things work out or survive while most do not. Is there a divine unchanging purpose in this process at every stage, or is "purpose" found in the process itself? If the purpose is in the process of creativity itself and the future is truly open to chance and necessity—and failure as well as success—then how do we *define* that process and what is the methodology necessary to establish its validity?

The very idea of randomness or chance is of quite recent origin. Dennett suggests that in earlier times,

> there was no way of even *suspecting* that some event was utterly random; everything was presumed to mean something, if only we knew what. Deliberately opting for a meaningless choice just to get *some choice or other* made, so one can get on with one's life, is probably a much later sophistication, even if that is the rationale that explains why it was actually useful to people. In the absence of that sophistication, it was important to believe that *somebody somewhere who knows what's right is telling you.*[326]

If God is involved in every moment giving purpose and direction—even if only by persuasive influence—how do we account for the "failures?" This is certainly not a classical deity who is all-knowing or all-powerful. The classical God would know at the beginning that most things attempted would not work out and would therefore avoid those things. Being all-powerful and all-knowing, this God would not work through a trial-and-error process, since God could not make mistakes. It is therefore increasingly difficult to defend any traditional notion of God as all-powerful and/or all-knowing. The failures and dead-ends in the evolution of the world are simply natural developments that did not or could not survive for various reasons. One example of such "failures" would be the estimate that 98% of all species on Earth have perished. If God works by experimentation—going through several models in order to achieve one success, how does that affect the religious understanding of a "personal" God who interacts to guide and inspire?

Deism is rejected by traditional dogma—but the dogma is flawed. Of course, it is much more comfortable letting others do our thinking for us and spoon-feed easy answers as difficult questions arise. It is even easy to affirm that "something" had to light the fuse for the Big Bang—a first cause. Limiting God to this function is unsatisfactory for most religious people. Without a divine presence guiding (and responding) to them, they are lost children without a parental God to rely on. Without such a God, persons are forced to see themselves as creatures responsible for who they are and who they are becoming. This means that we, to some degree, create our own future and, therefore, are responsible for at least a portion of the future direction of evolution—however large or small the effect. Moreover, we are responsible for each other. We have to grow up! Without a deity giving personal direction, we are forced to rely on the rest of "creation" to develop and implement that direction. Nature is self-organizing, and therefore we are the ones who create purpose and meaning.

Without a sense of a divine presence outside of ourselves, many are nevertheless filled with awe and wonder at the cosmos—and this awe and wonder opens us to a mystical/spiritual level of experience. Awe and wonder cannot be easily measured or analyzed. How do we explain these emotions beyond their chemical components? "Is this love?" is not the same kind of question as "Is this metal?"

Ian Barbour writes, "Evolutionary history does indeed show a *directionality*, a trend toward greater complexity and consciousness . . . ."[327]

Does Barbour's directionality satisfy the religious quest for a sense of the divine in the evolutionary process, or is that "directionality" simply an aspect of the self-organization of nature? It seems that not even complexity *necessarily* counts in the argument for directionality. If purpose is not *inherent* in the evolutionary process, can it be the result of consciousness? And if so, does that mean that nonhuman life must have some form of consciousness? Directionality might be understood as a built-in survival goal, something we see in the smallest of viruses that adapt to and fight against the best of our antibiotic medicines. Directionality, then, is a survival mechanism inherent in the brain.

What does it mean to say that God acts—or even thinks? Is it possible that creativity occurs without "thought" and that purpose is created within the process? If this is so, what would it mean to say that God acts, creating intention or purpose only in the developing process, taking each development as it comes and creating possibilities for each moment, each "droplet of occasion," so that what works endures and what does not work at any particular moment does not endure? In addition, if God "acts" in any manner, how do we distinguish between God's activity and any other activity? If God is said to work through natural and human activity, how is the concept of God, especially in its classical expression, even relevant? If God is the sum of all things (pantheism), or if God encompasses all things but is not identical to the sum of all things (panentheism), what is the distinction between God and creation? And is that distinction even important? We will address this question in the next chapter.

Summary

The myths of science, like the myths of religion, point toward broader truths. With this realization, we can begin to understand science as a worldview. Through the "evolutionary epic" science helps us find our place in the world and gives us a sense of meaning for life. The scientific history of life and the development of the cosmos are the creation story for our time. This story is not the narcissistic triumphant march of humankind, but the even grander story of the evolutionary development of not simply the Earth but of the universe—or the multiverse.

This cosmic "creation" story is important for persons of faith. For the past several decades, both theology and science have been forced to deal seriously with nature in terms of the network of relationships between the natural world and human life that exist in an interdependent relationship.

It is all too common to affirm that humans are story-telling animals. Our ancestors sat around campfires, gathered in courtyards, meditated under trees, and taught on temple steps, telling stories about beginnings and developments. Tradition remembers some of those stories—some about real people while others are about persons who are symbolic of larger ideas. These stories are not grounded in experimentally-proven facts, but are rather conversations that seek to answer in their own ways the "why and how" questions. They are "expressions of what moved people, excited them, hurt them, made them feel grateful."[328] While these stories were told from their particular perspectives of the world, there is a sense in which they transcend their time and continue to have influence in other generations and in other geographical locations to help persons who are facing similar questions. Because of this, these transcending stories have symbolic and metaphorical value.

What is common to all metaphors is also true of God metaphors. They are limited and when pushed to extremes, or taken literally, are misleading. As Rabbi David Nelson reminds us, "Shepherds do not care for sheep out of altruistic motives. Rather, they use the sheep, shearing their wool and occasionally slaughtering them for food . . . . Similarly, kings are often subject to palace intrigue and to conflicts with neighboring kings . . . . Fathers are humans, too. Sadly, many of us have to watch our fathers grow old and weak, and then care for them."[329] We are always limited by our worldviews. Xenophanes (d. 470 BCE) wrote, "If they could, horses and oxen would think of the Gods as horses and oxen." It really is a matter of perspective.

CHAPTER 8

Can God Really . . . ?

"We should do well to give up using the word 'God' for a generation, so impregnated has it become with a way of thinking we may have to discard if the Gospel is to signify anything."

—John A.T. Robinson

All of existence is a process directed toward survivability. While there is a large amount of determinism, there is also an openness and indeterminism within all of creation. There are choices to be made, possibilities to be actualized, and responsibilities to be assumed.

The search for meaning is basic to human life and is an aspect of survivability. At its heart, spirituality in its broadest sense is a search for meaning. The Christian doctrine of providence, built on the notion of creation from nothing, holds that God provides purpose, direction, and destiny for every aspect of creation. Because God is in control of everything, God is the ground of all meaning. The concept of human freedom in this scheme comes as a gift of God's self-limitation. The Christian argument is that we discover meaning and direction when we act in accord with predetermined divine purposes. Discovering and doing God's will is said to be the chief end of human existence.

Science, on the other hand, argues that evolutionary advance has equipped us with the ability to think, choose, and make decisions. Consciousness is an aspect of this evolutionary advance and through this consciousness, we create and discover and transmit purpose and meaning.

In the previous chapter, it was argued that pure creativity does not possess purpose in the normal sense. There is no one specific destination or Omega Point (Teilhard de Chardin) toward which creation is being drawn. There is only possibility filled with a complete range of options from which choices are made and to which potential is employed. Neither the possibilities nor the potentials can be fully known prior to their moment of realization.

What does it mean, then, to speak of the "will" of God? If there is no foreknowledge, and if purpose does not preexist but is discovered in process, then that which is referred to as divine will arises from the assumptions we draw from our reasoned experiences. The evolutionary drive rewards certain characteristics—characteristics that change according to adaptation and current reality. For example, an early evolutionary behavior that was rewarded was simply remaining alive. That meant kill or be killed. Over time, survival evolved beyond kill or be killed to mutual safety and protection, and then on to strength being discovered in cooperative effort. This is a lesson humans are still striving to understand and learn.

If it is true that through the evolutionary drive we discover and adopt certain characteristics that are beneficial to survival (both individual and corporate), then what we refer to as divine will ("immaculate perception") is in reality our collective experience and adaptation of those things that lead to fullness of life at a basic level and for *all* of creation on a more advanced level. We experience added value when selfishness gives way to sharing—realizing, of course, that there is a selfish benefit in cooperation. Because this is characteristic of the survival mode for life, sharing/giving is a transcending value. Value is created in the process of learning experiences that are in turn attributed to the higher/highest good that leads to survival.

Creativity encapsulates a degree of spontaneity and novelty. Creativity is basic to life and is present in all of existence. Its presence is essential for all interaction—from quarks to humans to rocks. Creativity is the glue that holds all things together because of its continuous presence and because of its spontaneous element.

Then what does it mean to say that God "permits" or "allows?" God "allows" human freedom. God "permits" the weather to happen. God does "not allow" corruption to ultimately hold sway over humans or for death to hold them captive. God "reveals" to "chosen" ones. God "grants" humans freedom of will. God "hardens" the hearts of many.

It does not make sense to say that God permits or allows anything at all. The notions of free will and decisionmaking are intrinsically temporal. Is a God who relinquishes some power—to nature or to humans—still omnipotent? If the universe is in some aspects indeterministic or random, does that mean that God's power is thereby limited, and therefore, indicates God's inability to predict or decide what the outcome will be beyond potential or possibility? What does this imply for an understanding of God? Is it possible to understand creativity as operating in purely natural ways? The implications of such a concept are not trivial.

The argument established in the previous chapter is that God is not a *who* that acts but is the name we give to *creativity* itself that has neither mind nor purpose. Rather, purpose is discovered and developed within the creative process itself.

Most recently, religion has been called the "sleep of reason." Karl Marx criticized religion, and specifically Christianity, by calling it the "opiate of the people." It is not difficult to demonstrate that religion often encourages people "to accept injustice by teaching them that the present order is divinely ordained and that the sufferings of this world are unimportant in comparison with the glory of the world to come—a time in the future when we will see, as Luther said, that everything had been as it ought to have been."[330]

Theologians continue to give credence to Luther's notion that God acts in history, nature, and human activity through "patient and silent presence," giving all creation the power and the freedom for self-development. "All systems of matter and life are complex systems with a fixed actuality/past and, in each case, a specifically open future/scope of possibility."[331] It would be more honest to say with Stephen Pope that "God as 'creator' is not . . . the reason why we have five fingers rather than eight. The Creator is neither a superpowerful planner who arranges every detail of natural history nor an omnipotent and omniscient manager of a business that is called the 'creation.'"[332]

After more than 150 years of debate and the presentation of convincing evidence for it, a majority of Americans still consider evolution incompatible with belief in God. This issue is polarizing. Those who consider them incompatible include atheists as well as religious fundamentalists. Even for evolutionary theists, there is a strong debate over how much independence and freedom God "gives" to the evolutionary process. Indeed, if we hypothesize that that which we call divine is not an agent or entity that acts but is simply the creativity of the cosmic evolutionary process, there is no "giving" of independence and freedom since the concept of giving suggests that the gift issues from one agency to another. Independence and freedom are, then, essential elements of creativity, as are interdependence and inheritance.

By way of the scientific method—"the rule of evidence, open communication and peer review, repetition of observations and experiments, isolation of variables, avoidance of bias, scrupulous scholarship"[333]—twentieth century science discovered that the universe itself has a history. It is obvious that the cosmos itself is very different today than it was in the past, and in the future, it will be very different from today. Science has discovered that "space is relational and not absolute; that the passage of time and judgments of simultaneity are observer-dependent assessments; . . . [and] the universe is perceived as relational and endowed with becoming."[334] These scientific discoveries influence our theology.

In his book *Why Christianity Must Change or Die,* Spong reflects the feeling of a growing number of Christians that the creedal formulas were "fashioned inside a worldview that no longer exists" and are "quite alien" to the world in which we live. He urges the church to start a dialogue with those who can no longer accept premodern theological concepts that are bound to literal understandings of both scriptures and creeds. Peter Young also urges us to understand that "God is not out there anywhere or everywhere. Nor is God some external presence, but more likely a love force stirring within each of us."[335]

Arguing from within the church, Spong states that theistic thinking was born at the exact moment when human self-consciousness first emerged from the evolutionary process, that it became the inevitable human response to the terrors of self-consciousness. "Powerful divine figures could also be placated, bargained with, flattered, or appeased," he writes. "Frail and frightened human beings thus could ingratiate themselves with these external powers so that instead of being victimized by them, they could move the deity to protect or spare them instead."[336] Human beings "have evolved to the place where the theistic God concept can be and must be cast aside." Searching for another way to speak about transcendence, Spong points to Alfred North Whitehead who argued that "the divine process [came] into being within the life of this world."[337]

Prayer

Persons within the Abrahamic faiths, and others as well, generally reject this kind of understanding. They need a God who is personal and who will take care of them. They need a God that can be manipulated through prayers and offerings and good deeds. Moving away from the more comfortable images of a loving, external deity throws us upon our own resources. Young speaks for many when he writes, "Many of us, imbued since childhood with the idea of God as father protector/punisher, are sometimes hesitant even to challenge such theistic images. Somehow, we still feel we might get punished."[338]

Russian novelist and playwright Ivan Turgenev (1818-1883) wrote: "Whatever a man prays for, he prays for a miracle. Every prayer reduces itself to this: 'Great God, grant that twice two be not four.'" There is no doubt that there is something about prayer that seems to work. Prayer often provides a meditative means to work through a problem. Through this focusing, we are able to review what has happened to us and to discern a way of moving more positively into the future. Prayer clearly provides solace and comfort to persons. However, the good results do not argue convincingly whether an "answer to prayer" is a divine response or some other psychological phenomena. The most that can be said is that it makes us feel better and thereby increases our sensitivities in such a way that we find the answer.

In his chapter on "The Meaning of Prayer in a World with No External Deity," Spong writes, "The deity I worship is rather part of who I am individually and corporately. So praying can never be separated from acting . . . . Prayer is the recognition that holiness is found in the center of life, and that it involves the deliberate decision to seek to live into that holiness by modeling it and by giving it away."[339] As Young writes: "Faith, we are taught from our first day in Sunday school, is all that counts. I would argue . . . that a rational, grown-up faith must contend with a God that is an integral part of who we are, the love force that knits us to our neighbors, and offers the only hope for human salvation."[340] Or, as Michael Benedikt argues, "God is the good we do."[341]

A personal God *needs* our constant attention, but any God that expects or demands constant attention and adoration is immature and unworthy of worship. A God—any God—that relies on flattery is an egotistical bore! In his 1963 book, *Honest to God*, John A. T. Robinson suggested that we should consider giving up using the word "God" for a generation, because it has become so entangled with inadequate and untrue meanings that make the biblical witness insignificant. How much truer that is a half century later!

Jurgen Moltmann raised the interesting question of how can we experience ourselves in relationship with God if God is supposed to mean everything to us while we are not supposed to mean anything to God? Classical theology has taught, in the words of the old liturgy: "We are not worthy to gather up the crumbs from under Thy table, O Lord . . . ." It has taught that we are worthless and wretched worms, the scum of creation. One can relate to this God only as a victim of divine abuse.

Omnipotence

The theory of divine omnipotence has always been a trouble spot for theology. Theodicy is a major part of that problem. Can God prevent evil, sickness, catastrophe, etc.? If not, why bother with such a God? But if so, why does God fail to do so? If God determines all things, then evil, sickness, catastrophe, etc. must necessarily be part of God's will or purpose. And if things are "going to hell in a hand basket," then God is responsible for this abysmal failure as well.

To argue that scriptures are right or wrong is irrelevant since these embedded traditions present conflicting views side-by-side, suggesting that one can prove practically any argument by looking selectively at sacred texts. Scriptures may preserve the wisdom of the traditions, but the wisdom of one time and place is not applicable everywhere and at all times. The wider view is that evil will be rectified in an afterlife where God has "real" power to act. God is powerless in this physical world of time and space and truly powerful only in the next.

The problem of evil and its relation to God (s) has plagued religious thought from the earliest of times. Around 300 BCE the Greek philosopher Epicurus wrote in his *Aphorisms*:

> The gods can either take away evil from the world and will not, or, being willing to do so cannot, or they neither can nor will, or lastly, they are both able and willing. If they have the will to remove evil and cannot, then they are not omnipotent. If they can, but will not, then they are not benevolent. If they are neither able nor willing, then they are neither omnipotent nor benevolent. Lastly, if they are both able and willing to annihilate evil, how does it exist?[342]

The term theodicy was coined by Leibniz in the eighteenth century and literally means "the justification of God." It is the defense of God's goodness in spite of the obvious existence of evil. On November 1, 1755, an earthquake that was followed by a tsunami and fire leveled the Portuguese city of Lisbon, killing up to 100,000 persons. This event also affected many other cities in the region. Many philosophers and theologians saw this as the result of God's anger against a sinful population. Voltaire was prompted to ask where God was in terms of this megadisaster. In his *Candide* he questioned the notion that "all is for the best in this, 'the best of all possible worlds,' a world closely supervised by a benevolent deity."[343]

The earthquake also affected Rousseau's thinking. His response was based on a naturalistic understanding, arguing that the severity of the devastation was not an act of God but rather occurred because there were too many people living within the city. And Immanuel Kant sifted through the available data and science of his day and concluded that the reason for the earthquake was due to natural, not supernatural causes. The earthquake also influenced Descartes whose certainty about many things changed to doubting and questioning all things.

To affirm that there is a cruel streak in the biblical God says more about embedded traditions that it does about deity, and yet these embedded traditions are the foundations on which human faiths are built. They assume that God is responsible for everything. Nothing happens that God has not in some manner knowingly and willingly caused or permitted to happen. Thus, when disaster struck, it was believed that God was punishing the people for something they did to offend God's honor or something they allowed to happen that was offensive to God. When tragedy came upon a person, it was likely caused by their sin or the sin of someone responsible for them. For instance, when the child of David and Bathsheba died days after its birth, it was considered punishment for their adultery and David having her husband Uriah killed. When pharaoh would not set the Hebrew slaves free, it was because God had "hardened his heart." And when Jews did not respond to the new Christian movement, it was because God had hardened their hearts (Romans 9-11). However, a God who hardens the heart of people, thus *preventing* them from doing the right thing, is not a righteous God at all.

Jesus glimpsed the insight that God does not act that way. It is reported he taught that the rain falls on the just and the unjust alike, and that persons killed by a falling tower were simply in the wrong place at the wrong time. Nevertheless, this belief in a sinful cause and negative effect continues to guide persons of all religious persuasions. In reality, the arguments defending God or accusing God are meaningless since they are based on a prescientific worldview in which God—however defined—interferes with and controls all worldly affairs.

Evil

Evil is not a noun; that is, it is not a force with an independent existence, any more than our thoughts have independent existence. Evil is an activity performed by persons, or persons within groups, that has a negative effect on others. This activity arises from either conscious or unconscious human decisions. As such, "if there were no humans, there would be no evil."[344]

Some would consider that there are natural evils—events that are painful and destructive and that are not the direct result of human decisions or choice. This would include tsunamis, earthquakes, hurricanes, volcanic eruptions, etc. These events are not evil since they are naturally occurring phenomena. A gray area would include human manipulations of the landscape.

A good historical illustration of human manipulation comes from the Sumerian period between 2037 and 2004 BCE. A crisis arose when there was a shortage of fertile wheat fields necessary to feed the burgeoning population. The engineers began digging channels from the riverbanks into reservoirs. The rising waters would flow into these storage areas. During the dryer months, the water was channeled out to the fields. "But the waters of the Tigris and Euphrates, although fresh enough to support life, were very slightly salty. When this faintly brackish water sat in reservoirs, it collected more salt from the mineral rich land. It then ran out over the fields and stood in the sun. Most of the water soaked into the earth, but some evaporated, leaving slightly more salt on the ground than had been there before."[345]

Over time, this led to such a concentration of salt in the ground that crops began to fail. The farmers of Sumer realized "the only solution was to avoid planting every other year, in a practice called 'weed fallowing'—allowing weeds with deep roots to grow, lowering the water table and allowing salt to wash back down beneath the topsoil." This, of course, created another problem—a lack of food. "In the absence of weed fallowing, fields could grow so toxic that they would have to be abandoned entirely, for as long as fifty years, to allow the soil to recover."[346]

Evil is defined by degree. The term evil is reserved for those human acts that are particularly heinous. Since it does not have an existence that is independent from individuals or groups of individuals, it is related to the issues of free will and determinism. For those who see evil as a force originating outside of humanity, i.e., such as Satan or other such "evil force," evil will always be with us and humans will never be able to overcome it. Many within the Abrahamic faiths regard Satan as a source of power independent of God, implying either that "the devil is an equally powerful, autonomous separate God, which is no longer monotheism, or a part of God himself, which is no longer omnibenevolent."[347]

The sense of evil as an independent force that can find incarnation in persons and nations has been expressed in recent history by President Ronald Reagan (an "evil empire" that would end on the "ash heap of history") and President George W. Bush ("axis of evil"). By applying the religious implications of evil to persons and nations with whom they disagreed, these leaders not only closed off channels of diplomacy, but also dehumanized their enemies. When we call someone evil we clearly identify *ourselves* as the standard of good. Jim Wallis wrote that close friends of President Bush said that after 9/11, Bush found his *mission in life*. "The self-help Methodist slowly became a messianic Calvinist promoting America's mission to 'rid the world of evil.'"[348] This messianic Calvinism arises from our Western tendency to see things in black and white, and to believe that things are unchanging in their essence. It is based on the logic that "A is A" or "A is not A." That is, a thing cannot be both A and not A. Today, we know the fallacy of such notions. Things do change. "Essence" is only temporary. With the exception of process thought, Christians have largely refused to admit that this applies not simply to things and all life forms, but to God as well.

The issues of free will and determinism are not isolated from each other. There is neither total free will nor total determinism. Rather, we are a mixture of the two; a mixture that is so complex it cannot be sorted out. If we have total free will, then we also have total responsibility. On the other hand, if we are totally determined, then we have no personal responsibility. The truth of the matter is to be found in the gray areas of complexity. Perhaps Shermer is correct when he writes that the question of free will versus determinism "may be a 'mysterian' mystery, where our brains are sophisticated enough to conceive of the problem but not advanced enough to solve it."[349]

Free will is not an either/or issue. By arguing that we have some degree of free will, "we are already in some sense entertaining the idea that there may be a random element to reality . . . ." Thus, free will lies somewhere between randomness and determinism. "It's clear that neither pure randomness or pure determinism would leave any room for free will. If the world is completely random, then by definition we have no control over what will happen, and if the world is completely deterministic we also similarly have no control over what will happen as it would all be pre-scripted."[350] Free will (or randomness) and determinism are two sides of the same coin. This is demonstrated in quantum theory that suggests every quantum event is fundamentally random, yet large objects behave deterministically. "How can this be? The answer is that sometimes when we combine many random things, a more predictable outcome can emerge. This may seem paradoxical at first . . . but this is not necessarily the case."[351]

Just how determined are our lives? Shermer argues from chaos and complexity theory that we have "a type of free will from ignorance, ignorance of all the determining causes in our lives, such that we are, de facto, free because when we make choices we cannot know all the causal variables." Because the variables are such a complex mixture of genetic, environmental, and historic causes, "We are each and every one of us, unique and different from every other of the six billion members of our species . . . . Human freedom arises out of this ignorance of causes."[352]

Will God Repent?

I first came across this question in 1980 when I read Elie Wiesel's *The Trial of God*. It is Purim and three actors get lost, ending up in Shamgorod that had just suffered a pogrom. The only Jews left are the innkeeper and his daughter who had been raped and tortured. The Innkeeper convinced the three actors to perform a mock trial of God for the terrible things he and his daughter have just endured. He wants to play the prosecutor and the three actors agree to be the judges. Just then, a stranger enters and agrees to be the defense attorney. God's defense attorney turns out to be Satan.

If humans are accountable for their actions, for their role in human suffering, then perhaps it is time for God to repent. Rabbi Shmuley Boteach tells this story:

> The great Hasidic master, Rabbi Levi Yitzchak of Berditchev, was known for his unconditional love for humanity. One year on the eve of Yom Kippur, when hundreds of people who came to pray with him were waiting for him to begin the Kol Nidre prayer, Rabbi Levi Yitzchak stood standing with his back towards the congregation. He stared silently at the holy ark where the Torah scrolls were kept. The congregation waited one hour, two hours—people were standing on their feet and beginning to sweat. Finally the shamas went over to Rabbi Levi Yitzchak and said, "You know, Rebbe, the people have to get home." So the great Rebbe said, "OK, I'm done."
>
> Rabbi Levi Yitzchak then turned to the people and said, "I want to bring you into the conversation I was having with G-d. I said to G-d, 'I come here before you on Yom Kippur, the Day of Atonement, to ask that You atone for my sins.' But then it suddenly struck me that in the past year, I haven't brought any plagues upon any part of the world. Nor have I made any woman a widow. Nor have I made any child an orphan. Nor have I caused anyone to go bankrupt and thereby not be able to sustain and support their children. Yet, G-d has done all of these things. And then it struck me, why isn't He coming to us and asking us for forgiveness? So I said to G-d, 'In the past year, I have caused no death. I have brought no plagues upon the world, no earthquakes, no floods. I have made no women widows, no children orphans. G-d, you have done these things, not me! Perhaps You should be asking forgiveness from me. So I'll make a deal. You forgive us, we'll forgive you, and we'll call it even.'"[353]

We might ask with Boteach, if God is omnipotent, why are we not more demanding of the divine? Why should we focus on our own need for repentance when God does not, even in the face of catastrophes and holocausts? "Where are the modern day Abrahams," he asks, "to declare before G-d, 'Shall the Judge of the entire earth not act justly?' Where are the modern Moses' who demand, upon hearing that G-d intended to wipe out the Jewish nation, 'Remove my name from the book you have written.'"[354]

> Some apologists tell us that God remains hidden from us so as not to coerce our worship. But God is not hiding out of solicitude for our freedom. We have not forgotten Job: therefore we understand that God is hiding out of cowardice. God is hiding because He has too much to hide. We do not seek burning bushes or a pillar of smoke. No—we wish to see God. Can God stand before us? Can God see the face of suffering humanity—and live?[355]

The implications for God's omnipotence might best be illustrated by a comparison with the dilemma posed by the old question: Can God create a rock so large that God cannot move it? Either way the question is answered limits God's power—not that this is a bad thing! Of course, our understanding relies on whether, in fact, God is omnipotent, and just what that term might mean for us. In the final analysis, the issue is meaningless since God is not an actor but an action. However, for religious people, a belief in the omnipotence of God as actor leads into the realm of God being utterly superior and in total control of everything that happens.

Perhaps we understand divine power from what we have learned about parental power. It doesn't take us long as children to get a sense that our parents are omnipotent and omniscient. In this relationship, we grow up only to discover that our parents have their faults and are neither omnipotent nor omniscient. Since there is a part of us that finds it difficult to live with uncertainty, we seek another dominance hierarchy that we are told will not fail or disappoint us. This new dominant figure (that can be found in a variety of forms) will do for us, care for us, and keep us from having to make so many decisions for ourselves. Some find this in religion while others find it in the military or in some dominant interpersonal relationship.

Abusive Power

Our Western ways of thinking glorify power. Power divides persons into winners and losers. When we use this metaphor to speak of divine power,

God becomes associated with every sort of paternalism and paternalistic intervention. Catherine Keller writes, "The prophetic expectation of a historical end to the causes of suffering, requiring the full collaboration of the people, was eventually exaggerated into the end-time hope for supernatural intervention. At the eschaton, everyone would see who had had the power all along."

Despite the innumerable historical failings of these desired divine interventions, persons still yearn for some messiah to come and save them. Since God or God's messiah or God's imam will not save the people, human powers are more than ready to assume a Godlike "stance of dominance, defined according to the standards of power by which God fails." This has resulted in various vicious theo-secular cycles of power, and "the more the powers of dominance succeed, the more God fails; the more God fails, the more the power of dominance fill the vacuum . . . . In other words, assuming the dominative-possessive view of power invariably sets God up in an abusive relationship to the world."

This failure of the omnipotent God, writes Keller, "has normally been disguised by some sort of eschatological deferral." She suggests that an alternative model to this dominative-possessive picture of God and God's relationship to the world should feature neither an all-powerful divine parent nor a powerless child-victim as paradigms of salvation. We recognize "such figures as complementary poles in the historical cycle of abuse. The abuse of power, collectively entrenched in the preconscious and nearly universal repetition-compulsion sometimes called original sin, can be seen at every level of the social orders dominating the planet."[356]

Reflecting on the socio-political situation of the late 1990s, Keller writes that powerlessness is "a dire social problem, threatening democracy in the U.S. and socializing masses of young people into futurelessness." Pointing to widespread "incest and other primordial violations," she writes that "it is not surprising that generations of children grow up expecting ever more grown-up levels of the abuse of power."[357] The secular failure of power to redeem is clearly seen in U.S. politics. The more power fails to conquer, the more it tries to shore itself up with all means of self-protection—i.e., lies, secrecy, bigger guns, military surges, manipulation of public opinion to selfish purposes, fear, etc. We live in a culture of fear that produces a sense of powerlessness and a heightened desire for a savior. When people turn to religion for answers, they are fed a spirituality that feeds this sense of powerlessness.

If theology is to stop justifying abusive power, it must emphasize that the answer lies in terms of human responsibility and point the marginalized to sources of power that are available to them. As Salvadoran activist and theologian Marta Benevides writes, "The poor do not need to be empowered. They already have power. They need to recognize and release it."[358] This is the clear message of liberation theologies, especially in their use of Exodus imagery and in their economic and class analyses that exposes how traditional piety cooperates with ecclesial and political hierarchies in maintaining the powerlessness of the poor. For liberation theologies, God does not change the situation for the people. Rather, God is the inspiration encouraging them forward in their struggle.

As theology continues to point to a future fulfillment "in God's good time," how viable is the promise? Moreover, how can we avoid the sense of human powerlessness as we wait for God to act? Indeed, does not the eschatological promise perpetuate the power of the oppressing forces while giving the oppressed a false hope? The uncertainty of the too-much-delayed eschatological day of justice can be devastating. The promise may give some persons hope and the courage to act, but it is precisely that hope and courage that inspires people to take responsibility for their own futures.

The biblical witness is that God is both Creator and Destroyer. When that vision of earthly salvation did not materialize as expected, it slowly shifted from the power of God to the power of the church and the state. "The aching void . . . of the failure of the God of power and might" was filled by earthly power. It is this "apocalypse myth of power" that has "dominated the Western theological imagination, a destructive anthropomorphism that must now be discarded."[359]

While the problem of how God can act in the world is not a new one for theology, the Holocaust and the bombings of Hiroshima and Nagasaki forced a new understanding. Why should God intervene to wither a fig tree yet allow millions to die in concentration camps and bombed-out cities? There is an apparent contradiction between understanding the world as determined by natural causes and claiming that God may, on occasion, "break into that causal order like a rogue elephant."[360]

This rogue elephant image may seem excessive to some, yet the traditional understanding of God as omnipotent points toward the violence of God—the existence of unmerited evil in the world. Many would agree that the violence of God "seems permanently bound up with his maleness." Of course, the problem of evil will not be solved by simply removing these dominant images from God-language. Nevertheless, the male-dominated God-language contributes to the problem. The debates over language indicate the need for new metaphors, although the debates continue to be tied to traditional categories. This is not helpful in dealing with the larger and more important identity issue.

God as Abuser

Jewish author and teacher David Blumenthal and Julie Shoshana Pfau, at the time a graduate student at Emory University, had an interesting e-mail dialogue concerning the question of God's violence. This notion grows out of the traditional argument of an all-powerful God.[361] Pfau writes, "I have a prior commitment to not worshipping that which is evil . . . . To worship and praise evil is destructive—to the self and to the world. The only thing that could ethically be done in relation to an abusive God is protest . . . . Abuse is such a grievous flaw that it negates any good qualities." Blumenthal responded that "in order to pursue the process of protest, one must indeed develop a sense of the redeemability of the other—which is why one worships. One does not worship an abusive God or an evil God; one worships (in the sense of praise) the non-abusive side of God. Also, one 'worships' the abusive side but with protest prayer . . . ."

This notion of an abusive God arises out of an understanding that God is all-powerful. This God does not exist, and protest against "him" is not only unnecessary but also ultimately tilting at windmills. I am certain that many persons do worship—and excuse—an abusive God because they are not *directly* on the abusive end of divine misconduct. In Pfau's image, they are not the one's being raped and they are grateful for that. As long as the abuser stays focused elsewhere, these persons are content to let the abuser abuse.

Pfau writes that she would not protest since protest "requires a belief that the abusive one would change. It also requires trust. I would not 'talk back' to someone (God) who could crush me and lacked the self-control not to do it. I only challenge people whom I trust. On the other hand, I suppose I do trust God enough to be able to get angry at Him and protest." Pfau was associated for a time with Vineyard, an aggressive, charismatic Christian denomination. During her time there, she was made to feel even more sinful for wanting to argue with this God. Since converting to Judaism, she writes, "I am glad that I can challenge and protest to God and that I can feel angry at God without it meaning I am possessed by demons (as the Vineyard people thought), but it is so much easier to deny God's power. My mind knows that it isn't logical that God could have the power to create a world but doesn't have enough power to stop evil." She also writes: "A god that kills his son is the worst because he doesn't just allow evil, he ordains it." She understands the theology behind the idea of Jesus' death, "but I couldn't get past the view of its abuse." Abused children, she writes, sometimes "idealize their abusers because they can't retain sanity knowing that their lives depend on someone who is evil. They blame themselves instead. This is what some religious people do in relation to God." To fear God would be to experience the ultimate in terror because God is inescapable and overwhelmingly powerful. Pfau writes:

> Before Abraham, God was acting in ways that covered the spectrum of good and bad. God chose to create humans with the ability to disobey and do evil things. Then God placed temptation before them, when God could have done otherwise. A good term for this is entrapment! When humans did disobey, God's punishments were excessive and included even future generations who were not guilty of the crime at hand. Later, God chose favorites—with terrible consequences—and killed off most of humanity in the flood . . . . Maybe God typically overreacts in an abusive way and then tries to justify it after the fact by blaming it on the victims.

"Now look what *you've* made me do!" proclaims this God. "I have no choice but to punish you. Now if you will just do as I say, things will be ok." And after the punishment, he says: "Come here, now, and give daddy a hug and a big kiss." And the cycle of abuse continues. Sometimes the abuser will choose someone close to you and punish him or her in front of you, just as God punishes Jesus for what you have done.

Blumenthal writes that in Judaism, "there is no intermediary between us and God—no son of God, no mother of God, to appeal to. To be Jewish is to face God, Face-to-face, or at least to avert one's eyes from a face-to-Face look."

The need for an intermediary has been a problem for me ever since my college days. At the crucifixion, the veil in the Temple was torn apart. This, I was taught, meant that we no longer needed a priest or a sacrifice to approach God. All that separated us from God was now destroyed with the death of Jesus. And then the church immediately sewed up that torn veil, so to speak, and created its own barriers to God—especially Jesus. This notion was, of course, based on the relationship that persons had with their earthly kings. One could not approach the king directly. To do so could mean death. Thus, there was a need for an intermediary, someone who could prepare the way in a proper manner. I totally agree with Pfau when she writes, "I would rather face God personally and speak my mind directly . . . ."

It is obscene to believe that God arbitrarily rewards some and not others, that some are blessed while others are made to suffer horribly. Religious persons respond that we cannot expect to understand this since God's ways are not our ways. However, it does not take much to see that the ways of God are the ways of the ancient kings and potentates. The claims that God somehow acts in history and nature are not only challenged by what we now know to be true. They are also open to moral and religious doubts.

Characteristics of God

All characteristics of God begin with what we want or need God to be, and we then work to fill in the gaps with what we experience and what we believe the meaning of that experience *should be*. If we determine that God should be loving rather than damning and capricious, then we look for indications that this is so. If we want a God who cares and is affected by who we are and what we experience emotionally, physically, mentally, etc., then we will construct a notion of God that fulfills that need. If we need a God to help defeat our enemy, we will construct a God who is a great warrior—one who is on *our* side! Nations do this every time they confront an enemy.

In this quest for God's identity, we need to ask: Is a particular characteristic *true in all times and in all places*? Is it as true in the palace as it is in the furnaces of Auschwitz? Is it as true in my comfortable home as it is to the homeless in the city's streets? Is God's relationship different between human and other aspects of creation, or is it just as true for the birds of the air and the fish of the sea and the animals that roam the earth? Was it as true for the universe 15 billion years ago as it is today? Indeed, is the notion of a divine undefeatable love consistent with universal human experience?

It seems inappropriate to speak of any specific act of God. Since it is we who posit the existence of God, and further give this God characteristics that we most desire or need, then we also have the responsibility for what we have created. Pedraja addresses theodicy in this manner:

> The difficulty we face in recognizing evil in our midst is that evil manifests the same creativity and destructive power we find in God; for to create something new, we must destroy the old. Evil often bears the same structures, depths of meaning, mystery, and creativity, as well as the same sense of awe we experience before the creative power of God, except that in the demonic it is "infused both with horror and the frenzy and ecstasy of the destructive impulse." Thus, the most difficult question in understanding the nature of evil comes in our inability to recognize it as such.[362]

As stated earlier, "natural evil" is nothing more than a human perception. It is simply part of nature's evolution. Augustine argued that evil does not exist apart from its embodiment in the human will and in the structures of society. Thus, the issue in natural disasters is not evil but human suffering. The issue is *tragedy* not evil. Evil can be applied to these things only insofar as humans are complicit in their creation. Even then, it is not the event itself that is evil, but the human actions creating the context for such destruction.

Does faith require a belief in the reality of justice? Or is justice an ideal toward which we choose to move? Is the notion of justice best understood as a developed means of survival? Injustice, then, would have short-term success for the individual but would produce long-term failure for the rest of the species. Injustice cannot be promoted as a survival model. This can be seen in instances of tyranny. While this type of governance may rule the day for decades or even for hundreds of years—brief moments in the evolutionary process—its injustice feeds on itself and eventually destroys from within. This may explain the case but in and of itself provides little hope or comfort to the victims of injustice.

The existence of evil is a reality. A further reality is that the world is not organized to meet human needs, ends, and values. Justice is not written into the atoms and is not a law of nature, but rather a learned survival mechanism. Therefore, one learns not only to hate but also to love. If it is true that values reflect the sort of beings we are and have become, then values such as justice are the things that may keep us from destructive arrogance. Such a naturalistic perspective can lead to increased ethical living because we understand that justice is something that humans are responsible for. God does not bring justice. It must come through us. God does not make justice happen, but creativity produces possibilities through which the evolutionary adaptations and tools for justice occur. Humans cannot just sit back and expect someone or something from the outside to make justice happen—either here through some messiah, alien force, or in some afterlife. *We are responsible.*

One theological answer to the problem of evil has been that God suffers—at least metaphorically—the pains of a suffering world. In doing so, it is said, God transforms our suffering. But what does it mean to say that God suffers in our ordeal—or is affected by our pain—when God is understood as creativity or even traditionally as spirit, neither of which can "experience" nor "suffer?" In the past, I tried to make the argument that God's suffering somehow transforms the suffering experienced in our world. However, I no longer find that argument satisfying or intelligible.

Summary

God can no longer be understood as a predetermining, all-powerful agent, nor a personal entity in complete control of everything that occurs in the world. At the quantum level, the processes of the world are random, chaotic, and at times self-creating. In the same manner on an everyday level, there is no way to determine who is going to have an accident or a serious illness. We can talk about probabilities. But there is not an objective moral providence that benefits one group over another or one person over another—or even one world over another. These events are all contingent.

Therefore, since God is not moral in this sense, *we have to be*. We are obliged to redefine our religious commitment to the values that will make this world a better place in which to live. Is there poverty? Then it is we who will have to do something about it. God will not. Is there war and hatred? Then it is we who have to be peacemakers. God will not step in and keep us from destroying each other—or even our planet. Are there coastal storms that can wipe out large parts of cities or whole towns? Then it is up to us to either avoid those places or build the dikes and retaining walls high enough and strong enough. God will not do it. Are there devastating illnesses that rob us of friends and loved ones? We cannot expect divine miracles to replace the hard task of medical research. In addition, we must accept that death—for better or for worse—is a natural part of all existence.

The Greek Prometheus stole the fire of the Gods and brought it to human beings—a symbol of human intellect, culture, and technical advance. Eve took God's fruit of knowledge and brought awareness of the world to humanity. In both of these mystic heroes—and there are many others—humans courageously challenged the power of the Gods and became responsible and, as far as possible, self-determining.

SECTION THREE

PREFACE

The issues surrounding christology become problematic not only for those who no longer literally accept the biblical stories but also for those who no longer accept the classical notions of God. For many, christology is a way of implying that the traditional God no longer exists, and only that which we can be seen and touched has any real meaning. Of course, traditional christology does not specifically say this—and even less, admit it—but this is clearly revealed in the church's practice. The exclusive focus on Jesus (or more technically, Christ) within the church means that the notion of God is no longer necessary with the result being a type of atheism: There is no God but Jesus Christ.

How does one pull off the gymnastics required to understand many of the doctrines and practices of religion? In light of the methodology presented in the first section and the understanding of transcendence in the second section, many traditional doctrines become useless, if not completely meaningless.

The Trinity is one example. Theologian Leonard Sweet has referred to the Trinity as "the twilight zone of Christianity."[363] By maintaining this doctrine, how does one avoid falling into polytheism—in appearance, if not in fact? Patrick Miller writes that it is "impossible to imagine Christian theology being Christian without the claim that God is not fully revealed apart from Jesus Christ or that one can exhaust what is to be comprehended about God without the work of the Spirit."[364] But is it not true that, even for traditional theology, any God that is *fully* revealed in any manner is not God at all? The idea that Jesus was in some sense simply God demands an understanding of transcendence that is untenable. Any literal notion that the fullness of transcendence (or God) became human in the form of Jesus should be discarded as simply false.

Likewise, theologies of perfection, beginning with God and then transferred to humans in the Garden of Eden story and later to Jesus, cannot withstand the criticism of logical thought. There was no perfection at the mythical beginning of the world. The argument that there was continues to lead to a sense of helplessness and hopelessness in ever being good enough. And when Jesus reportedly says that we should be perfect as God is perfect (Matthew 5:48), an impossible expectation is laid upon persons that they can never live up to. And it does absolutely no good to promise us that we will be made perfect in some afterlife. Methodist founder John Wesley struggled with this in his doctrine of Christian Perfection as a goal to be achieved—if only momentarily—through a disciplined life.

Can we say that God suffers with us because God is identified/unified with humanity in Jesus? What sense can there be in arguing that God "suffers" with us when such suffering results in neither divine pain nor change in the human situation? Does it make any sense to argue that God "hurts as we hurt?" If not, this notion may provide psychological comfort for some, but it is little more than spiritual candy—bringing temporary comfort but letting us down after the sugar rush subsides.

Most religions argue that only God (s) can bring about a new world. Since it is argued by Christians that Jesus inaugurated a new world, the kingdom or reign of God, he must have been God incarnate. Rejecting that notion, we come to realize that it is not God or some divine messiah or divine imam who brings about change but human beings who choose from a wide array of possibilities. Humans are expected to mature and develop. We are not expected to stay at the level of children, waiting for a parent's permission or help to do the things that will make a difference in the world. To argue that we cannot do it without God's help is like a whining child or an immature adult. This is not to deny the importance of community and our need for each other. On the contrary! It amplifies the importance of community. Of course, one advantage of this continuing immaturity is that we have someone to blame for our "inability" to do the right thing and thereby avoid taking responsibility.

Traditional doctrines of salvation are to be rejected. It seems very odd, indeed, that a God who had the ability to envision the creation of a universe of universes would wait for more than 15 billion years or more—until the birth of Jesus—to decide what the goal of that creation should be. That seems to be incredibly shortsighted on God's part. At best, it would perhaps be better to argue that the very human Jesus, building on all that went before him, offered an expanded vision of what human life could be. To argue that the notion of "the reign of God" entered history in Jesus is a denial of the vision that was present in the prophetic traditions that preceded Jesus. Jesus understood and stood within those prophetic roots. It is also clear that Jesus understood that this vision would be accomplished through human action following what he understood to be the divine vision. The power of that vision is in the very human actions it inspires.

Sinfulness is no longer to be seen as a rebellion against God but rather any action or attitude that negatively impacts another or destroys the ecosystem necessary for life. Sin is rebellion against life. The term "sin" is so religiously burdened that if one rejects religion one is also tempted to reject the notion of sin. What alternative term/concept needs to be utilized in order to remove "sin" from its religious moorings with eternal and otherworldly consequences to a new mooring with this-worldly implications and consequences?

CHAPTER 9

How Did that Nice Jewish Boy Become a Platonized Gentile God?

Jesus turns to his disciples and asks, "Who do people say that I am?" Various people reply, "John the Baptist" or "Elijah" or "one of the prophets." Then Jesus asks, "But who do you say that I am?" And Peter answers, "You are the Christ."

—*Mark 8:2.*

"Jesus is our paradigm."

—*Gary Wilson*

William Inge, Dean of St. Paul's Cathedral, was once asked to write a book about the life of Jesus. "He declined, saying that there was not nearly enough solid evidence to write anything about him."[365]

Indeed, one of the main problems we have in understanding the story of Jesus is that there are no first-hand or eyewitness accounts of him. The Gospels, written toward the end of the first century may contain earlier sources or oral traditions, but the earliest direct material we have about him comes from the Apostle Paul that was written at least twenty years after the death of Jesus.

When the Romans executed Jesus, the story changed. It was not simply the story he told, "but the one told about him" and what they now understood as his significance. The Jesus story was told in light of his Jewish heritage, and the images used in telling the story were common for that time. For instance, it was not unusual for the kings of the Middle East to refer to themselves as "Shepherd" of the people, and the Mesopotamian kings were often referred to as "King of Kings" and "King of the Universe." They were called Gods and Sons of God. Their stories included the images of virgin births and resurrections. The social, cultural, and historical contexts affected how the stories were composed and told.

Retelling the stories for new audiences in new places "inevitably brought other changes as elements of local culture or native dialects filtered into the telling." And it must also be emphasized that the Jewish homeland "was religiously diverse and socially stratified."[366]

Who is this Jesus that all Christians revere and many—if not most—worship as God? This question is as old as Jesus himself. His own contemporaries wondered if he was the prophet Elijah returning, as had been prophesized, to establish a new era for the nation of Israel. Or, perhaps, others thought, he was the resurrected John the Baptizer—a prophet who was killed about the time Jesus was starting his ministry. Was he a prophet or just another rabbi? Could he be a messiah—like the Persian King Cyrus (ca. 600-530 BCE)[367]—who would liberate Israel from its Roman occupiers?

The church has wrestled with this question for two thousand years. The Council of Laodicea incorporated four different views of Jesus in the four different gospels it included in the canon of scripture—plus other views, including those of Paul, Peter, and John of the Apocalypse. Not to be outdone, the church came up with its own views through Council pronouncements, Reformation interpretations, and numerous variations due to political, cultural and economic circumstances. And today the influences of other world religions add to how we view the man called Jesus.

The writer of Hebrews (13:8) argued that Jesus is the same yesterday, today, and forever. It is obvious that this is not the case, since the historical Jesus is hidden by so many layers of differing understandings. He is, as Stephen Prothero suggested, "something of a chameleon." Some would argue that what we tend to see in Jesus is simply an expression of our own hopes and fears—both personal and national. Can we ever know who Jesus really was or even who Jesus is for us today? Rejecting the notion that Jesus was God, we might nevertheless ask if he was especially open to a sense of transcendence—Did Jesus have a specially heightened insight into the meaning of what it means to be human in an often cruel, inept, and bewildering world? And if so, what was this understanding and when did it occur? Further, what was the worldview that influenced, and limited, his teachings?

This chapter does not seek to do an overview of the search for the historical Jesus. There are numerous such studies available. Nor is this an attempt to write yet another christology from a traditional point of view. From what has been argued thus far, any talk of the divinity of Jesus is meaningless. There is no more of the divine in Jesus than in any other human. Like a few others throughout history, he may have been more sensitive to the unity of creation and the separations that cause misery among persons, but he was as fully human as any of us. In fact, the WWJD (What Would Jesus Do?) fad of the past decade makes no sense if Jesus was not fully human. The challenge is to understand what continuing significance Jesus might have without making any supernatural claims for him. It can certainly be argued that separating the Jesus of history from the Christ of the church undermines confidence in the Bible, creeds, and other traditions. This is not denied. In fact, the Bible itself undermines all attempts of literalness. The search for clarity that utilizes reason, logic, and experience is not intended to undermine or undo faith as much as to establish a firmer ground for faith that is free from unreasonable claims. The biblical injunction to be prepared to give an account for what one believes seems to demand such an approach.

To argue that what we believe about Jesus should meet the criteria of experience, reason, tradition, scripture, and historical verification may seem obvious, but there is also the criterion of scientific method that we expect "truth" to meet in every other area of life.

Some scholars have concluded that the only clear thing we can say about Jesus is that he ate and drank with sinners! There are so many interpretations of the historical Jesus that it may be impossible to ever discover the "real" Jesus. All attempts to discover the *one and true* Jesus will be futile. Our own faith interpretations are drawn from what we "need" to see and experience in any given context. This can be clearly seen when we examine the proofs for Jesus' uniqueness that are selectively drawn from Old Testament sources through the methods of typology and prooftexting—applying images to Jesus that initially referred to others. Experience alone can lead us into odd places and emphases, but reason forces us to consider sources and consequences. Higher criticism, roughly the scholarly equivalent of the scientific method, forces us to ask questions and probe for the truth within the stories. However, even here, it will be impossible to discover Jesus apart from the two thousand years of accumulated dogmatism that surrounds him.

In the end, the christology developed by Church Councils have resulted in a sort of atheism since they implicitly concluded that there is no need for a God that is not "enfleshed," no need for a God we cannot see and touch. There is only a need for a human being to which we attribute the status of God. The doctrine of the Trinity was an attempt to correct this religious blunder, but it only complicated the matter.

It should be clear from the start that Jesus did not intend to be the founder of a new religion. Indeed, what we understand as the formal religion of Christianity did not get established until the turn of the first century—a church that Jesus would not have recognized or approved of. The Jesus movement was a sect within Judaism and was a product of this context. There were numerous other religious sects and political parties in first-century Judaism. Judea was part of the Roman empire and Judaism's (and Christianity's) religious understandings were influenced by this uneasy relationship. As Michael White points out:

> One problem that often occurs when people approach the world of Jesus is that they assume the political and religious climate was essentially the same as that of ancient Israel. Nothing could be further from the truth. The kingdom of David and Solomon had long since passed away, and the "golden age" of Israel, if there really was one, was long gone. Yet romantic ideas of Israel's past glory and future hopes were very much alive. The political changes that occurred after ancient Israel fell to the Babylonians in 586 BCE were far-reaching, but, if anything, the religious changes were even greater.[368]

The Social/Political Context

Historical studies over the past couple centuries have challenged traditional religious belief as much as scientific discoveries. To understand Jesus, one must also understand the context in which he lived. Christianity emerged not only as a sect within Judaism, but also within Greco-Roman culture. Christianity was not a new religion replacing a dying Judaism or a corrupt paganism. Both of these factors challenge "the patristic conception of Christians as a 'third race,' distinct from both Jews and pagans." Further, the eventual success of Christianity was at least partially the result of changes already taking place within the Greco-Roman religion, politics, and culture. The Christian religion, then, might be viewed "as a child of Hellenism [with] its conscious (and sometimes not-so-conscious) adoption of Platonist philosophical categories . . . [and] its adoption of Graeco-Roman rhetoric."[369]

We now understand in a much clearer way that religious ideas do not emerge in a vacuum. Rather, they are responses to existing concerns and conceptions of the world, and they are articulated in language that their contemporaries understand. The religious, social, and political conditions in Jesus' homeland were affected by complex influences coming from the vast expanse of the Roman Empire. It is important to understand this as we seek to understand the world in which Jesus lived and how this history affected his thinking.

When people approach the world of Jesus, they too often assume that it is essentially the same as that of ancient (or Old Testament) Israel. However, this is clearly *not* the case. Although the mythical "golden age" of the kingdoms of David and Solomon were in the far distant past, the memory of past glory and the hope of future restorations were very much alive. The political and religious changes that occurred after ancient Israel fell to the Babylonians in 586 BCE were great.[370] "There is no unbroken line of tradition from ancient Israel to Jesus or the rabbis." Nor is there an unbroken line from Jesus to today. The problem is that many assume that "one could jump directly from the prophets, such as Isaiah, who lived well before the Babylonian exile, to the second century CE without considering any intervening historical developments and influences." False conclusions are reached because of a profound ignorance of the historical and social changes occurring over hundreds of years.[371]

The northern kingdom of Israel and the southern kingdom of Judah were under the rule of several other nations during much of their existence. The Maccabean stories tell of the struggle in about 170 BCE against the Seleucidian king Antiochus Epiphanes. The Jewish cause was strengthened when Judas Maccabeus made an alliance with the Romans who were more than willing to help out since it was anxious to check the Seleucid power. About a hundred years later, in 66 BCE, Pompey, conquered the Syrian holdings (that included Israel and Judah) of the fading Seleucid empire. In Jerusalem, Pompey gave the temple priests control of the city.

> Under this new arrangement, Jerusalem would be part of the Roman province of Palestine, and would no longer have a Hasmonean king. Instead, Pompey appointed a priest names John Hyrcanus (known as Hyrcanus II) to be "High Priest and Ethnarch," a combined religious and secular office. The priests would run Palestine for Rome, and would report to a Roman governor who had changed over all of Syria, Rome's newest acquisition.[372]

Hyrcanus reported to the Roman governor, Herod the Great. In 40 BCE, the Parthians swept through Syria into Palestine, intending to kill Herod, but he escaped to Rome. They cut off the ears of Hyrcanus, and he was unable to continue as High Priest because of the mutilation. Three years later Mark Anthony drove the Parthians out of Palestine, and in 37 he installed Herod as a vassal king in Jerusalem—"a secular king of the Jews, doing away with a combined priesthood and kingship."[373] Herod the Great "used his authority to turn the shabby, rebuilt Second Temple into a showpiece of his greatness as a king," although he served at the pleasure of Rome.[374] Herod the Great also turned Judea from a relatively insignificant backwater of the Roman Empire into a gateway to the Middle East for shipping and trade. "His new harbor at Caesarea Maritina was a remarkable achievement complete with the aid of Augustus' own architects and engineers. Caesarea was a thoroughly Roman city lying within the borders of the Jewish homeland."[375]

The Roman Empire was immense and required efficient systems of roads and communications in order to maintain the flow of goods and services throughout the far-flung provinces. As soldiers and merchants traveled throughout the empire and beyond, they carried with them literature, art, philosophy, and religion.

Jesus was born sometime between 7 and 4 BCE during the kingship of Herod the Great. When Herod died in 4 BCE, "rather than choosing one of Herod's three sons to succeed him, Augustus divided Palestine into three parts; perhaps the size of the Temple had revealed family ambitions that needed to be squelched."[376]

When Augustus died in 14 CE, Tiberius succeeded him. By 31, it was obvious to Tiberius that civil war was a real possibility, and so he instituted a purge "that swept up hundreds of citizens of Rome, including his own young children . . . . From that time on, Tiberius' self-indulgence began to turn into cruelty . . . ."[377] It was about this time that a wandering Galilean prophet named Jesus came to the attention of "a large and powerful group of priests in Jerusalem." He challenged the way they were controlling the religious life of the Jews and their complicity with Rome. Since the office of High Priest and Ethnarch had been abolished, the priests no longer had any significant political power, but they were particularly sensitive to any threat to the limited influence with Rome they still had. These priests sought help from Herod Antipas, claiming that Jesus had called himself "King of the Jews." While this undoubtedly irritated Herod, who was legally King of the Jews as a vassal of Rome, he "had probably heard of the purges going on in Rome [and] was not about to do anything that smacked of independence; not when Tiberius was busy wiping out resistance."[378]

Herod Antipas sent the issue of Jesus directly to the Roman procurator Pontius Pilate "with the message that the Romans, not he, had better do something about this problem." However, Pilate was no more certain of his own safety than Herod was. "He too did not want to be suspected of doing anything that might undermine the power of that distant, angry, unpredictable princeps. A revolution in Palestine on his watch was not going to do him any good. So he agreed to execute Jesus." Just a few short years later, in 36 CE, he followed the same better-safe-than-sorry policy by reacting "to a similar mild threat from a bunch of rebelling Samaritans by executing them all. This produced a backlash of anti-Roman sentiment in Palestine. The Roman governor of Syria, Pilate's superior, yanked him off the job and sent him back to Rome in disgrace."[379]

White suggests that there were at least seven major crises during the period of 300 BCE and 200 CE that produced great change and upheaval in the development of Jewish life and culture:

1. Outside Political Domination
2. Homeland and Diaspora
3. Reforming Moments Undertaken with Religious Motivation
4. Increasing Tendencies Toward Sectarianism
5. Compilation of Scriptures
6. New Modes of Piety and a Heightened Sense of "Observance"
7. A Sense of Destiny and History Revealed

New patterns of belief, social organization, and religious practice resulted in response to these crises. The impact of outside political domination on

Jewish life and belief was tremendous. The Jews were originally part of the Western Semitic tribes that moved from place to place in the general area. The area that became known as Judea was only a "nation" for relatively brief periods of time. This was true especially during the reigns of the judges, David, and Solomon. At all other times they were part of other kingdoms, including the Philistines, Assyrians, Armenians, Babylonians, Egyptians, Persians, Seleucidians, Parthians, and the Romans. With each new occupation, political and social structures changed, and these changes produced cultural transformations as well, forcing numerous adaptations. Despite this, there was a continuing and growing sense that independent self-rule under religious leadership would someday be restored.[380] This resulted in numerous rebellions, revolts, and an increasing number of messiahs, each promising a return to a "golden age" of self-rule.

The religious landscape of Judea was further complicated by two interrelated factors: (a) There was a growing proportion of the Jewish population that lived *outside* the traditional homeland, and (b) there were sizeable populations of non-Jews who lived *inside* the homeland.[381] Both of these factors impacted Jewish identity as both groups were influenced by a diversity of language, culture, and custom.

There was also an increasing tendencies toward sectarianism—with as many as 70 clearly identified Jewish sects in the first century CE. Although initially experienced negatively, this "diversity and sectarianism gave way to a new sense of uniformity as the rabbinic movement grew out of the post-revolt reconstruction. Sectarians became heretics."[382] This sectarianism presented problems for the doctrine of election and the concurrent sense of chosenness, a major aspect of national identity that was as old as the people itself. This national consciousness was dealt a severe blow "when, contrary to divine promises, both the Davidic throne and Solomon's Temple were destroyed by the Babylonians. The theological response to that event was to reinterpret the promises of God regarding the future of the nation." It raised the question that was reflected by Paul in his letter to the Romans: Has God abandoned the Jewish nation? "Or was this outside oppression a punishment for abandoning God's ways? This response, known as the Deuteronomic theology, would become important in later generations and in the interpretation of successive crises."[383] This resulted in a sense of expectation: if it was indeed a punishment for abandoning God's ways, then a return to God's ways certainly would restore the nation.

Sectarianism resulted in various groups that considered themselves as the "righteous remnant." From this sense of expectation emerged the view of a divinely ordained history known as *apocalyptic*. It also involved messianic deliverers—somewhat as the Persian king Cyrus had been in the sixth century BCE.

This expectation of the restoration of the Davidic kingdom resulted in an increase in the number of rebel leaders and groups. These groups fed the growing rebellion that led up to what is referred to as the first revolt in 66-74 CE. Some of these rebels claimed miraculous powers, others appealed to prophecy to justify themselves, and all had the charisma to gather a popular following. It should be no surprise that Jesus was easily seen by Rome as one of these dangerous rebels or by the Jewish leaders as one of the religious deceivers. Also, Jesus grew up in Nazareth in Galilee, an area that Rome clearly identified as a hotbed of rebellion, insurrection, and assassins.

During this period of time, there was a new translation of the Jewish scriptures. The process of translating the Hebrew scriptures into Greek began as early as the third century BCE with the books of Torah, called the Septuagint. Later translations such as Daniel and Esther, and Jeremiah had lengthy additions composed in Greek, while others such as Tobit, Judith, and the Wisdom of Solomon were Greek compositions from the start.[384] This was accompanied by new modes of piety and a heightened emphasis on "observance."

Finally, there was a new sense of destiny. As a new sense of urgency emerged, the people began to believe that God was about to initiate radical changes that would restore their nation to its "former glory" and permanent independence. For a few, this restoration would be brought about by Jesus, whom they called Son of David.

At the social level during this period, Judah was experiencing of time a "growing economic rift between the landed aristocracy (including both Jews and non-Jews) and the rural masses (predominantly Jews). There was also a rift between urban centers and rural village life."[385] This is significant since "the life of Jesus was set entirely in the region of broader Judea under Herodian and Roman rule" while Paul, in contrast, "lived largely in the Diaspora. Although he was also thoroughly Jewish, he spoke and wrote predominantly, if not exclusively, in Greek. The Pauline mission—which would prove so significant to the ultimate shape and success of the

Christian movement—relied almost entirely on the mobile population of Greek cities under Roman rule."[386]

The Pax Romana was an important aspect of this first-century context. This was an important point for Origen who "considered Jesus' birth in the principate of Augustus to be a sign that the *Pax Romana* was God's way of preparing the world for the gospel."[387] "Despite their renown as warriors and conquerors, the Romans coveted peace; however the word 'peace' meant far more than just a condition of relative tranquility or an absence of outright warfare. Instead, it was the code word or symbol for an ideology; it meant bringing Roman culture and administration to all parts of the world."[388] White reminds us that this was similar to the American slogan: "Making the world safe for democracy." While bringing peace and empire was seen as a positive by Rome, not everyone shared this view—just as the "nation-building" of the US is not positively received in most places in the world. "The same imperial ideology might easily feel like oppression instead. Such was the case increasingly in Judea, where the memory of self-rule and an equally strong sense of divine destiny fostered revolutionary, apocalyptic sentiments."[389]

"In the eastern empire, it was common to incorporate imperial cult processions into local religious festivals and to offer sacrifice and signs of reverence to the statue of the emperor. In effect, the reverence for the emperor and deified Roma were signs of loyalty (*pietas*) to Rome."[390] Such worship of the emperor, however, became a scandal to Jews and Christians alike—and even to some Romans.

The growth of the Empire produced a syncretism not only in the character of Judaism and the new Christian movement, but also in the character of Greco-Roman religion. This had been occurring for some time, as the Romans leaders adopted many of the elements of local cultures and "Romanized" them.

There was a sense that history was "moving according to a divine plan toward its scripted, teleological outcome produced the Western notion of linear time." It also resulted in an expectation of "end times," called *eschatology*. It did not originally refer to the end of the world, but rather to the end of the present evil age. However, it eventually developed into the vision of "a final battle between the forces of God and Satan. From this notion also came the idea that a warrior figure, like David of old, would come to lead the triumph over the forces of evil."[391] For the early followers of Jesus there was a direct connection between the impending eschatological judgment on those who are opposed to God and to God's chosen, and the immanent return of the risen Jesus from heaven.[392] According to the Gospel of Matthew, Jesus taught that this eschatological event was to be fulfilled within the first generation of the movement (Matthew 10:5-7, 22-23).

It was into such a religious and political context that Jesus came preaching.

Incarnation(s)

Is Jesus the one incarnation, or as in Hinduism, one of many incarnations? Did God wait for millions of years to send one person—Jesus—for all times, or have many such persons risen up to encourage us in behaviors that reflect our goodness or godliness? A once-for-all incarnation as traditionally understood severely limits an infinite God and makes that God even more distant from the world. But it is also irrational and meaningless.

In my book *The Divine Activity*, I argued that there was not just one pivotal incarnation. Rather, incarnation was an ongoing process from the very beginning of creation. In more traditional language, I argued that incarnation was God's self-witness to the world, a vision for the world that was manifested through natural observation as well as through the witness of human leaders who were especially open to the vision. While my thinking has changed on the nature of "God," I continue to affirm, against the tradition, that there is no single incarnation.

Living in terms of supernaturalism, one does not have to choose whether or not to believe in the miraculous. That is a given. One has only to choose from a wide assortment which miraculous account to believe. "Son of God" is one of those notions. Belief in supernatural events requires one to decide *which* Son of God myth to follow—whether one of the many Egyptian, Chinese, Persian, Greek, Roman, or Christian. Indeed, there is the myth that the Greek mathematician and philosopher Pythagoras (sixth century BCE) was a Son of God—son of the Greek God Apollo. The Jewish David was called son of God.

The birth of Jesus was not unlike the birth of other human beings. One thing that can be clearly stated is that the birth of Jesus reminds us that every great leader begins as an insignificant infant, born into a culture and environment that they would someday seek to understand and then attempt to overcome. It is only in retrospect that one can say that this particular birth is a glimpse into the wonders of new life and the fragility of all of life.

The story of his virgin birth was believable in the first century, since it was similar to many neighboring religions that reflected divine "indwellings" with human beings. The Greek Perseus was born when the God Jupiter visited the virgin Danaë. Horus was born of the virgin Isis. Mercury was born of the virgin Maia. Romulus was born of the virgin Rhea Sylvia." But this did not occur only in the Greek, Roman, and Christian myths.

> The god Buddha was born through an opening in his mother's flank. Caticus the serpent-skirted caught a little ball of feathers from the sky and hid it in her bosom, and the Aztec god Huitzilopochtli was thus conceived. The virgin Nana took a pomegranate from the tree watered by the blood of the slain Agdestris, and laid it in her bosom, and gave birth to the god Attis. The virgin daughter of a Mongol king awoke one night and found herself bathed in a great light, which caused her to give birth to Genghis Khan. Krishna was born of the virgin Devaka.[393]

Any consideration of Jesus' uniqueness must be considered metaphorically. His significance lies in the transcending values and ideals that have been drawn from his orally-transmitted teachings. The importance, then, is not a divine Jesus or even the historical Jesus but the transcending principles he represents.

Long after the discoveries of Copernicus, Galileo, and Newton, the church continues to insist on maintaining the ancient worldview in which the concepts of magic, miracle, and divine intervention are accepted as valid explanations. The problem is, that worldview can no longer be defended with intellectual integrity. With this change in the way the world is understood, thinking people are forced to enter into and embrace a reality vastly different from the one found in the traditional language and images of their faith traditions.

When Darwin began relating human life to the world of biology more significantly than any of his predecessors, persons were challenged by a new way of understanding the world, an understanding filled with concepts diametrically opposed to the traditional Christian view of reality.

The church had assumed that God created a finished and perfect world. It was in this perfect world that the first human parents disobeyed God and thereby fell from the perfection of their creation. Through their act of cosmic disobedience, they led all of humanity into "original sin." However, under careful examination, Darwin, who had studied theology, reluctantly concluded that the natural world was unfinished and evolving, and it was thus "imperfect" from its very inception. There was no perfect state of Eden.

Nevertheless the Abrahamic faiths continue to insist on a literal Adam and Eve who literally lived in moral and spiritual perfection until they sinned and got kicked out of a literal Eden. From that point on, everyone has had to live with the consequences of their actions. Despite the fact that God had laid this sin upon us, we have the choice to escape this sinful nature. But we have that choice because God had allowed us to have it. And so we might wonder if the choice, or the sin, is really ours, and if we can claim anything for ourselves. "All we can do is seek the kind of humility that edges on humiliation,"[394] and spend our lives not only continually repenting of the slightest transgression, but living in fear that we might miss one and be dammed.

Following this line of thinking, it is not hard to see why the church demonized evolutionary theory. If human beings did not fall from perfection into sin, but were instead the result of millions of years of evolution, then the basic theme of Christianity—that Jesus was the divine presence in human form that came to earth to redeem humanity from the fall, i.e., their original sin—is no longer viable. And along with that, many related parts of the church's story are also rendered inoperative, especially the church's interpretation of the crucifixion of Jesus as the moment of divine sacrifice when the ransom for sin was paid to an angry and disillusioned God. Today a growing number of Christian thinkers are coming to understand that the cross as "the sacrifice for the sins of the world" is a barbarian idea based on archaic sacrificial concepts that must be dismissed.

Needless to say, Jesus and all of the disciples were Jewish and their scriptures were the Jewish texts of the Tanakh. We now know that there were many Judaisms in the first century and that Jesus stands clearly within one or more of them—most likely the Pharisees. Jesus was thoroughly Jewish from beginning to end. And yet, this fact has rarely been affirmed. It is hard to imagine, but even in the middle of the last century serious scholars were debating the Jewishness of Jesus. And throughout the history of the church, even when the Jewish identity of Jesus was not denied, it was compromised, overlooked, or ignored. Further, there is the continuing question of what kind of Jew he was.

> Is the historical Jesus best understood as a Jewish rabbi, who, like other rabbis, taught his followers the true meaning of the Law of Moses? Or as a Jewish holy man, who, like other holy men, could claim a special relationship with God that gave him extraordinary powers? Or as a Jewish revolutionary who, like other revolutionaries, urged an armed rebellion against the Roman imperialists? Or as a Jewish social radical, who, like other social radicals, promoted a countercultural lifestyle in opposition to the norms and values of the society of his day? Or as a Jewish magician, who, like other magicians, could manipulate the forces of nature in awe-inspiring ways? Or as a Jewish feminist, who, like other feminists, undertook the cause of women and urged egalitarian structures in the world? Or a Jewish prophet, who, like other prophets, warned of God's immanent interaction in the world to overthrow the forces of evil and bring in a new Kingdom in which there would be no more suffering, sin, and death?[395]

There are as many "Jesuses" as there are hopes and as many hopes as there are promises. To the list above, we might add Jesus as CEO.

The earliest written traditions we have about Jesus come from the writings of Paul, and his reflections are often at odds with those of the gospels. Paul had never met Jesus and, in his writings, he did not spend much time describing what Jesus had said or done. In fact, it might be said that Paul's letters "proclaim the gospel of, well, Paul." He points to the crucifixion and resurrection of Jesus as "the beginning of a new age in the history of the world, the most immediate practical effect being the end of the Jewish law—quite a different stance to that taken by Jesus in the Sermon on the Mount . . . (Matthew 5:17)."[396]

We now have over two hundred years of research trying to flesh out the historical Jesus. The problem is that much of this research has been defined by theological presuppositions. Even the "new quest" or the "third quest" for the historical Jesus focuses on the theological question of "continuity or discontinuity between the historical Jesus and the preaching of the early church." However, with a more global framework, the questions now are more "related to the broad sweep of human history and experience," leading us to ask how Jesus is similar or dissimilar from other religious figures.[397] But perhaps the real task is to search for a Jesus who no longer serves as an instrument of religious domination and control. We need only look at history to see why this should be so.

Again, the fact that Jesus is reinterpreted for various audiences throughout the centuries is not new or particularly surprising. Reinterpretation is found within the very bedrock of the scriptures themselves, demonstrating that the scriptures are interpretative. The various interpretations found within the four gospels and the letters of Paul are clear evidence of this.

> Mark, for example, lays particular stress on Jesus' contests with demons, for such contests demonstrate that already in this world the Son of God operates victoriously. According to Paul, Christians are taken into living communion with the risen and exalted Christ; they are adopted through the Spirit just as Jesus was established as the Son of God by the Father at the resurrection. Matthew sees in Jesus a second Moses who, in both continuity and discontinuity with the Torah, establishes a new teaching: he intends to integrate Jews and Christians into "a *corpus permixtum*, with internal tolerance and outwardly an 'aristocratic' self-confidence to be the 'light of the world.'" Luke sees Jesus—already filled with the Spirit even before his earthly birth—gaining human beings through the Spirit for the reign of God. Finally, John's Jesus wants to bring human beings into his eternal communion with the Father through a new birth in the power of the Spirit. This new birth occurs in the midst of a conflict between the Roman lords of this world and the true authority of Jesus, who acts as servant and friend.[398]

In my classes I would often ask, "When did Jesus become Messiah? When did he become the Christ?" Most gave an answer from the viewpoint of John's Gospel. I would then refer them to five or six basic texts, point out to them that for Paul, the earliest writer, Jesus was made Christ at the resurrection. For Mark, the next oldest book, Jesus was made Christ as the baptism. For Matthew and Luke, it occurred at the conception, while for John, written at the very end of the first century CE, it occurred at the beginning of creation. Someone would always ask, "Which is true?" to which I would respond, "Yes." As Rabbi Steinman taught, there may be truth in all of them. They are all subjective and temporally conditioned. Each is conditioned by self-interest.

To answer the question posed in this chapter's title, "How Did a Nice Jewish Boy Become a Platonic God?" we must realize that it is hard to say where Jesus ends and the church begins. As Leonard Sweet reminds us, "the closeness of identification between Jesus and the Christian community is more than metaphorical."[399] As the early Christian movement developed, it soon came to realize that Jesus needed to be more than a popular rabbi or even another prophet of Israel. Briefly stated, for the purposes of self-identification, the Christian movement saw the life and message of Jesus as the fulfillment of the Judaic messianic promise. As time passed and the messianic promises did not materialize, the movement regained its energy by reinterpreting the importance of Jesus in terms of interior changes rather than external changes, while still holding out the hope of a second coming of Jesus. (A friend, Rabbi Rose, used to remind me that Jesus will do on his second trip what the true Messiah will do on his first!) The struggle between these new messianic Jews and traditional Jews was intensified with the Roman persecutions. During these troubling times, the Christian movement put further distance between itself and its parent. As the movement developed into a structured church toward the end of the first century, the lines of demarcation became more clearly drawn.

With each movement away from its parent, the Christian movement reinterpreted or refined its understanding of who Jesus was. The first three centuries of the church saw the movement away from the historical Jesus and his earthly message to the theological Christ and its related heavenly promises. Thus began the movement away from the nice Jewish boy toward the platonic God enshrined by the Council of Nicaea. We will deal with this development in more detail later.

The Jesus of Theology

The Jesus of theology is not really about the historical Jesus at all but about the Christ into which the Jesus story developed. In 1936, Paul

Tillich (1885-1965) wrote that even if Jesus never existed, the Christ idea was enough to be the center of history. In fact, the Christ idea was already present in the Greek Logos philosophy, from which the author of the Gospel of John "borrowed" his idea of Jesus as the divine logos. Leonard Sweet draws a parallel between Tillich's comment and Eugene C. Debs (1855-1926), "who announced in 1915 that even if Jesus were pure myth, his principles of 'the kinship of races, the democracy of nations, and the brotherhood of men' made him 'the greatest moral and spiritual force in the world.'" In short, writes Sweet, "Christians didn't really have to deal with Jesus, only with what he said or what was said about him." The "Death-of-God" theologies of the 1960s "only pushed this thrust to its logical conclusions."[400]

To underscore the fact that christology has taken the place of theology, we need look no further than Neo-Orthodox theologian Karl Barth (1886-1968) who argued that our language about God should begin with language about Christ, for the incarnation is God's revelation and union with humanity. However, beginning with Christ is to argue backward from conclusions already made. Throughout the centuries, Christians have tried to make this argument from the Christ event and have therefore found it necessary to construct a Jesus to fit their current needs and then to prove how the evidence of scripture and tradition supports their construct. While it is not historically honest, it has nevertheless been the acceptable task of theology.

In the early twentieth century, Ernst Troeltsch (1865-1923) rightly observed that christocentrism is the theological counterpart of an earth-centered cosmology. The Christian proclamation, "*Our* religious history is the sole hope of salvation for the rest of humanity," has been viewed by Christians as divine election, "but to the rest of the world it looks like another example of the Western will to dominate. And now that the supporting ideology of colonialism has collapsed, the absoluteness of Christianity appears ready to collapse with it."[401] While private spirituality is still relatively strong, the institutional church appears to have collapsed in much of Europe, although both are still strong in the United States and in many African countries.

In rejecting the idea of a truth given once and forever, we are nevertheless led to affirm that a number of spiritual leaders throughout history have, through their keen investigations and profound insights, helped humanity to advance toward a fuller understanding of the value of life. Among them is Jesus. The importance of Jesus is not his accomplishments but a symbolic significance of self-transcendence, a symbol that seeks to assure persons that human life is meaningful.

Traditional christology has focused almost exclusively on Christ's atoning work, with the "Savior" converted into a heavenly being with little or no reference to the historical and very human Jesus. His birth, life, and death are transformed into myths of his miraculous birth, crucifixion, and resurrection. Over against this vague and shadowy picture, three centuries of biblical research have presented us the image of a man who lived in the mundane world of the average human being of that time. This Jesus, we were assured, understood our problems and sympathized with us. Doing his own method of biblical criticism, Albert Schweitzer questioned the historical reliability of all those "lives of Jesus." Summarizing Schweitzer's critique, Piper writes:

> Yet if historical accuracy was slighted in these portraits and biographies because their authors read too much of their own experience and perplexity into the record, *there was definitely gain in relevancy*. The laity began to realize again that Jesus had been less concerned with the moral faults of people than with the possibility of a rich, profound, and meaningful life. As a result of this historical reconstruction, Jesus had become a contemporary of modern [persons], offering [them] advice, guidance, and encouragement in the most difficult situations of life.[402]

This led to the friendship emphasis in one's relationship to Jesus and the divine. This is found in popular hymns like: "What a Friend We Have in Jesus," "Just a Closer Walk with Thee," "In the Garden," "Jesus Loves Me," "O How I Love Jesus," to name but a few. It is no accident that many of the contemporary Christian songs are filled with physical love and sensuality in referring to Jesus.

"Jesus is Lord"

The church's classical proclamation that "Jesus is Lord," continues to be the definitive claim that the divine aspect of Jesus is the determining factor of his life—with the overwhelming belief that there was nothing in his mental or physical life that could negate this overpowering presence and direction. The argument has traditionally been that if Jesus had been simply just another human being, his influence in history would gradually be lost, even if he had been "the greatest of men." However, if this were true, then how can one explain the continuing influence and driving force of other great leaders like Moses, Abraham, Homer, Plato, Aristotle, Confucius, Lao Tzu, Mohammed, and others?

The classical argument also asserts that as the Son of God, Jesus has not only proven his superiority over the forces of evil, but he has vanquished them. Listen to any of the Easter hymns to see this. Piper claims that Jesus as the resurrected Christ "succeeds in molding human life in full agreement with the will of the Father. He continues his earthly ministry in the history of [humanity] by keeping his Church permanently oriented toward the goal for which he lived and died."[403] This statement is really reaching! If this were true, the church would be less concerned with self-preservation and doctrine and more concerned about the physical and psychological needs of people. To argue that "this ongoingness is another evidence of the finality of his earthly work," is not a viable argument. It could just as well be argued that the philosophies of Aristotle, Plato, Moses, Confucius, and others are final since they are *even older* than Jesus!

Another argument is that the finality of Jesus is deterministic since "nothing is to be expected in the future, including the parousia, that is not already intended and implied in his earthly ministry and his resurrection . . . . It is by the accomplishments of his earthly life that he proves his qualification for his heavenly lordship."[404] This argument is so filled with emptiness that it hardly deserves comment!

Piper argues, "The novelty of the Gospel is not to be found in the fact that its subject matter differed from the divine work recorded in the Old Testament nor in the fact that its content was not yet known to the Jews." Rather, its newness was "in its historical *accomplishment*, namely, in the fact that with Jesus the execution of God's redemptive purpose had entered into its decisive and final stage. In Jesus' ministry the Old Testament is 'fulfilled.'"[405]

Fulfillment statements like this are clearly bogus. In Piper's argument, it would seem that Judaism has little to stand on without the Christian add-on. He writes: "In the light of the Gospel story the events of the Old Testament are seen as something provisional, namely, foreshadowing the coming of the redemptive age—hence the references to promises and predictions fulfilled—yet also as not yet able to bring the process to its intrinsic goal or offering what renders life truly meaningful . . . ."[406] However, if the new redemptive age has not brought the promises to any kind of apparent fulfillment, how can it be convincingly argued that the Old Testament was fulfilled in Jesus? Again, the fulfillment statements are not built on facts but on wish fulfillments—like "Mission Accomplished" slogans.

The tendency of historic Christianity is to focus almost exclusively on the divinity of Jesus. This can be traced to the political and ontological development of Christian faith and doctrine that occurred between the original belief that Jesus was the Jewish messiah and the councils of the Fourth and Fifth Centuries that transformed this understanding of Jesus into the Greek or Roman Christ. This process was undertaken by the church leaders who were influenced by their own religious, political, and cultural contexts. Again, the concept of the God-man had been in continuous use by various religious expressions for thousands of years before Jesus. However, the Roman emperor Constantine's adoption and creation of this new Christianity ensured that "the triumphalist dimensions and possibilities of the received narrative would be given pre-eminence," since "no respectable empire wants to set up as its primary religious symbol the spectacle of a broken, publicly despised, and officially criminal human being, particularly one whose execution the empire itself effected!" It was inevitable, then, that given this influence, the power and divinity of Christ would triumph. "Little of the Hebrew Bible's critique of power (the power of kings and military heroes and alleged deities) found its way into Christian christological reflection."[407]

When affirming the full and complete humanity of Jesus, the question arises whether this stress does not really obscure or eliminate the divinity of Christ. Doesn't this make Jesus a "mere man?" Such a question betrays a largely negative view of what it means to be human. It is a view growing out of the concept of original sin—a concept that arose out of an understanding of a perfect creation that we now know to be utterly wrong.

According to Irenaeus and a small number of others, being created in God's image means that human beings have the potentiality to grow into the likeness of God. This argument suggests that humanity has the capacity to reach out toward the Infinite. If this is true, then our understanding of the divinity of Jesus is cast in a different light. That which is described as divine in Jesus can be viewed as the human potential for transcendence in the context of a fulfilled life. By fulfilling his human potential to a high degree, others were able to discover meaning or purpose in life through who he was and what he represented. As my colleague Gary Wilson said in a theological study group, "Jesus is our paradigm."

Traditionalists will argue once again that this makes Jesus a "mere man" and, as such, simply a good man, perhaps even the best man who ever lived, but not the Son of God or the divine Logos. My response is: "So, what's the problem?" John Macquarrie argues that this "mere man" issue can be addressed in the same way that the earliest disciples addressed the question, by looking at how "everything turns on the very different ways in which two human beings, the first Adam and the new Adam, realize or fail to realize their human potential."[408]

Of course, Macquarrie's statement falls back into mythological language to make his point. Who was this "first Adam" meant to represent—humans as we now know them or the first humanoids who lived more than two million years ago—ancestral species *who are now extinct*? Jesus as the "new Adam" is obviously an idealized form of remembrance.

Great persons are always remembered greater than they were. My father died when I was 20 years old. While he was a tremendously important person in my life, over the years I have remembered him in a way just short of his walking on water! I have absolutely no doubt that the same sort of selective and then idealized memory applies to Jesus. An idealized memory can provide vision and impetus toward a larger vision when properly used, but it does not express "facts."

Again, traditionalists will argue that such a christology suggests that human beings, including the human Jesus, may achieve goodness through their own efforts, or through their own capacity for transcendence without divine assistance. Again I ask: "So, what's the problem?" One created "in the image of God" *should* be capable of achieving goodness to the extent to which their lives are defined by "grace."

Traditionalists raise a third question. "Doesn't this whole approach minimize the difference between Christ and other human beings? Doesn't it make the difference one of degree rather than of kind . . . ?" It may sound like a broken record, but once again I ask: "So, what's the problem?" Macquarrie writes that "perhaps it is a difference of degree, for if it were a difference of kind, would that not make Jesus Christ one of an alien race, and therefore quite irrelevant to us human beings?" He goes on to remind us that "sin is not of the essence of humanity, but a corruption of that essence."[409]

A fourth question is: "If we acknowledge the difference between Jesus Christ and other human beings to be one of degree, then are we saying that incarnation is also a matter of degree, and are we not thereby robbing the incarnation of its uniqueness in world history?" If anything, it leads us to see the importance of human responsibility.

Traditionalists reject efforts to deconstruct essential conceptions of Christianity arguing that such deconstruction contributes to the declining influence of their witness in the world. It will definitely challenge their cherished notions. However, it might also result in a positive process that can have the effect of clearing space for new and more adequate formulations of the church's witness. In this sense, it is important to remember that there is more than one history of the world and that each new age looks forward to a different future and remembers a different past.

Fulfilled Prophecy

Throughout the centuries, Christianity has been built upon its claims of supersession over Judaism. From the beginning, Christians have selectively chosen prophecies from the Tanakh to prove that God's plan for human salvation reached its fulfillment in Jesus. At the same time, it has also rejected other prophecies, such as the return of Elijah. It does not take too much effort to demonstrate that the New Testament writers—and the church from that point on—read Jesus *into* the prophecies they quoted. Despite the fact that today persons are fascinated by prophecies, astrology, and the paranormal, it is important to remember that history is not written ahead of time but is created as it is lived. The whole notion of prophecy, in the sense of prerecognition, violates our sense of time, an open future, and the primal sense of cause and effect. Effects occur *after* the cause, not vice versa. On the other hand, the future is in some sense calculable in terms of possibility and probability. Therefore, we understand that to honestly respect the embedded traditions of religions requires us to understand that the prophets were speaking to their own times, with messages that they and their audiences understood in relation to their own situations—messages that were sometimes way off target.

Respect for the embedded traditions requires us to understand the Christian writers on their own terms as well. It was common at the time for the words of the prophets to be treated as coded messages that have significance beyond the prophets' own understanding. Then, too, many who claim to be able to foresee the future cast prophecies in such broad and nebulous language that their words can apply to a wide range of events. The believer must choose from among the many candidates which one is the true prophet and also which of the prophecies have been fulfilled. Those who through the centuries have predicted the end of the world use this method of reading scripture. This includes not simply books like *The Bible Code* and books by popular preachers and speakers such as Hal Lindsay and John Hagee, but also the prophecies of Nostradamus and the fictional "Left Behind" series. The Abrahamic faiths received this method of appropriating the prophets from the ancient Greeks, "who believed that their prophets spoke under the influence of a 'spirit of prophecy' that overrode the speaker's own rational capacities."[410]

It is unlikely that exposing the falsehoods of "fulfilled prophecy" would change the mind of anyone who is already inclined to believe that Jesus was the messiah. Indeed, most who accept this as true do not know what the prophets really said or the context in which they were uttered. In fact, for those who are convinced that Jesus fulfilled the Old Testament prophecies, no demonstration of the facts would matter. And this is true not only for the more conservative believers but most mainstream believers as well. And it is further true not only for Christians but for Jews and Muslims and others as well. For Christians, this is nowhere stronger than in Advent/Christmas and Lent/Easter liturgies and sermons.

> *The early Christian belief that Jesus fulfilled prophecy arose after and because of the belief that he was the promised messiah.* This very important finding needs to be emphasized. The belief that Jesus was the messiah was the basis for the belief that he was the fulfillment of prophecy. It was not that people noticed that Jesus had fulfilled a series of prophecies and so concluded that he must be the messiah. The process worked the other way around. It was because Christians were convinced that Jesus was the messiah that they went searching through the scriptures to discover which prophecies he had fulfilled.[411]

The New Testament writers designed their "fulfilled prophecy" arguments to support the faith of the early Christian-Jewish communities, not to convert outsiders, although it was later used for that purpose. All of Christian history has been marred with the ugly consequences of the anti-Judaism resulting from the supersessionism of the fulfilled prophecy notion. Christians have the intellectual and moral responsibility to abandon these obsolete, self-serving, and damaging beliefs.

The Story is Transformed

Jesus, the nice Jewish boy, became Christ, the platonic God, because of the needs of the early church near the end of the first century CE. In Acts, we hear a speech of Peter in which he declares it was when God raised Jesus from the dead that Jesus became the Christ. To this extent, the words of Peter are in agreement with the words of Paul in the opening verses of the letter to the Romans. In this view, Jesus became the Christ at some point *after* his death on the cross, that is, at his resurrection. This is not an objective verifiable historical event, but rather an "act of God," which is to say it "belongs to the category of a human judgment or interpretation . . . ."[412]

Of course, the biblical writers were not in agreement on the issue of when Jesus became Christ. As mentioned earlier, Peter and Paul declare that Jesus became the Christ at the resurrection. Mark says that it happened at the baptism, while Matthew and Luke declare that it occurred at his conception. All of these views, when evaluated against their theological implications, *were declared heretical.* They became heretical for the simple reason that these earlier teachings were over-ridden by changes in the developing tradition. The Gospel of John, written at the end of the first century—and the most theological of the gospels—declared that it occurred at creation. Thus, for John's gospel, it is no longer a case of Jesus "becoming" the Christ or "being made" the Christ. Rather, Jesus was always the eternal Christ or Logos. In the Fourth Gospel there is, therefore, no need for a birth story—let alone a *virgin* birth story. Such a story would have been meaningless for this gospel writer—indeed, it would have undermined his logos philosophy.

By the time of the Ecumenical Councils and the formulation of the doctrine of the Trinity, the Christian message underwent substantial changes. The story started with the simple affirmation that Jesus was the Jewish messiah. Twenty years or so after his death, the emphasis began to shift away from the Jewish political messiah who had come to liberate the people. We can see a change in the apocalyptic tone of Paul's earliest letters to the Thessalonians and his later writings. The more the scholarly Paul thought about it, the more he moved in the direction of a spiritual messiah concerned with the liberation of the individual soul from sinfulness. It was with Paul that the man Jesus became less important as the more technical concept of Christ became paramount. Once that direction was established, it would not be reversed.

"As the gospel stories were gathered and recorded and positioned according to the author's theological argument, they, too, took up this redefinition. The affirmation now revolved around the issue of how to affirm that God was present in the man Jesus." By the end of the first century CE, the writer of the Gospel of John began the process of incorporating the spiritual Christ into the Godhead, although his efforts were mixed. The spiritual Christ and the human Jesus were both present. Thus, writes Geering, "within the space of about seventy years the chief 'act of God' by which Jesus supposedly became the Christ has moved from after his death, back through his ministry, baptism, birth, to beyond the creation itself, as the final creedal term 'begotten, not made' makes clear."[413]

The traditions surrounding the idealized memory of Jesus are a succession of subjective judgments. However, once this transition from Jesus to Christ was set in motion, some church leaders began to realize they had been painted into a theological corner by claiming too much. Now they struggled to explain how Jesus could be fully and completely human at the same time he was fully and completely God. There was no escape clause in this doctrinal development the church had engineered. Many different notions were suggested but rejected as heretical, since they simply did not fit the mold that had been created. Beginning with the issue of how Jesus related *to* God, the issue was changed by asking how Jesus could *be* God.

A literal understanding of incarnation was believable in the earliest generations of the church simply because it was heavily influenced by the Roman culture of the time; and Paul was a Roman citizen. However, the biblical incarnation is no longer believable. It has little more claim to being factual than the miracle stories of the Egyptian, Greek, and Roman religions. It is no more factual than Narnia, Harry Potter, or other modern parables. It may *contain* an element of truth, but it is far from being factual.

If it is true that Jesus was an ethical teacher, much like a first-century Gandhi or Martin Luther King Jr., seeking to implement justice on earth, then what difference does Jesus of Nazareth make for Christian faith and life? The question is crucial for Christians, for if one cannot speak meaningfully about Rabbi Jesus who walked the pathways of Israel during the late twenties and early thirties of the first century CE, and who was crucified in Jerusalem at the order of the Roman procurator, then any speech about the post-Easter Jesus loses much of its meaning.

But is it important for the Christian faith to be anchored in the real history of Jesus of Nazareth? If not, can faith be anchored in the transcending significance we see in the stories and traditions associated with him? Can faith be anchored in the symbolism of the Christ that points beyond himself and his human actions to those principles that transcends his life and actions?

One thing we can say about Jesus of Nazareth is that he was a respected teacher. This is the title that is most commonly used in addressing him in the gospels. Taken at face value, the Gospels report that he quoted many wise sayings, most—if not all—being simply lifted from the pages of the Tanakh. He was obviously a very good communicator, using a variety of metaphors and parables drawn from everyday life that were easily remembered. Many of these teachings are able to nourish the human spirit and give a particular perspective on life. He was also, at times, controversial. "Jesus cannot conceive of any rule or tradition that would prevent him from doing good or saving life on the Sabbath."[414]

Of course, Christianity has never been content to think of Jesus as a teacher, however profound and life-changing his teaching may have been. Indeed, it might be argued that Jesus "was not a timeless religious teacher . . . . He spoke for his own age, about concrete conditions, responding to the strivings of the life that surged about him. We must follow him in his adjustment to the tendencies of the time, in his affinity for some men and his repulsion of others."[415] What made Christianity distinct, and all too soon caused Christianity and Judaism to go their separate ways, were the claims made by Christians with regard to Jesus himself.

Nor has the church been content with thinking of Jesus as a prophet, even though he evidentially saw his purpose as establishing the kingdom of God on earth through changed lives that were focused on reconstituting the social and religious life of Israel. Like the prophets before him, such proclamations were almost always met with indifference and even hostility. By the end of the first century, the writer of the Gospel of John has Jesus envision a time when "the old burning issue of the true place of worship would be antiquated and dead" (John 4:19-24). In the Gospels it is apparent that Jesus valued the temple as a place of prayer for all people, but he was opposed to the misuse of the temple and any religious duty that did not serve the needs of humans. Like the prophet Micah, he resented the fact that religious observances often got in the way of true observance, and in the process, formal religion became "a parasite on the body of morality and was draining it instead of feeding it."[416]

With the Jesus of Nazareth left behind, Christians began to use the language of Wisdom in reference to the Christ who had taken on cosmic proportions. In using this Wisdom language, they were claiming for Christ what Greek philosophers had written and what Jewish writers had already claimed for the Torah. Christians simply took an existing metaphor and used it for their own purposes. They also took existing Jewish writings and Christianized them, such as the letter of James.

Dunn argues that a Jesus who was "merely" a great teacher would probably not have been crucified. But history convincingly proves that assertion wrong. Great teachers throughout history have been "crucified" for their teaching. Dunn argues that "there is no obvious reason why a Jesus who was simply a great hero would have been thought to have conquered death as no other hero before him had." But that, too, does not ring true when one takes into account the transcending stories of other religious and cultural heroes who conquered death by coming back to life.

Man of His Times

Jesus was a man of his own time and struggled with age-old prejudices. In the summary of his teachings called the Sermon on the Mount, Jesus instructed his disciples: "Do not give dogs what is holy; and do not throw your pearls before swine" (Matthew 7:6). Later, when he is sending his disciples out to preach about the coming Kingdom of God, he told them to go to Israel, but to avoid Gentiles and Samaritans (Matthew 10:5-6). In Mark's gospel, a Greek woman came to Jesus seeking healing for her sick child. Jesus rebuked her with these words: "Let the children [Israel] first be fed, for it is not right to take the children's bread and throw it to the dogs" (Mark 7:25-30).

These attitudes are at variance with the later advice Jesus gives about taking the Kingdom message to all the world (Matthew 28:19). This change in mission reflects a change made acceptable by Paul's ministry and the Jewish missionaries to the Gentiles who preceded him As Geza Vermes states:

> I suppose that from the moment when Paul was acknowledged as "apostle of the gentiles" (Rom 11:13; Acts 9:15) and a mission directed at gentiles had been approved by the leadership of the church in Jerusalem (Acts 15), the original direction of Jesus' work was remodeled radically. Non-Jews join the church in large numbers, and she did her very best, in accordance with the proselytizing model prevailing in Judaism at that time, to meet the new demands and to adjust to the changed situation . . . . Another decisive change that transformed the substance was due to the transplantation of the Christian movement to gentile territory, which affected the status of the Torah, which had been the source of inspiration and the rule of life for Jesus. Despite an express order by Jesus, Torah was declared not binding, abolished, nullified and outmoded. Jesus had understood Torah with such simplicity and depth and had lived it with such integrity for what he saw as its internal truth. Paul defined it with regard to its actual effect as an instrument of sin and death.[417]

In his article, "Jesus Was Not an Egalitarian: A Critique of an Anachronistic and Idealist Theory," John Elliott argues that "the currently-advanced theory that Jesus was an egalitarian who founded a 'community of equals' is devoid of social and political plausibility and, more importantly, of textual and historical evidence." Moreover, he writes, "it distorts the actual historical and social nature of the nascent Jesus movement and constitutes a graphic example of an 'idealist fallacy.'" Thus, the biblical texts really show Jesus and his followers "engaged not in social revolution, democratic institutions, equality, and the eradication of the traditional family, but in establishing a form of community modeled on the family as redefined by Jesus and united by familial values, norms, and modes of conduct."[418] Jesus did not eliminate status differentiation. While inverted, the statuses of first and last, master and slave, rich and poor remained. "Within the Jesus movement, children did not in fact become leaders in the movement, though they were favored by Jesus. Slaves were not in fact liberated and made equal to masters. Women were not put on a social parity with men. The disparity between poor and rich did not cease to exist among those in Jesus' group."[419]

Elliott carefully delineates how the arguments for equality are inferred, while at the same time showing how they fail to take into account the fact that the teachings of Jesus (and Paul, for that matter) nevertheless presuppose social and economic disparity. He cites at length several examples:

- A disciple is not above (or equal to) her/his master (Luke 6:40/Matt 10:24-25/John 13:16, 15:20);
- Male household owners are superior to and control slaves (Mark 13:34-37;Luke 12:42-48; 16:1-8; 19:11-27, etc.);
- Parents are superior to their children and deserve honor (Mark 7:11-13/Matt 15:4-6; Mark 10:19/Matt 19:19/Luke 18:20);
- Husbands are superior to their wives; the former can divorce their spouses, the latter cannot (Matt 5:31-32; 19:9; contrast the secondary version of Mark 10:12);
- Older sons are superior in social rank to younger sons (Luke 15:11-32);
- Certain slaves enjoy higher rank than others (Luke 19:12-27);
- Jesus presumed differentiated places of honor and status (Luke 14:7-14, 15-24);
- Economic disparity between the healthy and the infirm (hence his healings "for free") and between the wealthy and the poor (Luke 6:20-26; Mark 14:7/Matt 26:11 etc.);
- Jesus called for generosity (Matt 20:1-15), almsgiving (Matt 6:1-4) and the sharing (not the equalization) of resources (Luke 6:34-36; cf. also Luke 4:18, 7:22-23 etc.);
- In the kingdom of heaven (and the new family of faith symbolizing the kingdom), there are "lessers" and "greaters" (Matt 5:1-20).

Jesus was the product of his own time, and urged conduct that would relativize but not eliminate social and economic disparities. "Suffering and want caused by inequity were to be alleviated by generosity, almsgiving, and compassion toward one's fellow human beings, but Jesus engaged in no program to eradicate altogether the causes of such disparities." This was to occur in the near future, "before the present generation passes away." It would occur when God's reign, the kingdom of God, was established on the Earth in its fullness. In terms of ethnic differences, "Jesus distinguished between the House of Israel on which he focused his mission and the Gentiles excluded from that mission (Matt 10:6), a view at variance with that of Matt 28:19 and the composer of the Matthean Gospel."[420]

Summary

There is an old rabbinic story about the death of Moses. Moses resisted the angel of death and demanded his right to enter the Promised Land. God had to intervene and reason with him. In effect, God said to Moses: "Look, Moses, I know that the real reason you are reluctant to die is that you are uncertain what will happen to this people you led out of Egypt at My direction. If I can assure you that everything will turn out well in the end, that there will be a succession of competent leaders, will that satisfy you?" Moses agreed. To achieve this, Moses was projected a thousand years into the future where he saw Akiba, the greatest teacher of the time. Akiba was teaching the essence of Judaism to thousands of his disciples. Moses sat in the class listening, but to his great horror, he could not understand a word that was being taught! Was this the Torah he had brought down from Sinai and what he had taught his people? The Midrash said that Moses was angry until the following event occurred. A student arose and asked Akiba: "Master, from what do you deduce this teaching?" Akiba replied: "It is according to the teachings of Moses at Sinai." At that, Moses was pleased and ready to die.[421]

Like Moses, Jesus was a great teacher who cast a vision for a new social order based on his understanding of the Kingdom of God. His disciples took up this vision and changed it in ways that were both positive and negative. Today the world has inherited that vision, but Jesus would not recognize it. It is no longer the vision of a humble prophet from Nazareth but the imperialist vision of the triumphant Christ.

CHAPTER 10

Did Jesus Die For Your Sin?

"If we are to believe that God deliberately sent his only son into the world to be brutally tortured and crucified, then I take that to be transcendental child abuse, and I will not have it."

—*John Dominic Crossan*

"No one dares suggest that neon signs blinking the message that 'Jesus Saves' may be false advertising."

—*R. Laurence Moore*

In *The Age of Reason: Being an Investigation of True and Fabulous Theology*, Thomas Paine—a British radical and an important voice in revolutionary America—wrote a profoundly religious work that stirred up great hatred against him from the churches. Like Roger Williams had argued more than a hundred years earlier, Paine argued for a separation of Church and State and for a conception of equality based on the divine "sonship" of every human. This faith was the basis for his arguments against any claims to divine partiality by a "Chosen People," a Priesthood, a Monarch "by the grace of God," or an Aristocracy. Paine's *Age of Reason* was an expansion of the Quaker's "inner light" theology that influenced his formative years. He was critical of institutionalized religion, as was Williams—especially its efforts to acquire political power and control. Unlike Williams, Paine challenged the inerrancy of the Bible, argued for reason over revelation, and supported deism (a form of belief in natural religion that was popular with almost all of the American founding leaders).

Paine also had a keen interest in astronomy. Meditating on the vastness of the universe, he wrote:

> From whence then could arise the solitary and strange conceit that the Almighty, who had millions of worlds equally dependent on his protection, should quit the care of all the rest, and come to die in our world, because, they say, one man and one woman had eaten an apple! And, on the other hand, are we to suppose that every world in the boundless creation had an Eve, an apple, a serpent, and a redeemer? In this case, the person who is irreverently called the Son of God, and sometimes God himself, would have nothing else to do than to travel from world to world, in an endless succession of death, with scarcely a momentary interval of life.[422]

I mention Paine here because he spoke not only for many in his day but also for an increasing number in our own who have serious questions about how science and religion can honestly interact with each other.

A growing awareness of other religions and the widespread knowledge of their transcending stories require that we ask comparative questions. It is not difficult to demonstrate that the Christian faith has many similarities to the classical mythologies in which there is the figure of a dying God. Dionysos was torn limb from limb, and the body parts of the Egyptian God Osiris were widely scattered. Dionysos was resurrected and his followers were promised that they, too, would find new life. Of course, it is argued that the death of Jesus was different since this God-man *voluntarily* died for the sake of others. What is the quality of the difference?

Christians do not agree about the meaning of the death of Jesus. Mark Heim writes:

> Protestants historically take their stand on the confession that they can be reconciled with God because of the sacrifice of Christ: "We preach Christ, and him crucified." Roman Catholics point to the same event as the sacramental center of Christian life, with the words from the Gospel of John, "the Lamb of God, who takes away the sins of the world." Eastern Orthodox positions the significance of the death in relation to resurrection, proclaiming in the Easter liturgy that "Christ has risen from the dead, by death trampling upon death and bringing life to those in the tomb."[423]

Of course, there are those Christians who see the value of this death as purely symbolic, much like the God-deaths of other mythologies. However interpreted, the death of Jesus is the central event of the Gospels, and church traditions center on it.

The death of Jesus as sacrifice for human sin cannot be understood apart from the sacrificial acts that took place at temples throughout the ancient world. Indeed, the writer of the book of Hebrews talks about the perfection of Jesus not in moral terms but in sacrificial terms. The sacrifice was made pure at its death. According to the writer of Hebrews, the same thing was true of Jesus, who became perfect in death.

The idea of sacrifice is rooted in the primitive notions of providing food for the Gods and of soothing divine anger with various kinds of offerings. It is also understood as the way of cleansing a person of sin. The Apostle Paul used sacrificial metaphors to describe the significance of Jesus' death. The idea of sacrifice continues to persist in religious and military arenas.

Many Christians today find the crucifixion an embarrassing, primitive barbarism. The theory of substitutionary atonement raises more questions than it answers. It argues that we humans are guilty of sin against God, and there is nothing that we humans can do to establish an unbroken relationship with this offended God. We are unable to bridge the gap between God and ourselves. Because of human helplessness, reconciliation is left up to God. Thus, we get the transcending story of Jesus as the Christ, the suffering messiah, who does what no human being could ever do. If God alone can bring about this sin-removal, and if Jesus performs this "something" that no human being could ever do, then he must be more than human. If God provided the sacrifice, then Jesus would not be anything more than a human substitution for an animal, and the sacrificial act would not have been voluntary. However, Christians affirm that "Jesus voluntarily gave himself up for our salvation." If Jesus was able to effect this, then he must be God—or really, really close to being God.

Heim argues that there are many reasons to be uncomfortable with not only the doctrine of substitutionary atonement but with atonement theology in general.

> Most people are no more likely to regard Christ as a sin offering who removes our guilt than they are to consider sacrificing oxen on an altar in the neighborhood playground as a way to

> keep their children safe. We can hardly imagine God planning the suffering and death of one innocent as the condition of releasing guilty others. Moreover, it would be worse if we could do so, for a God about whom this is the troth is a God we could hardly love and worship. A good part of atonement theory today for Christians consists in conjuring up some idea of sacrifice that we can half-believe in long enough to attribute meaning to Christ's death. Once it has served that transitory purpose, we drop it as swiftly as possible as, at best, a metaphor.

The classical understandings of Jesus' death rest upon categories that are no longer acceptable. In legal terms, sin incurs a debt that must be paid to release the sinner from its burden. Human sin, then, is an affront to God's honor, an offense against the divine King that must somehow be atoned for. The question arises about the emotional stability of a God who is so easily offended. God's displeasure becomes a form of "rogue rage." Both of these categories are troubling. "If the debt is actually paid, in what sense is God merciful? If it is God who in fact pays the debt humans owe, how is justice truly satisfied?"[424] To compound this problem, there are internal problems in the biblical explanation of what the death of Jesus means. Is the cross a good thing or not?

> Jesus sets his face to go to Jerusalem. Jesus teaches his disciples, to their horror or disbelief, that he must die. Despite his own reluctance, he goes to his execution out of obedience to God—"not my will but thy will be done"—and does not lift a finger to oppose it. Yet the Gospels are equally emphatic that Jesus is innocent, that his arrest and killing are unjust, that those who dispatch him are quite indifferent to truth and treat Jesus as a pawn in larger political or social conflicts, that it is shameful for his friends to betray and abandon him. Jesus says, "The son of man goes as it is written of him, but woe to that man by whom the Son of man is betrayed. It would have been better for that man if he had not been born" (Mark 14:21).[425]

While the death of Jesus is said to save the world, it hard to see the difference between God's will and the will of evil persons.

What about the toxic psychological and social effects that are the result of the emphasis on the cross? Do we not glorify innocent suffering in exalting the death of Jesus and encourage people to accept their own suffering passively by imitating Jesus? The church has made that demand of its members. Again, Heim's criticism is direct. By making the cross *God's* solution to human sinfulness, we paint God as a violent and merciless despot. Indeed, this "solution," in which the divine Father punishes his innocent child in order to redeem the world, looks like approval for child abuse. After all, our behaviors are to reflect those of God. Further, "Is the invitation to identify with Christ's death and suffering a kind of therapeutic malpractice, fostering morbid fantasies? The cross has been carried at the head of crusades and pogroms, even as it was offered to the weak as a model of how they ought to accept their suffering." Heim suggests that perhaps the cross should carry a label: "This religious image may be harmful to your health."[426]

Yet, there are many who reject the idea that the cross is "a mandate for passive suffering" in the face of evil and abuse. There are the powerless ones who experience a source of comfort in believing that the crucified Jesus displays an example of self-respect and integrity, which the rulers of this world cannot take away. In a world that regards them as nobodies, they see God's concern for them in the cross "the most powerful affirmation of their individual worth." The fact that God in Christ was "willing to suffer and die specifically for them is a message of hope and self-respect that can hardly be measured, and that transforms their lives. That God has become one of the broken and despised ones of history is an unshakable reference point from which to resist the mental colonization that accepts God as belonging to the side of the oppressors."[427]

Nevertheless, our childhood question remains: If Jesus is God, and he really died on the cross, does that mean that God died on the cross? If not, then did Jesus really die? If Jesus is of "one substance with the Father," then how can we possibly avoid the notion of God's death on the cross? This, of course, leads to a death-of-God theology, whether the scholarly or the childhood type.

The church's traditional notion of the trinity cannot answer this question adequately. This fourth century notion of a trinity argued that it was really God who suffered, but that presents its own set of problems. Moltmann makes the argument that "the sacrifice of the cross is not a punishment to appease God's justice, but God's act of identification with humanity and the source of a new hope for the human future. The sacrifice is not directed to God: it takes place within God."[428] It seems that Moltmann leaves the language of the substitutionary theory largely intact.

It is obvious that the understanding of God presented in these pages leaves no room for this notion of the trinity or for any notion of a God-man. The notion of Jesus as God-man reminds me of Clark Kent as Superman. There was an episode—and this accident probably occurred in several episodes—where Superman confronts the crooks. They shoot at him, but the bullets just bounce off his chest. Then, in frustration, they throw their guns at him—*and he ducks*! Why does he duck? Is he really not what he appears to be? This notion of Jesus as God-man also reminds me of the Wizard of Oz who seems to be all-knowing until the curtain falls away and we see a man like everyone else. It is the same with the church's claims about Jesus. When we look behind the curtain erected by centuries of tradition, we discover that he is not who we have been taught that he is.

A major alternative to the substitutionary theory is to view the death of Jesus as heroic—an act that appeals to our conscience in the same way that Gandhi's willingness to suffer brought about a change in the status quo. In this view, the death of Jesus is not a transaction but an *inspiration*.

Perfection and Imperfection

Christian tradition considers human nature to be evil, broken, fallen, and in many cases even totally depraved. At creation, everything was perfect. Then humans were created and immediately screwed things up. Of course, it was the woman's fault! Wanting to explore their world, wanting to know good from evil, wanting to enjoy the pleasures of sex, meant breaking the rules and incurring the penalty of death. Not willing to remain ignorant and infantile, they matured by taking the risk, and the result of breaking the rules was a broken relationship with God. This, we are told, was not simply their sin. Their actions had universal application. Now, all of their descendants—all of humanity—who would likewise want to "know," would also participate in their same sin. Because of their desire to grow up and explore the possibilities of the wider world, that world became a hostile place in which humans had to struggle for livelihood.

This original sin mentality has contributed to a passive dependency in our traditions. As several writers remind us, this is the reason Christianity considers human beings to be "miserable sinners" who, in the words of the old liturgy, are "not worthy to gather up the crumbs under your [God's] table." Humanity, then, is unworthy and wretched. Spong convincingly asks:

> Would any human enterprise designed to provide training for effective parenting operate from this point of view? If modern parents told their children daily that they were miserable sinners, fallen creatures, lost, hopeless victims who could do nothing except await a parental rescue effort, would that rhetoric produce healthy children who would become healthy adults? Would we not see that parenting advice as destructive, sick and pathological? But has that not been the Church's primary definition of our humanity? Is it any less destructive or less pathological if it is done in the name of a God called Father?[429]

Does this argument advocate that human beings are innately good? No, nor does it advocate that humans are innately bad. Human beings are neither. As Spong writes: "I am . . . convinced beyond reasonable doubt that the traditional explanations offered by Christian theology to interpret human life as fallen and thus predisposed to evil is not just an inadequate anthropology, but it is hopelessly flawed, pathologically distorted, wrong, and it therefore must be abandoned.[430] For Christians, the remedy for this brokenness was the incarnation of God—enfleshed in human life—very similar to the Greek and Roman transcending stories that Christians have so strongly rejected as being pure myth.

There was no perfect creation and, therefore, no fall from this good and perfect state into a state of sin. Instead, creation is an ongoing process, still evolving and expanding. Therefore, we are not fallen creatures but rather "evolving creatures." We have emerged out of millions of years of evolutionary history in which the struggle to survive was intense. One result of that struggle is that human beings have become "radically self-centered," bearers of what Richard Dawkins calls "the selfish gene." This survival mechanism has shaped our consciousness, and salvation—if we are to continue using the term—is to be seen in moving beyond our fears and tribal boundaries and the human prejudices engendered by our evolutionary past. Salvation can never be a rescue from a fall that never occurred, a sin incurred and biologically passed by Adam and Eve who never existed, or a restoration to something we have never been. It is rather a call to move beyond our limits.[431]

We need to proclaim boldly that human beings are not fallen, sinful people who deserve nothing but punishment and destruction. Nor, in transmitting our transcending stories, should we denigrate the mythological first parents who ate of the tree of knowledge. Our sense of separation and aloneness is not a mark of our sin but rather an awareness of our potential and the distance we have to go to actualize it. Our struggle to move beyond radical self-centeredness is not the result of original sin, but a sign of our emerging consciousness.

This being true, we must conclude that Jesus did not die for anyone's sins. This notion is a human creation and draws on ancient metaphors designed to give persons some hope for a different future. However, the mantra, "Jesus died for my sins," is repeated so often and in so many places, it really does not lend itself to question or debate—at least in the church. Yet, this phrase is all but nonsensical. To compound the problem, this phrase is tied to a fetish about Jesus' shed blood in which we are washed and thereby cleansed of our impurities. The sacrificial payment for the sin of the world presents us with a God who is "sadistic and bloodthirsty." Yet this barbaric concept is so deeply engrained that it is seen as the whole substance of Christianity. Without it, traditional Christianity asserts, there would be nothing left.

However, this cannot be true. After rejecting the notion of being rescued or saved by the sacrificial death of an innocent person, and rejecting the notions of original sin and being restored to a perfection that never existed, we are left with a more humane faith. In this faith, we are called to maturity and responsibility. We are called to eat of the fruit of the tree of knowledge. We are called to value human community and cooperation in order to grow beyond self-centeredness, and to transcend the aura of fear that self-centeredness creates. We are called to abandon prejudice and parochialism, and we are called to live in self-giving ways, which the transcending principles that the great spiritual leaders like Jesus encouraged.

The life, death, and resurrection of Jesus are the central transcending concepts of Christianity. Nevertheless, the church is divided between those who are certain about the atoning value of the death of Jesus and others who are very uncomfortable with any suggestion of blood sacrifices of any kind. However, an essential question remains for Christians. Is it true that the suffering of Jesus was like anyone else's suffering except that he was entirely innocent, unlike others whose nature is human?

In his article, "Can Buddhism Save?" Christopher Brown argues that Buddhism and Christianity are two religious outlooks that are simply incommensurable. "Each embodies a distinct grammar, or set of linguistic and doctrinal rules, leaving little basis for common reference between the two. One looks in vain for point-for-point correspondences. While parallels seem to present themselves, the divergent frameworks within which they occur make direct correlation a questionable undertaking."[432] I would argue that the same argument of incommensurability is also true between different groups within Christianity. While the language may sound similar, the definition of words and understandings of the language are often quite divergent. Confusion results when this is not understood.

Nearly a half century ago, Jesuit theologian Karl Rahner (1904-1984) argued for the concept of "Anonymous Christianity" that, while retaining the conviction that Jesus Christ is the unique mediator of salvation, would extend the possibility of salvation to those who have not embraced the Christian faith. He admitted he could not find a better term, given the limits of Roman Catholic dogma. He wanted to affirm "the universality of Christ's redeeming action," and at the same time include in that salvation those whose lives reflected the hope and love of grace to those who have no knowledge of Christ. A loving God who wants everyone to be saved (1 Timothy 2:4) would certainly not consign all non-Christians to hell. Therefore, these non-Christians have received grace without realizing it. Since "*salvation cannot be gained without reference to God and Christ*," he wrote, "it must in its origin, history, and fulfillment be a theistic and Christian salvation."[433] He could not escape his belief in the uniqueness of Christ and the Catholic Church as founded by God through Christ. He wrote that the Catholic theologian "is *bound by the terms of his own Catholic belief* to hold fast to the fact that *God truly and effectively wills all men to be saved* . . . . And yet *it is only in Jesus Christ that this salvation is conferred*, and through Christianity and the one Church that it must be mediated to all men."[434]

Rahner's argument was an elaboration of what Vatican II (1962 to 1965) had affirmed in the Constitution on the Church. "Those also can attain to salvation who through no fault of their own do not know the Gospel of Christ or His Church, yet sincerely seek God and moved by grace strive by their deeds to do His will as it is known to them through the dictates of conscience."[435] For Rahner, this meant that even atheists and polytheists could be saved.[436] He knew that people often use the same word to mean different things. "Someone who denies God, for instance, perhaps merely denies something which does not even exist in the opinion of the theist . . . ."[437] In another place, he wrote:

> For if a given individual *rejects* the Christianity brought to him through the preaching of the Church, *even then we are still never in any position to decide whether this rejection as it exists in the concrete signifies a grave fault or an act of faithfulness to his own conscience* . . . . Thus *we can never say with ultimate certainty* whether a non-Christian who has rejected Christianity and who, in spite of a certain encounter with Christianity, does not become a Christian, is still following the provisional path mapped out for his own salvation which is leading him to an encounter with God . . . . [438]

For Rahner, a person showing love for the neighbor is evidence of love for God, since First John teaches that a loving relationship between a person and the neighbor is a loving relationship between the person and God.

However good and sincere his intention, Rahner's approach denied the "historical actuality" of non-Christian religions. In the same manner, John Hick's argument for the universality of salvation also fails to allow each religion to speak for itself. We can applaud their efforts. They are not alone in trying to understand how that ultimate reality—which Christians, Jews, and Muslims refer to as the one God—can be present in a multitude of expressions.

Resolving a Crisis in God's Life

Jack Miles provided a literary critique of christology by suggesting that Christ, as God Incarnate, resolves a crisis in the life of God.[439] The crisis in God's life is at least twofold. On the one hand, God is feeling remorseful and guilty. God is a masculine figure "who knows that he has been vengeful: his punishments have often been wildly disproportionate to the deed." For instance, the curse of work and pain and death itself were inflicted upon humanity for eating some fruit from God's tree—that is, for desiring knowledge—and God sent killer snakes among the Israelites during their sojourn in the wilderness because they had complained about bad food. God has ordered the slaughter of peoples, the bashing of the heads of babies against a city's walls, and has broken promises. How can these things be justified? Indeed, ask Miles, How can God atone for this?

Miles argues that the resolution to this crisis is the death of Christ as God Incarnate. This death is God's sacrifice of God's own self in atonement for God's own sins. This is in direct conflict with conventional Christian thought: Christ dies not for the sins of the world *but for the sins of God.* Thus, Christ is God's repentance and penitence, "a remedy for God's own past ruthlessness." Miles presents a story that holds the Bible and its God of justice to an accounting, much like the Jewish literature that has called upon God to account for evil and suffering, for instance, Elie Wiesel's play, *The Trial of God.*[440] Miles writes neither history nor theology, but his literary creation raises the kind of questions that many have thought or asked over the centuries—questions that theologians and religious leaders have creatively evaded or dismissed.

Every year between the beginning of Lent and Easter—especially Holy Week and Good Friday—Christian preachers and teachers try to arouse in their listeners a sense of grief at the spectacle of Jesus' suffering. Beginning with the "Last Supper" farewell speech to the disciples the story moves through his betrayal, arrest, humiliation at the hands of the Roman soldiers, the stumbling walk to the site of the crucifixion, the agony of the crucifixion, and his abandonment by everyone—including God. This is same angry God who demanded Jesus' death. Rarely will preachers and teachers have us look at the cross and there see God's own self crucified. God had to die upon the cross because, as Camus suggests in *The Fall*, "he himself knew he was not altogether innocent." Jack Miles echoes this sentiment. For many Christians, these Lenten efforts meet with decreasing success. This can be because the scene has lost its edge, being all too familiar year after year. It can also be because many no longer find the image of an angry God demanding human sacrifice believable. It can also be because people see so much suffering taking place in the world today that it is difficult to see how the suffering of Jesus is any different—*or even as tragic.*

The notion of blood sacrifice for atonement is no longer acceptable. The death of Jesus was a very human event to which Christians have attached a divine significance. However, it was not something that God did to Jesus or demanded in some divine retribution for human sin. That kind of God is indefensible. The crucifixion of Jesus was an execution by the Roman authorities—just one among thousands of such executions.

So why is the death of Jesus different? Christians say that the resurrection was the cosmic victory of Christ over the powers of evil. However, that, too, seems to be a hollow claim in the face of continuing suffering and the evils of our day, such as racism, genocide, terrorism, and imperialistic wars. This claim of cosmic victory is proven wrong by simple observation. Overcoming evil requires discipline by humans, not an act of atonement by a God-man.

We must reject the notion that the death of Jesus was the final expression of God's wrathful condemnation of sin. Nor was the death of Jesus the ultimate expression of God's loving choice to be with sinners, in all the physical and spiritual sufferings that "burden human life in its sinful condition." Nor is the death of Jesus "the agonizing birth of the new creation," as the Apostle Paul argued. On the cross, we see a man laying down his life for the things he believed in, hoping that through this act, others would come to see the importance of these things and be encouraged to live out their lives in obedience to what they believe to be the vision of God for the world.

Who was responsible for the crucifixion of Jesus—God, the devil, the Romans or Roman authorities, the Jews or Jewish authorities, the whole world of humanity, or was it Jesus himself? There are models of atonement, each reflecting a different responsible agent, but it seems clear from the embedded traditions we have received and from the historical records, that Jesus was seen as a threat to the already unstable state of things in Jerusalem by both the Romans and the Jewish leaders responsible to "keep the peace." The fact that the disciples of Jesus were armed at this time would indicate that they were about more than simply meditating on the "lilies of the field."

Even for those who believe in a personal God, the God who demands the death of a righteous person to appease his anger or to provide a way for humans to relate to his Godness is certainly unappealing. Such a God is clearly more concerned about his own offended dignity than the sufferings of the world. God the Selfish Parent cares more about himself than about his children.

While obedience unto death may be a marker of the supreme dedication of the martyr, death itself may be a major impediment to the mission.

Focusing on Jesus' mission directs us to the fact of human alienation in all its religious and political aspects. In and of themselves, death and suffering have nothing good about them. There is nothing particularly saving going on in the crucifixion.

Salvation

Then what is salvation? Can we still use that term? According to the Christian scriptures, Jesus and the early Apostles spoke of salvation in terms of a life in the kingdom of God, which encompasses all of creation—a kingdom over which a physical God would reign as an earthly king. Salvation was something that begins now and continues into whatever may follow this earthly existence. That understanding of salvation was changed into a theology that understands salvation either primarily in terms of heaven after we die or primarily in terms of social and economic liberation on earth.[441] While those two extremes do exist, in reality most of the church has sought a middle way, often emphasizing one side or the other. An example is The United Methodist Church that was one of the most vocal advocates of social justice in its earlier days. This was its strength; however, by the 1970s it began to decline as it took on the conservative trappings of doctrinal religion.

Salvation is a way of life that provides a greater sense of wholeness in all of life and overcomes the domination of negativity in our daily lives. In this sense, salvation can be a character-transforming process. This is necessary since human beings are so prone to settle for less than what they are capable of. Salvation is not becoming perfect. Indeed, theologies of perfection lead to a sense of hopelessness, since no one can ever measure up to that standard. When Jesus reportedly said that we should be perfect as God is perfect (Matthew 5:48), an impossible expectation was laid upon humanity that led to despair. Nor does it do any good to promise that we will be made perfect in the afterlife. The church's emphasis on perfection keeps us groveling as "poor, wretched, and blind" subjects of a God who prefers to keep us in a childlike, submissive state.

Salvation is the result of the graciousness of human relationships and in the beauty of creation. There are times when acceptance or forgiveness comes to us in circumstances where we have done nothing to deserve it, as well as in circumstances where we cannot make the first step in reconciliation. In such cases, grace is experienced in the gift of acceptance, forgiveness, or reconciliation. It is more difficult to understand grace on the level of transcendence. We can easily understand when we have broken a relationship with others, with nature, or even with our own selves. It is less easily understood when we talk about a broken relationship with an offended God, especially when we cannot understand specifically what that offense is. It is better to speak of our disappointment in not living up to our potential and our tendency to give in to destructive temptations.

Every religion has practices that aid in one's growth toward full personhood, deeper spirituality, "an ever-deeper re-formation of our inner personality," and so forth. Christians historically call these practices "spiritual disciplines." These include various expressions of fasting and prayer, study and service, submission and solitude, confession and worship, meditation and silence, simplicity, humility, frugality, secrecy, sacrifice, celebration, protecting animal life, integrity, courtesy, and the like. Rather than simply honoring God, most of these practices can just as easily be understood as ways of honoring self, one another, and nature. Religious people tend to see God taking "our little offering" and producing through them changes that one could hardly hope for or imagine. However, God is hardly a necessity in making these changes occur within the self or in others.

The characteristics Paul listed in his writings are the same characteristics also sought by non-Christians and nontheists: love, joy, peace, patience, kindness, generosity, faithfulness, gentleness, and self-control. In the same way, non-Christians and atheists also share the characteristics he listed as being harmful: sexual immorality, impurity, debauchery, idolatry, hatred, discord, jealousy, fits of rage, selfish ambition, dissentions, factions, and envy. These characteristics are either community building or community destroying. They either strengthen or weaken relationships. They do not require a Savior in order to be effective or effected.

The understanding of traditional Christianity is that "we cannot, by direct effort, make ourselves over again into the kinds of people who are able to live fully alive to God."[442] Only God, who is omnipotent and therefore has *all* the power, can accomplish this in and for us. We are so screwed up (depraved) that God, and only God, can change us. We are helpless children who will never grow strong enough to care for ourselves or for others. However, we are told that God can and does help us through the agency of Jesus.

Is that true? Do not the efforts of others help to transform our brokenness into wholeness? Does not a better understanding of ourselves—through counseling, friendships, personal meditation, etc.—happen through nonreligious means? Nonreligious people achieve transformation without the need of a deity to do it for them. Of course, the traditional argument is that God is working unconsciously through other people and through our "souls" to "get in touch" with our own thoughts and purposes. This is what Karl Rahner was trying to say in his notion of anonymous Christianity.

Nevertheless, what is there to demonstrate the truth of this? Is not this "need for God to do for us what we cannot do ourselves" simply a creation of the human mind to counteract the impulses of our selfishness? Is it not true that some of the religions, including Christianity, have argued for human dependence on a divine being in order to maintain power and control over their adherents? Lifelong dependency on an earthly parent would certainly be abhorrent. If a good parent knows better than this, why would God as Supreme Parent (Father, Mother, Whatever) do less? This sense of dependence reveals a disfunctionality in God who as a parent figure refuses to allow his children to grow up. Furthermore, religious leaders more often than not take advantage of their constituents by mirroring this divine disfunctionality. However, this "you need me" often masks the underlying reality, "I need you."

Foster writes: "We do not, for example, become humble merely by trying. Action on our own would make us more proud of our humility. Instead, we train with spiritual disciplines appropriate to our need—for instance, numerous acts of service for others that will incline us toward the good of all people." Is not the act of training with the spiritual disciplines *precisely* something that *we* are doing, and are not the resulting changes a product of *our efforts*? Why should God be offended when we are able to walk rather than crawl, to make decisions on our own without having to ask continually for help? Why would God be offended when we do things on our own rather than giving him all the credit for everything? Perhaps God has not yet heard: "Divine pride goes before the fall."

Again, when Foster argues that "God uses the various difficulties and trials we face in daily life to produce in us a kind of patient endurance,"[443] is it not more honest to say that we learn patience, humility, and endurance in the face of such difficulties? Is it not true that we are able to do this because of the ongoing process of life lessons and our relationships?

This leads Gurion to a therapeutic vision of salvation that "can assist us in ordering the goods of life appropriately and proportionately in relation to a compassionate, forgiving, and healing divinity."[444] This, of course, is nothing new. One of the great spokespersons for this point of view was Basil in the fourth century. Today—for both religion's good and ill—"therapeutic ideas about wellness, wholeness, and fulfillment proliferate in our culture, and they certainly have found their way into the churches and the consciousness of ordinary Christians."[445] However, much of the therapeutic and self-help movement of the past half-century has done this from a secular stance without the need of introducing God into the equation.

Rabbi Arthur Green has written that mysticism is often a spiritualized version of messianic narcissism. That is, in this kind of spirituality, all fantasies are allowed and all our dreams come true. He also argues that it is we who must "redeem the Messiah." It is we who must unify creation. Upon us all depends, with us all becomes possible.[446]

What Is Sin?

I agree with Sidney Callahan when she writes, "As a practicing sinner I don't need to be convinced of the reality of personal sin. Whenever I give in to the dreary enslaving powers of sin, it's not a question of ignorance or mental incapacity . . . ." Like most nice people, she writes, "I specialize in sins of omission. We lukewarm believers choose sloth and selfishness rather than commit mayhem. Only dedicated crusaders for evil reach the depths, or heights (?), of sin."[447] Our human proclivity toward negative behavior is explained by the church in the doctrine of "original sin."

How does a Christian who accepts the scientific findings that support an evolving universe make sense of this traditional teaching? Callahan argues that an understanding of the human condition should incorporate all the sources of truth available from scripture, church teaching, scientific evidence, and human experience. "I am firmly convinced that all human beings, even the most adored and adorable, possess not only a hunger for love and goodness, but innate inclinations toward selfishness. The collective experience of history, especially of the deadly twentieth century, makes the point all too well."[448]

Evolutionary theories give support for an inherited "mixed motivation" in the human species. "On the one hand, humans cannot survive or function as a social species without parental altruism and group bonds that produce sacrifice for others. On the other hand, each individual inherits a strong competitive drive toward self-interest, dominance, and an impetus toward pleasure and survival." From an evolutionary perspective, humans are the result of mutations, natural selection, and other contingencies that produced increasingly complex organisms. Over time, this included human self-consciousness and an abstract sense of self. With this development, humans achieved the capacity "to choose freely and consciously between alternatives."[449] With this capacity for self-consciousness, rationality, and intense emotions, humans achieved the ability to evaluate the worth of their acts by symbolic and moral standards. With the ability to understand good and evil came shame, guilt, and pride as well as inner conflict and temptation. There was also an awareness of human weaknesses, impotence, fear, inner divisions, and mixed motivations. These things are all inevitable aspects of life.

If evil is the result of harmful choices made by human beings, then it is obvious that human beings create evil. If humans create it, then it can also be overcome when persons make right decisions. Can an individual intentionally live in such a way that their actions are motivated in some sense by the needs of the other and at the same time take care of one's own needs?

Again, it appears that this is possible. Sin is that which alienates us from others, world, and self—as opposed to the minuscule picking apart of the human action and psyche. For most of us, the choices we make will sometimes hurt self or others or creation, and our "success" may be intermittent. Nevertheless, are these instances "sin," since even our best intention can cause hurt, and even a "sinful" act can lead to good? Is it the act or is it the outcome that is judged as being wrong? The answer lies in the debate as to how much freedom humans really have, how many of our decisions are really our own, and to what extent outside influences contribute to the decision-making process.

Toward the end of the thirteenth century, with newer understandings of the human body, the Augustinian belief was challenged that original sin was transmitted through sex, but the belief has persisted. For most theologians of the time, even Mary the mother of Jesus was not exempt from original sin. Aquinas taught that original sin was passed through the generations just as human nature is. The infection of original sin, he said, takes place at the point when the soul unites with flesh in the womb of the mother. Since Aquinas believed that the soul is what gives life, the soul's entry into flesh is at the point of the fetus' animation. Thus, "before a rational soul is injected into the flesh, a body is not accountable for mistakes."[450] Of course, we might well wonder what kind of "mistakes" or sins a nonviable fetus might commit!

Summary

There were millions of Jews in the Roman Empire. Why should the humanness of any one of them have been celebrated? Was Jesus of Nazareth inherently so much more humane than his Jewish contemporaries—for example, Hillel—that he deserved this privilege?

I have never felt comfortable with any understanding of sacrifice that saw it as the appeasement of an angry God. Abusive punishment does not in any way constitute or effect redemption. When we realize the extent to which all punishment involves revenge, the maintenance of power, control, and scapegoating, we can begin to affirm that only love and mercy are supreme. Salvation is a refusal to accept the judgment of those in power who erect the crosses upon which they crucify the good. It is an insistence on the survival principle that life will eventually win over death.

Jesus was not God and, despite centuries of theological and biblical claims, it is highly improbable that he ever claimed to be divine. People who did not know Jesus first-hand wrote the biblical letters and gospels, and gradually introduced the deification of Jesus. The most that Christians can claim is that in Jesus we catch a glimpse of what wholeness might mean, realizing that his teachings come from a specific time, within a certain religious, social, and political context. He was not free of prejudiced and limited insight. He was a prophet who spoke out of a deep commitment to human justice and righteousness. The traditional arguments that Jesus is the true and only mediator between God and humanity, the true liberator from all forms of human and demonic oppressions, and the true healer from all forms of sicknesses are greatly lacking in credibility, as are similar claims in other religious traditions.

When speaking of the good growing out of the death of Jesus, Christians need to be reminded of the words spoken by El Salvadoran Archbishop Oscar Romero just prior to his own death:

> As a shepherd, I am obliged by divine mandate to give my life for those I love—for all Salvadorans, even for those who may be going to kill me. If the threats are carried out, from this moment I offer my blood to God for the redemption and for the resurrection of El Salvador . . . . Martyrdom is a grace of God that I do not believe I deserve. But if God accepts the sacrifice of my life, let my blood be a seed of redemption and the sign that hope will soon be a reality. Let my death, if it is accepted by God, be for my people's liberation and as a witness of hope in the future.[451]

The witness of Jesus calls us to lives of responsibility, and because of that, Christians are called to begin with ethics, not theology.

CHAPTER 11

The Survival of Personal Identity

> *"Should I believe that at some time at the end of days the individual cells of my remains will be reconstituted? How many bodies have I already worn out in only one lifetime? We keep on changing. I cannot claim that this body will rise at the time of the resurrection. Which one of my bodies would it be, from which incarnation, from which time in history?"*
>
> —*Zalman M. Schachter Shalomi*

> *"Beyond the grave they will find nothing but death. But we shall keep the secret, and for their happiness we shall allure them with the reward of heaven and eternity."*
>
> —The Grand Inquisitor in Feodor Doestoevski, *The Brothers Karamazov*

In *The Physics of Immortality* (1994) physicist Frank Tipler argued that modern physics supports the idea that in some far-off future time God will resurrect every person who ever lived—as well as every person who *could have* lived! Mixing a healthy dose of science fiction with his science, he suggested that our brains will be preserved like "computer simulations," and we will all be given new spiritual bodies to live happily ever after in the biblical Paradise.

It is hard to imagine what it was like when our earliest ancestors first felt the need to give the natural event of death a supernatural explanation. Coming to grips with one's own death is a heavy reality. It forces us to give up the delusion that we will live forever. But wait! Perhaps this is not all there is. Perhaps my life can somehow be extended. Perhaps if I plead to the Gods I can bargain for a life after death, perhaps another shot at life in another time or another place. And, perhaps I will be able to continue the meaningful relations of this life in that beautiful Isle of Somewhere. We resist the idea of death, fearing that our extinction will render our lives as meaningless and worthless. Therefore, we seek to discover a way that we can live forever. We convince ourselves that there is something more after we draw our final breath. The basic argument is: "I believe it, therefore; it must be true."

Understood as a journey, life is filled with religious images, such as: the journey from slavery to freedom; from bondage to liberation; from simple appearances to a new reality; from confusion to insight; and from darkness to light, where we will see as God sees. The emphasis on an immortal soul says that the *here* is not as important as the *there*, that the *now* does not matter as much as the *then*. The result is that *we impoverish our humanity*.

The notion of an immortal soul attempts to rob death of its totality and has the ability to make us less ethical. Justice not meted out in this life is rectified in the next. A life cut short will find fulfillment in the next. An embryonic cell that never had the chance to develop into a mature life here will be fully developed in the next. In that "somewhere," perhaps over the rainbow, there will be no sorrow, sickness, pain, or sense of alienation—at least for the righteous. For the not-so-righteous, these things will be enhanced and no relief will ever come for them.

The belief that we have an immortal personally identifiable soul may certainly help to alleviate the fear of the unknown, the fear of alienation or separation that death brings. The belief includes a heaven that validates all that has been good about us. Because of this wish, religious persons will often try to give assurances that we will see our loved ones again in "heaven" where we will all be together again. As the old gospel song puts it: "When we all get to heaven, What a day of rejoicing that will be." Imagine getting to know the thousands of embryonic children you may now have, cells that in the afterlife will have developed into full persons. How will you know them, since you have never seen them, or even knew they existed?

When confronted with multiple marriages, most Christians, at least, ignore the teaching of Jesus that in heaven there is no marriage or recognition of relationships. For the writers of the Bible, heaven serves only one purpose and that is to give endless praise to God. Thus, our lives and our salvation are important for this same purpose. God is the sole focus. The "new traditionalists" say that it is similar to the state we experience in a dream where we can be "with" someone while being "present" to many others at the same time. Indeed, the argument goes, we can intimately be present to a hundred others at the same time, and it will seem as though there are only two persons intimately present. (Talk about parallel universes!)

The spiritual worldview is at variance with such ideas, but it, too, raises its own questions. If we are spirit when we die, how will we recognize each other in the afterlife? Further, if it takes a brain to enable the recognition function, how will that take place in a spiritual state that has no location or form? (It's a mystery!) This is why Tipler argues that the brain will somehow survive death. The biblical writer Paul says that we will have a spiritual body. As a "body," it seems to indicate recognizability, but it also understands spirit not in spiritual terms but in terms of material definitions. Of course, we are told, these issues are all moot since God will make it all happen in just the way *we* want it to happen.

When we look at the issue of personal survival beyond death, most persons do not think about survival of their entire personality. They do not want their more negative attributes to survive, although they do want to maintain their positive attributes. However, the negatives are just as important in making us who we are as the positives. While sexuality in the absence of a physical body would be a virtual reality experience, the emotive senses of love and physical attraction are nevertheless strongly desired. However, with so much of the physicality important in this life absent in the afterlife, what would be left? Would there remain any real personal identity?

Discussion of the soul in the Abrahamic faiths, especially Christianity and Islam, is strongly focused on personal identity and is definitely filled with physical and material promises. This is not true of most Eastern religions where reincarnation is a central belief, and the recurring soul does not maintain any personal continuity. In Western thought, though, the individual is central and the owner and controller of experiences and feelings and thoughts. My thoughts and my experiences belong to me; yours belong to you. One of the most fundamental properties of the self in Western thought is that the self is indivisible and discrete. "*I* am *one* individual, and *I* am quite distinct from *you*." This, again, is in contrast to an Eastern understanding of the self.

However, current studies lead us to affirm that the classical Western individualistic understanding of the self misses the mark. We are social selves, defined by our experiences. Since our concept of self is strongly rooted in the memory of past experiences, the self would not exist in the absence of memory. In fact, a person could not act coherently without memory since body movements could not be coordinated in any conscious pattern. The person would be completely incapable of making any sense of their perceptions, and could not even begin to order the experiences of the world around her. "No pattern or regularity in events would be apparent, and no concept of continuity—especially personal continuity—could be maintained."[452] It is through memory, then, that we realize a sense of personal identity. It is though memory that we recognize ourselves as the same individual from day to day. This does not mean that the self remains constant throughout life. Just as the body is constantly changing, so is the personality. Nevertheless, the question remains: If a sense of self depends on memory—a function of the brain—how can a sense of personal identity survive the death of the brain? (I know! I know! It's a mystery that only God understands!)

The Soul

For centuries, religious persons have agreed that there is something of the human person that survives death, and this something has been called the soul—a soul that would be saved or damned by God. The second century theologian Mathetes wrote in a Letter to Diognetus (c. 130-200 CE): "The soul hath its abode in the body, and yet it is not of the body."[453] In fact, the soul has been understood to be that which defines the human person. Because of its importance, the soul has been understood, in various ways, to be an intelligence that was at work throughout the body. The soul is what made the body grow to its destined shape, made it alive and warm, and reproduced its own form in procreation.

Early on there were spirits everywhere, not just in the human person. This belief was adopted from animistic beliefs that all things contained spirits that helped the host grow and survive. When the spirit was absent, death resulted. The more one's search expanded beyond persons, trees, and rivers, the more one began to understand that spirits guided the world itself. This idea was prevalent up through the 1700s and continues to operate today in astrology. One can look at the moon and planets and understand something about their own lives because even the cosmos has a soul. This cosmic soul or cosmic spirit is channeled through these heavenly bodies to enact its will, and those who truly are in tune can harness this power. "With each breath, the world's spirits entered the human body and infused it with life and intelligence, uniting the soul of the microcosm with the soul of the macrocosm."[454] Isaac Newton "saw a causal role for spirits (for example, producing every fifty thousand years or so angelic corrections to the motion of the solar system, which otherwise, he thought, might wobble apart . . . ."[455] By the end of the 17th century, all of these beliefs were deeply challenged and severely weakened.

The Greek philosopher Empedocles (ca. 490-430 BCE) understood the soul in terms of reincarnation. He described the soul as "the thing that thinks, feels pleasure and pain, and gives the living body its warmth. At death, it leaves the body and searches for another home in a fish or a bird or even a bush; during its time in the human body, it resides around the heart."[456] This idea was close to the Eastern idea of reincarnation. Cutting open a cadaver was avoided in the ancient world, fearing that the soul would not find rest in the afterlife.

Plato understood that the cosmos was a living entity that was divinely endowed with a soul. Lesser Gods known as demiurges designed human beings. The souls given to humans were immortal. He taught that the Gods began by creating the head first, since, like the cosmos, it was spherical. The divine seed was planted in the brain so that it could sense the world through the eyes, ears, and nose. With the information it gathered through the senses, the soul then implemented its divine mission of reasoning. The purpose for this reasoning was "to reproduce the harmony and beauty of the cosmos in its own thoughts."[457] Souls or spirits of another kind were inserted into the human to do the work of the master rational soul.

Aristotle, on the other hand, rejected the notion that the head was the seat of the chief soul and made the heart the core of his philosophy. He reasoned that the soul is responsible for "everything that a living creature does to stay alive. And since different organisms have different ways of life, they must have different souls . . . each with its own set of faculties or power."[458]

The Greek physician Galen (129-ca. 199 CE), whose influences reigned in the area of medicine until the 17th century, studied human skeletons and the serious injuries of gladiators, and he apparently dissected an animal every day. Through these observations, he concluded that he had found evidence for Plato's description of the chief soul and its lesser souls.

According to the Old Testament, the soul is simply life itself, residing in the blood and disappearing at death. In its break from Judaism, the Church adopted the Greek understandings about how the soul and the body worked, and Galen's explanations best served that purpose. Galen's work was absorbed into church dogma and doctrine. By accepting the teachings of Galen, the Church declared that the Old Testament soul was Galen's lower souls of the liver and the heart. "The immortal soul had no physical dimension, but the church fathers put its faculties in the empty ventricles of the head, where they could not be corrupted by weak, mortal flesh." For Christians, the heart "became not only the seat of the passions, but also the site of moral conscience, an organ with powers of perception beyond the senses. It is no coincidence that Jesus if often pictured with an open heart but never an open brain."[459]

The Greek philosopher Epicurus (341-270 BCE) argued that the world was filled with atoms that were "invisibly small, indestructible particles of different shapes and sizes." The church rejected this notion since it undercut its understanding of the soul. Epicurus believed that atoms were moving throughout the cosmos without supervision or purpose, clustering in countless different ways, and producing an infinity of worlds. For him, "the Gods were indifferent to human affairs; the world carried on thanks only to the jostling and mixing of invisible particles." For him, "the soul was no different from the rest of the cosmos; it was made of atoms concentrated in the chest. As these atoms leaked from the body . . . they were replenished with every breath. Death came when the atoms of the soul suddenly fled the body, taking life with it."[460]

Christian theologians were outraged over the idea that the world required no cosmic soul providing purpose or providence—much the same response that the Church is making today to similar scientific claims. In the 13th century, Italian theologian Thomas Aquinas (1224-1274) rejected this notion of the blind actions of atoms, arguing that everything in creation has a purpose that is given by the Creator. Aquinas "opted for Aristotle's idea that the soul is the form of life, whether that life is plant, animal, or human." However, the human soul was different in that it alone survived death. While the soul's faculties, such as memory and imagination, were located in the ventricles of the head, Aquinas "made it clear that no physical organ could produce self-awareness or any other human thought." This God-given responsibility belonged to the soul alone.[461]

Throughout history, the definition, location, and function of the soul took many turns. With each scientific development, especially in biology and astronomy, beliefs were challenged and, at times, changed. Carl Zimmer's *Soul Made Flesh* is an excellent source for understanding this history. Today, the search for the soul, for "spirit in physical places," seems very quaint, even though these failed experiments continue to be taken seriously in the religious community.

Following the Old Testament view, there have been those who hold that the soul is material and dies with the body. This idea was popular for decades among the common people, but was considered by the intellectuals as "slum religion." Even the popular religious writer John Milton considered that the soul was limited to the life of the body. The argument was that "if the soul were immaterial, it would have no way to break out of a material body at death." Such a belief was seen as a threat not only to the eternal salvation of the unbeliever but to the very survival of the *nation itself*, since it was believed that persons without a concern for the afterlife would be free to live as they pleased in all manners of immorality. If enough people believed this and lived in this way, the nation would fall under the weight of its collective "sin." This argument continues to be widely used against those who do not agree with church doctrine.

In the afterlife, the belief is that the soul becomes free of all things that define life: hunger, thirst, bodily functions, aging, sweat, toil, etc. It is bereft of stimulations, challenges, and decisionmaking. In heaven one experiences perpetual joy without its opposite. It is an eternal "high." Fulfillment is achieved without something to struggle against, without that something against which to measure the joy. It is like being zoned out on a bipolar medication where the highs and lows of life are no longer experienced.

When does the soul begin? If the soul preexists, when is it "connected" with or implanted in the person? Does it happen in the embryonic cell or in the potential that is present in *every* cell? This question has been addressed since the time of Aristotle and has changed according to the "scientific" knowledge of the day. Theologian Don Cupitt, an Anglican priest and emeritus professor of Philosophy of Religion at the University of Cambridge, states that we have to give up the belief in substances, including the belief that we are or have immortal souls. "So long as we think that a bit of us is not of this world and has to be preserved unsullied for another life elsewhere, we will fail to commit ourselves completely to this world and this life." Only then will we begin to see that "the world is all ours, and that we wholly belong to our world." Only then will we begin to take responsibility for it. Only then will we realize how profoundly every aspect of our being is interwoven with it. "Every last bit of us is situated in the here and now, biologically, historically, and culturally. We are not detachable from our world, and it comes as no surprise that those contemporary novelists who have wished to use the idea of heaven have been obliged to picture it as being simply a fantasy-continuation of this life."[462]

Philosopher Nancey Murphy of Fuller Theological Seminary writes: "Science has provided a massive amount of evidence suggesting that we need not postulate the existence of an entity such as a soul or mind in order to account for life and consciousness."[463] Recent studies in neurology strong suggest that our memories, emotions, and thoughts—all of which make up our personality, our personhood—reside in the physical interactions of the brain. Murphy is correct in seeing that this poses a serious theological problem since it asserts that the dualisms on which traditional theology is built are no longer tenable.

A problem for many Christians (and others) is the fact that memories, emotions, thoughts, etc. are physical activities. If these functions are simply extensions of our physical bodies—of our brains—what does that mean for the soul to which they have been attributed, or at best, functions that survive in the soul? If these things are physical activities, the soul loses its functional purpose.

In his review article, "The Soul Problem," Michael Shermer presents the problem of the soul in this way:

> In June 2002, baseball legend Ted Williams died. It would have been a short-lived news story had Williams' son not whisked the body away to Phoenix, where it was cryonically frozen at negative 320 degrees, the ostensible hope being that "Teddy Ballgame" would one day be resurrected to play again. The episode raises an intriguing question: If Williams' body were reanimated, would the cranky perfectionist live again? In other words, is the soul of Ted Williams in deep freeze along with his brain and body?[464]

One's answer depends on what is meant by the soul. Do we mean "the pattern of memories, habits, and dispositions that constitute personality," or is the soul "an ethereal entity that is independent of the body?" If it is independent of the body, is it not also independent of memories, habits, love, and personality—those things that define us?

The notion that the soul can leave the body probably came from the belief that when a person dreams of traveling to a place, the soul actually leaves the body and journeys there. Thus, when death occurs, the soul leaves the body for the last time. This dualism comes from Greek philosopher Plato who in the fifth century BCE taught that the body was simply a mortal vessel containing an immortal soul that left the body at death. The church adopted this kind of thinking from the Jewish Pharisees and taught that the soul lives on after physical death, retaining all the powers of perception and feeling despite being separated from the sensual body.

Jay Taylor understands the concept of the eternal soul as a source of fear itself, and not just a fear of hell since the soul, "our very essence and truth and eternity, does not even belong to you. You yourself do not belong to—yourself! Your soul is nothing more than a piece of property waiting to be claimed by one of two gods," either God or Satan. Either way, you are nothing more than property without any freedom.[465]

Atheists like Taylor are not alone in disdaining such an image of the afterlife. I still remember hearing the college chaplain during my freshman year say that if all heaven amounts to is sitting on a cloud, strumming a harp, and singing hymns for all of eternity, he didn't want to go. Coming from a rather conservative background, my shock at what he said was enormous. I fought with that idea for a long time, but a few years later came to the same conclusion.

If humans have eternal souls, do other conscious animals also possess eternal souls? As children often ask, "Does my dead pet go to heaven?" Did prehistoric and now extinct anthropoids, who existed millions of years ago, have souls? Where in the evolutionary process were souls introduced? This is a sticky wicket for the religious mind. Can disembodied spirits/souls experience joy or pain? If not, it would seem that without physical bodies capable of such feelings, the joy of heaven and the fury of hell are meaningless. How can an *immaterial* entity be affected by *material* promises and threats? (Once again, it is a mystery!)

Resurrection of the Body

This, of course, is why many theologians throughout the centuries have maintained that there is a literal resurrection of the body at some point after death. The Apostles' Creed concludes with these words: "I believe . . . in the resurrection of the body, and the life everlasting." This has been traditionally interpreted to mean that the human body will be raised from the dead at some undetermined point in the future. The bodies of those who have decomposed will be reconstituted. This includes any body part that was lost at any time during the life cycle, such as parts lost due to amputation, disease, or simply deterioration. The argument has been that since these body parts participated in the goodness or the sin of one's life, they ought also to participate in the heavenly bliss or the hellish suffering of eternity. As Rabbi Shalomi rightly asks: "Should I believe that at some time at the end of days the individual cells of my remains will be reconstituted? How many bodies have I already worn out in only one lifetime? We keep on changing. I cannot claim that this body will rise at the time of the resurrection. Which one of my bodies would it be, from which incarnation, from which time in history"[466]—or if it should prove to be true, from which of the parallel universes?

The resurrection of the body seems to be in conflict with the notion of an eternal soul. The conflict arose early in the church's history, since Paul addressed it in his first letter to the congregations in Corinth (chapter 15), one of the earliest documents we have. He declares that at the resurrection, the physical body is changed into a spiritual body that then takes on the nature of immortality. While that has not been the argument of the church in its doctrine of the resurrection of the body, the fact remains: belief in an immortal soul is little more than "life" insurance, just in case the body is not resurrected! Belief in a soul is a backup plan.

Olaf Blanke, a neurologist from the University Hospital of Genf, Switzerland demonstrated that the near-death experiences many religious writers use to prop up the arguments for a soul can be naturally induced. A 2003 article in *Nature* reported that when an area of the brain called the Gyrus Auqularis is stimulated with electrodes, the subjects experience themselves as floating about the bed looking down on all that is in the room. Other researchers have reached similar results. (Another argument made to prove that there is a soul has been put to rest by the scientific method.)

In 1869, Pope Pius X reversed the Catholic Church's centuries old position that the soul arrived into the infant in the womb in the fifth month of pregnancy. He declared, instead, that it arrived at the moment of conception. This was based on the scientific finding that humans did not begin as miniatures in the womb but rather as eggs fertilized by sperm. That must mean, Pius concluded, that life begins at conception, "When Sperm meets Egg."

A hundred and fifty years ago, the understanding was that sperm had little babies curled up in it. Thus, masturbation, or sex for pleasure, was the destruction of these possible life forms.

> Now we know about DNA and reproduction, and we can literally grow whole organisms in about three weeks from an embryonic stem cell. We can engineer genes that do all sorts of things, and on and on. This has absolutely changed our view of ourselves. A lot of things that were left to 'God' or to the mysteries of the Great Out There, are now in our control. And it's kind of frightening. We don't always know what to do, what would be moral or immoral. I think the problems in genetic research are small compared to the problems that will happen as neurotechnology matures.[467]

The question arises for the skeptical: If only one soul is infused into the single zygote, what happens when the zygote splits into two separate pieces and each develops into a complete fetus, producing identical twins? Does the soul also reproduce and divide, so that both "share" a part of the one soul, or is another soul infused later than the first, or are two souls infused at the beginning?

What about "fetus in fetu," the rare abnormality in which a fetus is trapped inside its twin? It is so rare that less than a hundred cases have been recorded in medical literature. "The trapped fetus can survive as a parasite even past birth by forming an umbilical cordlike structure that leaches its twin's blood supply until it grows so large that it starts to harm the host, at which point doctors usually intervene."[468] Do both fetuses have a soul or do they share one?

When an early-term miscarriage occurs, does that soul exist for eternity without any discernable traits or identity to distinguish it from all the others that *God* has aborted—or as the anti-abortion groups would say, murdered?

The concern about personal identity in heaven helps explain, at least in part, why most people find little or no comfort in God-focused portrayals of heaven. Mark Ralls offers a personal experience to illustrate this.

> A few months ago, a man who had lost both his wife and son to cancer spoke up in a Bible study group: "I remember hearing a preacher say that we would recognize our families in heaven but we would not have any family relations. They would be familiar, but we wouldn't share intimately as we had done on earth. And I thought to myself, How awful! I would hate to pass my son or my wife on the street in heaven and then go back to my own little house. I know this is a terrible thing to say, but if that is true, then heaven sounds a lot like hell to me."[469]

The immaterial or spiritual aspect of God, heaven, souls, etc. are constantly translated into the material and carnal in religious thought. This is doubtlessly because persons have trouble believing what they cannot see, or at least understand in terms of their daily existence. Therefore, heaven is pictured as an actual, physical place where God is seen as physically sitting on a king's throne giving orders, keeping records, and receiving endless praise, while the human soul is viewed as a material substance leaving the body at physical death with full powers of recognition and recognizable features.

Our western religious ancestors believed that the heart was the seat of feelings and intellect. While ancient philosophers "knew the brain plays a role in paralysis, seizures, and behavioral derangement, that knowledge was regularly overlooked for the following 2,000 years." To be sure, no one then really knew what the brain did or how it functioned, and it was natural that our religious ancestors began talking about spirits and souls. The soul, for them, "was the name for what animated something, what gave it goals and the ability to make things happen. Just as people now distinguish hardware from software, anatomy from physiology, brain from mind, nouns from verbs, and form from function, it was once commonplace to distinguish body from soul." It was also believed that there were "little souls" that controlled the functions of the body's organs.

Today we know that the "little soul" is simply the function of an organ, not something separate from it. However, they did not.[470]

As our religious ancestors began accepting aspects of the scientific developments of their day, the soul moved from the heart to the brain. However, physiologists argued that the functions of the body and all of the organs did not arise from the soul—little souls or one big soul—but rather "arises from the emergent properties of a 'committee' of cells . . . ." The control once thought to be the responsibility of the soul was now understood to be "one of the brain's higher functions."[471]

This new scientific understanding brought about some obvious conflicts with and within the religious community that adamantly believed the soul was in control of the body. It called into question the afterlife—and if there is an afterlife, just what is it that succeeds the physical human body? Since the locus of the soul kept being moved around—from liver to heart to brain—what was now left? The religious community began redefining the soul from a controlling substance to a spiritual life-force to the personality. Caring for souls is a big business—a vested interest that had to be protected at all costs. The result was that those who disagreed with the "party line" were ostracized and worse. Old notions, even when they are disproved, do not easily die.

For most persons, there is nothing more important—or more comforting—than the idea that there might be something—whatever that may be—that transcends the physical here and now. This is intimately tied to one's definition of what it means to be human as well as to one's conception of God.

What distinguishes humans from other animals? At one time, it was said to be the soul, but in earlier centuries, it was believed that animals also had souls, and even earlier, that everything in the world has souls of some sort. Today, some Christian theologians question the existence of a soul. Everything traditionally attributed to the human soul is now shown to be biological processes. For centuries, philosophers, theologians, and scientists have probed, seeking to know where the soul is located in the body and what happens to it at death. This has included autopsy of animals, the weighing of the live and then dead human being, and the use of MRI and x-rays.

That which was once attributed to the soul is now identified with the self and with the functions of the brain. In fact, the 1967 edition of the *Catholic Encyclopedia* defines the soul as the "source of thought activity." It remains that the soul is considered a thing or substance that is nevertheless sharply distinguished from the body.

Nancey Murphy has said that there was a three-way controversy in the 1920s:

> The vitalists were saying that you had to postulate a vital force or an entelechy—which I think is just another word for an Aristotelian form—in order to understand how you can get life out of nonliving material. That view has been as thoroughly rejected as anything can be in philosophy. The second possibility was that reductionism is true, and you could eventually explain living processes in simple, biological terms. The third suggestion was the postulation of emergence—that you get something genuinely new when you get to the level of life.[472]

The religious theory of vitalism was largely abandoned in the early 19th century when it was demonstrated that biological organisms are made from perfectly ordinary atoms. Indeed, part of the organism's "metabolic function is to acquire new substances from the environment and to discard degenerated ones. An atom of carbon, hydrogen, oxygen, or phosphorus inside a living cell is no different from a similar atom outside, and there is a steady stream of such atoms passing into and out of all biological organisms."[473]

> What you are is an assemblage of roughly a hundred trillion cells, of thousands of different sorts. The bulk of these cells are "daughters" of the egg cell and sperm cell whose union started you, but they are actually outnumbered by the trillions of bacterial hitchhikers from thousands of different lineages stowed away in your body. Each of your hot cells is a mindless mechanism, a largely autonomous micro-robot. It is no more conscious than your bacterial guests are. Not a single one of the cells that compose you knows who you are, or cares.[474]

This notion is too much to handle for many who see it as "trading in mystery for mechanism." They believe that not only does it diminish the truth of the Bible and their faith, but it also impoverishes a positive vision of human possibility. However, this is not necessarily true.

The idea of all things being constituted by atoms is nothing new. It originated with the Greeks in the fifth century BCE. This idea took hold twenty-four centuries *later* when 19th century chemists provided indirect evidence that all matter consists of atoms. A century later, it was proven. Sometimes it takes a hypothesis a long, long time to move from idea to direct evidence—what science calls a theory. In 1905, Einstein wrote a paper in which he demonstrated how the dimensions of an atom could be determined.

Vitalism

But how can these inanimate atoms become animated? Some have argued that this is impossible—life does not come out of non-life. This notion stood fairly secure until recently. Nevertheless, the argument continues to be that there must be something added, some nonmaterial ingredient, a life force of some sort. This vital force or vital spark that gives life was seen by many as the soul—the very breath of God in human life.

Vitalism has a long history in medical philosophy. Traditional healing practices believed that disease was the result of some imbalance in the vital energies that distinguish living from non-living matter. In Western tradition, these vital forces were identified as the humors, while eastern traditions called these forces *ch'i*, *ki*, *prana*, etc.

The notion of ch'i is rooted in Taoism. Lao Tzu taught that it was the yin and yang that brings balance to existence. Ch'i is what gives life. Moltmann explains: "The *ch'i* is the omnipresent, formless, but all-forming power of existence, of all living things, and of human beings, too. Because it is formless, it can form everything; because it is empty, it can take in all things. Because it is the 'between' of all things, it can bring about the universal sympathy of living beings."[475] Ch'i can be understood in the words of Star Wars' Obi-Wan Kenobi as "an energy field created by all living things. It surrounds us and penetrates us. It binds the galaxy together."[476] As Robinson explains: "In Taoist thought there is neither absolute good nor absolute evil, but rather good and evil are relative conditions of one another. As Obi-Wan puts it, 'You're going to find that many of the truths we cling to depend greatly on our own point of view.'

From a Taoist point of view, it is not possible to have the light without also having darkness . . . ."[477]

In the 16th century, the invention of the microscope allowed scientists to challenge vitalism with the development of a germ theory of disease. The more science understood how the body functioned, the less power vitalism had in explaining things. In the past couple decades, a return to vitalism can be seen in the current arguments of intelligent design.

Daniel Dennett, Director of the Center for Cognitive Studies and Professor of Philosophy at Tufts University, defines vitalism as "the insistence that there is some big, mysterious extra ingredient in all living things." Vitalism holds that "the laws of physics and chemistry alone cannot explain life functions and processes." It is opposed to the thesis that life emerges from a complex combination of organic matter.[478]

The soul is "the ghost in the machine." Religious tradition argues that the soul occupies a *place*, meaning that it occupies some sort of *space*. Moreover, if it occupies space, we may then ask about its size, shape, orientation, and motion.

Abrahamic traditions argue that there is a time when the soul does not exist. Other religious traditions have beliefs that include reincarnation and the idea of the soul transcending death. However, the dilemma continues with a discussion of immortality. On the one hand, we desire the continuation of our personality after death, but we do not want this to be simply a static existence. We desire an afterlife that involves some sort of activity and growth. Jesus spoke of *life everlasting*, the unending passage of time." On the other hand, these concepts of the soul, life everlasting, and related concepts, are tied to our perception of time in the physical world.

Moltmann writes that eternal life has nothing to do with timelessness. Rather it is "fulfilled life in the experience of the moment." It is the human longing for an "*eternal present*."[479] Thus, there is no "eternal" dimension to the "kingdom of God" or the "reign of God" except in the "eternal moment."

To expect God to bring about justice in an afterlife is to expect God to do what humans should be doing in this life. Situations of injustice are intentionally or unintentionally created where human beings are seen as commodities and nature exists to be exploited. Because this is the path that religions have often chosen to follow, they are not only part of the problem, but also sometimes a major source of the problem.

While it is true that many religious persons have intentionally focused on justice issues, their energies are depleted by others who focus on justice in an afterlife. Energy for transformational action is further depleted by an undue focus on institutional maintenance and survival. In my own denomination, for instance, the effectiveness of pastors and churches is based on how well they raise funds to maintain the denominational structures. In this sense, local churches are little more than cash cows when they should be agents of social transformation. If we operated as though this life is all there is, our efforts would be focused on how transformative justice might happen. We would be more concerned about the future of our children and grandchildren will inherit. We would find ways to encourage and comfort one another in meaningful ways.

Summary

Most persons throughout the centuries have believed in a soul that transcends death in one manner or another. For some, the survival of personal identity has been paramount. When that has been true, there is an emphasis on being with one's loved ones in the next life. For a few, the glory of God has been paramount. When this has been true, personal recognition has taken a back seat to being lost in the heavenly choir.

Each time new discoveries forced a change in the location of the soul, it was moved from one place to another within the body, but its existence was not questioned. It was concluded that the soul was simply impossible to pin down. So strong is the desire for continuation of personal identity beyond death that all sorts of beliefs have been devised to guarantee it. The fact is, persons today will have no more success in finding the soul than did their predecessors.

I must admit that there is no one who would be happier than I if there is some sort of survival of a recognizable personal identity after death. There are those I deeply miss and would love to meet again. However, I do not believe that this is or will be the case.

CHAPTER 12

The Golden Rule and Moral Responsibility

"My call for a spiritual revolution is not a call for a religious revolution. Nor is it a reference to a way of life that is somehow otherworldly, still less to something magical or mysterious. Rather, it is a call for a radical reorientation away from our habitual preoccupation with self; it is a call to turn toward the wider community of beings with whom we are connected and for conduct that recognizes others' interests alongside our own."

—*The Dali Lama*[480]

"My sense of the holy, insofar as I have one, is bound up with the hope that someday, any millennium now, my remote descendants will live in a global civilization in which love is pretty much the only law."

—*Richard Rorty*

One day a graduate student of Ludwig Wittgenstein said how much he regretted the Church's condemnation of Origen's doctrine that God would eventually abolish hell and redeem everyone in the world—including the demons. Wittgenstein quickly stopped the student by responding that it was right for the church to reject Origen's thought. "It would make nonsense of everything else. If what we do now is to make no sense in the end, then all seriousness of life is abandoned."[481] If there is neither a heaven to hope for nor a hell to shun, why be good? That is an age-old question.

In what has become known as "Euthyphro's Dilemma," Plato posed the troublesome question of which comes first: Are pious persons loved by the Gods because they are holy, or are they holy because the Gods love them? Is something moral because the Gods command it, or do the Gods command it because it is moral? Are we good because that is what God demands, or are we good and in turn attribute our good behavior to God? Is justice determined by God and dependent on God, or is justice embraced by God and independent of God? This seems like the "chicken-or-the-egg" kind of argument, although most persons choose rather quickly.

On the one hand, there are those who claim that they are good because God demands it, and because rewards or punishments accompany the demands. This is a barter deal. If I am good, God will reward me. I am good in order to get something for my goodness. The danger in this understanding is that it asserts that any command of God, no matter how terrible it might seem, is just if God authorizes it. The history of religion clearly demonstrates that God and the Gods have authorized all sorts of atrocities.

On the other hand, there are those who claim that they are good without this divine command and its promise-or-threat consequences. I am good because it is the right thing to do regardless of the consequence—and whether or not there is a God.

This kind of dilemma is found even in a strictly scientific explanation of morality. "If morals have a natural instead of a supernatural origin, then there apparently can be no transcendent being or force to objectify them with absolute standards. If there are no absolute standards, then morality must be relative."[482] Harvard evolutionary biologist Edward O. Wilson presented the dilemma this way: "Either ethical percepts, such as justice and human rights, are independent of human experience or else they are human inventions." Those who claim that they are independent of human experience argue that moral guidelines exist outside the human mind. Those who claim that ethical precepts are human inventions understand they have evolved through the ages out of human experience, natural law, and biological wiring. Wilson writes, "I believe in the independence of moral values, whether from God or not, and I believe that moral values come from human beings alone, whether or not God exists."[483]

Shermer attempts to provide a middle way between these two approaches. He writes: "The moral sense in humans and the moral principles in human cultures are the result of laws of nature, forces of culture, and the unique pathways of history; theists who embrace the findings of science may assume that God created and utilized the laws of nature and forces of culture to generate within humans a moral sense and within human cultures moral principles." The moral sense "evolved out of behaviors that were selected for because they were good either for the individual or for the group." Negative or immoral sentiments were often isolated because they were bad for the individual or group. The most basic moral feelings "are largely under biological control, whereas the more social and cultural human needs and moral feelings are largely under cultural control." Unlike the Calvinist and similar theological strains who declare that humans are totally depraved and without any goodness in themselves, I share the view with Shermer that

> Humans are, by nature, moral and immoral, good and evil, altruistic and selfish, cooperative and competitive, peaceful and bellicose, virtuous and nonvirtuous. Such moral traits vary within individuals as well as within and between groups . . . . But all people have the potential for all moral traits. Most people most of the time in most circumstances are good and do the right thing for themselves and for others . . . . Religion was the first social institution to canonize moral principles, but morality need not be the exclusive domain of religion. [484]

Moral principles are not absolute. That is, they do not apply to all people in all cultures under all circumstances all of the time. But neither "are moral principles relative, entirely determined by circumstances, culture, and history. Moral principles are provisionally true—that is, they apply to most people in most cultures in most circumstances most of the time." Perhaps one of Shermer's best contributions to this topic is his discussion of provisional morality. Provisional means confirmed to such an extent it would be reasonable to offer assent.

> In provisional morality, we can discern the difference between right and wrong through three principles: the ask-first principle, the happiness principle, and the liberty principle. The ask-first principle states: *to find out whether an action is right or wrong, ask first.* The happiness principle states: *it is a higher moral principle*

> *to always seek happiness with someone else's happiness in mind, and never seek happiness when it leads to someone else's unhappiness.* The liberty principle states: *it is a higher moral principle to always seek liberty with someone else's liberty in mind, and never seek liberty when it leads to someone else's loss of liberty.* To implement social change, the moderation principle states: *when innocent people die, extremism in the defense of anything is no virtue, and moderation in the protection of everything is no vice.*[485]

Our sense of what is moral has evolved through millions of years, especially in the last 200,000 years. This moral sense evolved through the laws of nature, the forces of culture, and the contingencies of history. Because morality is the result of an evolved psychology, the moral sense transcends individuals and groups and belongs to our human species.

It has been my habit for many years to pick up litter, to put a product back on the shelf that has fallen to the floor, or even occasionally to take a paper towel and dry off the sink countertop in the restroom at my favorite Panera restaurant where I do most of my writing. I have come to realize the reason behind this is a philosophy my parents taught me: always leave things better than you found them. In recent years, I attached this to the concept of excellence in my leadership seminars. I believe it is also tied philosophically to the concept of doing for others what you wish someone would do for you.

As children, we learned the Golden Rule: "Do unto others as you would have them do unto you."[486] I saw this lived out by my grandmother, Dora Ward Snyder. When I was quite young there was a "ragman" named Clarence who would come though Maineville, Ohio with his old white horse and wagon. That was a real oddity in the 1940s. Clarence collected scrap iron, rags, and just about anything else he could sell. I remember one day when my cousin Dale and I chased after him throwing gravel from the road toward the horse. Our grandmother saw us and immediately took us into the house. Sitting us down at her kitchen table, she proceeded to talk quietly to us about the golden rule. "How would you feel?" she began. "How do you think Clarence felt?"

In the 1960s, President Kennedy addressed the nation's whites about the issue of segregation. He asked them to imagine that they were black and unable to attend school, vote, or eat in restaurants. How would it feel to be denied these things? Could *they* accept this second-class status?

One of the defining questions at the beginning of the Bible is: "Am I my brother's keeper?" The answer that developed, "Do unto others," is an ethic of reciprocity that is found in the scriptures of nearly every religion. It is often regarded as the most concise and general principle of ethics. It is a condensation in one principle of all longer lists of laws. A few quotes will illustrate this:

- You shall love your neighbor as yourself. (Judaism, *Leviticus 19:18*)
- In everything do to others as you would have them do to you. (Christianity, *Matthew 7:12*)
- Not one of you is a believer until he loves for his brother what he loves for himself. (Islam, *Forty Hadith of an-Nawawi 13*)
- A man should wander about treating all creatures as he himself would be treated. (Jainism, *Sutrakritanga 1.11.33*)
- Try your best to treat others as you would wish to be treated yourself, and you will find that this is the shortest way to benevolence. (Confucianism, *Mencius VII.A.4*)
- One should not behave towards others in a way that is disagreeable to oneself. This is the essence of morality. All other activities are due to selfish desire. (Hinduism, *Mahabharata, Anusasana Parva 113.8*)
- Comparing oneself to others in such terms as "Just as I am so are they, just as they are so am I," he should neither kill nor cause others to kill. (Buddhism, *Sutta Nipata 705*)
- One going to take a pointed stick to pinch a baby bird should first try it on himself to feel how it hurts. (African Traditional Religions, *Yoruba Proverb* (Nigeria)

The religions of the world have claimed special pipelines into the mind of God, giving them the right to tell the rest of us how to live and defining what is right and wrong. The argument that universal moral standards can come only from one's own particular God is clearly not true. The data from my studies indicate that religious and nonreligious persons generally agree on a basic set of moral standards. Steven Pinker argues, "Morality, at heart, is the idea that one's own perspective is not privileged—that the only coherent code of behavior takes a disinterested perspective that applies equally to oneself and to others."[487] Arguing that part of the innate structure of the human mind is the ability to take someone else's perspective, to believe that "other people are people in just the way we are," Rebecca Goldstein writes, "We need this belief to make sense of other people's actions and relate those actions to life. But there's a moral element in our acknowledging that other people have all the aspects of subjecthood that we do."[488]

Principle among the basics is the logic of reciprocity. "If we live in a world in which each of us, in the fullness of time, will be in a position to do the other a favor—or at least refrain from hurting each other—and if we both end up better off if we help each other than if we hurt each other, then certain moral emotions are expected to evolve."[489] Not only does this appear in some form in all of the major world religions, but it also appears to be part of all life forms. This suggests that the rule may be a universal moral truth. The philosopher Peter Singer argues that there is a universal capacity for empathy. At its earliest stages, people applied it "only within the narrow circle of the family or village or clan. Over the millennia, the moral circle has expanded to encompass other clans, other tribes, and other races. The question is, Why did this happen? What stretched our innate capacity for empathy?"[490]

There is a neural mechanism that "says" in our very nervous system: "You will feel better if you do unto others as they would have you do unto them."[491] The notions embedded in the notion of a Golden Rule are fundamentally about well-being—the well-being of oneself, of others, the groups to which one belongs, and even to other animals. There are no neutral-value actions or behaviors in this rule. Everything matters because we are all interrelated.

Jen

Confucius taught: "Human goodness, the Jen, consists of loving others."[492] The main characteristic of *jen* is a person's ability and duty to be in relationship with others. The term consists of two characters, "man" and "two." The foundational meaning of *jen* is "people," "human beings," or "common people." The literal translation is often "man-for-man," and is usually translated as benevolence or humanness, but is also variously translated as human heartedness, goodness, benevolence, man-to-man-ness, and that which gives human beings their humanity.

Confucius made *jen* the centerpiece of his philosophy. Its basic understanding is that we are to see others as we see ourselves, since our shared humanity is representative of the relationship between all persons. Since all of human life is defined in terms of relationships, *Jen* has a unique value and priority. In *Analects*, Confucius affirmed: "The man who possesses *jen* is the one who, in strengthening himself, strengthens others, and wanting to grow, causes growth in others."[493]

While very early the concept referred to the Emperor's relationship with his people, by Confucius' time, the concept had come to include all the obligations people had to those that were near to them, such as family. "Although Confucius offers several definitions of *jen*, it is perhaps no exaggeration to consider the Confucian *Analects* as one long extended definition of the concept of *jen*."

> First of all, it is the quality that all superiors (those in ruling positions) should have in order to govern well; if the mandate of Heaven decrees that government is for the welfare of the people, then all governors first and foremost should display the quality of *jen*. Principally, *jen* consists of *shu* and *chung*, "reciprocity or self-analogy" and "doing one's best." In the first instance, one should use oneself as an analogy when attempting to determine what is owed to others or what is beneficial to others: what you wish done for yourself, you should do for others, what you do not wish done for yourself, you should not do to others. But knowing this isn't enough; you should exert yourself to the best of your abilities (*chung*) to accomplish what you owe to others—this doesn't mean that you'll succeed: it is sufficient to have the right intent and make the right effort in order to have the quality of *jen*.
>
> Secondarily, *jen* consists of all those other qualities which are part of a moral life: *li*, or properly doing all the rituals that govern day to day life; *yi*, or right action; *hsin*, or making one's words conform to one's deeds (this includes speaking the truth and not speaking if one does not know the truth); *ching*, or "reverence," "seriousness," or "the sense of awe in the face of one's obligations to others."

In other words, "government ideally should be run by ethically superior human beings who concentrate solely on the welfare of the people they govern."[494] Politicians worldwide need to take a lesson from these pages, since they seem to be more interested in their own gains and careers than in the people they represent.

"*Jen* is something one learns rather than something one is born with. One learns morality by listening to moral precepts (*hsüeh*) and by thinking through them in order to determine if they are applicable to the situation you find yourself in (*ssu*); the key to morality in Confucius is always *thinking* since the world is constantly changing."[495]

Mo Tzu took exception to the limited application of *jen* by both Confucius and his philosophical heir Mencius. These teachers taught that one's moral obligations applied to a relatively small number of persons, such as to family, one's immediate neighbors, and to the politician's constituency. "Against this, Mo Tzu asserted that our obligations to the well-being of others extend to every human being and that we should individually pursue the well-being of every human with whom we have contact. Generally translated as "universal love," this concept "is really the logical extension of *jen* as encompassing an even greater range of people."[496]

Fr. Yves Raguin (1912-1998) wrote that in this world we are not meant to be anything other than human. To be human means being able to see another *as Other*. This Other is not necessarily a deity. The Other is that which is not me, but is part of me, and I of it. In Buddhism, self is understood in the image of running water whose only continuity is the flow itself.

Jewish philosopher Martin Buber argued in his philosophy of dialogue that we can only discover meaning when we move beyond self toward the Other who is outside us and yet is not us. Buber spoke of the I-Thou relationship, which stresses the mutual existence of two entities who meet without qualifying or objectifying the other. The I-It relationship, on the other hand, is where the two are treated as objects and where the self is the primary focus. Buber saw the I-Thou mode of relating as a dialogue, whereas the I-It was a monologue. We do not operate out of just one mode but rather use both at different times, although the I-It mode is used most of the time. This is similar to Lakoff's strict and nuturant modes of thought.

The traditional language of immanence and incarnation points to this by arguing that that which transcends us, and is not us, nevertheless encounters us and is part of us—and in a paradoxical sense, is an integral part of who we are.

A common example of this might be the experience of friendship that leads us into an ever-widening universe by the discovery of someone else. It is also illustrated in the loving relationship in which the two lovers give themselves to each other without losing their selves in the process. The strength each shares builds up the strength of the other. There is a synergy in which the two together become more than they were alone.

Thus, we have an obligation as one human being to another to do no harm. We have a duty, insofar as possible, to make something good happen in each situation we encounter. This arises out of the unconditional acceptance of the other simply because she or he is human. Every person deserves respect. Beyond this, respect is extended to other life forms including the inanimate aspects of nature. This common ground transcends religious belief. To demean another or to destroy nature is always counterproductive at some point.

This human obligation to one another is primary. Belief in a soul or God (s) or otherworldly notions of rewards and punishments can interfere with our responsibilities to each other to the extent they distract us from our own humanity. When we expect God to take care of the poor, the hungry, the prisoner, the environment, and so forth, we refuse to assume our own duty to do these things. As Carl Sagan said in the 1985 Gifford Lectures, "The more likely we are to assume that the solution comes from the outside, the less likely we are to solve our problems ourselves."[497]

Selfishness

Richard Dawkins argues that we are born with a "selfish gene." It comes as part of our survival equipment. The selfish gene refers to the fact that every gene is "concerned" to replicate itself. In using this phrase, Dawkins obviously does not believe that genes have consciousness or intention. It is a metaphor. Despite their inherent selfishness, "a gene gains nothing by going off selfishly on its own. Its only route to the next generation is via contributions to what Leigh has called 'The Parliament of the Genes.' Genes would pursue their interests selfishly if they could, but they can't. Success comes only from cooperating with other genes to benefit the whole organism."

However, this emotionally powerful metaphor "conceals the vast differences between our [individual] interests and those of our genes."[498] We have the power to defy and overcome this selfishness, writes Dawkins. "We are built as gene machines and cultured as meme machines, but we have the power to turn against our creators. We, alone on earth, can rebel against the tyranny of the selfish replicators."[499]

Affirming this, the question then becomes *Cui bono*? Who benefits? Dennett argues that one can care for others, or for a larger social structure, while caring for oneself. "There is nothing that restricts me to *me* as contrasted to an *us*."[500]

This seems to contradict the traditions that speak of "selfless" caring. However, striving for pure selflessness is guaranteed to fail. Jesus, and other spiritual leaders like him, did not operate with completely selfless motives. If Jesus cared about the welfare of others, making personal sacrifices helped him to fulfill those conscious and unconscious desires, thereby benefiting both others and himself. This would be a good kind of selfishness. But again, the defining criteria of pure selflessness are too elusive. Not even God as traditionally understood is purely selfless.

Dennett stuns the average religious devotee by saying that an altruist should not simply sacrifice herself or himself for no gain—"that's just being stupid." He then illustrates this by considering the statutory safety briefing to passengers on airplanes: "If you are traveling with a child, when the oxygen masks descend, first put on your own mask, then tend to your child." The logic is clear: by taking care of yourself first, you will be in a better position to take care of your child. Taking care of your child first may actually disable you from being of any further assistance to your child and to yourself. Since your child's welfare is what matters most to you, take care of yourself in order to better take care of your child. The other side of this is selfish desire.

> If you, selfish daydreamer that you are, prefer savoring in your imagination the future prospects of your child—if you prefer this activity to all others, and will take whatever steps are necessary to preserve the credibility of these parental flights of fancy by protecting your child, then you are no different from the miser who risks death to save his treasure chest from sinking to the bottom of the sea. If you have made the mistake of trading in your altruistic concern for your child for a selfish

> concern for your own peace of mind as you reflect on how you are sacrificing everything for your child, you are no true altruist. You're just taking all these steps in order to feel good about yourself.[501]

Mirror Neurons

Antonio Damasio demonstrated in the early 1990s "that morality could be studied using the then new technology of fMRI, and also that morality, and rationality itself, were crucially dependent on the proper functioning of emotional circuits in the prefrontal cortex." We cannot understand the fMRI studies unless we embrace the principle that "our brains, like other animal brains, are constantly trying to fine tune and speed up the central decision of all action" by approach or avoidance. We learned this in psychology 101. What Damasio helps us understand about this is that we have "intuitive reactions to almost everything, particularly to morally relevant stimuli such as gossip or the evening news. Reasoning by its very nature is slow, playing out in seconds." Conscious reasoning, on the other hand, is much slower, taking seconds rather than milliseconds. Because of this, it is rare that we use "reasoning to override our initial intuitions," perhaps less than five percent of the time.[502] Observations of infants suggest that mirror neurons are innate, since babies can imitate behavior two to three weeks after they are born. They can imitate a mouth opening, a finger moving or a tongue peeking through lips. Nearly twenty years before the term "mirror neurons" was coined, Andrew Meltzoff published his findings that a key mechanism in this early learning is by observing others. He argued that babies do not become social. Rather, they are social at birth.[503] His findings were novel at the time, flying in the face of Piaget's accepted understanding that infants begin life in "asocial isolation," and only slowly gain an understanding of the relationship between the self and other.[504]

There are many puzzling questions about the evolution of the human brain. The discovery of mirror neurons in 1992 began to unravel the mystery. This discovery is as important for the study of human behavior as DNA was for biology. These mirror neurons help us to "read the mind" of another; that is, they help us to understand the intentions of another in order to predict her/his behavior.

Mirror neurons in our brains re-create for us the emotions we experience in life. When we watch a film, for instance, we empathize with the fictional characters. We say that we know how they are feeling. In fact, *we do feel what they feel*—sadness, joy, pain, fear, and so forth. We are literally experiencing the same feelings. When we see someone fall, we flinch as if we are feeling his or her hurt.

> Our brain produces a *full simulation*—even a motor component—of the observed painful experiences of other people. Although we commonly think of pain as a fundamentally private experience, our brain actually treats it as an experience shared with others. This neural mechanism is essential for building social ties. It is also very likely that these forms of resonance with the painful experiences of others are relatively early mechanisms of empathy, from an evolutionary and developmental point of view.[505]

These moments of empathy, writes Marco Iacoboni, "are the foundation of empathy and possibly of morality, a morality that is deeply rooted in our biology."[506] Mirror neurons, which were first discovered in the frontal lobes of monkeys, help us to understand the intentions, mental states, and motivations of others.

> In the real world . . . neither the monkey not the human can observe someone else picking up an apple without also invoking in the brain the motor plans necessary to snatch that apple themselves (mirror neuron activation). Likewise, neither the monkey nor the human can even look at an apple without invoking the motor plans necessary to grasp it (canonical neuron activation). In short, the grasping actions and motor plans necessary to obtain and eat a piece of fruit are inherently linked to our very *understanding* of the fruit . . . . [Thus] perception and action are not separated in the brain.[507]

Thus, these mirror neurons are more concerned with the *goals* rather than with "the specific actions to achieve these goals."[508] Since they are a basic source of empathy, mirror neurons are fundamental to our social lives, allowing us "to share emotions, experiences, needs, and goals" with others.[509] Vilayanur S. Ramachandran, one of the discoverers of the mirror neuron, says that they blur the lines between self and others, "not just metaphorically, but quite literally, since the neuron can't tell the difference."[510] He and others have since discovered similar neurons for touch.

We learn by imitating. Of course, other animals also imitate the behavior of others, even of other species, but human imitations are more complex. As Iacoboni writes: "We have an instinct to imitate—to synchronize our bodies, our actions, even the way we speak to each other." Indeed, "imitation and 'liking' tend to go together. When someone is imitating us, we tend to like that person more." This gives some credibility to the old saying that imitation is the sincerest form of flattery. "Through imitation and mimicry, we are able to feel what other people feel. By being able to feel what others feel, we are also able to respond compassionately to their emotional states."[511]

Our brains are wired for empathy. They are also wired to affirm "our sense of being the agents of our own actions."[512] The two are bound together. One of the problems of Western philosophy—and especially the popular psychology of the street—has been the strong tendency to artificially separate self from other. However, it is clear that self and other are "co-constituted," as I argued in *The Divine Activity*.[513] As the philosopher phenomenologist Dan Zahavi puts it, "They reciprocally illuminate one another, and can only be understood in their interconnection."[514]

> How can we think of "self" except in terms of the "other" that the self is not? Without self, it makes little sense to define an other, and without the other, it does not make a lot of sense to define the self. And how could mirror neurons not play a role here? These are the very brain cells that seem to index (with their neuronal firing patterns) this unavoidable relationship between self and other, the inevitable interdependence . . . . Thus mirror neurons embody both the interdependence of self and other—by firing for the actions of both—and the independence we simultaneously feel and require, by firing more powerfully for actions of the self.[515]

Since self and other are so interrelated, isolation inhibits self-recognition. For a clear sense of self, one must have continuous relations and interactions with other individuals. In seeing other, we see ourselves. "Our neurobiology—our mirror neurons—commits us to others. Mirror neurons show the deepest way we relate to and understand each other: they demonstrate that we are wired for empathy, which should inspire us to shape our society and make it a better place to live in."[516]

Thus, we are deeply interconnected at a basic, prereflective level. So why is there so much atrocity in the world? Iacoboni suggests three main factors. First, is the phenomenon of imitative violence. "The same neurobiological mechanisms facilitating empathy may produce, under specific circumstances and contexts, a behavior that is the opposite of an empathetic behavior." Second, "mirror neurons are premotor neurons . . . and thus are cells not really concerned with our reflective behavior." The third factor as to why there is so much violence in the world, is that "the powerful *local* effects of mirroring and imitation [shape] a variety of human cultures that are often not interconnected with one another and therefore end up clashing."[517]

But what prevents us from blindly imitating every action we see? One answer is that there may be "frontal inhibitory circuits that suppress the automatic mimicry" when that action is deemed inappropriate. "Your left inferior parietal lobe constantly conjures up vivid images of multiple options for action that are available in any given context, and your frontal cortex suppresses all but one of them . . . . When these frontal inhibitory circuits are damaged, as in frontal lobe syndrome, the patient sometimes mimics gestures uncontrollably, a symptom called echopraxia." This overriding function creates "the null signal ('I am not being touched') from skin and joint receptors in your own hand blocks the signal from your mirror neurons from reaching conscious awareness." Speaking in more general terms, the overriding function "is the dynamic interplay of signals from frontal inhibitory circuits, mirror neurons (both frontal and parietal), and null signals from receptors that allow you to enjoy reciprocity with others while simultaneously preserving your individuality."[518]

Oxytocin, the Love Chemical

"What determines how humans interact socially? Why do we sometimes cooperate but at other times refuse to act cooperatively? Why are some people willing to trust a stranger, whereas others are mistrustful? Why do some people take risks to achieve their goals, whereas others prefer to stay on the safe side?"[519] These are some of the questions both social scientists and biologists are asking in order to discover the mechanisms that guide the social interactions of Homo sapiens.

Henry Dale (1875-1968) discovered the oxytocic action of pituitary extracts more than fifty years ago. However, it is only recently that oxytocin has been studied in terms of human interactions. Oxytocin is a naturally occurring hormone that is produced in the hypothalamus and stored in the posterior pituitary. It is released into the bloodstream and widely distributed throughout the central nervous system. It helps smooth muscle contractions in childbirth and in breastfeeding mothers. Recently, writes Michael Kosfeld, "we've discovered that its applications go beyond the maternal. It turns out that oxytocin also reduces social anxiety and helps people meet and bond with each other." For example, "A man and woman involved in the mating dance are releasing oxytocin, [but] so are friends having a good time at dinner."[520] He says that a number of animal studies have demonstrated that the oxytocin system mediates the ability to form normal social attachments.

Zak Lynch writes that oxytocin "helps us like each other, and makes us value being in social situations where trust, kindness, and love are mutually exchanged. You can think of it as the neurochemical basis of love, of all human attachment and bonding, and therefore of cooperation and teamwork on all levels."[521]

Paul Zak, director of the Center for Neuroeconomic Studies at Claremont Graduate University, argues that this "ancient hormone allows us to expand from strictly kin-based groups into villages, and then into small cities." We might ask which came first, an increase in oxytocin that produces a greater sense of trust, or the gradual increase of trust that increased the level of oxytocin? Regardless of the conclusion, it is clear that with the increased trust level, "survival was no longer everyone's full-time job. Learning and other advanced behaviors could flourish."[522]

The depth of oxytocin's effect has definite limits. "The love and trust it promotes are not toward the world in general, just toward a person's in-group. Oxytocin turns out to be the hormone of the clan, not of universal brotherhood." Carsten K. W. De Dreu, a psychologist at the University of Amsterdam, is currently studying the evolutionary aspect of oxytocin. "Besides loyalty to one's own group, there would also have been survival advantages in rewarding cooperation and punishing deviants."

If oxytocin underlies these behaviors too, it "would perhaps have helped ancient populations set norms of behavior." These findings support the evolutionary principles that no one who placed unbounded trust in others could survive. Psychologists have now concluded it is "the agent of ethnocentrism."[523]

Kosfeld emphasized that the effect of oxytocin is "specific to trusting other people and the willingness to take risks in social situations. Oxytocin does not affect human attitudes toward risk and uncertainty in situations where there are no other human beings involved."[524] Bruno B. Averbeck, an expert on the brain's emotional processes at the National Institute of Mental Health, explains this process of trusting.

> The brain weighs emotional attitudes like those prompted by oxytocin against information available to the conscious mind. If there is no cognitive information in a situation in which a decision has to be made, like whether to trust a stranger about whom nothing is known, the brain will go with the emotional advice from its oxytocin system, but otherwise rational data will be weighed against the influence from oxytocin and may well override it.[525]

Another interesting fact about oxytocin is that "stress actually increases its release, so a reasonable amount of stress can make a group of individuals bond as a family, a team, a company. This explains the lifelong friendships that can form among people who serve together in the military, for example. But too much stress will make people pull back from the group. Their brains will simply tell them to."[526]

As important as this oxytocin discovery is, we need to keep in mind that a large number of very complex biological processes influences human behavior. We automatically test the trustworthiness of others by studying their body language, eye movements, gestures, and so on. "That is why people like to meet in person whenever there's an important decision to be made, and why we see increased use of video-conferencing."[527]

Biological Basis for the Rule

Having examined how the brain, through mirror neurons and oxytocin, facilitates our empathetic responses, we now look at how this may have evolved. Life is a combination of determined and undetermined events. Some things we have no control over, while other things demand that we choose between options. In speaking of determined events, we do not mean that the events are divinely preordained but simply that we have no control over them. It is here that we speak of chance as playing a major role in the development of the universe as well as in biological development.

Dennett tells us that one of the most important innovations in biological evolution was the accident known as the eukaryotic revolution, which happened some billion years ago.

> The first living things, the relatively simple cells known as prokaryotes, had the planet to themselves for around three billion years, until one of them got invaded by a neighbor, and the resulting team-of-two was more fit than their uninfected cousins, so they proposed and multiplied, passing their teamwork on to their offspring . . . . These super-cells, eukaryotes, lived alongside their prokaryotic cousins, but were enormously more complex, versatile, and competent thanks to their hitchhikers. This was unwitting cooperation, of course. The eukaryotic teams were utterly obviously the teamwork in which they engaged.[528]

Thus, from conflict came something new, and "the very selfishness of genes can give rise to cooperation. For among the potential resources that genes can exploit is the potential for cooperation with other genes. And if it pays to cooperate, natural selection will favour genes that do so. Thus selfish genes can come to be accomplished cooperators . . . . This cooperation arises not in spite of but because of genetic selfishness." Cronin goes on to point out, "each of these adaptations is incomparably more intricate, more effective than any gene could build alone. And each cooperative enterprise creates a platform for the next."[529] Such cooperation arises at the margins, and even small changes generate conflict. This means that "what might make for survival in one case does not necessarily make for survival in another."[530]

An aspect of the eukaryotic revolution, the advent of multicellularity, was cooperation: "Why do these individual cells submit so selflessly to the good of the whole team? They have *become* hugely dependent on each other, of course, and cannot survive long on their own excerpt in the particular environment they usually inhabit, but how did they get that way?"[531] This is important for our discussion of human interactions. Sober and Wilson ask: "If communities of genes and cells can evolve a system of rules that allow them to function as adaptive units, then why can't communities of individuals do the same? If they do, then *groups will be like individuals* . . . ."[532]

As we look at the evolution of this rule of cooperation, we discover that "the brain is a physical system with built-in neural circuits designed to generate environmentally appropriate behavior. These neural circuits are specialized for handling different adaptive problems, and most brain functioning is unconscious."[533] Our sense of what is moral involves a number of different faculties in the brain and entails a "mentality of autonomy and interchangeability of interests." Morality is associated with notions of purity and defilement as well as notions of conformity to community norms. As Pinker writes:

> People, for example, tend to equate morality with high rank. We see that in the language: words like noble, which are ambiguous, [meaning both] high ranking and morally exalted. We see it in celebrity worship: People think that Princess Diana and John Kennedy Jr. were highly moral people, but they were pretty average. People tend to blur good looks with morality. You can give them a bunch of photographs and ask them to judge how nice they think the people are. The better-looking people are judged as being nicer.[534]

At least a portion of what we consider moral seems to be written into our human genetic structure. However, it is easy to confuse the metaphorical motives of the genes with the real motives of the whole person. A common mistake we often make is confusing correlation with causation. This is most clearly seen when dealing with statistical data. It can also be seen clearly in supernatural and magical ways of explaining things. For instance, one prays that God will heal her friend of a serious illness and the friend gets well. She claims that the prayer worked and God healed her friend. However, other "causations" were also present and the correlation claim is flawed.

Just because people may be selfishness, prejudice, shortsighted, or self-deceived does not mean that significant reforms cannot take place in the world. Significant reforms have taken place, including the end of slavery in most of the world. Reform is possible because even if we do have some motives that cause us to be selfish, prejudice, or shortsighted, we have *other* motives that can counteract them.

Human moral sensibility has flexible parameters. People in all cultures have the ability to respect and sympathize with other persons. Nevertheless, throughout history this has often been done selectively. While our moral sense may be programmed to sympathize with only members of our family or clan or village, over time that has shifted to include larger and larger circles of acceptable acquaintances. The development of an ever-widening circle is an example of how we can move beyond our initial "moral settings." Biologists and primatologists have reported observations where this occurs in the animal world as well. As Darwin wrote: "Any animal whatever, endowed with well-marked social instincts, the parental and filial affections being here included, would inevitably acquire a moral sense or conscience, as soon as its intellectual powers had become as well developed, or nearly as well developed, as in man."[535] One of the basic problems we encounter with all types of fundamentalism is that the circle is drawn too small. Fundamentalists maintain control by keeping the circle as small and tight as possible. Censorship and secrecy are essential to such designs. If persons are allowed to think and decide for themselves, so the argument goes, they will choose to enlarge the circle and lessen the tyrant's capacity to control and manipulate.

People bring at least four basic fears to the issue of explaining in terms of genetics how the brain works and the resulting human behaviors: inequality, imperfectability, determinism, and nihilism. But none of these should be taken seriously if we simply remember that even if there are parts of the brain that compel us to do things, there are *other* parts of the brain that caution us not to act and thereby hold us responsible for our behaviors. When we hold each other responsible for our actions, we are demonstrating that behavioral change can take place.

While the theory of natural selection describes an evolutionary process in which creatures compete to promote their own survival, biologists have nevertheless observed that animals and even lower organisms often behave altruistically. Darwin himself was puzzled by this. He wrote that animal altruism was "one special difficulty, which at first appeared to me insuperable and actually fatal to my whole theory."[536]

Erica Klarreich reports that a vervet monkey who spots a leopard, for instance, warns its fellow monkeys, even though the call may attract the leopard's attention to the individual. Clearly, there is more than self-interest involved here. Likewise, a vampire bat that has hunted successfully shares nourishing blood with a fellow bat that failed to find prey. The wild dogs of Africa are considered the most efficient hunters on the continent. They are very social animals, living in packs of 10 to 40 dogs. Cooperating in the hunt, they split up into various groups, circling the prey in order to outflank it and to cut off its means of escape. Once there is a kill by any group, the victorious dogs will call out to the rest of the pack to stop their chase and come to the feast.

Such behavior goes beyond self-interest and points toward the interest of the species. This does not mean that selfish animals do not take advantage of their peers. They do. However, the truth seems to be that generous actions help to advance the larger group. Somehow, writes Klarreich, "the altruistic behaviors observed in the wild must benefit the giver as well as the receiver."[537]

The evolutionary perspective admits that other animals have varying degrees of altruism, or what some call "pre-morality." As we study this in other animals, we begin to discover how human moral sentiments possibly developed. In passing, this perspective also gives other animals and life forms greater dignity and status than does a nonevolutionary perspective. As Frans de Waal argues in several places, it turns out that cooperation is a good strategy, especially among primates.[538] The following characteristics appear to be shared by humans and other mammals: "attachment, binding, cooperation and mutual aid, sympathy and empathy, direct and indirect reciprocity, altruism and reciprocal altruism, conflict resolution and peacemaking, deception and deception detection, community concern and caring about what others think about you, and awareness of and response to the social rules of the group."[539]

Frans de Waal tells about experiments that were carried out with capuchin monkeys. The experiment consists of two monkeys in two cages facing one another with a mesh screen between them. Individual A is given a bowl of cucumber slices while Individual B is given a bowl of apple pieces. The monkeys are forced to wait for whatever the other brings close to the partition, allowing them to reach for it. While most primates would stay in their own little corner and jealously guard their food, the capuchins bring lots of food to where the other can get at it and occasionally even push it through the mesh to the other. De Waal writes: "We found that if Individual A had been generous with its cucumber, Individual B was more likely to share its apple." They also performed a "labor market" experiment. This was done by placing food on a movable tray with a counterweight too heavy for a single monkey to pull. Each monkey sat in its own side of the test chamber, ready to pull the bar connected to the tray. The food was placed in front of only one of the monkeys, meaning that all benefit went to this individual. "Being true cooperators," writes de Waal, "they coordinated their actions perfectly to pull the tray." De Waal concludes: "Winners were more generous after cooperation than if they had obtained food for themselves. They seemed to realize when help was needed and rewarded those who provided it."[540]

Michael S. Gazzaninga, a neuroscientist specializing in split-brain research, observes, "It seems that half of the scientific world sees the human animal as on a continuum with other animals, and others see a sharp break between animals and humans . . . . We either see the similarities or prefer to note the differences."[541] Both aspects are important in understanding who we are as human beings as well as living organisms. One thing is basic: The human mind is built to think socially. The fact is, we have evolved with the brain capacity to assess social behavior in large groups in order to determine the value of cooperation, the risk of noncooperation, and so on. In his study of natural selection, Darwin noticed that, paradoxically, many creatures make themselves less fit in order to allow the group to survive.

Game Theory

Interestingly, some of the most illuminating ideas of how this works are coming from game theory, the field of mathematics that studies strategic behavior in competitive situations. For decades, the basic paradigm for understanding cooperative and competitive behaviors is the scenario called the prisoner's dilemma, in which each player has a powerful incentive to exploit the other. The idea of the prisoner's dilemma addresses the notion that "every circumstance in nature in which something like *cooperation* arises requires explanation."[542] The game is set up so that cooperation is best for the group, but each player individually does better by taking advantage of the other. A growing body of mathematical analysis and computer modeling now suggests that in many circumstances, those who cooperate can survive in the prisoner's dilemma.[543] Dennett observed that persons with genuine moral sentiments are better able to act in their own interests. "People with good reputations can thus solve even nonrepeated prisoner's dilemmas. For example, they can cooperate successfully with one another in ventures when cheating is impossible to detect. Genuine altruism can emerge, in other words, merely on the basis of having established a reputation for behaving in a prudent way."[544]

In the April 2004 issue of *Nature*, researchers argue that under certain conditions, a cooperator can infiltrate, and eventually take over, a population of cheaters. The game works like this:

> In the prisoner's dilemma, the police are separately interrogating two accomplices. Each criminal has two options: to cooperate with the other by keeping quiet or to defect by squealing on the other. If both cooperate, they'll each receive a 1-year sentence. If each incriminates the other, they'll both get 5 years. But if one cooperates and the other squeals, the cooperator will land a 10-year sentence, while the squealer will get off with only 6 months in jail. Chase through the options, and you'll find that no matter what course one prisoner chooses, the other will do better by defecting. So, if the two players are perfectly rational, both will inevitably squeal.[545]

This game encapsulates the cooperation paradox: Even though cooperation is the best plan, it often not adopted, since cheating benefits the individual.

In biological versions of the prisoner's dilemma organisms compete for increased fitness and reproductive success. It is not necessary to assume that the "players" are rational, only that they follow their inbuilt genetic programs. If one strategy outperforms the others, the individuals using that strategy will tend to have more offspring, who will also follow the superior strategy. After many generations, the weaker strategies will have been weeded out, and the players will be using the strategies that rational thinkers would have come up with. This can be demonstrated with an example using RNA viruses.

> In fact, a variation on the prisoner's dilemma can take place with participants—RNA viruses—about as far removed from high-level reasoning as imaginable. In 1999, Paul Turner of Yale University and Lin Chao of the University of California, San Diego mixed two different strains of a virus called phi6. They had chosen one strain that abundantly manufactures the molecules the virus needs for reproduction, and another that puts fewer resources into making these molecules and instead grabs the molecules that the other viruses make. "They are cheaters, who exploit the viruses doing the heavy lifting," Turner says. He and Chao measured how the two strains' interactions affect their fitness. "It falls out that these selfish viruses take over the system, but when that happens, the average fitness of the population drops," Turner says. "It fits in exactly with the predictions of the prisoner's dilemma."[546]

Cooperation occurs more easily in situations where a participant plays the prisoner's dilemma repeatedly with the same opponent and learns from previous games. After all, it can be risky to exploit someone you know you are going to encounter again. In 1980, political scientist Robert Axelrod held a tournament at the University of Michigan in Ann Arbor in which he invited game theorists to submit strategies for repeated prisoner's-dilemma encounters. The computer-simulated tournament produced a surprise: The hands-down winner was one of the simplest strategies, a tit-for-tat rule.

> A player using the tit-for-tat strategy cooperates in the first round and then in each subsequent round mimics the opponent's behavior in the previous round. In a population containing a mix of defectors and tit-for-tat players, the latter generally do better, provided there are enough of them. When they meet another tit-for-tat player, both cooperate and get a high payoff. When they meet a defector, they get suckered once, but only once. If repeatedly losing the game translates into low fitness,

> often the defectors do so poorly that they eventually die out, leaving an entirely cooperative population.[547]

Researchers have shown that a single tit-for-tat player in a population of defectors can sometimes get a toehold and then drive the defectors to extinction, provided the population is fairly small. The researchers' reasoning goes like this:

> Although a single tit-for-tat player surrounded by defectors does worse than the defectors do, and so has less chance than the defectors of producing offspring, the chance is not zero. If that single player is lucky enough to have an offspring, there are now two tit-for-tat players in the population. In a large population—say, 1 million—having a second tit-for-tat player doesn't give either one much of a boost, since their odds of running into each other are practically nil. But in a small population—say, 10—the two tit-for-tat players have an excellent chance of encountering each other, cooperating, and getting a high payoff. Depending on the particular payoffs of the game, their fitness levels may soar, and they can expect to have more offspring with each generation.

Martin Nowak of Harvard University and his collaborators have shown that for a wide range of game parameters and population sizes, a lone tit-for-tat player actually has a better chance of its descendants eventually taking over the entire population than any individual defector does.[548]

Other game theorists are arguing that another test might be better. In the same issue of *Nature* (8 April 2004) researchers highlight another set of interactions, called the snowdrift game, in which players have incentives both to cooperate and to exploit each other. The new analysis of the snowdrift game challenges some accepted wisdom about which environmental factors encourage cooperative or exploitative behavior.[549] In this game, the scenario has two cars stuck in a massive snowdrift. Each driver can either shovel snow (cooperate) or simply sit in his car (defect). Unlike the prisoner's dilemma, in which defecting is the better strategy no matter what your opponent does, the snowdrift game requires each player to take into account the other's actions. If the other driver is shoveling, it's tempting to sit back and let him do all the work. However, if your opponent refuses to leave his car, then you'd better get out your shovel and start digging.

> Curiously, the phi6 RNA viruses, which play the prisoner's dilemma in certain conditions, play the snowdrift game in others. In 2001, Turner and Chao found that if the cooperative viruses evolve in isolation before being mixed with defectors, they become so good at making the molecules needed for reproduction that they thrive even when the defectors steal molecules. Then, as in a snowdrift game, even if the cooperators do all the hard work, they're not necessarily cut down by the exploitative defectors.[550]

Pointing to what he calls "evolutionary original sin," Dennett wonders how it cannot be rational to deflect in some situations.

> If the other guy deflects (or if "everybody does it"), then you're a patsy if you don't defect as well, and if the other guy doesn't defect, you make out like a bandit by defecting. And if everybody knows this, how can anybody ever cooperate? When payoffs are in the short term, how can evolution ignore them, and when we consider that life is short, how can we ignore these payoffs? Fear of punishment and a desire for acceptance will take us past the easy cases, by changing the expected payoff.[551]

Role of Religion

If a biological basis for reciprocity can be established, religions cannot be seen as its originators, but rather institutions that have taken on the role of applying it to broader groups—even though it can be amply demonstrated that almost all of the religions have often acted against this basic instinct by enforcing their exclusive claims. Despite their rhetoric, they try to keep the circle small in order to maintain power and control. When that happens, religion is destructive—and we can suppose that in the end they will destroy each other—or perhaps, all of us.

A little known fact for believers in the Abrahamic traditions is that the topic discussed in the Bible more than any other is hospitality. This includes welcoming the stranger, feeding the poor, reaching out to the prisoner, etc. Welcoming the stranger points to a willingness to make room for another. In a world where vulnerable travelers needed food, shelter, and protection, hospitality rules became paramount since one never knew when they themselves would be the stranger. This was especially true in nomadic society. Hospitality is an ethic of exchange implying at some level that human beings share a common dignity and vulnerability that at times causes one to be dependent on the generosity of others. The underlying assumption of compassionate reciprocity is that since I have at some point been a stranger and vulnerable, I should show empathy with the stranger who comes to me. One need not be religious to offer or receive hospitality, but for some religious people, it is in this act of hospitality that God is most intimately experienced.

Shermer points out that love of one's neighbor meant different things in the earlier bands and tribes and in the latter chiefdoms, states, and empires. In the Paleolithic social environment in which moral sentiments evolved, one's neighbors were family, extended family, and community members who were well known to all. To help another was to help oneself. In chiefdoms, states, and empires the biblical admonition "Love your neighbor" meant only one's immediate in-group. Out-groups were not included. In a group selection model of the evolution of religion and morality, those groups who were particularly adept at amity within the group and enmity between groups were likely to be more successful than those who haphazardly embraced total strangers.

This interpretation helps to explain the paradoxical nature of biblical morality, where "on one page high moral principles of peace, justice, and respect for people and property are promulgated, and on the next page raping, killing, and pillaging people who are not one's 'neighbors' are endorsed."[552] Thus, Deuteronomy 5:17 commands, "You shall not kill," whereas a few chapters later, the Israelites are commanded take their enemy's city, steal their cattle, enslave their citizens, and kill the men and rape the women who do not surrender (Deuteronomy 20:10-18). The paradoxical nature is seen also in Exodus 22:21 and Deuteronomy 10:19 where the Israelites are commanded to love the stranger by reminding them that they were once "strangers in the land of Egypt."

The French Jewish philosopher, Emmanuel Levinas (1906-1995) argued that all of our metaphysics and mythologies must be given a human face in order to be understood. They must be transformed into an ethical approach to the face of the "Other." Having lived through the Holocaust, Levinas challenged his readers to imagine watching a trainload of Jews traveling off to a death camp. You do not need to begin with some metaphysics to justify a strong reaction to such a situation. What could be more basic than the ethical demand made by that human face staring at you? Thus, our theology, philosophy, political thought, etc., should begin with an ethic of hospitality—how can we make the other feel at home? Conversely, how can we enter into their experiences of need and vulnerability?

In such a situation, one cannot approach the other with indifference, since seeing the face of the other encompasses our concern, interest, and feelings toward the other. Even the soldier torturing the prisoner is not indifferent, although their concern or interest is negatively applied. The face of which Levinas wrote is not simple a physical face. Rather, the face of the other represents a transcendence that is experienced in down-to-earth real-life relations between human beings. In the past, I have used the term incarnation to speak of this, but I now realize that the term is too laden with baggage to adequately express this thought.[553]

For Christians, the argument in the letter of First John is that one can know God only by reaching out to another. The face of God is discovered in the face of the other. Levinas argued this point, writing that it is only by orienting ourselves to the other that we can orient ourselves toward the Good. While he might not argue against the conclusion of First John, he certainly gave Christians no credit for understanding or applying that teaching. In one place, he wrote: "Being Christian, Europe could do nothing to put things right. Neither by what Christians did as Christians, nor by what, in Christianity, should have dissuaded people from performing certain acts."[554] The oppression of the poor, the widow, the orphan, and the stranger is repeatedly prohibited in the Bible, even though throughout history these things are invariably done *in the name of God*! The ethical obligation one has to the stranger arises precisely from the fact that the stranger is the person who has no ties, especially family ties, to me. The stranger has no claim on me except that she/he is human.

Since the Abrahamic faiths are required to deal with God language, it is important that the notion of God as mediator be abandoned. For traditional Christian thought, God is seen as the mediator between the "I" and the other so that one is able to be in relationship with another only because of God. *But the reverse is true.* We begin with human relationships and only then move to God. As the writer of First John implies, behind the face of every person is God.

The rule to do unto others is present not only in human society but is embedded in the evolutionary history of all life. Religious persons seem to feel that this rule is only valid because God commanded it. However, acting ethically is not the result of moral rules given from God. Indeed, the ethical always takes precedence, even over an apparent command of God.

Even following the law of reciprocity is not problem-free. Human actions not only solve problems, they also create new ones. Things often turn out in unexpected ways. Moltmann illustrates this in three areas: (1) Everything that can be used can also be misused. (2) Hopes can be disappointed if they are not fulfilled, but they can also be disappointed through their fulfillment. As the old adage said: "Be careful what you wish for." (3) Every step forward in any sphere of life puts the life-system of the whole out of balance. So when any individual piece of progress is made, the balance has to be restored.[555]

Why be Good?

Empathy is the single moral value that underlies progressive social and political decisions. However, empathy is ineffective without taking responsibility in specific acts of caring and justice. Caring is not simply a feeling, but the courage to act, the courage to reach out to another. In the political arena, "care requires that government have two intertwined roles: protection and empowerment. Protection is more than just the army, police, and fire department. It means social security, disease control, and public health, safe food, disaster relief, health care, consumer and worker protection, environmental protection." Lakoff describes these functions as the moral mission of government, with protection guaranteeing freedom from harm, from want, and from fear; and empowerment is maximizing your goals. American democracy, he writes, "is rooted in empathy, in connecting viscerally with others . . . allowing us to share experience with others and therefore to comprehend a common humanity as the basis of equality."[556]

The tragedy of 9/11 provided a window into the soul of not only the citizens of the United States but also into the soul of the citizens of the world. Initially, a majority of the world mourned and governments sent condolences for the tragedy that had occurred. However, as soon as it occurred, fundamentalists on both sides were quick to claim that it was done in Allah's name or had been decreed by God's will as punishment of a sinful nation. At that point, Muslim and Christian fundamentalists spoke with one voice. In a *Newsweek* article, Jerry Adler quoted Richard Dawkins as saying that after hearing once too often that "to blame the attacks on Islam is like blaming Christianity for the fighting in Northern Ireland," he responded: "*Precisely*. It's time to get angry, and not only with Islam." Adler commented:

> Dawkins and [Sam] Harris are not writing polite demurrals to the time-honored beliefs of billions; they are not issuing pleas for tolerance or moderation, but bone-rattling attacks on what they regard as pernicious and outdated superstition . . . . They ask: where do people get their idea of God? From the Bible or the Qur'an. "Tell a devout Christian . . . that frozen yogurt can make a man invisible," Harris writes, "and he is likely to require as much evidence as anyone else, and to be persuaded only to the extent that you give it. Tell him that the book he keeps by his bed was written by an invisible deity who will punish him with fire for eternity if he fails to accept its every incredible claim about the universe, and he seems to require no evidence whatsoever."[557]

Being kind and generous is not, at its foundation, a "religious" act, although one's beliefs may help promote such acts. As was argued earlier, moral values, including empathy, pity, sympathy, and reciprocity evolved as part of our survival kit. Even when an action is counterproductive to one's own survival, it may be productive in saving others in the group. As part of the evolutionary development, altruism does not need a deity as "the source of all goodness and love." Moreover, pointing to a natural source for goodness and love certainly does *not* mean the end of morality.

Stuart Kauffman argues that there are two major strands of modern Western ethics. One is based on moral law and the other is based on the consequences of our choices. Neither can stand alone. "Even biological evolution shows this. Certain brain lesions change our moral reasoning" from one to the other. This implies that natural selection has "operated to tune human morality."[558] Despite this fact, many continue to insist that without belief in God, all morality would cease and the world would freefall into chaos. Indeed, much of the resistance to evolution as fact is the fear that without God to create the universe and to authorize moral law for its governance, civilization would be untenable.

Sucking Up

Many claim that if there is no God, there is no reason to be good. The Apostle Paul addressed a similar argument in his letter to the Romans where people claimed that if there is no threat of hell or promise of heaven, there would be no reason to be good. We could respond with Paul (loosely translated!): "Do you really mean the only reason you try to be good is to gain God's approval and reward? That's not morality, that's just sucking up" (Romans 6:15). Anyone who says, "If God is dead, nothing matters," is a spoilt child who has never looked at another with compassion.[559]

The Euthyphro Dilemma reappears as we ask why we should be good. Those who say, "If there is no God then there is no reason to be good," are addressing the wrong question. Asking, "Why should we be good?" is like asking, "Why should we be hungry?" or "Why should we fall in love?" The answer, says Shermer, is that being good is as much a part of being human as being hungry, having sex, or falling in love. This sense of doing something good for someone else is an evolved moral sense.

The better question is this: if you were convinced there was no God, would you begin committing robbery, rape, and murder, or would you continue being a moral person? The argument here is that it is a higher level of morality to be good *for its own sake* than because of the rewards that may result from being good. "Humans deserve life, liberty, and happiness, not because God said so but because we are human. Period. These rights and values exist because we say they exist, and that is good enough. They are inalienable because we say they are, and that suffices."[560]

The traditional religious argument is that people will not love their neighbors in this life unless they have something personally to hope for or to fear after they die. However, this conclusion is what Berdyaev called "the most disgusting morality ever conceived." Is a system of rewards and punishments really necessary to induce persons to behave in a socially redeeming manner? The ancient Jews did not think so. Many modern Jews do not think so. Nor do atheists and nontheists. Controlling human behavior by threats and rewards relies on a belief in naked self-interest. In reality, this is nothing less than a *confession of disbelief* in love as the highest principle of life. What do threat or promise have to do with love of neighbor or doing to others what one wishes for oneself? "If we love people we want to help them. How can doing what we want to do require a reward, beyond the satisfaction of having a rational aim and capacity to realize it? Unless being loving is its own reward it is not really loving."[561] Love of others is indirect self-love. "We are members one of another" should be motivation enough.

The notion that God is the all-in-all of our motivation undermines the Golden Rule. Many of us have heard this exclusivist kind of love taught in the church: A good performed that is not based in love for God counts for nothing. I once heard a Sunday School teacher explain to her adult class that all the good done by Gandhi counted for nothing because he was not a Christian.

Buddhists, on the other hand, seem to have a much clearer understanding of the Golden Rule since, for them, personal identity includes, at the least, a partial identity of the other. Buddhists call this the "no soul, no substance" doctrine. This reflects the notion that "we are members one of another," but not just as human beings, but all of creation. When we really think about this, we know they are right. What is the self apart from what others have added to our lives? Indeed, what is the self apart from what other animals and the rest of nature have added to our lives? We are social selves, and apart from all these things, we are nothing. As Hartshorne wrote, "It is our love that makes us anything worth mentioning."[562]

It is "altruism" that explains self-love, not the other way around. "Sympathy, the root of altruism, is the common principle of all love and all senses of identity."[563] An ethic of love can contribute a corrective to a world that seems bent on destroying itself—with major help from religion. It can relieve us of the fears that seek to control and destroy life.

The Golden Rule is a value of equality, but this value "does not mean that we do not for practical reasons have special responsibilities for our own welfare. There are many benefits which no one can give to us unless we give them to ourselves . . . . Those who neglect their own health or other conditions of happiness will end up being a nuisance or worse for others."[564]

The imperative of the Golden Rule grows out of the day-to-day life of the average person. It describes a rather conventional way of acting. However, does the Golden Rule express or surmount simple self-interest?

It would seem that it does not break with the best of the ancient maxims that preceded it, nor from what we have learned from the social and biological sciences. Indeed, social scientists make the strong argument that social relations are by definition relations of reciprocity. It would seem that there is a benefit present—either to the individual or to the larger community. For instance, friendship "is established and maintained by mutual benefaction. Accepting and reciprocating benefits maintains a state of mutual obligation, essential to the social bond between partners in the exchange."[565] We are bound together by mutual benefit. We may initiate a relationship without any sense of fulfilling an existing obligation, but the benefit accrued arises from the challenge to reciprocate. By accepting the favor or benefit, whatever that may be, one enters into a moral obligation to make some returning favor or benefit. In this way, the relationship can be ongoing. Conversely, overt rejection or failure to reciprocate, signals either a breach of the relationship or the continuation of a state of non-relationship.

Thus, "A person who acts flagrantly selfishly even once may be ostracized for months. Conversely, a person who acts altruistically in cooperative ventures may gain huge benefits in the long run."[566] As we saw in our discussion about game theory, altruists can be exploited, but it is equally dangerous to be perceived as selfish.

Much of our helping others is not consciously calculated for maximum gain, but is performed out of our emotions of concern, duty, or guilt. "People make and keep commitments, sometimes even more when there is no real enforcement mechanism. Furthermore, making commitments to do things that are not in your interests can be a powerful strategy of social influences."[567]

The reciprocal act, however, need not be returned to the initial giver. It can become a "pass it on" or "pay it forward" type of response. In this way, the goodness of the initial act is multiplied—increasing the circle, so to speak. The benefit to the initial giver may be the indirect joy of seeing the goodness continue. On the other hand, it may be simply the knowledge that others will receive some benefit, some joy, from my action.

During the 2007 Christmas season, there was an incident at a Starbuck's where a person in the drive-up paid for the coffee for the persons in the car behind. The "miracle" was that each succeeding driver did the same thing—so that up to 100 drivers kept the gift going. The benefit to the initial driver—who could know the extent of his or her gift only indirectly through a news report—was the satisfaction of doing something kind for another person without hope of repayment. The wider benefit, which could not have been anticipated, was the countless times this "random act of kindness" was repeated in other places.

Like all maxims, context is still essential. The general rule is a starting point that stimulates the kind of interaction necessary to bring into existence the kind of social relations that contribute to survivability.

Summary

We can neither look up nor look back to know how to act. The rule of reciprocity is a transcending concept that is based on the survival mechanism of self-interest and self-fulfillment. Ethical responsibility precedes being itself. A biological base for this can be seen in that care for the young—the most intimate other—is essential for survival. In this sense, ethical obligation precedes the moment of conscious choice. Morality and ethics have evolved over time based on the biological needs of individual entities and their concerns for survival. The values that we consider ethical and moral grow out of the coping and survival needs of human beings. These become accepted for the wider group as they pass the time-testing experiences of life. What may have started as the need for survival and the reproduction of individual cells, became the need to protect one's young. It evolved as the social groupings enlarged. As individuals began to band together, there arose a need for rules of living and dealing with others. These rules were relatively simple since everyone in the group or tribe knew one another. Initially these rules were mostly instinctive. This worked well when everybody in the social unit knew everybody else.

However, about 35,000 years ago, communities were being created, and with this new development, sets of ethical principles were required. One now had to learn to deal with strangers. These principles of right and wrong transcended the individual, and morality was now tied to the larger group. Although morality clearly exists outside of religion, religion was one of the institutions that were developed to enforce these principles and the rules and laws that they engendered.

CHAPTER 13

Playing God

> *"It is not the answers of science that provide transcendence, but the quest for those answers."*
>
> —*Michael Shermer*

Today we are confronted with new and far-reaching research and experimentation in genetics such as gene therapy, cloning, transgenetics, stem-cell research, prenatal screening, artificial insemination, and so on. Some oppose this research because this is playing God; that is, it is doing something that is the sole right and responsibility of God, the Gods, or God's earthly representative. The reality is that whenever we hold people responsible for their actions, we are already "playing God." However, what if God as traditionally understood is removed from the equation?

There is little chance of that happening any time soon. The positions of the Roman Catholic Church have taken a strong hold on American sexual and reproductive issues. Indeed, much of Protestant Christianity has adopted the Catholic position in large part over the past five decades. Richard Doerflinger, head of Pro-Life Activities for the U.S. Conference of Bishops recently defended this. "We are not imposing a Catholic vision on America. We are offering a more human vision."[568] That "more human" vision includes papal restrictions against embryonic stem-cell research as abortion, as well as in vitro fertilization (IVF), birth control, and AIDS-prevention methods.

Dignitas Personae

The new updates are in *Dignitas Personae: On Certain Bioethical Issues*, released by the Vatican in December 2008. The document states: "The desire for a child cannot justify the 'production' of offspring, just as the desire not to have a child cannot justify the abandonment or destruction of a child once he or she has been conceived." IVF is ethically unacceptable to the Church because it "*dissociates procreation from the integrally personal context of the conjugal act*: human procreation is a personal act of a husband and wife, which is not capable of substitution."[569] In other words, human procreation can only morally take place by the physical male penile penetration of the female vagina. (One can only assume that this act is to be performed in the "missionary position" in order to assure the domination of the husband!) Naturally, procreation sought outside of this relationship is considered an act against nature and therefore a sin. It is, therefore, "*ethically unacceptable to dissociate procreation from the integrally personal context of the conjugal act.*"[570] On this basis, the Catholic Church does not allow the treatment of infertility by means of artificial fertilization. Intracyto-plasmic sperm injection (ICSI) is rejected on the same basis. Cryopreservation of embryos (freezing them at extremely low temperatures so that they might be used later) is rejected because it is an affront to the dignity and humanity of the embryo that is considered by *Dignitas* as a human person—undifferentiated from a fetus, infant, child, youth, or mature adult. "Cryopreservation is *incompatible with the respect owed to human embryos*; it presupposes their production *in vitro*; it exposes them to serious risk of death or physical harm . . . ; it deprives them at least temporarily of maternal reception and gestation; [and] it places them in a situation in which they are susceptible to further offense and manipulation."[571]

Using embryos for research and for the treatment of disease in unacceptable to the church because this treats the embryo as mere "biological material" and results in her/his destruction. In the same way, preimplantation diagnosis (testing before being transferred into the woman's womb) for the purpose of ensuring that only embryos free from defects are chosen, is nothing more than selective abortion. Further, "such an attitude is shameful and utterly reprehensible, since it presumes to measure the value of a human life only within the parameters of 'normality' and physical well-being, thus opening the way to legitimizing infanticide and euthanasia as well."[572]

Interceptive methods such as the IUD and the "morning after" pill (and all other artificial forms of birth control) are techniques of abortion and are therefore immoral and unethical. In November 2010, Pope Benedict urged bishops around the world to make the first Advent service a vigil for "nascent human life." He declared, "Science itself has shown how autonomous the embryo is, how it interacts with the mother and develops in a coordinated and complex way." He went on to firmly state, "It's not an accumulation of biological matter, but a new living being, dynamic and marvelously ordered, a new individual of the human species."[573]

Genetic Engineering

In a *Newsweek* column, George Will echoed *Dignitas* by warning that genetic engineering will result in nothing less than "the abolition of humanity." Genetic engineering, he argued, can be seen as the human attempt to affect evolution since, theologically speaking, the beginning of creation is the creation of conditions for the *potentialities* of history. "Naturally produced" possibilities are both constructive and destructive. Human engineering is no different. As *Dignitas* affirmed: Genetic engineering is "the attempt to create *a new type of human being*," and therefore recognized as "an *ideological element* in which man tries to take the place of his Creator." It is also viewed as "*an unjust domination of man over man.*" (The church's use of male terminology here is significantly revealing.)

In the same way, *Dignitas* also argues that "human cloning is intrinsically illicit in that, by taking the ethical negativity of techniques of artificial fertilization to their extreme, it seeks to *give rise to a new human being without a connection to the act of reciprocal self-giving between the spouses*, and more radically, *without any link to sexuality*." Human cloning for reproduction "imposes on the resulting individual a predetermined genetic identity, subjecting him . . . to a form of *biological slavery*, from which it would be difficult to free himself."[574]

Dignitas argues that if a zygote is "naturally aborted" in the womb, or if a child is born with three heads, God planned it that way and we do not have the right to change or alter that divine plan in any way.

> The originality of every person is a consequence of the particular relationship that exists between God and a human

> being from the first moment of his existence and carries with it the obligation to respect the singularity and integrity of each person, even on the biological and *genetic* levels. In the encounter with another person [the zygote], we meet a human being who owes his existence and his proper characteristics to the love of God, and only the love of husband and wife constitute a mediation of that love in conformity with the plan of the Creator and heavenly Father.[575]

Of course, we should treat the zygote, embryo, and fetus with dignity and respect, but not because they are considered persons in the sense of viability. Nor does it mean that we value it in the same way as a child at birth or a mature adult. However, *Dignitas* warns, researchers who experiment with or interfere with the development of that zygote or embryo cooperate in "evil and scandal."

Cloning

Nick Bostrom, philosophy professor at Oxford University, asks us to imagine that we are one of the human clones that will be born at some point in the future. Imagine also those people who opposed your birth and who even now consider your very existence a crime against humanity and an affront to God. Historically, he writes, many of the great medical breakthroughs that we now accept as blessings were in their own time condemned for one reason or another.

> Such was the case with anesthesia during surgery and childbirth. People argued that it was unnatural and that it would weaken our moral fiber. Such was also the case with heart transplantations. And such was the case with in vitro fertilization. These "test tube babies" would be dehumanized and would suffer grave psychological harm. Today, of course, anesthesia is taken for granted; heart transplantation is seen as one of medicine's glories; and the public approval rate of IVF is up from 15% in the early seventies to over 70% today.

These historical examples should indicate to us how "immediate emotional reactions to medical developments are an unreliable indicator of their morality. We are prone to prejudice and to narrow-minded underestimation of the long-term benefits of technological development.[576] It is understood that we ought to perfect the methods of cloning before trying it on humans. Nevertheless, looking at the issue from a future perspective gives us a different slant on the matter. It also reminds us of the importance of seeing the cloned person as a unique human being worthy of full human dignity.

Looking beyond the emotions of the moment, we might see that cloning will not significantly change the world. "Some people will owe their lives to this technology, and some infertile couples will be grateful for having had the chance to raise a child of their own." Moreover, we will realize that science does not stand still, and our technology will continue to advance at a rapid pace, with some future developments overshadowing the issues of cloning and genetic engineering. Indeed, it is not too much to believe that one day "we will have the option of extending our intellectual, physical, emotional, and spiritual capacities beyond the levels that are possible today. This will be the end of humanity's childhood, and the beginning of what one might call a 'transhuman' era."[577]

The misuse of cloning by a very small minority is an obvious risk we will have to take. In the *New Republic*, University of Chicago bioethicist Leon Kass wrote that "it is not at all clear to what extent a clone will truly be a moral agent," since its autonomy would be subverted by "the very fact of cloning, and of rearing him as a clone."[578] Indeed, *Dignitas Personae* indicates that the clone is "a new type of human being," and as such will certainly be viewed as different, and not seen as fully human. The fact is that the clone would be raised as a carbon copy of the donor, or at worst, raised as not fully human. Raising a child in the image of another is nothing new since many parents, usually unconsciously, treat their "natural born" offspring as younger versions of themselves or even at times as a replacement for a deceased sibling. However, the cloned child would have different formative experiences. Even more compelling, writes Cathy Young, the cloned child would not even be an exact physiological replica. "The donor egg into which the genetic material is inserted still contains its own mitochondrial DNA in its outer membrane; this material will affect the development of the embryo, as will the womb environment.

Even identical twins, who do share the same genetic makeup and the same womb, can have very different traits and personalities."[579]

At present, the real ethical issue is the resulting congenital abnormalities that result at a very high rate in such processes. But for now, "mammalian genetic engineering" is only in its infant stage. "Although the human genome has been mapped, scientists are very far from exact knowledge of which genes affect which traits, under what circumstances, and in what combination."[580]

Nevertheless, some will ask what happens to our notions of self-determination if the human person is simply reduced to biological material. "What happens to the belief in individual freedom if individuality can be reduced to a software program written by other people"—an engineer of "human souls?" Does it make a difference whether these characteristics are produced by chance, i.e., unaided sexual intercourse, or by human design?[581]

It seems that for many ethicists and philosophers, the major issue is not the process of genetic engineering in and of itself, but how this technology will be utilized. If one begins with the presupposition that all the "bad" things we envision will most certainly take place—that if something can happen, it will—then none of the past accomplishments of science and health care could have occurred. For instance, would we be better off if Willis, Bole, or Pasteur had been prohibited from their inquiry, experimentation, and actions? All of these were opposed in their own day on moral, ethical, and religious grounds. Although it rarely occurs, one could just as well begin with the presupposition that all the "good" things we envision will take place—and more—without, of course, discounting the warnings and cautions of the negatives that are also possible.

There are those who oppose genetic engineering on religious grounds, arguing that it puts scientists in the position of God. Many theologian/ethicists have argued that genetic engineering is like building the Tower of Babel—we are trying to be our own creators and in the process to be our own God(s). This type of an argument usually comes from those who want to argue that God is an omnipotent God who is in control of literally everything. But if this is true, does such a God really need protection from human usurping of divine prerogatives? Fundamentalists such as Pat Robertson certainly think that God needs *their* help. That is a true oxymoron for a traditional doctrine of God! (Of course, fundamentalists—like the rest of us—are highly selective in their orthodoxy!)

As scientists understand more about our genetic makeup, they are exploring "genetic determinism"—the possible links between genes and behavior. This raises serious questions for theologians and ethicists. If behavior is to some degree determined by genes, to what extent do humans have responsibility or the possibility to control this genetic influence? If the influence is strong, then what becomes of free will? And, how can one be held accountable if genetic determinism is compellingly strong? If a predisposition is genetically compelling, then how can it be wrong, or how can it be sin—since it is certainly "God-given?" Would there be a difference in the way we address, say, a gene for violence, a gene for homosexuality, or a gene for a devastating disease? Will we at some point in the future screen everyone at birth—or at an early stage of pregnancy—in order to somehow prenatally treat or terminate these "difficult pregnancies?" It is hard to avoid the obvious conclusion that genetic engineering is challenging our ideas about what it means to be human—and challenging them in often disturbing ways.

Francis Crick, a co-discoverer of DNA, boldly challenged religious people and their concept of the soul when he wrote: "You, your joys and your sorrows, your memories and your ambitions, your sense of personal identity and free will, are in fact no more than the behavior of a vast assembly of nerve cells and their associated molecules."[582] While such reductionism is certainly shocking to religious sensitivity, it need not be the final word. The whole is more than the sum of its parts. Human beings are more than a collection of cells, nerves, etc. While the conclusions of science cannot finally dictate how life is to be lived, religious persons ignore the implications of scientific discoveries at their own peril. The result is that their theology is weaker and their message will become increasingly irrelevant to a world that will eventually move away from it.

D. Gareth Jones writes, "A scientific study of the nervous system by itself will not tell us all we want to know about people and their functioning." Yet, "when confronted by a barely functioning brain on account of immaturity at the beginning of life or degeneration at the end of life, neural activity cannot be ignored. The lack of any functioning of the central nervous system, no matter what state one's body may be in, must have implications for our assessment of the meaningfulness of that human life." It is erroneous, he continues, "to regard ourselves as *composed of* a brain, plus various other organs, and an immaterial something that constitutes the real me (mind or soul). On the contrary, our brains represent us. They make us what we are only in the sense that we make them what they are. Far from being a machine-based model, this is a person-model."[583]

Embryonic Stem Cells

The religious and political efforts to restrict embryonic stem-cell research are based on the argument that "if a cell begins to divide, even if only six or eight cells, that a 'soul' of a person is already implanted, and that any effort to experiment with this is 'immoral.' The postulation of a soul to prohibit scientific inquiry is reminiscent of the suppression of Galileo and the teachings of Darwin."[584] The fallacy of "the little person inside," or the "ghost in the machine," has led to a lot of confusion. The religious debate about the morality of any research on any potential human life form deals with the timing of "ensoulment."

Many conservative religious teachers, both Catholic and Protestant, argue that the soul pops out of a starting gate at the moment the sperm enters the egg. Building on this argument, the controversy currently taking place concludes that a single cell has achieved *legal personhood*. Pope Benedict XVI declared that "embryos developed for in vitro fertilization deserve the same right to life as fetuses, children, and adults—and that that right extends to embryos even before they are transferred into a woman's womb." While in the past the Vatican had held that human life begins at conception, Benedict's comments were significant because he specified that even an embryo in its earliest stages is just as much a human life as an older being. *Dignitas* states, "although the presence of the spiritual soul cannot be observed experimentally, the conclusions of science regarding the human embryo give 'a valuable indication for discerning by the use of reason a personal presence at the moment of the first appearance of a human life' . . . ." That first moment of life is "the moment the zygote has formed," and the zygote demands the same "unconditional respect" as a mature adult.[585]

While that may seem ludicrous to many, "it's only another small leap to claiming that any interference with such a one-cell stage of a fertilized human egg is manslaughter or murder"[586]—a conclusion already reached by many "pro-life" groups. From a reasoning point of view, one must take into account the fact that God seems rather careless with early embryos.

Many embryos are naturally and spontaneously aborted in the first several months. God is undoubtedly careless with the embryos that the Pope and other religious leaders now declare to be human persons in the fullest sense. While affirming that these fertilized eggs should be handled with respect, reason demands that a fertilized egg and its genome *do not* constitute a person.

Charles Hartshorne wrote: "It is not a mere opinion that *there are enormous (I am using words carefully) differences between a fetus and an adult human being, differences that are similar to those by which we judge ourselves to be more valuable than even the apes.*" He was adamant: "Of course the fetus is alive! So are puppies and kittens [and dust mites!]. Of course it is human . . . if 'human' here means that its origin is in the union, in a human womb, of a human sperm and a human egg cell." The real question, he argued, concerns not the fetus, "but the value of the actual stage. Not everything that can be is, and the 'equal value of the actual and the possible' is not an axiom that anybody lives by or could live by."[587] This can be illustrated by the fact that in most places it is considered a more serious crime to kill an adult than to kill a child. "Would it not be well," wrote Hartshorne, "if some of the rhetorical tears shed over the dying of fetuses were saved for the tragic sufferings, in many cases the deep misery, of women, many of them very young, who against their intentions and wishes, have become pregnant?"[588]

Ethical judgments should be arrived at without intentionally misstating facts in order to satisfy one's religious beliefs. Nor should they be arrived at through ambiguous arguments. Twenty years ago, Hartshorne argued that "pro-life" literature is "mostly a string of verbally implied identifications of fertilized egg cell with fetus, or fetus with infant, infant with child, child with youth, youth with adult." Any cause is suspect, he wrote, which ignores or denies "distinctions so great as that between even a child and an animal form (say a three—or four-month-old fetus) in actual functioning far below the higher mammalian level, or which collapses the contrast between 'actually valuable' and 'potentially valuable' as though 'capable of becoming such and such' were no different from 'actually being such and such.'" The journey, he stated, "from less than nothing of rational personhood to the fullness of personhood . . . is the progressive *creation* of value, with no fixed value there from the start."[589]

For centuries, Christianity has *wrongly* argued that a person is simply one reality from conception through death (and beyond). However, we have known for decades that this "one" reality changes and has different qualities over time. With each change in the process of development, there is a new concrete reality.

The current resistance to embryonic stem cell research is based on an unstated assumption. We tend to believe that a thing either is or is not a human being. This either/or perception of life, writes Lee Silver, professor of molecular biology at Princeton University, arises from a literal interpretation of the Bible, especially Genesis 1:27, "God created man in His own image." A literal interpretation of this can lead one to believe that God created humans instantaneously. For this line of thought, "there can be no such thing as gradual creation, because then you have partial man, and man would not be in the image of God. There is no such thing as a partial God. God is absolute."[590]

The current stem cell debate is given high priority among those who believe that a zygote is a human being. Of course, those who believe this are ignorant of the fact that "stem cells are part of every living thing. They can develop into any type of cell and make up the earliest form of a living thing."[591] Alan Padgett, professor of systematic theology at Luther Seminary in St. Paul, Minnesota, writes that while the term "persons" is notoriously difficult to define, "we also need some sense of what a human is. At the end of life, there is general agreement that a human person needs, among many other things, some brain activity. When brain activity ends, the human's life is over. Applying this to the start of life, some brain or neural activity would seem to be necessary for an embryo to be a person."[592] In a letter to the editor of *Science & Theology News*, Padgett writes:

> I use the criterion of having some brain activity because it is what we use in medical ethics at the end of a person's life. I do not at all mean mental powers or intelligence, but any brain activity at all. This criterion is absolute—either there is some or there is none. The degree of brain activity is irrelevant; we are not talking about mental abilities or consciousness. Finally, we can prove quite simply that the proto-embryo does not pass this test.[593]

The fourth and fifth centuries held a widely divergent variety of thoughts about when life begins. The arguments, then as now, centered around the soul. Some theologians argued that human life began at conception, while others, following Aristotle, held that the spiritual soul was "infused" at forty days or so, while still others held that the timing of the infusion of the soul was a mystery known to God alone. In the seventh century, "Penitentials" there was a graded level of penance for abortion according to whether the fetus was formed or unformed. In the same way, canon law in the Roman Catholic Church during that time imposed excommunication only for the abortion of a fetus that had developed a human form. Thomas Aquinas, the most authoritative theologian during the Middle Ages, explicitly argued "that the human embryo did not possess a spiritual soul and was not a human being (*homo*) until forty days in the case of males or ninety in the case of females."[594] By the middle of the nineteenth century, most of Western Christianity agreed that the human embryo possessed only a relative value, depending on the level of its in utero development. Even though the embryo was not yet fully human, it was held that the human embryo should never be attacked deliberately. Thus, while the church did not teach that the early embryo was a person in the fullest sense, it did teach that the embryo should always be treated with respect.

> From the seventeenth century, the classical biology of Galen and Aristotle had begun to be displaced by a variety of other theories. One, in particular, gave a more equal role to the female and male elements in generation, and therefore increased the significance of "fertilization," that is, the moment of the union of male and female gametes. This theory was finally confirmed in 1827 with the first observation of a mammalian ovum under the microscope, a scientific development which informed the decision of Pius IX in 1869 to abolish the distinction in legal penalties between early and late abortions. By the mid-nineteenth century the prevailing opinion, among both Reformed and Roman Catholic Christians, was that, most probably, the spiritual soul was infused at conception.[595]

The proper moral question, Padgett argues, is not "When does life begin?" but rather, "When does an embryo become a human person?" And while the status of the fetus does seem to be in question, the same is not true for the zygote and the "proto-embryo" of the first two weeks after conception. He argues:

> I can find absolutely no reason to believe that this small collection of identical cells—the stem cells—is a person, or has any neural activity. It does not even have a brain cell yet. [Robert] Song's idea that it could be a "person with potential" turns on the assumption that a zygote could be a person. I find this assumption impossible to accept . . . . A zygote is not a person. Personhood, therefore, does not begin at conception. The zygote deserves our respect, as the seed of a human body, but this does not mean that research on zygotes is automatically immoral.[596]

The argument that a cell *could be* a "person with potential," while true, is at the same time ludicrous. Again, for religious persons to use this argument makes God the worst of all abusers, or, using the line of thinking of anti-abortion protesters, God is a serial killer of the worst kind. Embryonic stem cells have the *potential* to develop into an actual person. "Yet based on the molecular signals that you give the cells, the cells can change from embryonic to nonembryonic and back to embryonic." So then, it is like asking the "How-many-angels-can-dance-on-the-head-of-a-pin" type of question. "How many human beings are there in a dish of embryonic stem cells?" Suppose that there are a million cells in the dish. If you "separate all the cells, then you have a million human beings. But you can then put them back together to form a single organism. What happened to the 999,999 human beings? Robert George would say they all died. Scientists would say that this is not a scientific question, but a theological question.[597]

I would hope that theology would answer that this is not a question for them either since the organism is a life form but only as *human-in-potentiality*. One must address the issue of viability of personhood, *not* potentiality for life. To declare that potential for human life is the same thing as human life itself is absurd. Carried to its logical point, the argument for granting human rights for *potential* life forms causes us to identify God as violating "His" own moral code. When a woman gives birth, why doesn't the church demand that the placenta be given a proper funeral (since it contains living cells and *potential* human beings) rather than approving that it simply be thrown in the garbage? Again, we might ask: Why does God allow the "seed" of men and women to be wasted in sexual relations?

When an argument is taken to the extreme, as *Dignitas* does, the answer also borders on the extreme.

The political and legal issues surrounding what constitutes personhood affect not only abortion but also determining end of life issues. The Terry Shivo case in 2005 demonstrated the extent to which uninformed politicians will go to push a conservative religious agenda at the expense of medical and scientific judgments. Kenneth Hendrickson writes:

> Because a rigid definition of person could endanger access to abortion, the courts are moving toward a logical but frightening resolution: revisiting the unvarying interest of the state to protect life. Most Americans have no problem with early-term abortions, when fetal life displays no apparent personhood. But the issue is no longer early-term abortion. In reviewing euthanasia laws, U.S. District Court judges have for years invoked abortion law to justify variable degrees of state interest in preserving adult lives. Writing for the majority of the Ninth Circuit Court of Appeals in 1996, Judge Stephen Reinhardt argued that the state's interest in equal protection varied with relevant circumstances. Reinhardt cited *Roe v. Wade*. The case had, he said, enshrined the doctrine of variable state interest. Just as opinions about the value of a fetus could differ relative to the development of the fetus, so opinions about the worth of an adult could differ relative to the health, mental state, or even self-opinion of the adult.[598]

In September 2007, the Vatican stated that administering food and water to a patient in a vegetative state is a moral obligation. It further reiterated that removal of feeding tubes from persons in a vegetative state is an immoral act since it is taking the life of the person. Many popular authors support this conservative religious agenda. In his book, *Denial of the Soul: Scriptural and Medical Perspectives on Euthanasia and Mortality*, M. Scott Peck wrote that while secularism is an understandable phenomenon and not particularly alarming until it comes to the issue of euthanasia. Why? Because it reveals secularism's "denial of the soul." This, he says, bodes ill for our future, since those who have a secular outlook on life and the world are self-centered while the religious person knows that God is the center of the universe. This Godview leads Peck to conclude that since we have been created or designed with a purpose, we do not "own" ourselves but are rather the "property of God." Thus, in terminating one's life through euthanasia, one denies God and "God's timing and right to my life."[599]

Genetic Patenting

Science and religion have their distinctive conceptual and methodological approaches, and this presents barriers to conversation and mutual understanding. "Science and religion have very different mandates and approaches to the world. It may sometimes seem that practitioners of the two fields are speaking different languages even when using the same words."[600] One of the problems has been that religious leaders commenting on scientific issues have not paid close enough attention to the subjects on which they comment and pass judgment, making them seem to the scientific community as intellectually irrelevant.

In 1989, the World Council of Churches published *Biotechnology: Its Challenges to the Churches and the Word* that explicitly opposed the patenting of life forms: "The patenting of life encodes into law a reductionist conception of life which seeks to remove any distinction between living and non-living things . . . . This mechanistic view directly contradicts the sacramental, interrelated view of life intrinsic to a theology of the integrity of creation."[601] However, biotechnology does not deny that all of life is intrinsically related. Indeed, it demonstrates just the opposite. As Chapman observes: "As with many other scientifically based issues, only a small number of persons within various church agencies and theological institutions have paid attention to relevant developments or followed debates among secular experts . . . . When issued, these [religious] statements have lacked specific references to then current subjects."[602]

In the 1980 landmark decision of Diamond v. Chakrabarty, the Supreme Court ruled in a 5-4 decision that "genetically modified living organisms were patentable as a new and useful manufacture or composition of matter." Prior to this decision, "life forms were considered to be 'products of nature' and ineligible for patent protection."[603]

One basic argument against genetic patenting was that it "represents the usurpation of the ownership rights of the sovereign Creator." Southern Baptist theologian Ben Mitchell made "a careful distinction between the role of God, 'the true Inventor of every living creature,' and the contribution of the scientist, who at best reorganizes or manipulates some of the genes. According to Mitchell . . . patenting biological materials as the stuff of human artifice risks obscuring the revelation of God in the created order." On the other hand, science understands that "respect, even recognition of intrinsic worth, does not necessarily make something sacred, not even a little bit sacred."[604]

Sociologist John Evans puts this debate into context by speaking about *frames*, which is a "schemata of interpretation" that allows people to "locate, perceive, identify, and label" occurrences in the world. The insight here is that we cannot simply absorb all that occurs in our daily experience, and so we categorize them to help us in analysis. This helps us avoid reinventing the wheel at every moment. So, for instance,

> When people hear of a new issue that they do not understand, they try to put it back into a schemata of interpretation, or frame, in order to understand it. This is one reason why the abortion debate seems to seep into other issues. As the most readily available frame for understanding the political aspects of reproduction, new reproductive technology questions often are considered using the frame of the abortion debate, with its pre-packaged cognitive categories (conflict of rights between different forms of life) that may or may not be the best way to consider the new issue. The debate then focuses on the parts of the phenomena that have categories (e.g., conflicts over rights) while ignoring other parts.

He also points to the issue of smoking. "The issue frame determines who legitimately makes the decisions. If nicotine is a drug, cigarettes become a policy issue decided by legislatures, the courts, and executive branch agencies. If it is a lifestyle choice, the decisions remain with individuals."[605]

Just as issues are framed, so are the types of arguments that we make. Argumentative frames "are the assumptions or preconceived cognitive categories that highlight what part of a phenomenon is important. These include assumptions about the grounds for evaluating arguments as legitimate or illegitimate." As a general orientation, "claims in the ethical frame are micro, while claims in the prophetic frame are macro in nature.

While the ethical frame seeks to prescribe what one is supposed to do in particular circumstances, in the prophetic frame the claimant is concerned with exposing the roots of what is perceived to be fundamentally and systematically right or wrong."[606] Ethical arguments focus on immediate concrete acts while future questions are put off until they become immediate. Prophetic analysis seeks to deal with future issues in the present.

> The ethical frame uses the application of principles to cases and the sharpening of distinctions between cases. Arguments using the prophetic frame often question the very principles that are used in ethical discourse. Subjective claims such as emotion and perception are bracketed as either unimportant or unusable in the ethical frame. The prophet, on the other hand, often considers emotional response to be signs of wisdom.[607]

The claim that changing the human genome is playing God is a prophetic claim. To the scientific mind, this argument about playing God is senseless since scientists have "played God" for as long as persons have asked, "What if?" In fact, "the whole development of medicine . . . is in fact playing God, keeping people alive . . . who otherwise would have died."[608] However, most people have moved beyond referring to medicine as "playing God."

There are four basic arguments against granting patents on human genes: (1) ownership of human genes infringes on human dignity because it is equivalent to ownership of humans; (2) because it commercializes body parts which should not be commodified; (3) because it cheapens that which defines human identity; and (4) because it would lead to inappropriate modifications in our genetic integrity.[609]

In point one, we see that for some, ownership of a single human gene is the equivalent of ownership of an entire human body. Religious leaders say they reject reductionist arguments, and yet this argument is clearly reductionist, just as the papal argument that a single cell is a person is reductionist. Dan Eramian, responded to this: "I must confess I never quite understood the basis for their argument that 'no one should own life' since I know no one who does claim to 'own life' . . . . Some of the religious members of our group felt that our technology was perhaps developing so fast that there was no time to assess the moral and ethical questions that day-to-day discoveries were generating."[610]

The second argument is based on the assumption "that the ownership and sale of human genes through a patent system, like the ownership and sale of certain body parts (e.g., organs for transplantation) or certain physical services (e.g., surrogate motherhood) is an inappropriate commodification (being treated as a commercial commodity) which weakens human dignity."[611] This argument was also used against paying for blood transfusions and kidney transplants. However, "since the material from which the genes are isolated usually is abandoned tissue or fluids, there is no giving up because of poverty of something useful, no exploitation, and no resulting impairment of dignity, at least as long as the donor knows that the material which would otherwise be discarded will be used for scientific/commercial purposes."[612] Indeed, the donation of the material for genetic research should be seen as a caring and sharing act.

The third argument can be formalized as follows: "(1) it is wrong to commodify that which defines human identify because doing so impairs human dignity; (2) human genes define human identity; (3) patenting human genes involves patenting that which defines human identity; (4) therefore, patenting human genes is wrong because it commodifies that which defines human identity." This argument is "connected with the individuation of persons for the sake of assigning rights and responsibilities, rather than the notion of identity connected with individual and/or social conceptions of self,"[613] again something that traditional religious thought argues against.

The fourth argument that it leads to "inappropriate modifications seems to grow out of the negative history of the eugenics movement in which the leaders of that movement sought to "improve" human beings. Their efforts did in fact lead to a failure to respect the dignity of many who were perceived as "flawed" human beings. While this is a concern that deserves attention, the more important concern is to make certain that safeguards are in place to prevent it.

Theologian Ted Peters summarizes the issue by arguing that "patenting knowledge of human genes is not likely to violate human dignity when we define dignity as treating each individual human person as having intrinsic worth." As we have argued, the human person is much more than DNA. "What applies to gene sequences is not necessarily the same as what applies to a human being as a whole."[614]

Summary

The idea of "playing God" in genetic engineering and embryonic research is principally a problem for the Christian West since in the East, especially in Buddhism and Taoism, there is no God with a master plan. Thus, the idea of playing God for them is meaningless. The notion of playing God makes sense only in the context of the traditional monotheism of the Abrahamic faiths.

The argument made in this chapter surrounds the fundamental issue of viability. Viability is the definition of personhood. The question of the soul is a non-issue for many since there is no proof that one exists. Viability includes the presence of brain activity; without it, there is no identity or personhood. The notion that humans cannot make life-and-death decisions—that we are the subservient property of God, and therefore God alone has the right to make such decisions—is based on a faulty premise.

When we address the issue of abortion, we might take a clue from Carl Sagan and Ann Druyan. In their popular article, "Is It Possible to be Pro-Life and Pro-Choice?" they argued that the facts "concerning the evolving characteristics of a human fetus" should be weighed "to judge the point before which abortion could not reasonably considered murder and beyond which it could."[615]

The fundamental issue of human viability must be addressed in terms of scientific inquiry and ethical standards untethered from the strictures of religion. Religion can help to ask the questions and to suggest solutions, but religion is only one source among many—and no one source is absolute.

CHAPTER 14

Is the Church Really Necessary?

"Control is, by its nature, a feature of doctrine, because as soon as you declare what's true you declare what's false."

—Trevor Greenfield

"Ignorance is the mother of devotion."

—Roger Williams, Puritan minister

At one point in Chaim Potok's novel *The Promise*, Abraham Gordon, a skeptical Jewish scholar, muses on a typical modern discontent while talking with Reuven Malter, an Orthodox rabbinical student: "Of course, that's the problem . . . . How can we teach others to regard the tradition critically and with love? I grew up loving it, and then learned to look at it critically. That's everyone's problem today. How to love and respect what you are being taught to dissect."[616]

That has been my struggle with the church. I have had a love/hate relationship with the church for nearly all of my adult life. On the one hand, I have appreciated the great potential it has for good; while on the other hand, I have seen its small-mindedness, political maneuvers for power, advantage, and retribution, and its destructiveness to the human psyche. I have seen the lives of persons changed for the good—alcoholics, addicts, and others have found new direction for their lives and the ability to control their dependencies. Faith can inspire persons to noble acts. It can make persons more effective in their daily lives and give them strength to bravely confront temptations, despair, misfortunes, and death. The Church can provide strong social bonds that permit persons to achieve together what they could not achieve separately.

At its best, the Church has encouraged the creation of beautiful art and music, inspiring stories and comforting ceremonies. Since the church is more than hierarchies and structures, we should also note that the daily actions of religious people have accomplished innumerable good deeds, and they have tried to change the world by alleviating suffering, hunger, illness, and poverty. There is also the comfort of belonging and companionship that helps persons know that someone who cares is walking beside them.

At its worst, I have also seen church-sponsored and church-supported bias and prejudice poison the social environment with fear and hate. The church has a history of violence against those who do not believe in the right way, a violence that includes heresy trials, torture, witch-hunts, pogroms, crusades, inquisitions, and holy wars. It has fought against the civil rights of various groups and has stirred up hatred in the name of God. It has used its power and influence to encourage persons to accept inferior status to a God who will punish them like a Mafia boss if they do not do what the God-appointed authorities say. It has, and in many places continues to, assign women to a second-class status and to advocate the principles of Social Darwinism (not to be confused with Darwin's biological evolution). It has raised enormous amounts of money to build and maintain "cathedrals"—money often received from those who could afford it the least.

Thus, religious institutions have provided structures that are noble and positive as well as structures that are despicable and destructive. Therefore, we must ask: How can the church be an agent of transformation if it is not itself transformed? If the church is to be a positive force in the world, it must provide a model of social healing that holds humanity responsible for both the continuing existence of injustice and the creation of justice. Is that possible? Only time—perhaps centuries—will tell. Change does not come quickly or easily to institutions—whether religious, political, or otherwise—especially when they understand themselves to be ordained by God. The church is largely a tradition-bound reactionary force rather than a humanity-focused leader.

It is not the community of faith, the people, that receives my deepest criticism, but the hierarchies and local authorities who misuse their trust and put blinders on the eyes of their members so that they will not ask deep, penetrating questions. In order for the church to be a force for good, it must be released from the shackles of idolatry to ignorance and the past. The same is true of other religions.

In the opening pages of *Breaking the Spell*, Daniel Dennett compares this sort of task to being at a concert where you are really caught up in the moment. You are awestruck and breathless as the music of your favorite artist carries you away to another place. Then somebody's cell phone starts ringing! Breaking the spell. Hateful, vile, inexcusable. This inconsiderate jerk has ruined the concert for you, stolen a precious moment that can never be recovered.[617] The spell of unreflective believers must be broken.

A survey reported by AP writer Rachel Zoll indicates that fifteen percent of Americans claim to have no religious affiliation. In 2001, the figure was 14.2% and a mere 8.2% in 1990, according to the American Religious Identification Survey (ARIS). The number of persons claiming no religion rose in every state, and in the state of Vermont, the figure was 34%. The margin of error in the survey of nearly fifty-five thousand adults has a margin of error of 0.5 percentage points.

In a 2008 study by Trinity College, formal religious observance was sharply down in the United States. Surveying more than fifty-four thousand adults, it was found that those calling themselves Christian had fallen by ten percent since 1990. It fell from 86.2% down to 76%. In addition, the percentage of those who claim no religious affiliation had almost doubled, from 8.5% to 15%. While there are slight differences between these two surveys, their similarity is striking. So many Americans claimed no religion at all that this category now outranks every other major religious group in the US except Catholic and Baptist. In a nation that has long been mostly Christian, a 2008 ARIS survey reported, "the challenge to Christianity . . . does not come from other religions but from a rejection of all forms of organized religion."

The ARIS survey found that traditional organized religion continues to play less and less a role in many lives. "Thirty percent of married couples did not have a religious wedding ceremony and 27 percent of respondents said they did not want a religious funeral." Further, about 12% "believe in a higher power but not the personal God at the core of monotheistic faiths."[618] These persons are the new deists.

Hans Christian Anderson's fable, "The Emperor's New Clothes," is a good example of what is happening today. For most, the falsehoods and myths that are "common wisdom" survive simply because exposing them for what they are is taboo. "An indefensible mutual presumption can be kept aloft for years or even centuries because each person assumes that somebody else has some very good reasons for maintaining it, and nobody dares to challenge it."[619]

What this recent ARIS survey tells us is that for an increasing number of persons, religion has become a personal way of life that can be lived outside of the ecclesiastical structures. For many others who are still in the church, it has become a social practice, a community ritual, in which they find a certain sense of acceptance and support—despite the theology expressed. For a growing number of the 96$^{+/-}$percent who believe in God, this is not the classical God but rather a belief in "a force in the universe that nonetheless seems to shine inside us with a power that is inexplicable but real to all who witness it, and gives meaning to life . . . ."[620]

It might seem to some that the church is expendable. Its social vision and passion for the poor and weak have been lost, while cultural and scientific forces have exposed the untenability of much of the church's doctrine. It is weighed down with many trivial notions in doctrine and ritual that obscure the great central truth that is wholly relational—"Do unto others . . . ." Everything else is superficial when compared to this great truth.

The church claims a divine origin in order to achieve a greater significance and relevance, denying that it is a human creation. However, it is no longer possible to maintain this claim of a unique and nonhuman origin for the church—or for any other religion, government, or social institution.

Exclusivism

That, of course, does not stop persons from making exclusive claims. Within Christianity alone, there are thousands of different denominational interpretations, and there are even varying interpretations between churches in the same denomination. When a Southern Baptist pastor in my area not long ago integrated his congregation with the congregation of another denomination, a letter to the editor from another Southern Baptist pastor criticized the action, saying:

> Southern Baptists do not align themselves with any other denominations. Southern Baptists have, until recently, always demanded that those entering our churches from other non-Baptist groups to be baptized by a *true* Baptist church . . . .

> The Rev. Pierce has gone against the beliefs and practices of the Southern Baptist Convention, Illinois Baptist Association, and Metro-Peoria Baptist Association. He will be excluded from these organizations, or should be.[621]

It is impossible to avoid the reality that the church is a human organization created by humans and maintained for the spiritual and physical welfare of its adherents. Human religious sensibilities have evolved over thousands of years, and they continue to develop today—often outside of religious institutional structures. As a human organization, the church has been—and continues to be—culturally and politically formed. Indeed, religious belief historically is established through political and military means and is then supported by cultural forces supported by political forces—and by further military and political means as necessary. As such, the church—and all other religious institutions, for that matter—is to be evaluated and justified in the same way that all human institutions are evaluated; that is, its contribution to human life. Ideally, the purpose of the church is not the propagation and maintenance of static dogma but the ethical pursuit of humanizing existence.

Many will protest, asking how one can be passionately committed to a church that is no longer recognized as having a divine origin. The simple answer is that we need only look around us and we can see that persons are passionately involved in many social organizations and causes that do not claim to be divinely-ordained—some of which do at least as much good as the church. These people will sacrifice for the things they believe in—even giving their lives for things that have nothing to do with religion.

Religious conviction need not depend on the belief that a deity uniquely endows its religion. There is an illustration I first heard from Krister Stendahl, which was later retold by Paul Knitter in his book *No Other Name*.

> Exclusivist . . . language is much like the language a husband would use of his wife (or vice versa): "You are the most beautiful woman in the world . . . you are the only woman for me." Such statements, in the context of the marital relationship and especially in intimate moments, are certainly true. But the husband would balk if asked to take an oath that there is absolutely no other woman in the world as beautiful as his wife

> or no other woman whom he could possibly love and marry. That would be using a different kind of language in a very different context.[622]

While such exclusivist language may be appropriate for private devotions and communal liturgy—whether religious or political—it is inappropriate in other circumstances. The context determines whether poetic or empirical language is appropriate. For most religious people, the failure to recognize this distinction only reinforces their exclusivity.

Morality

Many claim that without a divine origin for religion in general, or for the church in particular, all sense of morality will be lost. People will do whatever they please since religious authority will no longer be the "voice of God" to mortals on earth. Without divine sanctions, the church would have no authoritative voice by which to "enforce" their moral convictions. I find this argument offensive and without any basis.

Religious people do not have a corner on the morality market—although they do seem to enjoy being morality police and running other people's lives! In fact, on some levels it appears that religious people are not as moral as nonreligious persons are. While the messages of love and justice and equality have been a staple of the church in its good times, it is obvious that the church has no special competence in framing moral judgments. The same is true for other religions as well. Ethics can be based on rational equality apart from a deity. As research has amply demonstrated, the more strongly religious beliefs are held, the more incidents there are of child and spousal abuse. This strongly relates to the belief in male dominance and the view that women and children are property.

Whitehead once noted that the true foe of morality is not change, but stagnation. "It is true that the defense of morals is the battle cry which best rallies stupidity against change." In attempting to defend absolute and unchanging moral laws, the "pure conservative is fighting against the essence of the universe."[623]

The question arises whether it is possible to divorce moral and ethical judgments from their religious roots—however imperceptible that relationship might be. Some will argue that when the culture embraces religious understandings of morality and ethical behavior and then secularizes them, they are still rooted in religious insight. However, the deeper issue is whether morality and ethical behavior are *in fact* rooted in religious insight. A convincing argument can be made that they are not, although it does appear that religion and morality may have developed together. Ethical behaviors have grown out of the process of evolutionary development and adaptation, and religions have taken up the role to accept and enforce them. Moreover, when a culture no longer considers a behavior immoral or unethical, aspects of the religious step in and try to interpret the change in religious language, so that even newly adopted standards are "baptized" in the process of acculturation.

Paul Krutz, Chairman of the Center for Inquiry and Professor of Philosophy Emeritus at State University of New York at Buffalo, states:

> Recent scientific polls of belief in European countries—France, Germany, England, and others, even Japan—indicate that the level of belief in a theistic being and the institutionalized practice of organized religion have declined considerably; yet these highly secular societies exemplify good moral behavior, and are far less violent than the United States. The view that without religion you cannot have a meaningful life or high motivation is thus thrown into question.[624]

Throughout history, the basic purpose of religion has been to help individuals cope with the existential yearnings for meaning, especially in the face of despair and hopelessness that arise in response to human tragedy. The church is not necessarily good or right or just. Rather, it is an evocative attempt to provide comfort, meaning, and purpose. At its best, the church provides an ethical way for humans to live together peacefully.

Like every other system of belief, the church is the product of creative human imagination. It traffics "in fantasy and fiction, taking the promises of long-forgotten historical figures and endowing them with eternal cosmic significance." This is not belittling since the roles of creative imagination, fantasy, and fiction are "among the most powerful expressions of human dreams and hopes, ideals and longings . . . . The creative religious imagination weaves tales of consolation and of expectation. They are dramatic expressions of human longing, enabling humans to overcome grief and depression."[625]

Brief Historical Glimpse

Jesus proclaimed the coming of an era of peace and justice and righteousness, calling it "the Kingdom of God"—a term that has been spiritualized even more in recent decades by being changed to "reign of God." While still using the language of kings and the political dominance of the strongest, the "reign" metaphor nevertheless changes the image from a changed material world—and the resulting rectifying of the plight of the poor, homeless, powerless, etc.—to an image of power and control in a single king, albeit a divine king. It unwittingly changes the focus from helping the powerless to supporting the powerful—indeed, the all-powerful! The change de-emphasized male dominance—an honorable and much needed change in the church—but the dominance remained. It is no longer the vision of a material world changed with the help of human cooperation, but a vision of a spiritual world dominated by a regal God—a God who, as discussed earlier, seems to have power only in a spiritual world.

Jesus announced that this divine kingdom would be established on Earth within the lifetime of his hearers (Matthew 16:28; 23:36; 24:34; Mark 9:1), and when that did not occur, his words were interpreted in a way that fit the changed circumstance. By the mid-second century, the earthly kingdom of God proclaimed by Jesus was relocated either to the church itself or to a heavenly world beyond death. In order to protect their positions of control, the clergy were given "the keys to the kingdom"—and they became the mediators of religious favors. By the end of the fourth century, the church controlled the keys not only of the spiritual kingdom but the earthly kingdom as well by compromises made with the State in exchange for favors. In this way, "there was no longer any danger of the clergy's being made redundant by the arrival of the Kingdom on earth." After the relocation of Jesus' message from earth to heaven, anyone who taught the possibility of immediate religion could be described as a "gnostic," a "mystic," a "heretic," or whatever, and were duly persecuted. The church soon proclaimed that the promised kingdom could be found only within its structures and leaders.[626]

History demonstrates how the relationship between politics and the church had changed the way salvation is understood. Constantine's victory at the Milvian Bridge in 313 CE changed the meaning of the symbol of the cross. The emperor ordered that the banner of the cross be carried at the head of each of his armies as they went into battle. The historian Eusebius of Caesarea (ca. 260-339) described the vision inspiring Constantine's order:

> He said that about noon, when the day was already beginning to decline, he saw with his own eyes the trophy of a cross of light in the heavens, above the sun, and bearing the inscription, CONQUER BY THIS. At this sight, he himself was struck with amazement, and his whole army also, which followed him on this expedition, and witnessed the miracle . . . . And while he continued to ponder and reason on its meaning, night suddenly came on; then in his sleep the Christ of God appeared to him with the same sign which he had seen in the heavens, and commanded him to make a likeness of that sign which he had seen in the heavens, and to use it as a safeguard in all engagements with his enemies.[627]

In this way, the humble cross of Jesus became "the victory-granting cross," a magic charm, so that after Constantine the cross became filled with symbolic meanings of the earthly triumph of the church, and jeweled crosses began to predominate. This has continued to the present day so that even Protestant churches that shun ornateness have the conquering and triumphal symbol of a shiny brass cross—in contrast to a crude and humble wooden one. We follow Constantine's example in another way. He continued to emboss "Sol Invictus," the sun God, on his coins and he remained the chief priest of the Roman state cult until his death. Christians, too, claim the magic charm of the cross while continuing to worship the Gods of their own choosing.

Following the example of Constantine, the church in the Middle Ages poised the cross as a conquering sword during the Crusades. The Crusades clearly demonstrate the baser nature of the church. In violation of papal policy, "the crusaders raped, and pillaged, and murdered 'infidels' closer to home, i.e., the Jews."[628] As Marc Saperstein comments, "the cross, the symbol in which the massacres were perpetrated, acquired powerful negative associations for Jews that linger to this day." The anti-Jewish violence of the Crusades, he writes, was "symbolic, if not symptomatic, of a profound change."[629]

During the Second World War, imprisoned theologian Dietrich Bonhoeffer tried to get closer to the Jesus ideal by arguing for the possibility of a "religionless Christianity." Pushing this idea further, English theologian Don Cupitt writes:

> The kind of religion that Jesus came to preach was abolished in his name, being replaced by a curious idolatry of the Church and of the spiritual power that had come to be vested in the higher clergy. In time, people completely forgot the idea that what is called "orthodox Christian doctrine" was merely a way of thinking appropriate for a transitional period of training or discipline, when people are under authority, and that it existed in a state of ardent longing for its own supersession by something much better. Instead, people honestly began to think that Church doctrine is the Truth, forever.[630]

In 1904, Father Alfred Loisy (1857-1940), a modernist director of the Institute Catholique in Paris, wrote: "Jesus foretold the kingdom, and it was the Church that came."[631] Modernists in the 1800s and early 1900s "believed that the historical scholarship conducted during that time had made many church dogmas impossible to maintain, dogmas such as the founding of the Church by Jesus, his virgin birth, and his divine sonship—in essence, Jesus' very divinity."[632]

In order to fight this modernist movement within the Church, Pope Pius IX called together the Council of Bishops, and on July 18, 1870, the dogma of papal infallibility was made official—even though less than half of the bishops approved of it! It was a secret agenda item that was not made known to them before their arrival. Baigent writes that the bishops gathered and found themselves subjected to strong-arm tactics. "The cost of criticism was immediately apparent: the loss of Vatican stipends was the least that a dissenting bishop could expect . . . . Certain church leaders who stood and spoke against [infallibility] were 'dealt with' by house arrest, while others fled. One leader was physically assaulted by the pope [Pius IX] himself."[633]

The popes did all they could to silence this modernist heresy. In 1902, Pope Leo XIII created the Pontifical Biblical Commission to oversee the work of all theological scholars and to make sure they did not stray from the teachings of the Church. Modernists were suspended or excommunicated, and their writings were placed on the Index, the list of books that Catholics were forbidden to read. Beginning in 1910, all priests and Catholic teachers were required to swear an oath against

Modernism. "Just to be sure that the ever-changing world outside would not intrude . . . , students at seminaries and theological colleges were forbidden to read newspapers."[634] Protestants have been no less closed to new understandings, and their means of control have been almost as stern, as their literally interpreted scriptures became a *paper pope*. The enforcement came in the person of strong charismatic leaders.

Because the church has often operated with a strict constructionist interpretation of its documents that are considered infallible, it has been necessary to make sure that the texts are immune from all change and all challenge that might subvert its absolute truth. The Bible was considered perfect because it comes from a perfect God. If it is the only source of true knowledge, then believers are superior to those who are not believers. Building on this, those who are superior among the believers have job security in their truth production and interpretation.

The argument that there is a singular source of true knowledge provides the grounds for "true" politics, "true" religion, and "right" belief. True politics follows from those proclaiming the truth, a politics that has the right to actively suppress all who disagree. Since scripture holds the highest position in any hierarchy of religious knowledge, all other knowledge and attempts to discover truth must be subordinate to it.

Referring back to the recent ARIS surveys, 78% of Americans believe the Bible is the "word of God," and 65% believe the Bible holds the answers to "all or most of the basic questions of life." Thus, the grounds for "true" politics, "true" religion, and "right" belief continue to be strong in the United States. This need for certainty in uncertain times calls for something that is secure throughout time, and many find it in an infallible sacred text.

There was no "original" Bible, but simply many writings, with some that were accepted and more that were rejected. The origins of what we know as the Bible were messy and "shaped by chance." The notion of an infallible Bible originated with the fundamentalist movement in the latter part of the nineteenth century. "Rooted in nostalgia for the mythical, romanticized image of sixteenth and seventeenth century Puritan piety, this movement believed that the Bible was the solution for all social, familial, and individual ills."[635] This yearning for a return to Puritan piety and control is present today and is supported by fundamentalist political agenda.

At some early point, the mission of the church took a 180-degree shift away from a prophetic emphasis on justice for the oppressed to the maintenance of ecclesiastical power and control. In recent history, this has been true of the United Methodist Church, once the largest and most politically and socially influential Protestant denomination in the United States. Beginning with its founder John Wesley, Methodism not only proclaimed a gospel of personal salvation, but it was deeply committed to social justice. The strength of Methodism was its ability to enlist its members in all sorts of social causes—slavery, poverty, racism, employment, health, etc. It began losing both members and the ability to influence the nation when it diverted its attention from social issues and put its efforts on doctrinal debates and strengthening hierarchal control.

The fundamentalist group largely responsible for this change in direction for the United Methodist Church is the Good News movement—bad news for the denomination. Beginning in 1966, Good News, the United Methodist "tea party" faction—focused on divisive doctrinal and social issues, set up an alternative church structure and publishing house, and threatened to leave the denomination unless their demands were met. While the denomination continues to negotiate a peaceful coalition, it is losing members, influence, and integrity. It is giving in to the pressure in order to protect power and property. This movement continues to be a "church within the church" with increasing financial clout as its major weapon.

Another indication of how far the UMC has drifted from its original purpose is the term "missional appointment." What this means in practice is that the bishop's appointment of a pastor involves a "troubled church," a pastor with whom the bishop has "issues," or both. The problem with the term "missional appointment" is that it is reserved for special cases whereas—as any real leader will confirm—*every* appointment should be missional, that is, related to fulfilling the church's mission, i.e., the vision of Jesus. *Every* appointment should be made based on how this particular match will fulfill not only the larger vision of the church but also the mission for the particular situation. Alas! This seems to be rarely considered.

Early in the history of the church—and down to the present day—anti-Judaism has been part of the Church's belief and practice—resulting in all sorts of laws, pogroms, persecutions, and death camps. Since Christians came to see themselves as the "new" chosen people of God, replacing the "old" chosen people (Israel), their "new" covenant also replaced the "old" covenant. The new holy priesthood within the hierarchy of the developing church claimed all truth and all priority. The church wrote and enforced legislation that Jews and other unbelievers could not have houses of worship—or even the right to worship *privately*. Eventually, even those Christians differing from "right belief" lost their rights, including the right to live—as witnessed in the crusades, inquisitions, witch trials, and heresy trials.

This same attitude is reflected in the current actions of militant fundamentalists within Islam. And I have no reason to doubt that *if unleashed*, the junkyard dogs of Christian fundamentalism would follow the same path. The Christian Right in the US is already walking down that path in terms of abusive legislation on issues including homosexuality, abortion rights, birth control, immigration, minority rights, immigration, rights of women, property rights, the Christian "yellow pages" that encourage Christians to buy only from Christians, and the encouragement of national isolationism. According to the Christian Right, those who are not chosen, those who refuse to follow the "true" word of God (whether in the church or in the government), should have no rights. This is clearly an attempt to return the nation to Puritan control. This leads us to ask about what part the church plays in persuading believers *to do wrong*. Does the church—and religion in general—encourage its members to discriminate against others, to spread hatred, lies, and so forth?

Governments often buy into religious exclusivity, believing that it not only helps to win votes but that it also brings about and maintains an orderly populace. It is acceptable to take away certain freedoms from the citizens in order to govern smoothly and to avoid the messy process of public discussion and dissent. As we saw in the McCarthy era in the United States, and in many ways since then, those who disagree with the God-appointed have been harassed, imprisoned, and even eliminated.

The church in many parts of the world enjoys state privileges. In return, the church supports the state. In the United States, religious institutions and their clergy enjoy tax-exempt properties even when some of these properties are not directly used for religious purposes or to promote the public good. This certainly increases the taxes on all other citizens, with a special burden for the poor.

The church discovered very early that "absolute truth requires absolute authority." If the Christian scriptures are absolutely true and beyond challenge, then its truth must have an absolute authority that can stand on its own. Since its truth is from God who is "beyond understanding," then there are things in the scriptures (and in Christian doctrine) that are beyond human understanding, things that cannot be explained and must be accepted on faith. Scripture contains its own validity because of its divine origin. The argument is a self-authenticating circle, and the power of the church is assured.

As the tension between the scientific and biblical descriptions of "truth" increased, the church employed a two-world theory to address new discoveries. In the past few centuries, it taught that the two realms must be held separately. This would prove to be difficult for many Christians who have simply closed themselves off from accepting anything that called into question the literal truth of the Bible. After all, they say, there could be no eternal truth if biblical truth was not eternally true. Moreover, if eternal truth as contained in the absolutely true scriptures could be challenged, then so could the eternal and absolute God who is the author of that eternal truth—as well as the absolute and eternal church. This resulted in circular arguments that said in essence: scripture is absolutely true because God is absolutely perfect and true. Scripture is eternal because God is eternal. God is eternal because scripture says that God is eternal.

This circular reasoning also applied to church authority. If all persons are not equally endowed with understanding, those who *are* so endowed should be the leaders of the church. Of course, the winners in the debates always claim to be so endowed—even though just who the winners were fluctuated with the tides of political power, charisma of the particular leaders in the debates, and the popularity contests in the streets. The practical effect of such a struggle for power and control among the believers resulted in the centralizing of authority.

Absolute authority requires winners and losers. The church under Constantine claimed to be the absolute earthly authority. Such churchly authority requires a malleable political landscape to maintain itself. In order to guarantee that political entities will properly protect the earthly authority of the church, the political authority must also submit itself not only to biblical authority but also to the authority of the church that alone has the right and power to interpret it. This means that no unbeliever can ever be allowed to rule over believers. This thinking continues to hold sway in the United States today.

Therefore, biblical truth requires that it is guarded by ecclesiastical authority that, in turn, is protected by the divinely appointed governmental entity (king, emperor, president, senator, etc.), which, in turn, must be supported by a believing populace. In order to maintain a believing populace, the government must give favored status to the church and must pass and enforce laws against unbelievers and their ungodly acts. The religious leaders of the people must in turn support the government in order to ensure the government's continuing protection. This seems to be a carefully conceived house of cards—and a very definite argument in favor of evolutionary theory as applied to systems. This house of cards is so interconnected that it begins to tumble when any one of its parts is unfaithful to the contract. Therefore, heresy cannot be tolerated in the church *or* in the state and must therefore be removed.

It would be difficult for any Christian to be unaware of the intensely political nature of the church. No one reading the history of the church can escape how even basic theology, doctrine, and dogma were dictated by, or at least developed in concert with, secular politics.

Two-Sword Theory

In order to establish the church's power and authority over political leaders and nations, it devised the two-sword theory. This is important to us today because the Religious Right is doing all it can to implement this in the United States and in other places throughout the world. The two-sword theory was derived from the gospel of Luke.

> Just prior to Jesus' capture, the apostles indicated their willingness to use two swords in order to resist arrest. Jesus, however, rejected the call to arms. When Peter used his sword to cut off the ear of the servant of a high priest, Jesus ordered that the sword be put away, healed the ear of the servant, and surrendered to the authorities. Rather than accept this story at face value, medieval commentators viewed the tale of Jesus' capture as an opportunity to find deeper meaning in Scripture . . . . One sword, in the words of Pope Gregory VII (1073-85), represented the sword of the divine word. The other sword stood for the power exercised by the king.[636]

A practical example of this was the struggle between King Philip IV of France and Pope Boniface VIII in 1306. Philip needed money to pay for an expensive war against England, and in order to do that he began taxing church property. This was sternly resisted, and the pope issued a document, *Clericis Laicos*, that prohibited the king from taxing the church.

> Rather than submit to the authority of the pope . . . Philip imposed trade sanctions on Rome and prohibited anyone from taking gold or silver out of France. This move cut directly into Pope Boniface's funding. The pope countered by issuing another official document, *Ineffibilis*, in which he claimed the right to supervise the king . . . . As the conflict escalated, both Pope Boniface and King Philip called special councils to have each other condemned . . . . In one of Boniface's best-known bids to assert supremacy over temporal powers, *Unam Sanctam*, he referred to the two swords and tried to claim them both as instruments that belong to the church.[637]

Boundaries, whether real or imagined, reflect the power structures that establish them. The church's theology is no different and bears the marks of politics and power. It is not, nor has it even been, pristine and pure, but is burdened by all the biases and prejudices that are part of the human condition. "Theology is an artificial enterprise . . . . We must always look to theology with the realization that at times the boundaries it draws and the colors it depicts are mere creations of human beings, reflecting their own frailty and not the truth of God."[638]

The decline of the church is not the result of biblical criticism but the fact that the Christian enterprise has not adjusted to the modern world. Catholic theologian Karl Rahner wrote that in the future, we would see an increasing decline of faith and practice, and the influence of the church will deteriorate. "We shall feel as though we are living among people thoroughly opaque to religion, talking to deaf ears and uncomprehending hearts . . . . We have too an unpleasant sense whenever we hear the sound of our own voice that it is not particularly surprising that no one listens to us. Doesn't a great deal of what we say sound strange in *our own ears*—outmoded, utterly out of date?"[639]

The language and images of the church are not only strange—they are at time barbaric. This is clearly true of the church's central activity, the Eucharist or Lord's Supper. As a young woman complained to me several years ago, the whole act of eating a sacrifice seems to hark back to cannibalism and the eating of the other in order to secure its strength and life. Even the wording of the liturgy suggests this, as we are instructed to eat the body of Christ and drink the blood of Jesus.

A few will argue that this imagery needs to be jettisoned, while others argue that the Eucharist should be reinterpreted as a meal in anticipation of the heavenly banquet that Jesus will someday share with us in the heavenly kingdom (Luke 22:17-18). In this latter sense, "do this in remembrance of me" will refer to remembering the purpose of Jesus' life and the vision he understood God to be casting for the world through him. Remember this vision, be empowered by the vision, enact the vision, in order that the vision will be fulfilled and we will all then share in the heavenly celebration dinner together.

A Positive Role for the Church

In talking about the church, we proceed from the simple fact that "no one, whether catholic, Hindu, or Muslim, or whatever, would submit to the decrees and directives of organized religion if they did not already accept a transcendental commitment and further accept that an earthly institution is the trustworthy authority on or manifestation of those eternal transcendental truths."[640]

This does not mean that religion is the problem per se. The problem is when religion in any of its multiple forms and expressions claims to be the sole heir to the "truth," as opposed to being *a* way to truth, and a way that can be challenged and corrected. All those who make exclusive claims are part of the problem. This is true of both religious and secular extremism. A basic purpose of religion in general, and the church in particular, is to encourage greatness of spirit and to avoid the intolerance of exclusivism. The Abrahamic faiths have inspired greatness not only in the area of service to others but also in the areas of creativity, science, reason, and justice. Judaism and Christianity have worked for freedom and secular political and economic systems. In addition, their best expressions have urgently worked for the separation of church and state.

It is not the right or role of the church to manipulate government, to dictate to it, or to seek privilege from it. The church has a prophetic role to challenge governments when their measures are unjust. However, it is all too easy to illustrate how the church has conformed to the worst practices of government and society. Consider the critique of Martin Luther King, Jr.:

> The erstwhile sanction by the church of slavery, racial segregation, war, and economic exploitation is testimony to the fact that the church has hearkened more to the authority of the world than to the authority of God. Called to be the moral guardian of the community, the church at times has preserved that which is immoral and unethical. Called to combat social evils, it has remained silent behind stained-glass windows. Called to lead men on the highway of brotherhood and to summon them to rise above the narrow confines of race and class, it has enunciated and practiced racial exclusiveness.[641]

Concerning this prophetic role of all religious persons, Rabbi Abraham Heschel wrote: "The prophet is a person who is not tolerant of wrongs done to others, who resents other people's injuries. He even calls upon others to be the champions of the poor."[642]

Throughout the millennia, religion has served two primary functions: providing a meaning to life and social cohesion. While some of its transcending stories are no longer relevant in an age of science, it can adopt new stories about the origins and nature of life. Life needs to be defined not simply in terms of our human species, but all forms of life. These new stories need to have a provisional or transitioning quality about them, drawing on the lessons we have learned from the evidence of science, historical research, and logical reasoning.

The time of absolutes is over. When we reflect on the fact that there are nearly 34,000 Christian denominations and about 10,000 distinct religions that can also be further subdivided, it must be clear that they cannot all be "right"—and all could possibly be "wrong." Regardless, it is obvious that no one person or group possesses the absolute truth.

The social cohesion function of the church has been often abused by the State seeking to produce social conformity—to convince people to be content with their lot—thus providing social stability and "proper" behavior. From a politician's point of view, religious doctrine is important to the degree that it brings about social stability—and, more importantly, votes. Within the church, and in religions generally, heaven and hell function to produce right behavior and are generally employed by those with power to control those who do not.

Today, this cohesive function of the church must include the positive encouragement of altruism, cooperation, and service to the larger community. It is imperative that this cohesive function operates as a unifying factor and that it be inclusive rather than exclusive. Anglican archbishop Desmond Tutu put it this way:

> If we could but recognize our common humanity, that we do belong together, that our destinies are bound up in one another's, that we can be free only together, that we can survive only together, that we can be human only together, then a glorious world would come into being where all of us lived harmoniously together as members of one family, the human family, God's family. In truth, a transfiguration would take place. God's dream would become a reality.[643]

The church should focus on bringing people together without demanding or even expecting agreement in thought. Otherwise, as Carl Sagan once said, "we run the danger of fighting to the death on ideological pretexts." We must understand and admit the deficiencies and inadequacies of our own belief if we are to begin to understand the belief of another. Speaking of both political and religious ideology, Sagan wrote:

> Our history is in part a battle to the death of inadequate myths. If I can't convince you, I must kill you. That will change your mind. You are a threat to my version of the truth, especially the truth about who I am and what my nature is. The thought that I may have dedicated my life to a lie, that I might have accepted a conventional wisdom that no longer, if it ever did, corresponds to the external reality, that is a very painful realization. I will tend to resist it to the last. I will go to almost any lengths to prevent myself from seeing that the worldview that I have dedicated my life to is inadequate.[644]

Religion has a socializing role. Most people attend religious services in order to explore the meaning and purpose of their lives in the context of like-minded friends and acquaintances. They attend in order to learn how to cope with the difficulties of life and to find encouragement. They come because they want to be better persons—more loving, more accepting, more forgiving, more giving, and more joyful. They want to find a place that accepts them for who they are in this moment and not judged for who they are or have been. They want to find a place where they will be challenged "to be all they can be," to use a military slogan. People bring their children so that they can grow up learning the same set of positive characteristics. Of course, for most of these people, Jesus is an important guide and most often their savior.

Rules are important in every society. At their best, these are formed to bring about moral and ethical living. The church can help persons discover and live out the things that are important for a happy and prosperous life. Beginning with the Golden Rule, the church can offer examples and support in understanding and putting into practice love for one another. In this role, the church needs to remember the flexibility that Jesus built into the law. When an adulterous woman was brought before him (notice that the accusers did not bring the man!), Jesus did not condemn her, but simple said to the accusers, "You who are without sin, cast the first stone." Jesus offered acceptance of the woman and forgiveness of her indiscretion. However, he did not make his forgiveness contingent on a change in her behavior. He did tell her to "go and sin no more. The reality is that when we are accepting, forgiving, and reconciling, positive behaviors begin to occur—in both the giver and the recipient.

The church can also encourage its adherents to expand this caring for one another to the caring of the earth and its resources. In the same context, the church can help define and fight for social justice. The church finds its lasting strength, then, when it focuses on these things rather than on doctrinal issues. The former requires cooperation and the application of the golden rule, while the latter seeks to divide and ignores the wider implications of the golden rule.

A Positive Role

The church will move closer to the vision of Jesus when it looks deeply into the faces of those in need—everywhere in the world. It will use reason and compassion to care for others and to work for their welfare, justice, and freedom. The church should be measured by how well it works for these things. It should be measured by its deeds, not by its pronouncements.

The church must seek its identity, not in that which once was, nor in that which never was, but in that which can be. Rather than escaping into end-time eschatology, it should firmly plant its feet in reality and hope. Rather than defending a literalism of its sacred texts—or just as bad, ignoring troublesome texts—it should embrace knowledge wherever it is found and strive to understand the world rationally. It should encourage the freedom to think, believe, and act in ways that do not infringe on the same freedom for others.

Searching for "the truth that sets us free" requires that we have people with different perspectives who will challenge our biases and irrationalities and help us to transcend them. After all, it was Jesus' main goal to get people to rethink their religious commitments and values—values that honored traditions more than persons in need.

The church should help persons understand that the search for truth never ends and therefore belief itself must incorporate a means of self-correction in the face of incompatible data. It should have some form of natural theology whereby doctrine is established, challenged, and changed by the ongoing process of reason, experience, and experiment.

The church should be more concerned about valuing those in need than giving undue attention to rules and regulations and doctrinal purity. The church should live its faith, not institutionalize it.

The church should help persons understand what Lao Tzu taught about transcendence; that is, "The Tao that can be told is not the universal Tao." This would be a move to recognize the mystery and wonder of all of life in the vastness of a universe of universes.

The church should help persons realize that prayer is not asking God that two times two not be four. Certainly, prayer provides comfort and can be a means of working through problems. It can be a way of reviewing current events and helping us perceive a preferred future. It can even be a meditative process of evaluating options and deciding on the best ones. It can be a means of keeping the vision of justice and peace alive in our everyday experience.

More difficult will be the need for the church to help persons move beyond a dominance way of viewing relationships. It will be difficult because the foundation of the church is laid on a dominance hierarchy. Traditional masculine ethics tend to operate outside of relationships and emotions, and this leaves little room for negotiations. It is relationships—not abstract principles—that are primary in a fulfilling life. Moving beyond a dominance hierarchy way of thinking, challenges the view of a God who is in absolute control of everything. It requires that we become responsible for our actions and for our world. If we wish to avoid annihilation of the human species on Earth, it is we who must work to change the course that the warlords of the nations have chosen.

Summary

Since at least the time of Constantine, the church has had to play—or has allowed itself to play, and has enjoyed playing—the role of Western culture-religion. As a result, the term "Christian" has obligated itself to stand for all sorts of things, both biblical and nonbiblical. A post-Christendom context that has been in formation since the 18th century will become the normal situation of the church in the third millennium. This presents a challenge to the church. Those who find little comfort in the traditional affirmation that "Jesus is Lord" will continue to withdraw from the churches and seek to fulfill their spiritual yearnings in ways that are more in line with their beliefs and values. This exodus, which has been experienced by the churches in Europe and can already be seen occurring in North America, appears to be inevitable as the pluralization of religion and the secularization of society continue to widen.

When the church's influence is inadequate to effect its desired changes in individual lives, it steps outside its commonly accepted bounds and seeks to force its desires upon the wider population through gaining control of the political process. Once that control is captured, it can impose its will on the rest of the population. Understanding itself as divinely chosen for this mission, the church uses every means at its disposal. The political idea of democracy is easily cast aside in pursuit of a theocratic autocracy—run, of course, not by God but by those who have crowned themselves as privy to the true will of God.

While this grab for power is not new in our time, it nevertheless continues to be an issue for those who believe in freedom *of* religion as well as those who believe in freedom *from* religion. It is an issue for those who believe that God has many children—children who do not all think alike and who relate to their divine parent in different ways.

In the same way, when the church's role of teaching children and youth about spiritual matters flags, the church tries to shove this role onto the public schools. It expects the schools to teach the church's particular views to the exclusion of all others. While it would be good for children to be exposed to a variety of religions in order for them to understand the diversity of peoples throughout the world, even these attempts are often high jacked by those who see this as an opportunity to evangelize—discounting all other options.[645]

Is it possible for the church to examine critically its forms and procedures and to purge its triumphalism and exclusivity? Can the church begin to define itself in terms of the humanitarian call of Jesus to feed the hungry, to give drink to the thirsty, to welcome the stranger, to clothe the naked, and to care for the sick and those in prison? Will the church find language and images to proclaim a prophetic message of peace and justice?

CHAPTER 15

Faith in the 21st Century

"Ignorance is nothing shameful; imposing ignorance is shameful."
—Daniel Dennett

"Just as right order requires that we believe the deep matters of the Christian faith before we discuss them rationally, so it seems to me to be an instance of carelessness if, having been confirmed in faith, we do not eagerly desire to understand what we believe."
—Anselm, Cur Deus Homo

Faith has an evolutionary purpose in that it supports internal cohesion for a group thereby enabling the group to better cope and compete with external challenges. Faith operates as a source of purpose and direction. For individuals, faith provides a sense of rootedness as well as purpose.

Belief must meet philosophical and scientific scrutiny, since there is nothing about religious belief that makes it immune from this requirement. Indeed, religious belief has relied on certain ancient "scientific" understandings of the world since the beginning. The way one understands the world is reflected in the way one sees oneself and transcendence.

Religious faith is a combination of belief and trust. It consists of those things that persons value and which give direction to life. Thus, it entails beliefs about how the world works, even when these beliefs are groundless. The credibility of a belief depends upon evidence. For much of religious faith, that evidence is anecdotal, meaning that it is "true" in some situations and not in others.

Like every other belief system, "religious belief has a stake in the truth." Those who seriously seek for truth "have a strong motive to get at the truth, to investigate, to think, to hypothesize, to consider objects, to engage in reformulations of the truth, in order to become as clear as they can about what it is that they believe; what it implies and what it does not imply."[646] While I believe he got the matter backwards, this is what Anselm was pointing to when he wrote that it was "an instance of carelessness" for persons not to "eagerly desire to understand" what they believe. Speaking to another time with a different understanding of the world and of faith, John Locke argued: "He that believes, without having any reason for believing, may be in love with his own fancies; but neither seeks truth as he ought, nor pays obedience due to his Maker."[647]

A religious faith that speaks to a 21st-century worldview must dissolve its traditional parameters. It must expand the definitions of its concepts and radically redefine or jettison some of its doctrines. Faith must be expressed in the context of the entire range of science and cultures. Beyond this, it must address what Ruether called "the fundamental contradiction" between our human existence and our "aspirational horizon of meaning and value."

Faith cannot be bound to creeds and doctrines, since they are not once-and-for-all answers to the questions of existence in general and relationships in particular. They are rather expressions that are found to be meaningful in particular times and within particular worldviews. Today, while couched in religious jargon, these questions are no longer particularly religious, since the issues they address are now dissolved into the whole human community. Religious language understood with secular meanings is becoming common. The sacred and the secular are bound up in one another. This is not to deny a transcendent horizon of life, but it does redefine it. A meaningful theology becomes secular as it seeks to integrate the transcendent and prophetic horizons of all the various ways of reflecting upon human existence. This vision of the theological function seeks to release theology from its moorings in old worldviews. There is no area of thought that is off-limits to extensive challenge and exploration if that vision is to be achieved.

The symbols and metaphors of the past have limited applicability in the 21st century. Many of these expressions of faith have lost their ability to project hope or to express mystery. In his *Letters and Papers from Prison*, Dietrich Bonhoeffer wrote that we were entering an age of "no religion at all," or at least religion as it had been defined in the classical imagination. Writing in the 1940s, Bonhoeffer rejected the dualistic mindset in which classical religion and its institutions were framed, arguing that a new way of understanding reality was superceding it. As Ruether wrote: "We seem to be emerging into a new stage of consciousness where what was previously called 'religion,' must find its place, not as a separate 'sacred sphere,' but as the transforming horizon of human existence. We have entered the era of the 'demise of heaven' . . . and of the God who was defined in terms of one side of these dualisms."[648] As Karl Rahner wrote in the 1970s, in the future we will see "a further decline of faith on the empirical level and of the practice of religion and the influence of the church as we have so far known it. We shall feel as though we are living among people thoroughly opaque to religion, talking to deaf ears and uncomprehending hearts . . . . We have too an unpleasant sense whenever we hear the sound of our own voice that it is not particularly surprising that no one listens to us."[649] We need to hear these prophetic voices in our own day.

Ruether argued that the classical concentration on individual repentance and salvation simply does not provide an ethical grasp, or the tools to deal with, the great structures of evil that affect us both corporately and environmentally. "In our 'private confession' we have, in effect, involved people in a process of kneeling down to examine a speck of dirt on the floor while remaining oblivious to the monsters which are towering over their backs."[650]

Faith in the 21st century must abandon the literalism of texts and metaphors. It must discover new metaphors that can be communicated and acknowledged in light of our current knowledge. Faith is a hope that is personally received *in the context of community*. It is the vision of a preferred future, not simply for the individual, but for the human family. We do not—indeed, we cannot—live as isolated individuals. We are social beings who live in the interconnectedness of all creation. Religions that are captivated by divisive squabbles—both internally and externally—cannot hope to present this vision clearly, and are, indeed, the enemy of that vision.

While it is couched in Platonic imagery, the prayer of Jesus is for the heavenly kingdom to become a reality on earth. Today we would certainly put this vision in different terms, but the intent would be the same: that the hoped-for vision of justice, equality, and freedom become a reality for all persons—indeed, for all of "creation." This vision does not require that one affirm or deny a deity, but it does require that human beings take responsibility for the future of the human race. We may not be able to give direction to the course of the stars, but we can give direction to human interactions. In the expression of a 21st century faith, perfection is not the measure of "success," since in all biological and mental development mistakes and chance are constants.

The Church highly overrates perfection. The challenge that Jesus called out to his disciples, and thereby to all who would follow him, is that we are to be perfect as God is perfect. But, are we perfectible? M. Eugene Goring suggests in *The New Interpreter's Bible* that it would be better to understand this reference to perfection as "wholeness" or to be "single-minded in devotion to the one God."[651] However, I am not certain that removing the command from its Platonic moorings makes the matter any easier. In current philosophy, perfectibility can be defined "either as the capacity to achieve perfection [end-state theory] or more modestly, as the capacity to progress indefinitely toward it [process theory]."[652]

We might even question whether perfection is an ideal worth maintaining. When I was ordained, the bishop asked all of us ordinands the traditional Wesleyan question, "Do you expect to be made perfect in this life?" We were expected to answer in the affirmative. Knowing that many of us had doubts, Bishop Webb said, "If you don't, just what do you expect?" Nevertheless, is this ideal to be our highest desire? John Wesley spoke of this in terms of being "perfect in love," something he believed possible even if only momentarily.

Carey suggests: "Perhaps the best possible world is not one that is perfect, but rather one in which, as Ralph Waldo Emerson put it, 'there is a force always at work to make the best better and the worst good.'" Ideals, she wrote, "provide the bull's eye to aim for, but . . . it is just as well that we can only approach, and not achieve them; for we *benefit* more from the approach than we would from the achievement." If we could live in a perfect state, one of two alternatives would result: "remaining forever the same, or worsening." With the former, "there is the problem of unrelenting boredom, which makes perfection itself look suspiciously like worsening. At the least, as Lovejoy sagely observes, 'it is not obvious that remaining forever unchanged should be regarded as an excellence."[653]

Civilization and religious culture are the products of a gradual development due to human interaction with nature and the social environment. Individuals are born into a particular culture, and they are largely molded by that culture. Human values have developed over hundreds of thousands of years and do not come from a supernatural source. Because of this, these values change over the course of time and are evaluated by their relationship to the nearly universal code of reciprocity.

All of human life has a "religious" aspect to it in that religion is the expression of those thoughts and feelings that point to awe and mystery. Consequently, a strict divide between the sacred and the secular can no longer be maintained. The value of religion is reflected in the degree to which its actions reflect the humane intention of the universal code of doing to others what one would like done to them. While this code has certain limitations, it is a part of the survival mechanism built into the process of life. Religion is a positive characteristic of life when it encourages personal fulfillment, the social welfare of all, and the care of the Earth. This is not religion as commonly understood, but an attitude of transcendence that finds in its experience of awe and mystery a concern for all of nature and life.

The either-or issue of the notion of God is avoided here since it is an issue that cannot be finally resolved one way or the other. Regardless of which way one leans, it is clear that responsibility for the world, to the extent that free will operates in the world, belongs to humanity. To say that God exists means, *at most*, that creativity produces a self-sustaining universe, and this creativity continues to create in every moment of time. However, this creativity is not identified with any traditional notion of God. Chance operates as an aspect of creativity, as do failed acts of novelty.

A 21st century faith is about a vision of peace, justice, and freedom for all humanity, based on nothing more that the belief that this is the right thing to do. We desire for others what we desire for ourselves.

Our admission that all images and symbols are limited and often inadequate does not need to result in despair. Rather, the more they are "mined" and refined in terms of our current worldview, the more confidence we have that they are rooted in reality and not fantasy. We live by faith in the ultimacy of truth and in the "intelligibility of reality." As such, we create new images in order to better interpret our experiences and discoveries.

Faith in the 21st century must learn from science and not be afraid of its proven results. Science is rooted in a fundamental faith in truth and value and "religion, especially theology, can benefit by learning to become as imaginative and honest as science in the pursuit of understanding."[654] In observing reality, science employs imagination as it creates images, symbols, hypotheses, and theories, to explain those observations. "In Galileo's time most people lived with an image of the physical universe as an intrinsically very unenergetic kind of reality. Everything physical was resistant to motion. Only continuing effort could sustain any movements. If the stars and planets moved, it was only because God unrelentingly pushed them, or at least assigned angels to do so."[655] That image was challenged and replaced. The same was true for Darwin and other scientists who changed our way of looking at things. The same must be true for religious images.

21st Century Affirmations

No doctrine is final or complete. All are conditioned by cultural context. The categories listed below form an outline for reinterpreting the Christian faith in a way that makes sense in today's world.

Creation. The physical universe/multiverse may be infinite, without beginning or end. This is no more difficult to imagine than an infinite creator is. To speak of a creator in the future will be to speak of creativity in a self-sustaining universe that is continually creating through energizing activity. The physical universe/multiverse continues to grow, with planets and galaxies both coming into existence and dying. The vastness of the universe has always engendered a sense of awe and wonder for persons. The current hypothesis of an infinite universe and alternative universes are difficult to conceptualize, but they definitely affect how we understand faith issues.

Purpose. The universe and *all* that is in it have evolved over billions of years. It evolves without initial design or purpose other than creativity, that is, reproduction. Purpose is created within the process of creativity and is not a pre-ordained given. Humanity, as we now know it, is not the highest purpose of the universe/multiverse, since it continues to change and evolve. Human purpose is created in the process of evolution, and therefore the highest purpose of life is whatever we decide that to mean. That purpose, nevertheless, would be limited to the present moment but not limiting to the future.

Creativity. Creativity is the source and energy of all things. Creativity is not a person, place, or even a force, but a process that operates more on the level of imagination. For religious persons, that which we call God (s) is to be understood as an activity or process, not a person or thing with human attributes such as caring, jealousy, anger, joy, etc., all of which are human projections. It does not "intervene" in the world since it is the ongoing process of creating that world.

Religion. Religion is a human creation and developed in its earliest stages as the by-product of a survival need, perhaps the need of trusting the judgments of the experiences of the elders. In this way, religion at its basic point has a survival value. The scriptures of all religions are human creations and are to be viewed as literature that may contain nuggets of wisdom or "truth." These writings are not infallible or divinely inspired. As social systems develop or evolve, they are increasingly focused on authority, control, and power. This is also true of belief systems. Therefore, religion has a history not only of good deeds but also as a primary source and support of violence against others.

Chosenness. There are no divinely chosen peoples or tribes, nor are there divinely given lands. "Holy" lands are captured or stolen from others, and claims of their divine origin are simply tools of control and power. There are no divine human beings or human incarnations of God (s). Those who are considered incarnations are those who possess or have attributed to them the same qualities we associate with our God(s). Jesus and all similar religious leaders were born like all other human beings with fathers and mothers. There is no "second coming" of Jesus, a messiah, or imam. No one can claim to possess or have access to special or secret transcendent knowledge.

Prayer. Prayer often acts as an effective placebo, offering its adherents comfort, challenge, and courage. This is used for both positive and negative purposes. Prayer can function as a centering focus. It can be a meditative means of personal and corporate reflecting on our relationship to one another and consequently become a means of increasing attitudes of caring and acts of reaching out with aid and comfort.

Afterlife. It is doubtful that there is any form of survival of personal identity following death. Consequently, there is no literal heaven or hell. These are notions created by humans to control and manipulate human behavior. The notions of heaven and hell can be considered positive and negative ideals humans strive for or against.

Relationship. Relationship is the chief source of satisfaction and goal in human life—and is, in fact, present in all of existence as the interdependence of all things. The concept of a "golden rule" is present in some form not only in all religions but also as a method of survival in the evolutionary process at even the most basic levels of life. Therefore, concern for the well-being of others should be the purpose of all groupings and institutions, including the religious.

Sin. There was no initial perfection from which humanity fell. Therefore, salvation, however it is defined, is not a restoration to a former perfection. It makes little or no sense to talk about "sinning against God," although it is highly meaningful to speak of sinning against another person, against nature/creation, and against one's own self. Since we take responsibility for our own lives and decisions, we will continually seek new knowledge and develop the means of involving others in our decisions.

Based on the above affirmations, faith in the new century must be fully committed to human rights, separation of church and state in political affairs, an expansion of global consciousness, and an approach to solving social problems that allows for the implementing of new alternatives. It must take into account emerging scientific and technological discoveries in order to exercise moral influence on these as they are developed. Because of this, life must be guided more by reason in the light of experience and critical observation. Moral and ethical decisions must be evaluated by their consequences. This, of course, recognizes an awesome human responsibility in which human choice decides what is true and good and desirable from among a myriad of competing criteria. We might use a well-known biblical story to illustrate this.

When Abraham was commanded to sacrifice his son Isaac, he represented the human situation. He was forced to decide whether his new God Yahweh or his old God Sin, the moon-God of his former home in Ur, had required this. Unable to be certain about which God was addressing him, Abraham had to take on "the mantle of ultimate valuator." He had to decide "the *source* of the command, and in the final analysis his judgment of the source determines the *value* of the command."[656] Is it the voice of the God Sin from whom he was moving away? After all, the fall of Ur was not simply the death of a city, but of an entire culture. Ur's collapse also showed the impotence of the God Sin and the Goddess Nanna. Or, was the God Yahweh, the God he was moving toward, addressing him? Clearly, only Abraham could make that crucial decision.

Just as there was a large element of uncertainty in Abraham's situation, so in our situations of life, there exists an element of uncertainty. We cannot escape the necessity and responsibility to determine what is right and wrong. We cannot appeal to God or the Gods or tradition or holy books for the right answer. Those sources may help to inform our decision, but the decision is ours nonetheless. This is both the blessing and bane of human freedom.

While we operate within the confines of our human limitations, we also operate within an understanding that the old certainties of classical belief no longer stand as an unquestioned foundation for decision-making. Once we understand that the future is truly open and filled with competing values between which we must choose, we can no longer maintain that God is implementing an inevitable historical vision that will ensure a more just and humane world. Injustice and atrocity are always live options. As John Cobb wrote in his excellent little book, *Praying for Jennifer* (which I used in every confirmation class since I was given a prepublication copy in 1983), God will not save us from destroying our planet or ourselves. Life is always held in our hands and the best of our efforts can be easily undone by the actions of others.[657]

A 21st-century faith will express its beliefs in an open and pluralistic environment. It will be intentionally focused on those things that will enable human beings to hope and believe that there is a way that we can live together without destroying each other or ourselves. As a result, dialogue must become the normal way of relating to others whose religious, political, and cultural beliefs are different from our own. This does not mean that anything goes, but it does mean that we will seek to gain from the experiences of others and try to have as complete an understanding of alternative points of view as possible. Only through dialogue and considered compromise can mutual understanding be achieved.

CHAPTER 16

Conclusions

The more we know, the more questions we have. It is a cliché to say that the most educated person in the world today knows less and less, but at least she or he knows less and less about more and more. A person asked me in a discussion group about the expansion of the universe: "If you go as far as you can, what is on the other side? What is the universe expanding into?" I admit that I have also asked that question and still do not fully understand Hawking's answer. For scientists like Hawking, this is not even a good question. Based on Einstein's 1917 argument that space can connect up to itself, Davies uses the curved surface of the Earth as an analogy. "The Earth's surface is finite in area, but unbounded: nowhere does a traveler meet an edge or boundary. Similarly space could be finite in volume, but without any edge or boundary. Few people can really envisage such a monstrosity . . . ."[658] *He is right!* Few can really understand such a concept. And yet, the fact is that most of our children know more about the natural order than any of the founders of the world's religions.

When we look at deep space with the most powerful telescopes currently developed, we can view only about five percent of the Universe. Recent observations not only revealed hundreds of billions of stars and galaxies but also revealed that the rest that is invisible to our telescopes is "composed of new kinds of particles called *dark matter* that is far more exotic than anything we have ever seen or created in even our most sophisticated laboratories." Beyond this is the even more outrageous "possibility that most of what exists in the Universe is not matter of any kind, but some strange new energy that is fueling the accelerated expansion of the Universe."[659]

This is not the place to discuss the implications of dark matter and dark energy—or even "thick-skinned gravastars." These recent discoveries "pulled the ground out from under our understanding of the cosmos." Scientists expected to confirm that gravity, which pulls mass together, would oppose cosmic stretching. However, what they discovered is that "the Universe is expanding ever faster toward an unknown future, powered by something that has been dubbed *dark energy*, whose existence was unexpected and whose presence remains unexplained." Evalyn Gates, Assistant Director of the Kavli Institute for Cosmological Physics and senior research associate at the University of Chicago, compares this discovery to science falling through a rabbit hole, "and the world in which we find ourselves is far more preposterous than any Carrollian adventure." [660]

If we understand that the Universe is incredibly dynamic—an active and often violent arena where nothing is even fixed in time and place—we are just as challenged by the complexity of biological systems. While biological systems have to obey all the laws of physics and chemistry, they nevertheless have qualities that cannot be derived from physics and chemistry. In his book *The Quark and the Jaguar*, physicist Murray Gell-Mann, who won the Nobel Prize for his quark theory, suggested that "complexity explains why all the action of the universe cannot simply be reduced to a few fundamental rules. Or, to put it differently, complexity theory says that, given a complete knowledge of the state of the universe at its inception and given a complete knowledge of the laws of physics and chemistry, it would still be impossible to predict the path of life on Earth."[661]

Knowledge of the physical world is necessary for us to speak meaningfully about religious concepts. Nevertheless, religions have consistently misrepresented the origins of human life and the universe. Indeed, 150 years after Darwin, 52 percent of Americans still deny the theory of evolution. While the theory has undergone several changes, it is one of the basic elements in our understanding the world in which we live. The church faced a similar challenge from Copernicus and others. The church had accepted Aristotle's worldview under the strong guidance of Thomas Aquinas. Later, when Copernicus, Bruno, and Galileo proved that Earth was not the center of the universe, their theories were seen as wrong because they denied the biblical worldview. If they were right, the authorities reasoned, then Earth would be demoted, along with humankind—not to mention a hierarchy that relied on this "truth." If these theories were right, we could no longer properly speak of *the* earth or *the* world, but we would be forced to speak of *an* earth, *a* world. Today we can no longer properly speak of *a* world but *a* universe, that is, simply one among millions. If these theories were right, what other parts of the church's teachings would be challenged?

Einstein presented another challenge with his theory of special relativity. This theory said that there is no center—there are no privileged frames of reference. Not only is our Earth not the center of the universe, it has no important position (except for us) or state of motion. We are, so to speak, an incidental aspect of the universe, a grain of sand on a seemingly endless beach.

Contemporary physics challenges religion to either change its images and metaphors or to abandon God-talk altogether. This challenge also includes all discussions about the beginning and end of the world as we know it. Indeed, even our traditional understandings of time are irrelevant and no longer possible to sustain.

It is not true that a world without God would be a world without ethics or morals, a world reduced to lawlessness and total disorder. Many throughout the centuries have made that argument, but the truth is that the existence of God(s)—or the belief in God(s)—does not necessarily make us more humane. It has been argued in these pages that values result as a natural part of the evolutionary social process of development, envisioned and idealized as factors contributing to survival and advance. This unconscious process allows for the mutation and adaptation of values that lead to survival.

The old argument that without belief in God—read "my" God—all things are permissible and immorality will rule the day. However, one might ask those who affirm this: If *you* were freed from the restraints of doctrine—especially the hope of heaven and the threat of hell, on which this belief is based—would *you* choose to lead a life of unrestrained immorality? This claim says more about the person who makes the claim than the reality of the situation. It may well reveal a suppressed desire for unbridled behavior.

How we view the value of art, nature, love, friendship, etc., is based on attributed value. But does the attributing of high value to something *necessarily* grow out of our belief in a deity of some sort? Or, are the views of even those who deny the existence of a deity of any sort nevertheless based on unconscious memes and traditions and values generated over innumerable centuries of embedding to the extent that they become a foundation that we never see or acknowledge but are there nonetheless? These value systems are like the bedrocks that support the foundations of various kinds of buildings with many different purposes and designs.

It is obvious that religious hierarchies have too much at stake to abandon, or even radically revise, their traditional beliefs, although individuals are increasingly taking this route as traditional views become so questionable they lose their credibility. Some beliefs are no longer acceptable in light of contemporary norms and values. When Pope John XXIII "opened the windows" of the church to let a fresh wind blow through, many were appalled, and when he died, the windows were quickly slammed closed. Change is hard to bring about in the church—even for a progressive pope!

Religions in general, and the church in particular, must be able to articulate beliefs in such a manner that adults can discover a deeper faith within a contemporary worldview. Whether that can happen is highly questionable. Religion tends to reject the evidence and reasoning of science. In its better times, reasoning and scientific evidence are simply tolerated as a separate realm of knowledge. Religions seem to take pride in their ignorance, affirming in the words of Ignatius Loyola: "We sacrifice the intellect to God." We can hardly imagine how much knowledge has been destroyed because it did not square with what the church—or other religion—believes.

The journey taken in these pages has at times been difficult. What began as an exploration of the effects of a quantum worldview on religions expressions turned into an examination of everything I have believed and taught. I have ended up in a new and strange land with few familiar markers. Questioning and probing have defined my life as far back as I can remember. More often than not, I sought to answer the questions within the bounds of an "acceptable" theology, even as I sought to push the limits. Now, I find myself more out of bounds than within them, more outside the circle, and much less related to what was once the center.

Our criteria for making judgments are always strategies of interpretation. For many years, I have employed a strategy of suspicion in approaching truth claims and pronouncements of authority figures—and not just religious claims. However, I had not yet approached the element of danger and threat to human life and nature that is found in many of the religious truth claims found in my own religious tradition. As one who has in the past tried to interpret these threats away, I now realize that doing so simply sweeps the problem under the proverbial rug.

Some of these truth claims are to be rejected outright and their danger brought to light. This would include, but is not limited to, notions of: sacred land; divine rights bestowed on persons; chosenness; the promises of heaven; the threat of hell; and end-of-time prophecies. Those who have an assurance of eternal life in heaven have little motivation to challenge or change the status quo since everything will be made right in the sweet bye-and-bye. Tertullian, one of the early church fathers, promised that one of the most intense pleasures of the afterlife for the redeemed would be the "endless contemplation of the tortures of the damned." Those who look for a bloodthirsty second coming as envisioned in the book of Revelation have no motivation to work against warfare, including the possibility of a nuclear holocaust. In fact, such a devastating situation is actually encouraged by many as a sign of the second coming of the messiah or the twelfth imam.

Most challenging to me has been the age-old question of the existence of God. I have concluded that it is no more difficult to believe in an infinite universe that has no beginning or end, than to believe in an infinite God without beginning or end. We might say with Taoism, which is nontheistic, that Tao is so great it doesn't even have to exist. Indeed, the God of the Abrahamic faiths is exceedingly small in comparison.

Traditional notions of God based on anthropomorphic images are to be rejected. In the past I argued in more traditional language that if God is spirit, these human attributes make no sense at all—even as metaphors. As a result of this journey, I am led to affirm the infinity of creativity as the source of all things. The traditional notions of "God" have so much baggage that I avoid identifying God with creativity. It is difficult but necessary to affirm that all traditional notions of God are projections of the human imagination, projections based on human desires and needs. This is like painting a bulls-eye around the point where the arrow has already landed. A God that we can easily conceive is a very small God—indeed, not God at all.

Tillich saw the divine as not inhabiting some transcendent world above nature, but is to be found precisely in the "ecstatic" character of this world. We no longer see the divine in light of our relationship to something or someone outside of our world but precisely to that which is an integral part of the world.

The traditional image of God as an all-knowing, all-loving, all-powerful parent is simply a human projection. I have taught classes on the necessity of using inclusive language in all areas of common and religious speech. At a deeper level, I have had trouble with God-as-Father language since it plays such an important role in the dominance theory of relationships. Like many others, I have said that God-as-Father is an image of endearment, speaking of the loving parent who wants only the best for his children. But the image is much darker when taken as a whole. It speaks of a relationship where we never get the chance to grow up. We are—and will always remain—dependent children. Authority figures of every stripe—king, emperor, pope, imam, president, and pastor—have taken full advantage of this "Father knows best" mentality of control and manipulation. We are continually reminded that we are children who need someone to think for us, to take care of us, to punish and reward us. Indeed, as children, we are simply property. We are not our own. We cannot even give ourselves, since we have nothing to properly give. People in all faiths—and in all political movements, for that matter—are considered children, since children are more malleable and gullible. Considering persons as children manipulates their wish—or perhaps their need—to be fooled. This ancient problem provides a means for those with power and authority to exploit us.

It has also been difficult to deal with the issue of the survival of personal identity, although I have been moving toward this for several years. Wrestling with this as a pastor, I would say to the grieving family, "As John lived in the life and love of God in this life, so shall he live eternally with God." It was the truthful statement of a Christian agnostic. I sincerely doubt there is survival of personal identity beyond death. Looking for hope in a quantum worldview, some have suggested there is hope in the idea of parallel universes. But this is just as speculative as the notions of heaven and hell. I must confess that there is no one who would be more excited than I if it were true—not so much that *I* would continue, but that I could once again spend time with those I have loved and admired. (In truth, such recognition in the afterlife is not even biblical!) But, alas! I am not at all interested in a heaven of endless hymn singing and praise. A God that needs endless praise is the most boring of egoists. I would want the opportunity not only to visit with others, but also to have the opportunity to discover, grow, and meet interesting people. Over the years, I have often said that when I die, *before* I go to heaven, I want to take a complete guided tour of the *entire* universe. If only that were possible.

It has been a really long time since I have felt comfortable with the traditional Jesus/Christ. The church claims to worship only one God, but most of its hymn and prayers are directed to this second God, Jesus/ Christ. The church, it seems, has little use for God other than as Creator. Once creation had taken place, the Christ of Nicaea was all that has been necessary. From my high school years, I have never been able to understand why, if God is so personal, we have any need for an intermediary—whether it is Jesus, or a priest or a hierarchy. Very early, I concluded that we do not have direct access to God if anything or anyone is required to intercede on our behalf. If an intermediary is necessary to protect either us from God, or God from us, then this God is unworthy of praise.

Wrestling with the future of the church has been challenging in the sense that I know it has the *potential* for both good and evil. The "true believers" in every religion will not be satisfied until the whole world bows the knee to *their* God—for Christians, that God is Jesus Christ. For the church, one only needs to open any hymnal to see how this is inculcated into the minds of the faithful. I have come to the unsettling conclusion that the church does not have the capacity to realize its great potential for good. Even when it is trying to accomplish something good—*and it does do a lot of good*—it is guided by its inherent exclusivism, judgmentalism, and moralism, creating in its wake a dependency upon itself in those it seeks to help. This is not to deny the good that the church does, but to decry its motives. The ceremonies and practices of religions in general and the church in particular are simply the "echoing repetitions of yesterday." Creeds and ceremonies are often substitutes for genuine virtue. Centuries ago, the prophet Micah warned against this, saying that God abhors sacrifices and ceremonies and instead desires acts of justice and mercy to others, especially to the poor. His God was not a self-centered egotist but a God who truly cared about people. Micah's God demanded that justice was a human responsibility, and more important than religious ceremony.

The church can be a valuable institution when it focuses on the basic needs of people, and not simply on its members or likeminded Christians. The characteristics I would hope to see in a new church include: supportive, listening, open to new discoveries, empowerment of people, role model for reaching out to those in need, commitment to learning, honesty, courageous, inclusive, and compassionate.

Who Can be a Christian?

Can one be a secular Christian or an agnostic Christian? At its core, being a "Christian" means consciously choosing to follow the teachings of Jesus, what the medieval theologian Thomas à Kempis (1380-1471) called *Imitatio Christi*, the imitation of Christ. However, it is not simply doing what Jesus did or would do, but using his received teachings as a guide. The writer of John's Gospel realized that we would be able to do *more* than Jesus did. With new understandings of relationships, we will do things differently from what he did. While many will disagree, being a Christian has little, if anything, to do with affirming a particular set of doctrines or beliefs. Nor does it ask the trite question, "What Would Jesus Do?" We can ask what he taught, but we have no right to make him say things that he would have had no knowledge of. We can ask if what he taught still applies in our time and place. We cannot claim that what he did and said was valid for all times and in all places.

To be a Christian, it is not necessary to confess the trinitarian Christ of Nicaea. It does means, at the very least, to seek truth wherever it may be found, to show compassion, and to seek justice for the powerless and the abused. It is sufficient to act in the humane manner that Jesus of Nazareth taught—love of neighbor, love of self, feeding the hungry, clothing the naked, welcoming the stranger, caring for the sick and needy, care for those cast off by society, care for the environment, and the refusal to allow religious beliefs and ceremonies to get in the way of doing these things. It is sufficient to discover "God" in the outreached hand of need and in the giving hand of sharing and lifting up.

When I was 13 years old, part of the Christmas activities in my father's church that year was a play, "Christmas in the Cobbler's Shop." It was based on Tolstoy's short story in which the cobbler receives an angelic message that the messiah will visit his shop that very night. He anxiously awaits the visit. While he works and waits, three persons come to his shop who are in need of help. (I played the role of a young boy who needed a pair of shoes.) As the day ends, the cobbler is disappointed since the promised visit by the messiah did not happen. Then he hears the message that the messiah had been there three times that night in the persons of those in need. Then, off stage, I sang quietly with the choir, "Where Cross the Crowded Ways of Life."

Where cross the crowded ways of life,
Where sound the cries of race and clan
Above the noise of selfish strife,
We hear your voice, O Son of Man.

In haunts of wretchedness and need,
On shadowed thresholds dark with fears,
From paths where hide the lures of greed,
We catch the vision of Your tears.

O Master, from the mountainside
Make haste to heal these hearts of pain;
Among these restless throngs abide;
O tread the city's streets again.[662]

This play and the words of this hymn had a profound effect on my life. Almost a decade later while I was a student at MacMurray College, Dow Kirkpatrick[663] spoke at a chapel service. The title of his sermon, based on Matthew 25, was "Behind the Face of Every Man Is God." That reinforced my growing faith that in the final analysis, it matters less what one believes than what one does. Action is always the measure of belief. Doctrine is worthless unless it leads to humanitarian efforts.

Later I would learn that the basis of Matthew 25 is the broader concept of hospitality. My family moved a lot as I was growing up, and I have moved my own family many times. Until now, I have never lived in one place longer than seven years. I was always the new kid, the stranger, the outsider. Each new situation was surrounded with unsettling tension for both me and the "established" others.

In every situation, the new is an unknown threat to the status quo. The status quo is cautious and often closed to the new, but when both are open to the other, communication begins, fears are reduced (or confirmed), and eventually, if one is fortunate, mutual acceptance occurs.

The effort in these pages is not to deprive persons of wonder and consolation. Indeed, the world is filled with wonder, mystery, and inspiration—all more astonishing than burning bushes, sudden creations, and miracles. While creativity has more random elements of chance than most might feel comfortable with, there is an ever-deepening sense of mystery in the cosmic and biological evolutionary processes as we come to know not only that we are composed of stardust but also how intimately we are part of the animal kingdom. Having said that, we need to remember how religions have acted in cruel and destructive ways when they were strong, how they manipulated the weaknesses of the people, enslaving the body and the mind. When we forget what that must have been like, we need only open a newspaper to see how it is when today's religious leaders have the power to dictate how things must be.

It is my belief that any God worth its salt would prefer honest doubt to unreasonable faith. It is my hope that these pages have raised questions for you and encouraged you to address them in your own way.

ENDNOTES

PREFACE

1 Anna Quindlen, "Still the Brightest," *Newsweek* 149:20 (21 May 2007), p. 82.

2 John Shelby Spong, *Why Christianity Must Change or Die*. New York: HarperSanFrancisco, 1998, p. 20. See also Peter A. Young, "Confessions of a Believer in Exile," *Cross Currents*, Winter, 1998 http://www.findarticles.com/p/articles/mi_m2096/is_4_48/ai_54064306

3 Theodore M. Snider, *The Divine Activity: An Approach to Incarnational Theology*. American University Studies, Series VII: "Theology and Religion," Vol. 63. New York: Peter Lang, 1990, p. 1.

CHAPTER 1—Imagining a World

4 Luis G. Pedraja, *Teologia: An Introduction to Hispanic Theology*. Nashville: Abingdon Press, 2003, p. 12.

5 Ann Druyan, "Editor's Introduction," in Carl Sagan, *The Varieties of Scientific Experience: A Personal View of the Search for God*. New York: Penguin Books, 2006, p. xi.

6 Richard Cohen, *Chasing the Sun: The Epic Story of the Star that Gives Us Life*. New York: Random House, 2010, p. 17.

7 Ibid.

8 Pedraja, *Teologia*, p. 14.

9 Francisco J. Ayala, "Biological Evolution: An Introduction," in James B. Miller, ed., *An Evolving Dialogue: Scientific, Historical, Philosophical and Theological Perspectives on Evolution*. Washington, DC: American Association for the Advancement of Science, 1998, p. 16.

10 Ibid. p. 320.

11 Ibid. pp. 319, 323, 324.

12 Vilayanur S. Ramachandran, *The Tell-Tale Brain: A Neuroscientist's Quest for What Makes Us Human*. New York: W.W. Norton & Company, 2011, 118.

13 Michael Dowd, *Thank God for Evolution: How the Marriage of Science and Religion Will Transform Your Life and Our World*. New York: Plume, 2009, p. 8.

14 Lera Boroditsky, "How Does Our Language Shape the Way We Think?" (12 June 2009) http://www.edge.org/3rd_culture/boroditsky09/boroditsky09_index.html

15 Richard Dawkins, "The Future Looks Bright," http://www.edge.org/3rd_culture/bright/bright_index.html

16 Thomas Friedman, quoted in Tom Nissley, "Where Were You When You Realized the World Is Flat? (Or Have You?): A Conversation with Thomas L. Friedman," http://www.amazon.com/exec/obidos/tg/feature/-/562744/ref=lbrc_inter2/102-6650176-4755342

17 Ibid.

18 H. L. Mencken, quoted in Greg Martinez, "Kitzmiller v. Homo boobiens," *Skeptical Inquirer* 31:6 (November-December 2007), p. 55.

19 For an extensive look at the roots of the separation of church and state, see John M. Barry, *Roger Williams and the Creation of the American Soul: Church, State, and the Birth of Liberty*. New York: Viking, 2012.

20 Debby Applegate, *The Most Famous Man in America: The Biography of Henry Ward Beecher*. New York: Three Leaves Press, 2006, p. 267.

21 Pat Duffy Hutcheon, "Beyond the Quest for Certainty—Mind-Matter Duality in Philosophy, Religion and Science," *Humanist*, (July 2001) http://www.findarticles.com/p/articles/mi_m1374/is_4_61/ai_76800134

22 Stephen Jay Gould, *Rocks of Ages: Science and Religion in the Fullness of Life*. New York: Ballantine Books, 1999, 319, 326.

23 Francisco J. Ayala, "Biological Evolution: An Introduction," in James B. Miller, ed., *An Evolving Dialogue: Scientific, Historical, Philosophical and Theological Perspectives on Evolution*. Washington, DC: American Association for the Advancement of Science, 1998, p. 11.

24 Herbert Spencer, "Progress: Its Law and Causes," *The Westminster Review*, 67 (April 1857): pp. 445-447, 451, 454-456, 464-65.

25 Barry Werth, *Banquet at Delmonico's: Great Minds, the Gilded Age, and the Triumph of Evolution in America*. New York: Random House, 2009, p. 26.

26 Ibid. p. 128.

27 Ibid. p. 50.

28 John D. Rockefeller, quoted in Werth, p. 123.

29 Werth, p. 89.

30 William Graham Sumner, quoted in Werth, p. 183.
31 Ibid, p. 186, 187.
32 Herbert Spencer, quoted in Werth, p. 244.
33 Ibid. p. 231.
34 Rita M. Gross, "Religious Diversity: Some Implications for Monotheism," *Cross Currents* 49:3 (Fall 1999) http://www.crosscurrents.org/gross.htm
35 Ibid.
36 Ibid.
37 Daniel C. Dennett, *Breaking the Spell: Religion as a Natural Phenomenon*. New York: Penguin Books, 2006, p. 107.

CHAPTER 2—Consciousness and Belief

38 Steven Pinker, *The Blank Slate: The Modern Denial of Human Nature*. New York: Viking Press, 2002, pp. 1-2.
39 Zach Lynch, *The Neuro Revolution: How Brain Science is Changing Our World*. New York: St. Martin's Press, 2009, p. 47.
40 Vilayanur S. Ramachandran, *The Tell-Tale Brain: A Neuroscientist's Quest for What Makes Us Human*. New York: W.W. Norton & Company, 2011, p. 37, 38.
41 Ibid. p. 46.
42 Ibid. pp. 47-48.
43 Ibid. p. 60.
44 Malcolm Jeeves, "Mind Reading and Soul Searching in the Twenty-first Century," in Joel B. Green, ed., *What About the Soul? Neuroscience and Christian Anthropology*. Nashville: Abingdon Press, 2004, p. 23.
45 Antonio Damasio, *The Feeling of What Happens: Body and Emotion in the Making of Consciousness*. New York: Harcourt Brace & Company, 1999, p. 4.
46 Ibid. p. 9.
47 Ibid. p. 12.
48 Ibid. pp. 16, 15.
49 Ibid. p. 16-17.
50 Ramachandran, *The Tell-Tale Brain*, p. 8-9.
51 Lynch, *The Neuro Revolution*, p. 50.
52 Michael Gazzaniga, *Human: The Science Behind What Makes Us Unique*. New York: HarperCollins, 2008, p. 126f.
53 Ibid. p. 128.
54 Michael Shermer, "Adam's Maxim and Spinoza's Conjecture," *Scientific American* 298:3 (March 2008) p. 36.

55 Ibid.

56 Ibid. p. 37.

57 Dan Ariely, *Predictably Irrational: The Hidden Forces that Shape Our Decisions.* New York: HarperCollins, 2008.

58 Sharon Begley, "When It's Head versus Heart, the Heart Wins, *Newsweek* 151:6 (11 February 2008) p. 34.

59 Frank Luntz, quoted in Begley, p. 35.

60 Begley, p. 35.

61 Gregory W. Lester, "Why Bad Beliefs Don't Die," *Skeptical Inquirer* (November 2000) http://www.csicop.org/si/2000-11/beliefs.html

62 Ibid.

63 Ibid.

64 Ibid.

65 George Lakoff and Mark Johnson, *Philosophy in the Flesh: The Embodied Mind and Its Challenge to Western Thought*, New York: Basic Books 1999.

66 Niels Henrik Gregersen, "The Naturalness of Religious Imagination and the Idea of Revelation," *The Online Journal for Philosophy of Religion* 3 (2003) http://www.arsdisputandi.org/

67 Ibid.

68 Ibid. See Lakoff and Johnson, pp. 45-73.

69 George Lakoff, *The Political Mind: Why You Can't Understand 21st Century Politics with an 18th-Century Brain.* New York: Viking, 2008, p. 82.

70 Ibid. p. 99.

71 Ibid. pp. 254-255.

72 Steve Odin, "A Post Modern View of Aesthetic Symbolism: Shingon Esoteric Buddhism and Whitehead's Theory of Symbolic Reference," paper delivered at the "Toward a Post-Modern World" Conference in Santa Barbara, California (16-20 January 1987): p. 1.

73 Alfred North Whitehead, *Process and Reality: An Essay in Cosmology.* David Ray Griffin and Donald W. Sherburne, editors. New York: Macmillan Company, 1978, p. 183.

74 Bruce M. Hood, *The Science of Superstition: How the Developing Brain Creates Supernatural Belief.* New York: HarperOne, 2009, p. 13.

75 James Alcock, quoted in Tom Genoni, Jr., "Exploring Mind, Memory, and the Psychology of Belief," *Skeptical Inquirer*, January-February, 1995. http://www.csicop.org/si/9501/belief.html

76 Susan Greenfield, "Making Up Our Minds," *New Statesman* (27 September 1999) http://www.findarticles.com/p/articles/mi_m0FQP/is_128_4456/ai_56749577

77 Read Montague, quoted in Lynch, *The Neuro Revolution*, p. 4.

78 Greenfield, "Making Up Our Minds." See also, Vilayanur S. Ramachandran, *The Tell-Tale Brain: A Neuroscientist's Quest for What Makes Us Human*. New York: W.W. Norton & Company, 2011.

79 Ted Peters, "How We Believe: The Search for God in an Age of Science," *Christian Century* (15 November 2000).

80 Michael Shermer, "Why People Believe in God: An Empirical Study on a Deep Question," *Humanist* (November 1999) http://www.findarticles.com/p/articles/mi_m1374/is_6_59/ai_57800244

81 Bruce M. Hood, *The Science of Superstition: How the Developing Brain Creates Supernatural Belief*. New York: HarperOne, 2009, p. 96.

82 Ibid. p. 97, 98.

83 Ibid. p. 111. See Stuart Guthrie, *Faces in the Clouds: A New Theory of Religion*. New York: Oxford University Press, 1993.

CHAPTER 3—A Quintrilateral Way of Discerning Truth

84 Emile Durkheim "Pragmatism & the Question of Truth," http://www.marxists.org/reference/subject/philosophy/works/fr/durkheim.htm. From his *Pragmatism & Sociology*. Cambridge University Press, 1983.

85 Stephen Bertman, *The Genesis of Science: The Story of Greek Imagination*. New York: Prometheus Books, 2010, p. 66.

86 Ibid. pp. 70, 68.

87 Ibid. pp. 99, 96.

88 Brian Greene, *The Hidden Reality: Parallel Universes and the Deep Laws of the Cosmos*. New York: Alfred A. Knopf, 2011, p. ix.

89 Ibid. p. 4.

90 Ebbe B. Ebbesen and Vladimir J. Konecni, "Eyewitness Memory Research: Probative v. Prejudicial Value," http://psy2.ucsd.edu/~eebbesen/prejvprob.html

91 Marc Green, "Errors in Eyewitness Identification Procedures," http://www.visualexpert.com/Resources/mistakenid.html

92 John Stuart Mill was the first to use this illustration.

93 Nassim Nicholas Taleb, *The Black Swan: The Impact of the Highly Improbable*. New York: Random House, 2007, p. xvii-xviii.

94 Ibid. p. xix-xxi.

95 Pedraja, *Teologia*, p. 83.

96 Ross L. Stein, "On the Possibility of an Immediate Experience of God," *The Journal of Liberal Religion* 3:2 (summer 2002) http://www.meadville.edu/stein_3_2.html

97 Alfred North Whitehead, *Process and Reality*, p. 113.

98 Stein.

99 Richard Dawkins, quoted in Liam F. Heaney, "The Essence of Language: Metaphorically Speaking," *Contemporary Review* (June 1995) http://www.findarticles.com/p/articles/mi_m2242/is_n1553_v266/ai_17381432

100 Rainer Maria Rilke, quoted by Alan Lightman, in Adam Bly, ed., *Science Is Culture: Conversations at the New Intersection of Science & Society*. New York: Harper Perennial, 2010, 56.

101 Alan Lightman, in Adam Bly, ed., *Science Is Culture*, p. 58.

102 Stephen Bertman, *The Genesis of Science: The Story of Greek Imagination*. New York: Prometheus Books, 2010, p. 1.

103 Martin Luther, "The Damned Whore, Reason," http://www.jesuscult.com/Luther_Anti-Reason.htm

104 Luther, quoted in Lynch, *The Neuro Revolution*, p. 136.

105 Pedraja, *Teologia*, p. 55.

106 James A. Sheppard, *Christendom at the Crossroads: The Medieval Era*. "The Westminster History of Christian Thought;" Louisville KY: Westminster John Knox Press, 2005, p. 33.

107 Dr. Robert Guthrie comments on this: "I would have loved to be the head of the Department of Sociology at a university in which Galileo was the head of the Physics Department and Aristotle was the head of the Philosophy Department. The 'argument rooms' would have needed to be soundproofed and the expletives deleted!" (Personal correspondence)

108 George Lakoff, *The Political Mind*, pp. 7-8.

109 Antonio Damasio, *Descartes' Error: Emotion, Reason, and the Human Brain*. New York: G. P. Putnam's Sons, 1994.

110 Lakoff, p. 232.

111 Ibid. p. 13-14.

112 George Ellis, quoted in Heather Wax and Gerald Shaw, "Master of His Universe," *Science & Spirit* 16:1 (January-February 2005): 33.

113 George Ellis, "On Rationality and Emotion, Faith and Hope," *Metanexus Cosmos*. (21 June 2004) http://www.metanexus.net/metanexus_online/show_article.asp?8916

114 George Ellis, quoted in Wax and Shaw, p. 36.

115 Fareed Zakaria, "Presidential Pony Show," *Newsweek* 155:25 (21 June 2010), p. 16.

116 Sharon Begley, "Don't Just 'Do Something'," *Newsweek* 155:25 (21 June 2010), p. 17.

117 Richard P. Feynman, *What Do You Care What Other People Think?* New York: W.W. Norton, 1988, p. 247. Quoted in Michael Shermer, "A Skeptical Manifesto," *Skeptic,* 1:1 (Spring 1992), pp. 15-21. http://www.skeptic.com/01.1.shermer-skep-manifesto.html

118 Paul Tillich, *Systematic Theology: Volume 1*, Evanston: University of Chicago Press and New York: Harper & Row, Publishers, 1955, p. 103.

119 Michael Shermer, "A Skeptical Manifesto," *Skeptic,* 1:1 (Spring 1992), pp. 15-21. http://www.skeptic.com/01.1.shermer-skep-manifesto.html

120 Bruce M. Hood, *The Science of Superstition: How the Developing Brain Creates Supernatural Belief.* New York: HarperOne, 2009, pp. 201, 205.

121 Michael Foucault, *Power/Knowledge: Selected Interviews and Other Writings.* New York: Pantheon Books, 1977, p. 52.

122 J. Wentzel van Huyssteen, p. 217.

123 Delwin Brown, quoted in van Huyssteen, p. 218. See Delwin Brown, *Boundaries of our Habitations: Tradition and Theological Construction.* New York: State University of New York Press, 1994, pp. 24-28.

124 Edward Dolnick, *The Clockwork Universe: Isaac Newton, the Royal Society, and the Birth of the Modern World.* NY: HarperCollins Publishers, 2011, p. 36.

125 Ibid. pp. 37-38.

126 Daniel Boorstein, *The Discoverers.* New York: Random House, 1983, p. 409.

127 Dolnick, *The Clockwork Universe,* p. 63.

128 Ibid. p. 60.

129 Philipp Blom, *A Wicked Company: The Forgotten Radicalism of the European Enlightenment.* New York: Basic Books, 2010, p. 43.

130 Pierre Bayle, *Pensées* (1683). Quoted in Blom, *A Wicked Company,* p. 43.

131 Blom, *A Wicked Company,* p. 43.

132 Michael Cronin, "Babel's Standing Stones: Language, Translation And The Exosomatic," *Crossings: eJournal of Art and Technology,* Volume 2:1 (March 2002) http://crossings.tcd.ie/issues/2.1/Cronin/

133 Dennis Ford, *The Search for Meaning: A Short History.* Berkeley: University of California Press, 2007, p. 29.

134 Mircea Eliade, *The Sacred and the Profane: The Nature of Religion.* "A Harvest Book," New York: Harcourt, Inc., p. 12.

135 Karl Marx, *The Eighteenth Brumaire of Louis Bonaparte* (1852). http://www.marxists.org/archive/marx/works/1852/18th-brumaire/ch01.htm The "Eighteenth Brumaire" refers to 9 November 1799 in the French Revolutionary Calendar—the day the first Napoleon Bonaparte had made himself dictator by a coup d'etat.

136 Pedraja, *Teologia*, p. 75.

137 Jeanette Rodríguez, quoted in Pedraja, *Teologia*, pp. 75-76.

138 Pedraja, *Teologia*, p. 76.

139 van Huyssteen, p. 224.

140 Connie Barlow, "The Way of Science—Exploring the Foundations of Humanism," *Humanist* (March-April, 1998) http://www.findarticles.com/p/articles/mi_m1374/is_n2_v58/ai_20430859

141 Richard Dawkins, quoted in Connie Barlow, "The Way of Science—Exploring the Foundations of Humanism," *Humanist* (March-April 1998) http://www.findarticles.com/p/articles/mi_m1374/is_n2_v58/ai_20430859

142 Barlow, "The Way of Science."

143 Susan Blackmore, "The Power of Memes," *Scientific American* (October 2000), 283:4.

144 Ibid. p. 54.

145 Joseph Poulshock, "Memetics, Language, and Theology," A paper given to the Society for the Study of Theology and Christian Philosophy at Tokyo Christian Institute, 26 June 2001, Hhtp://www.ling.ed.ac.uk/~naphtali/MLT.PDF

146 Susan Blackmore, *Waking from the Meme Dream.* Paper presented at The Psychology of Awakening: International Conference on Buddhism, Science and Psychotherapy, November 1996. http://www.memes.org.uk/meme-lab/DART96.HTM

147 Robert Aunger, editor, *Darwinizing Culture: The Status of Memetics as Science.* Oxford: Oxford University Press, 2001.

148 Connie Barlow, "The Way of Science."

149 Reference lost.

CHAPTER 4—It Was Said of Old—Embedded Tradition

150 William James, quoted in Clifton F. Guthrie, "So Human a Book: Pragmatism and Scriptural Authority," *Quarterly Review* 25:3 (Fall 2005): 258.

151 Tyron Inbody, "Methodism and Pragmatism: Promise or Peril?" *Quarterly Review* 25:3 (Fall 2005): 278.

152 Margaret D. Zulik, "Prophecy and Providence: The Anxiety over Prophetic Authority," *The Journal of Communication and Religion* 26:2 (September 2003): 205; quoted in Clifton F. Guthrie, "So Human a Book," p. 255.

153 Pedraja, *Teologia*, p. 19.

154 Michael Baigent, *The Jesus Papers: Exposing the Greatest Cover-Up in History*. HarperSanFrancisco, 2006, p. 70.

155 See Deuteronomy 4:2; 12:32; Proverbs 30:6; Revelation 22:18.

156 Bart D. Ehrman, *Lost Christianities: The Battles for Scripture and the Faiths We Never Knew*. New York: Oxford University Press, 2003, p. 231.

157 Baigent, *The Jesus Papers*, p. 79.

158 Ibid. p. 82, italics added.

159 Michael Cronin, "Babel's Standing Stones: Language, Translation And The Exosomatic," *Crossings: eJournal of Art and Technology*, 2:1 (March 2002): http://crossings.tcd.ie/issues/2.1/Cronin/

160 Robert Stanton, "Forum: The Reality of Reality," *Skeptical Inquirer*, May/June 1999 http://www.csicop.org/si/9905/reality-of-reality.html

161 James A. Sheppard, *Christendom at the Crossroads: The Medieval Era*. "The Westminster History of Christian Thought;" Louisville KY: Westminster John Knox Press, 2005, p. 23.

162 Bart D. Ehrman, *Misquoting Jesus: The Story Behind Who Changed the Bible and Why*. New York: HarperSanFrancisco, 2005, p. 7.

163 Ibid. p. 155. The entire book presents a good discussion of this. See also his *Lost Christianities: The Battles for Scripture and the Faiths We Never Knew*. New York: Oxford University Press, 2003, chapter 10, pp 203-227.

164 Ibid. p. 175.

165 Ibid. p. 11.

166 Justo L. González, *Manana: Christian Theology from a Hispanic Perspective*. Nashville: Abingdon Press, 1990, p. 99f.

167 Frans de Waal, *Chimpanzee Politic: Power and Sex among Apes*. New York: Harper & Row, 1982.

168 Donald M. Braxton, "Certainty and Self-Deception among American Fundamentalism," *Metanexus Anthropos* (2004.12.09) http://www.metanexus.net/metanexus_online/show_article.asp?9195

169 Ibid. See David Livingstone Smith, *Why We Lie: the Evolutionary Roots of Deception and the Unconscious Mind*. New York: St Martin's Press, 2004.

170 Ibid.

171 Ehrman, *Lost Christianities*, pp. 150-151.

172 Theodore M. Snider, *The Divine Activity*.

173 Teilhard de Chardin, quoted in Robert L. Faricy, *Teilhard de Chardin's Theology of the Christian in the World.* New York: Sheed and Ward, 1967, p. 116.

174 Michael Shermer, *The Science of Good and Evil: Why People Cheat, Gossip, Care, Share, and Follow the Golden Rule.* New York: "Owl Books," Henry Holt and Company, 2004, p. 185.

175 Sam Harris, *The End of Faith: Religion, Terror, and the Future of Reason.* New York: W.W. Norton & Company, 2004, 2005, pp. 12, 13.

176 Ibid. p. 19, 25.

177 Farley, "Fundamentalism: A Theory."

CHAPTER 5—Intuition as a Source of Knowledge

178 David G. Myers, *Intuition: Its Powers and Perils.* New Haven, CT: Yale University Press, 2002, p. 1.

179 David G. Myers, "Do What You Feel, Maybe: The Power and Perils of Relying on Intuition," http://www.incharacter.org/article.php?article=88

180 Lea Winerman, "What We Know Without Knowing How," *Monitor on Psychology* 36:3 (March 2005) http://www.apa.org/monitor/mar05/knowing.html

181 Gerard Hodgkinson, quoted in University of Leeds, "Go with Your Gut—Intuition Is More than Just a Hunch, Says New Research," *Science Daily* (6 March 2008). See Gerard P. Hodgkinson, J, Langan-Fox, J. and Sadler-Smith, E. "Intuition: A Fundamental Bridging Construct in the Behavioural Sciences," *British Journal of Psychology* 99 (2008), 1-27. http://www.sciencedaily.com/releases/2008/03/080305144210.htm

182 John Bargy, "Bypassing the Will: Towards Demystifying the Nonconscious Control of Social Behavior," in *The New Unconscious*, ed. R. Hassin, J. Uleman, & J. Bargh. Oxford University Press, 2004. Quoted in Tom Stafford, "Consciousness Exists to Make Itself Unnecessary," (3 March 2006) http://www.mindhacks.com/blog/2006/03/consciousness_exists.html

183 John A. Bargh, quoted in Bruce Bower, "The Mental Butler Did It," *Science News* (30 October 1999)
http://findarticles.com/p/articles/mi_m1200/is_/ai_57799547

184 Jon Hanson and David Yosifon, "The (Unconscious) Situation of our Consciousness—Part I," *The Situationist* (15 November 2007), http://thesituationist.wordpress.com/2007/11/15/the-unconscious-situation-of-our-consciousness-part-i/

185 Karen S. Peterson. "There's A Gut Feeling About This Whole Intuition Thing," *USA Today* (26 February 2003) http://www.usatoday.com/news/nation/2003-02-26-mind-intuition_x.htm

186 Benedict Carey, "Who's Minding the Mind?" *New York Times* (31 July 2007) http://www.nytimes.com/2007/07/31/health/psychology/31subl.html?_r=2&oref=slogin&oref=slogin

187 David G. Myers, "Do What You Feel, Maybe."

188 Lea Winerman, "What We Know Without Knowing How."

189 David G. Myers, "Do What You Feel, Maybe."

190 Ibid.

191 David Milner, quoted in David G. Myers, "Do What You Feel, Maybe: The Power and Perils of Relying on Intuition," http://www.incharacter.org/article.php?article=88

192 David G. Myers, "Do What You Feel, Maybe."

193 Ibid. Italics added.

194 Ibid. See David G. Myers, *Intuition: Its Powers and Perils*. New Haven, CT: Yale University Press, 2002.

195 Michael Shermer, *The Science of Good and Evil*. p. 178.

196 Pedraja, *Teologia*, p. 59.

197 James Warren "Jim" Jones (1931-1978) was the pastor, founder and leader of the People's Temple. Facing increasing scrutiny from the US and Guyana governments, on November 18, 1978 he ordered all of the members—more than 900 men, women, and children—to fatally drink poisoned Kool-aide and then killed himself. Nine other persons were killed at a nearby airstrip, including US Congressman Leo J. Ryan.

198 Alan Lightman, in Adam Bly, ed., *Science Is Culture: Conversations at the New Intersection of Science & Society*. New York: Harper Perennial, 2010, pp. 53-54.

199 Sharon Begley, "I Can't Think!" *Newsweek* 158:10 (7 March 2001): p. 30.

200 Ibid. p. 31f.

201 Joanne Cantor, quoted in Begley, "I Can't Think!" p. 32.

202 Begley, p. 32, 33.

203 Russell Stannard, *Grounds for Reasonable Belief*. Edinburgh: Scottish Academic Press, 1989, p. 169.

204 Daniel C. Dennett, *Darwin's Dangerous Idea: Evolution and the Meanings of Life*. New York: Simon & Schuster, 1995, p. 520.

205 Fred Hoyle, quoted in Paul Davies, *The Mind of God*, pp. 228-229. See Fred Hoyle, "The Universe: Past and Present Reflections," *University of Cardiff Report* 70 (1981), p. 43.

206 Ibid. p. 229.

207 Sheppard, *Christendom at the Crossroads*, p. 24.

208 Amazon.com, "Interview with Sam Harris: The Mortal Dangers of Religious Faith," http://www.amazon.com/exec/obidos/tg/feature/-/542154/002-5322908-3699212

209 Davies, *The Mind of God*, p. 227.

210 Ken Wilber, ed., *Quantum Questions*. Boulder: New Science Library, 1984: p. 7.

211 Davies, *The Mind of God*, p. 229-230.

212 Owen Flanagan, *The Problem of the Soul: Two Visions of Mind and How to Reconcile Them*. New York: Basic Books, 2002.

213 Peter H. Van Ness, "Introduction: Spirituality and the Secular Quest," in *Spirituality and the Secular Quest*, ed. Peter H. Van Ness, Vol. 22 of *World Spirituality: An Encyclopedic History of the Religious Quest* (New York: Crossroad, 1996), p. 2.

214 John Macquarrie, *Paths in Spirituality* (New York: Harper and Row, 1972), 40.

215 Sandra M. Schneiders, "Theology and Spirituality: Strangers, Rivals, or Partners," *Horizons* 13:2 (1986): 266.

216 Stanley J. Grenz, "Christian Spirituality and the Quest for Identity: Toward a Spiritual-Theological Understanding of Life in Christ," *Baptist History and Heritage* (March 2002) http://www.highbeam.com/doc/1G1-94160844.html

217 Ibid.

218 Dowd, *Thank God for Evolution*, p. 22.

CHAPTER 6—And Jacob Digged a Well

219 Lakoff, *The Political Mind*, p. 22.

220 Ibid. p. 43.

221 Ibid. p. 35, 37.

222 Ibid. p. 34.

223 Ibid. p. 25.

224 Ibid. p. 38.

225 Ibid, p. 56.

226 Ibid. p. 58.

227 Ibid. p. 71.

228 Barry Werth, *Banquet at Delmonico's: Great Minds, the Gilded Age, and the Triumph of Evolution in America*. New York: Random House, 2009, 62.

229 Ibid. p. 61.

230 Ibid. p. 61.

[231] Lakoff, p. 71.
[232] Ibid. p. 73.
[233] Ibid. p. 59.
[234] Ibid. p. 128.
[235] Kaku, *Physics of the Impossible: A Scientific Exploration into the World of Phasers, Force Fields, Teleportation, and Time Travel.* New York: Doubleday, 2008, p. 58.
[236] Manjit Kumar, *Quantum: Einstein, Bohn, and the Great Debate about the Nature of Reality*. New York: W.W. Norton & Company, 2008, p. 218.
[237] Vlatko Vedral, *Decoding Reality: The Universe as Quantum Information*. New York: Oxford University Press, 2010, p. 157.
[238] Kaku, *Physics of the Impossible*, p. 61. See, for example, Louisa Gilder, *The Age of Entanglement: When Quantum Physics was Reborn*. New York: Vintage Books, 2008.
[239] Adam Bly, ed., *Science Is Culture: Conversations at the New Intersection of Science & Society*. New York: Harper Perennial, 2010, p. ix.
[240] John Eddy, quoted in Richard Cohen, *Chasing the Sun: The Epic Story of the Star that Gives Us Life*. New York: Random House, 2010, p. xxii. See: John Eddy, "Climate and the Role of the Sun," *Journal of Interdisciplinary History*, 10:4 (Spring 1980): pp. 725-747.
[241] William Tucker, "Complex Questions: The New Science of Spontaneous Order—Complexity Theory," *Reason*, January, 1996 http://www.findarticles.com/p/articles/mi_m1568/is_n8_v27/ai_17779895
[242] Tad Hogue, quoted in William Tucker, "Complex Questions."
[243] Tucker, "Complex Questions."
[244] Samuel Butler, *Unconscious Memory* (1880), quoted in George Dyson, "Darwin among the Machines: Or, the Origins of [Artificial] Life?" *Edge* 7.8.97 http://www.edge.org/3rd_culture/dyson/dyson_p2.html
[245] Kaku, p. 105, 110-111.
[246] Ibid. p. 124.
[247] "Watson (artificial intelligence software)," http://en.wikipedia.org/wiki/Watson_(artificial_intelligence_software)
[248] Ibid.
[249] David Levy, quoted in Charles Q. Choi, "Not Tonight, Dear, I Have a Robot," *Scientific American* 298:3 (March 2008), p. 94.
[250] Choi, p. 94.
[251] Ibid. p. 96.
[252] Levy, quoted in Choi, p. 96.

253 Sherry Turkle, quoted in Choi, p. 97. See Sherry Turkle, *The Second Self: Computers and the Human Spirit.* Cambridge, MA: MIT Press, 2005.

254 Joel B. Green, *What About the Soul? Neuroscience and Christian Anthropology.* Nashville: Abingdon Press, 2004, p. 6.

255 Frank Tipler, "The Omega Point as Eschaton: Answers to Pannenberg's Questions for Scientists," *Zygon*, 24 (1989): 241-242.

256 Davies, *The Mind of God*, p. 117.

257 Harry Emerson Fosdick, *The Living of these Days.* New York: Harper & Brothers, p. 8.

258 Davies, *God and the New Physics*, p. 97. See also the "Brain in a Vat" experiments done by Thomas De Marse at the University of Florida.

259 Ibid. pp. 97-98. The question of the survival of the self or soul in transplants is dealt with in the interesting young adult book, *Unwind*, by Neal Shusterman. New York: Simon & Schuster, 2007.

260 Ted Peters and Martinez Hewett, *Evolution from Creation to New Creation: Conflict, Conversation, and Convergence.* Nashville: Abingdon Press, 2003, p. 176.

261 Stuart A. Kauffman, *Reinventing the Sacred: A New Vision of Science, Reason, and Religion.* New York: Basic Books, 2008, p. 3, 4, 5.

262 Philip Hefner, "Created to be Creators," *Metanexus Sophia* (19 December 2003) http://metanexus.net/metanexus_online/show_article.asp?8664

263 Stuart A. Kauffman, *Reinventing the Sacred: A New View of Science, Reason, and Religion.* New York: Basic Books, 2008, p. 6.

264 Philip Hefner, "Created to be Creators."

265 Jurgen Moltmann, *Science and Wisdom.* Trans., Margaret Kohl. Minneapolis: Fortress Press, 2003, p. 124.

266 Francis Fukuyama, *Our Posthuman Future: Consequences of the Biotechnology Revolution.* New York: Farrar, Straus, Gioux, 2002.

267 Hefner, "Created to be Creators."

268 Terrence Deacon, *The Symbolic Species: The Co-Evolution of Language and the Brain.* New York: W. W. Norton, 1997, pp. 1-2.

269 William James, "Reflex Action and Theism," *The Limits of Language*, ed. Walker Gibson. New York: Hill and Wang, 1962, p. 7.

CHAPTER 7—What Color Is an Invisible Dog?

270 A. P. Hotaling's whiskey warehouse survived San Francisco's 1906 post-quake inferno while many churches were destroyed. This prompted an unknown author to write these lines.

[271] William H. Swatos, Jr., review of "Acts of Faith: Explaining the Human Side of Religion," *Sociology of Religion* 63:2 (Summer 2002) http://www.findarticles.com/p/articles/mi_m0SOR/is_2_63/ai_89078713

[272] Nicholas Nicastro, *Circumference: Eratosthenes and the Ancient Quest to Measure the Globe*. New York: St. Martin's Press, 2008, pp. 35-36.

[273] Ibid. p. 34, 37.

[274] Reference lost.

[275] Stephen Bertman, *The Genesis of Science: The Story of Greek Imagination*. New York: Prometheus Books, 2010, pp. 95-96.

[276] Ibid. p. 151.

[277] Nicastro, p. 79.

[278] Sophocles, quoted in Nicastro, p. 80.

[279] Nicastro, p. 80.

[280] Ibid. p. 85.

[281] Tertullian, quoted in Nicastro, p. 160.

[282] Georgia L. Irby-Massie and Paul T. Keyser, *Greek Science of the Hellenistic Era*. London: Routledge, 2002, p. 17.

[283] Nicastro, p. 173.

[284] Christine Garwood, *Flat Earth: The History of an Infamous Idea*. New York: St. Martin's Press, 2007, p. 23f.

[285] Ibid. p. 24.

[286] William H. Calvin, "Concept Change after Contact. Old Notions Never Die. They Just Incorporate," http://williamcalvin.com/2005/CALVIN%20post-contract%20religion.pdf, p. 3.

[287] Ibid. p. 4-5.

[288] Kitty Ferguson, *The Music of Pythagoras: How an Ancient Brotherhood Cracked the Code of the Universe and Lit the Path from Antiquity to Outer Space*. New York: Walker and Company, 2008, pp. 23-24.

[289] Ibid. p. 108.

[290] Gregory J. Riley, *The River of God: A New History of Christian Origins*. New York: HarperSanFrancisco, 2003, p. 39.

[291] Riley, pp. 39-40.

[292] Ibid. pp. 40, 41.

[293] Susan Wise Bauer, *The History of the Ancient World: From the Earliest Accounts to the Fall of Rome*. New York: W.W. Norton & Company, 2007, p. 64.

[294] Ibid. p. 65.

[295] Ibid. p. 115.

296 Ibid. p. 231.

297 Ibid. p. 233.

298 Ibid. p. 234.

299 Riley, p. 42.

300 Carl Huffman, "Archytas," *Stanford Encyclopedia of Philosophy*, http://plato.stanford.edu/entries/archytas/

301 Ferguson, *The Music of Pythagoras*, p. 122.

302 Ibid. p. 240f.

303 Ibid. p. 241.

304 Riley, p. 42-43.

305 Ibid. p. 46.

306 Carl Sagan, "The God Hypothesis," *Skeptic* 13:1 (2007): 42.

307 Davies, *God and the New Physics*, p. 66.

308 Odin, pp. 6-7.

309 Paul Bloom and Deena Skolnick Weisberg, "Why Do Some People Resist Science?" http://www.edge.org/3rd_culture/bloom07/bloom07_index.html. See: Paul Bloom and Deena Skolnick Weisberg, "Childhood Origins of Adult Resistance to Science," *Science* 316:5827 (18 May 2007), pp. 996-997.

310 Gordon D. Kaufman, "Re-conceiving God and Humanity in Light of Today's Ecological Consciousness: A Brief Statement," *Cross Currents* 50:1-2 (Spring/Summer 2000) http://www.findarticles.com/p/articles/mi_m2096/is_2000_Spring-Summer/ai_63300896

311 John Shelby Spong, "Re-Imagining God in a Post-Tsunami World,": *Catholic New Times* 29:4 (February 13, 2005) http://findarticles.com/p/articles/mi_mOMKY/is_3_29/ai_n11838806

312 Toolan, David S. "Praying in a Post-Einsteinian Universe," *Cross Currents* 46:4 (Winter 1996-97) http://www.crosscurrents.org/toolin.html

313 Kauffman, *Reinventing the Sacred*, p. 19. See also Philip W. Anderson, "More Is Different," Science, New Series, 177:4047 (4 August 1972), pp. 393-396.

314 Carl Sagan, Introduction to Stephen Hawking, *A Brief History of Time: From the Big Bang to Black Holes*. New York: Bantam Books, 1988, p. ix.

315 Davies, *The Mind of God*, p. 15.

316 Hawking, *A Brief History of Time*, p.1.

317 David A, Pailin, "On the Significance of the Sovereignty of God," *Theology Today* 53:1 (April 1996), p. 37.

318 Carl Stecher, "Looking for God in All the Wrong Places," *Humanist*, May-June, 1998. http://www.findarticles.com/p/articles/mi_m1374/is_n3_v58/ai_20770510

[319] Pedraja, *Teologia*, p. 106.

[320] Michio Kaku, *Physics of the Impossible: A Scientific Exploration into the World of Phasers, Force Fields, Teleportation, and Time Travel.* New York: Doubleday, 2008, p. 135.

[321] Chris Stringer, quoted in Heather Wax, "Concerning Hobbits," *Science & Spirit* 16:1 (January-February 2005): 24.

[322] Wax, p. 24.

[323] Mike Morwood, quoted in Wax, p. 24.

[324] Vilayanur S. Ramachandran, *The Tell-Tale Brain: A Neuroscientist's Quest for What Makes Us Human.* New York: W.W. Norton & Company, 2011, pp. 9, 10.

[325] Luke 13:1-5; Matthew 5:45.

[326] Daniel C. Dennett, *Breaking the Spell: Religion as a Natural Phenomenon.* New York: Penguin Books, 2006, pp. 133-134. See also Julian Jaynes, *The Origins of Consciousness in the Breakdown of the Bicameral Mind.* Boston: Houghton Mifflin, 1976, p. 240.

[327] Ian Barbour, *Nature, Human Nature, and God.* Minneapolis: Fortress Press, 2002, p. 16.

[328] Willlem B. Drees, "Creation: From Nothing until Now, Part 1," *Metanexus: Views* (17 December 2001).
http://www.metanexus.net/metanexus_online/show_article.asp?5071.

[329] David W. Nelson, "God as Big Bang: New Way to Comprehend the Divine," *Science and Theology News*, 6:3 (November 2005): p. 34.

CHAPTER 8—Can God Really…?

[330] David Ray Griffin, *Two Great Truths: A New Synthesis of Scientific Naturalism and Christian Faith.* Louisville: Westminster John Knox Press, 2004, p. 57.

[331] Jürgen Moltmann, *Science and Wisdom.* Trans., Margaret Kohl. Minneapolis: Fortress Press, 2003, p. 66.

[332] Stephen J. Pope, "Christ and Darwin: a PBS Series and a New York Review of Books Essayist Fail to Take Seriously the Work of Leading Figures in the Field of Religion and Science—Back to the Evolution Wars?" *Christian Century* (2 January 2002).

[333] Paul R. Gross, "Neo-creationist Tactics Show Troubling Evolution," *Science and Theology News*, 6:2 (October 2005): 5.

[334] John Polkinghorne, "Natural Science, Temporality, and Divine Action," *Theology Today*, 55:3 (October 1998), p. 329.

335 Peter A. Young, "Confessions of a Believer in Exile," *Cross Currents*, 48:4 (Winter 1998) http://www.findarticles.com/p/articles/mi_m2096/is_4_48/ai_54064306

336 John Shelby Spong, *Why Christianity Must Change or Die*. New York: HarperSanFrancisco, 1998, p. 52.

337 Ibid. pp. 63, 64.

338 Peter A. Young, "Confessions of a Believer in Exile."

339 Spong, *Why Christianity Must Change or Die*, pp. 147, 148.

340 Peter A. Young, "Confessions of a Believer in Exile."

341 Michael Benedikt, *God Is the Good We Do: Theology of Theopraxy*. New York: Bottino Books, 2007.

342 Epicurus, *Aphorisms of Epicurus*, http://www.ag.wastholm.net/author/Epicurus.

343 "1755 Lisbon Earthquake," http://en.wikipedia.org/wiki/1755_Lisbon_earthquake.

344 Shermer, *The Science of Good and Evil*, p. 69.

345 Susan Wise Bauer, *The History of the Ancient World: From the Earliest Accounts to the Fall of Rome*. New York: W.W. Norton & Company, 2007, p. 139.

346 Ibid. p. 140.

347 Victor J. Stenger, *God: The Failed Hypothesis*. Amherst, NY: Prometheus Books, 2007, p. 223.

348 Jim Wallis, "Dangerous Religion: George W. Bush's Theology of Empire," *Sojourner's Magazine* 32:5 (September-October 2003), pp. 20-26 http://www.sojo.net/index.cfm?action=magazine.article&issue=soj0309&article=030910

349 Michael Shermer, *The Science of Good and Evil: Why People Cheat, Gossip, Care, Share, and Follow the Golden Rule*. New York: "Owl Books," Henry Holt and Company, 2004, p. 120

350 Vedral, *Decoding Reality*, pp. 154, 155.

351 Ibid. p. 155.

352 Shermer, *The Science of Good and Evil*, pp. 134, 135.

353 Shmuley Boteach, "Is It Time for G-D to do Teshuvah?" *Tikkun*, September-October, 2002.

354 Ibid.

355 Evan Fales, quoted in Stenger, *God: The Failed Hypothesis*, p. 240.

356 Catherine Keller, "Power Lines," *Theology Today* 52:2 (July 1995): 189.

357 Ibid. p 190. For the interaction of violence against children with apocalyptic Protestantism and the cultural expectation of mass doom, Keller refers us to Philip Grevin, *Spare the Child: The Protestant Roots of Child Abuse* (New York: Knopf, 1991).

[358] Marta Benevides, in a lecture at Drew University, November 1993. Quoted in Keller, "Power Lines," p. 190.

[359] Janet Martin Soskice, "God of Power and Might," *Theology Today*, 54:1 (April 1997), p. 20-21.

[360] Ibid. p. 21.

[361] Julie Shoshana Pfau and David R. Blumenthal, "The Violence of God: Dialogic Fragments," *Judaism*, 51:2 (Summer 2001), http://www.crosscurrents.org/blumenthal0701.htm. Julie Shoshana Pfau was a graduate student in religion at Emory University. David R. Blumenthal teaches and writes on constructive Jewish theology, medieval Judaism, Jewish mysticism, and holocaust studies.

[362] Luis G. Pedraja, "Suffering God: Theodicy in the Twenty-first Century," *Quarterly Review* 22:2 (Summer 2002): 168. See also Daniel Day Williams, *The Demonic and the Divine*. Minneapolis: Fortress Press, 1990, p. 13.

SECTION THREE PREFACE

[363] Leonard I. Sweet, *New Life in the Spirit*. Philadelphia: Westminster Press, 1982, p. 29.

[364] Patrick Miller, "A Strange Kind of Monotheism," *Theology Today*, 54:3 (October 1997), p. 293.

CHAPTER 9—How Did that Nice Jewish Boy Become a Platonized God?

[365] Baigent, *The Jesus Papers*, p. 11.

[366] L. Michael White, *From Jesus to Christianity: How Four Generations of Visionaries & Storytellers Created the New Testament and Christian Faith*. New York: HarperCollins Publishers, 2004, pp. 7, 13.

[367] Cyrus is mentioned 23 times in the Bible and alluded to many other times. See especially 2 Chronicles 36:22-33; Ezra 1:1-8, 3:7, 4:3-5, 5:13-17, 6:3-14; Isaiah 44:28, 45:1-13; Daniel 1:21, 6:28, 10:1, and 1 Esdras 2.

[368] White, *From Jesus to Christianity*, pp. 15-16.

[369] Jeffrey W. Hargis, *Against the Christians: The Rise of Early Anti-Christian Polemic*. "Patristic Studies," vol. 1; New York: Peter Lang, 1999, p. 1.

[370] Ibid. pp. 15-16.

[371] Ibid. p. 16.

[372] Ibid. pp. 683, 685.

[373] Ibid. p. 702.

[374] Ibid. p. 708.

[375] L. Michael White, *From Jesus to Christianity: How Four Generations of Visionaries & Storytellers Created the New Testament and Christian Faith*. New York: HarperCollins Publishers, 2004, pp. 40-41.

[376] Bauer, *The History of the Ancient World*, p. 709.

[377] Ibid. p. 718.

[378] Ibid. p. 720.

[379] Ibid.

[380] White, *From Jesus to Christianity*, p. 17.

[381] Ibid. p. 19.

[382] Ibid. See also: Marcel Simon, *Jewish Sects at the Time of Jesus*, Translated by James H. Farley. Philadelphia: Fortress Press, 1980.

[383] Ibid. p. 21f.

[384] Ibid. p. 86.

[385] Ibid. pp. 36, 39.

[386] Ibid. p. 42.

[387] Joseph W. Trigg, *Origen*. "The Early Church Fathers," London: Routledge, 1998, p. 55.

[388] White, *From Jesus to Christianity*, p. 42.

[389] Ibid. p. 46.

[390] Ibid. p. 50.

[391] Ibid. p. 73.

[392] Ibid. p. 125f.

[393] Christopher Hitchens, *God Is Not Great: How Religion Poisons Everything*. New York: Twelve, 2007, p. 23.

[394] James A. Conner, *Pascal's Wager: The Man Who Played Dice with God*. New York: HarperSanFrancisco, 2006, p. 106.

[395] Ehrman, *Lost Christianities*, p. 95.

[396] Baigent, *The Jesus Papers*, p. 73f.

[397] Sara Schechner, "The Riddle in the Skies," *UNESCO Courier* (May 2001) http://www.findarticles.com/p/articles/mi_m1310/is_2001_May/ai_75143876

[398] Michael Welker, "Who Is Jesus Christ for Us Today?" *Harvard Theological Review* 95:2 (April 2002).

[399] Leonard Sweet, "'Personal Lord and Savior:' Christology and the Devotional Image," http://www.leonardsweet.com/includes/ShowSweetenedArticles.asp?articleID=92

[400] Ibid.

401 B.A. Gerrish, "What Do We Mean by Faith in Jesus Christ?" *Christian Century* 116:26 (6 October 1999) http://www.findarticles.com/p/articles/mi_m1058/is_26_116/ai_56249457

402 Otto A. Piper, "Christology and History," *Theology Today* 19:3 (October 1962) p. 331 (Italics added).

403 Ibid. pp. 335-336.

404 Ibid.

405 Ibid. p. 337, italics added.

406 Ibid. p. 338.

407 Douglas John Hall, "Confessing Christ in a Post-Christendom Context," *Ecumenical Review* (July, 2000) http://findarticles.com/p/articles/mi_m2065/is_3_52/ai_66279081

408 John Macquarrie, "Current Trends in Anglican Christology," *Anglican Theological Review* (Fall, 1977) http://www.findarticles.com/p/articles/mi_qa3818/is_199710/ai_n8774191

409 Macquarrie, "Current Trends in Anglican Christology."

410 John J. Reilly, reviewer, "Daemonomania," *First Things* 111 (March 2001): 53.

411 Miller, quoted in Reilly, reviewer, "Daemonomania," p. 53.

412 Lloyd Geering, "How Did Jesus Become God—and Why?" *The Fourth R* 11:5 (September/October 1998) http://www.westarinstitute.org/Periodicals/4R_Articles/Jesus_to_God/jesus_to_god.html

413 Ibid.

414 James D. G. Dunn, "Jesus for Today," *Theology Today* (April 1995) http://www.findarticles.com/p/articles/mi_qa3664/is_199504/ai_n8725673

415 Paul B. Rauschenbusch, ed. *Christianity and the Social Crisis in the 21st Century: The Classic that Woke Up the Church.* NY: HarperCollins, 2007, p. 42.

416 Ibid. p. 59.

417 Geza Vermes, quoted in Gerhard Bodendorfer, "Jewish Voices about Jesus," *Jewish-Christian Relations* http://www.jcrelations.net/en/?item=738

418 John H. Elliott, "Jesus Was Not an Egalitarian: A Critique of an Anachronistic and Idealist Theory," *Biblical Theology Bulletin* 32:2 (Summer 2002) http://www.findarticles.com/p/articles/mi_m0LAL/is_2_32/ai_94332342

419 Ibid.

420 Ibid.

421 Hayim Goren Perelmuter, *Siblings: Rabbinic Judaism and Early Christianity at Their Beginnings.* Mahwah, NJ: Paulist Press, 1989, pp. 7-8.

CHAPTER 10—Did Jesus Die for Your Sin?

422 Thomas Paine, *The Age of Reason: Being an Investigation of True and Fabulous Theology* (1793), http://www.infidels.org/library/historical/thomas_paine/age_of_reason/part1.html#3

423 S. Mark Heim, "Christ Crucified," *Christian Century* 118:8 (7 March 2001) http://www.findarticles.com/p/articles/mi_m1058/is_8_118/ai_72094707

424 Ibid.

425 Ibid.

426 Ibid.

427 Ibid.

428 Ibid.

429 John Shelby Spong, "Christian Anthropology: Definition of Our Humanity, Or Ancient Pathology?" *Human Quest* (July/August 1999) http://www.findarticles.com/p/articles/mi_qa3861/is_199907/ai_n8853324

430 Ibid.

431 Ibid.

432 Christopher A. Brown, "Can Buddhism Save? Finding Resonance in Incommensurability," *Cross Currents*, (Summer 1999) http://findarticles.com/p/articles/mi_m2096/is_2_49/ai_55106736

433 Karl Rahner, *Theological Investigations, Vol 16.* Translated by David Morland. London: Darton, Longman & Todd, 1979, p. 218.

434 Karl Rahner, *Theological Investigations, Vol 10.* Translated by David Bourke. London: Darton, Longman & Todd, 1973, p. 31.

435 *Dogmatic Constitution On The Church* "Lumen Gentium" Solemnly Promulgated By Pope Paul VI, 21 November 1964. http://www.vatican.va/archive/hist_councils/ii_vatican_council/documents/vat-ii_const_19641121_lumen-gentium_en.html

436 Rahner, *Theological Investigations, Vol 16*, p. 202.

437 Karl Rahner, *Theological Investigations, Vol 6*, Translated by David Bourke. London: Darton, Longman & Todd, 1966, p. 38.

438 Rahner, *Theological Investigations, Vol 10*, p. 48.

439 Jack Miles, *Christ: A Crisis in the Life of God.* New York: Alfred A. Knopf, 2001.

440 Elie Wiesel, *The Trial of God: (as it was held on February 25, 1649 in Shamgorod).* New York: Random House, 1979.

441 Richard J. Foster, "Salvation Is for Life," *Theology Today* (October 2004) http://www.findarticles.com/p/articles/mi_qa3664/is_200410/ai_n9453164

442 Ibid.

443 Ibid.

444 Virgen Guroian, "Salvation: Divine Therapy," *Theology Today* (October 2004) http://www.findarticles.com/p/articles/mi_qa3664/is_200410/ai_n9453167

445 Ibid.

446 Arthur Green, *Seek My Face: A Jewish Mystical Theology*. Woodstock, VT: Jewish Lights Publishing; 2nd edition (2003), p. 187.

447 Sidney Callahan, "We're All Original Sinners," *Commonweal* 127:2 (28 January 2000) http://www.findarticles.com/p/articles/mi_m1252/is_2_127/ai_60054355

448 Ibid.

449 Ibid.

450 Sheppard, *Christendom at the Crossroads*, p. 85.

451 Reference lost.

CHAPTER 11—The Survival of Personal Identity

452 Davies, *God and the New Physics*, pp. 88-90.

453 Mathetes, *Letter to Diognetus*, 6:3. http://www.earlychristianwritings.com/text/diognetus-lightfoot.html.

454 Carl Zimmer, *Soul Made Flesh: The Discovery of the Brain—and How It Changed the World*. New York: Free Press, 2004, p. 6.

455 John Polkinghorne, "Natural Science, Temporality, and Divine Action," *Theology Today*, 55:3, October, 1998, p. 338.

456 Zimmer, *Soul Made Flesh*, p. 10.

457 Ibid. p. 11.

458 Ibid. p. 12.

459 Ibid. p. 16.

460 Ibid. p. 17.

461 Ibid. p. 18.

462 Don Cupitt, "The Radical Christian Worldview," *Cross Currents*, Spring-Summer, 2000 http://www.findarticles.com/p/articles/mi_m2096/is_2000_Spring-Summer/ai_63300893

463 Nancey Murphy, *Whatever Happened to the Soul? Scientific and Theological Portraits of Human Nature*. Minneapolis: Fortress Press, 1988, p. 18.

464 Michael Shermer, "The Soul Problem," *Psychology Today* (November-December 2002) http://www.findarticles.com/p/articles/mi_m1175/is_6_35/ai_92849367

465 Jay Werbinox Taylor, "Attacking the Soul Hypothesis," *American Atheist Magazine* (Spring 2004) http://www.findarticles.com/p/articles/mi_m0OBB/is_2_42/ai_n6100434

466 Zalman M. Schachter Shalomi, "Renewing God," *Tikkun* (September 2001).

467 Read Montague, quoted in Zach Lynch, *The Neuro Revolution: How Brain Science is Changing Our World*. New York: St. Martin's Press, 2009 p. 70.

468 ABC News, "Man with Twin Living Inside Him—A Medical Mystery Classic," (23 August 2006) http://abcnews.go.com/Health/story?id=2346476&page=1

469 Mark Ralls, "Reclaiming Heaven: What Can We Say about the Afterlife?" *Christian Century* 14 December 2004 http://www.findarticles.com/p/articles/mi_m1058/is_25_121/ai_n8702624

470 William H. Calvin, "The Fate of the Soul," June 2004 http://williamcalvin.com/2004/June04NaturalHistory%20download.htm

471 Ibid.

472 Nancey Murphy, quoted in Matt Donnelly, "Why Is there Something Rather than Nothing?" *Science & Theology News* 6:7 (March 2006): 19.

473 Davies, *God and the New Physics*, p. 59.

474 Daniel C. Dennett, *Freedom Evolves*. New York: Viking, 2003, p. 2.

475 Moltmann, *Science and Wisdom*, p. 191.

476 Walter (Ritoku) Robinson, "The Far East of Star Wars," in Kevin S. Decker and Jason T. Eberl, *Star Wars and Philosophy: More Powerful Than You Can Possibly Imagine*. New York: Barnes & Noble Inc, 2009, p. 29.

477 Ibid. p. 32.

478 Daniel Dennett, "Vitalism," http://www.skepdic.com/vitalism.html

479 Moltmann, *Science and Wisdom*, p. 96.

480 Dalai Lama, quoted in Janelle Lazzo, "Heaven, Self-Respect and the Golden Rule: Diverse Group Contemplates Reasons to be Good," *National Catholic Reporter* 39:7 (13 December 2002) http://www.findarticles.com/p/articles/mi_m1141/is_7_39/ai_95632000

CHAPTER 12—The Golden Rule and Moral Responsibility

481 Source lost.

482 Michael Shermer, *The Science of Good and Evil*, p. 18.

483 E. O. Wilson, quoted in Shermer, p. 18. See E.O. Wilson, *Consilience: The Unity of Knowledge*. New York: Knopf, 1998, pp. 238-265. See also E.O. Wilson, "The Biological Basis of Morality," *Atlantic Monthly* 281:4 (1998) pp. 53-70.

[484] Shermer, *The Science of Good and Evil*, pp. 19-21.

[485] Ibid.

[486] The golden rule is found in the Bible in various forms in the following places: Leviticus 19:18; Zechariah 8:17; Matthew 5:43; 7:12; 19:19; 22:39; Mark 12:31; 12:33; Luke 10:27; Romans 13:9-10; Galatians 5:14; and James 2:8.

[487] Steven Pinker, in Adam Bly, ed., *Science Is Culture: Conversations at the New Intersection of Science & Society*. New York: Harper Perennial, 2010, p. 29.

[488] Rebecca Goldstein, in Adam Bly, ed., *Science Is Culture: Conversations at the New Intersection of Science & Society*. New York: Harper Perennial, 2010, p. 29.

[489] Steven Pinker, in Adam Bly, ed., *Science Is Culture*, p. 29f.

[490] Ibid., p. 31.

[491] George Lakoff, *The Political Mind*, p. 101.

[492] Confucius, *Analects* 12:22.

[493] Confucius, *Analects* 6:8.

[494] Richard Hooker, "Jen," http://www.wsu.edu/~dee/GLOSSARY/JEN.HTM

[495] Ibid.

[496] Ibid.

[497] Carl Sagan, *The Varieties of Scientific Experience: A Personal View of the Search for God*. Edited by Ann Druyan. New York: Penguin Books, 2006, p. 129.

[498] Randolph M. Nesse, "Why a Lot of People with Selfish Genes Are Pretty Nice Except for Their Hatred of The Selfish Gene," in Alan Grafen and Mark Ridley, eds. *Richard Dawkins: How a Scientist Changed the Way We Think*. Oxford: Oxford University Press, 2006, pp. 208, 207.

[499] Richard Dawkins, *The Selfish Gene*. Oxford: Oxford University Press, 1989, p. 215.

[500] Daniel C. Dennett, *Freedom Evolves*. New York: Viking, 2003, p. 180.

[501] Ibid. p. 195.

[502] Jonathan Haidt, "Moral Psychology and the Misunderstanding of Religion," *Edge* (22 September 2007) http://www.edge.org/3rd_culture/haidt07/haidt07_index.html

[503] Andrew Meltzoff, Andrew and M. K. Moore, "Imitation of Facial and Manual Gestures by Human Neonates," *Science*, 198 (1977), pp. 75-78.

[504] Eric Jaffe, "Mirror Neurons: How We Reflect on Behavior," *Observer* (Association for Psychological Science), (May 2007) http://www.psychologicalscience.org/observer/getArticle.cfm?id=2167

[505] Marco Iacoboni, *Mirroring People: The New Science of How We Connect with Others*. New York: Farrar, Straus and Giroux, 2008, p. 124.

506 Ibid. pp. 4-5.

507 Ibid. p. 14.

508 Ibid. p. 41.

509 Ibid. p. 109.

510 Vilayanur S. Ramachandran, *The Tell-Tale Brain: A Neuroscientist's Quest for What Makes Us Human*. New York: W.W. Norton & Company, 2011, p. 124.

511 Iacoboni, *Mirroring People*, Ibid. p. 114.

512 Ibid. p. 132.

513 Theodore M. Snider, *The Divine Activity*. See especially Chapter 14, "The Social Self," pp. 219-234.

514 Dan Zahavi, quoted in Iacoboni, p. 132; see Dan Zahavi, "Beyond Empathy: Phenomenological Approaches to Intersubjectivity," *Journal of Consciousness Studies* 8 (2001): 151-167.

515 Iacoboni, *Mirroring People*, p. 133.

516 Ibid. p. 268.

517 Ibid. pp. 268-271.

518 Ramachandran, *The Tell-Tale Brain*, p. 124f, 125.

519 Michael Kosfeld, "Trust in the Brain: Neurobiological Determinants of Human Social Behaviour," *EMBO Reports* http://www.nature.com/embor/journal/v8/n1s/full/7400975.html

520 Michael Kosfeld, "Brain Trust," *Greater Good* (Fall 2008) http://greatergood.berkeley.edu/article/item/brain_trust/

521 Zach Lynch, *The Neuro Revolution: How Brain Science is Changing Our World*. New York: St. Martin's Press, 2009, p. 98.

522 Paul Zak, quoted in Lynch, *The Neuro Revolution*, pp. 106-107.

523 Nicholas Wade, "Depth of the Kindness Hormone Appears to Know Some Bounds," *New York Times* (11 January 2011), page D1.

524 Kosfeld, "Brain Trust."

525 Wade, "Depth of the Kindness Hormone...."

526 Lynch, *The Neuro Revolution*, p. 107.

527 Paul Zak, quoted in Lynch, *The Neuro Revolution*, p. 108.

528 Dennett, *Freedom Evolves*, pp. 144-145.

529 Helena Cronin, "The Battle of the Sexes," in Alan Grafen and Mark Ridley, eds. *Richard Dawkins: How a Scientist Changed the Way We Think*. Oxford: Oxford University Press, 2006, p. 15, 16.

530 Michael Ruse, "Richard Dawkins and the Problem of Progress," in Alan Grafen and Mark Ridley, eds. *Richard Dawkins: How a Scientist Changed the Way We Think*. Oxford: Oxford University Press, 2006, p. 148.

531 Dennett, *Freedom Evolves*, p. 150.

532 Elliott Sober and David Sloan Wilson, *Unto Others: The Evolution and Psychology of Unselfish Behavior*. Cambridge, MA: Harvard University Press, 1998, Quoted in Dennett, *Freedom*, p. 193.

533 Steven Pinker, quoted in Ronald Bailey and Nick Gillespie, interview with Steven Pinker, "Biology vs. The Blank Slate: Evolutionary Psychologist Steven Pinker Deconstructs the Great Myths about How the Mind Works," *Reason*, Oct, 2002 http://www.findarticles.com/p/articles/mi_m1568/is_5_34/ai_91475038

534 Ibid.

535 Charles Darwin, quoted in Victor J. Stenger, *God: The Failed Hypothesis*. Amherst, NY: Prometheus Books, 2007, p. 193.

536 Charles Darwin, quoted in Ullica Segerstråle, "An Eye on the Core: Dawkins and Sociobiology," in Alan Grafen and Mark Ridley, eds. *Richard Dawkins: How a Scientist Changed the Way We Think*. Oxford: Oxford University Press, 2006, p. 76f.

537 Erica Klarreich, "Generous Players: Game Theory Explores the Golden Rule's Place in Biology," *Science News* 166:4 (24 July 2004) http://www.findarticles.com/p/articles/mi_m1200/is_4_166/ai_n6151880

538 See Frans de Waal, *Good Natured: The Origin of Right and Wrong in Human and Other Animals*. Cambridge, MA: Harvard University Press, 1996. See also Frans de Waal, *Chimpanzee Politics: Power and Sex Among Apes*. Baltimore, MD: Johns Hopkins University Press, 1989.

539 Shermer, *The Science of Good and Evil*, p. 31. For an extensive list of human moral and religious universals, see his Appendix II, pp. 285-292.

540 Frans de Waal, *Our Inner Ape: A Leading Primatologist Explains Why We Are Who We Are*. New York: Riverhead Books, 2005, pp. 204-205.

541 Michael S. Gazzaninga, *Human: The Science behind what Makes Us Unique*. New York: HarperCollins, 2008, p. 7.

542 Daniel C. Dennett, *Freedom Evolves*. New York: Viking, 2003, p. 147.

543 Ibid.

544 Ibid. p. 215. See Robert H. Frank, *Passions within Reason: The Strategic Role of the Emotions*. New York: W. W. Norton, 1988, p. 91.

545 Ibid.

546 Ibid.

547 Ibid.

548 Ibid.

549 Ibid.

550 Ibid.

551 Dennett, *Freedom Evolves*, pp. 202-203.

552 Shermer, *The Science of Good and Evil* p. 36.

553 See my *The Divine Activity*.

554 Levinas, reference lost.

555 Moltmann, *Science and Wisdom*, pp. 133-134.

556 George Lakoff, *The Political Mind*, p. 47, 58.

557 Jerry Adler, "The New Naysayers," *Newsweek* 148:11 (11 September 2006): 47-48. See Richard Dawkins, *The God Delusion*. New York: Houghton Mifflin Company, 2006. See also Sam Harris, *The End of Faith: Religion, Terror, and the Future of Reason*. New York: W.W. Norton & Company, 2005.

558 Kauffman, *Reinventing the Sacred*, pp. 259-260.

559 Kai Nielson, *Ethics Without God*. Amhurst, NY: Prometheus Books, 1990, p. 227f.

560 Shermer, *The Science of Good and Evil*, p. 156.

561 Charles Hartshorne, *Omnipotence and Other Theological Mistakes*. Albany, NY: State University of New York, 1984, p. 99.

562 Ibid. p. 108.

563 Ibid.

564 Ibid. p. 124.

565 Alan Kirk, "'Love Your Enemies,' The Golden Rule, and Ancient Reciprocity: (Luke 6:27-35)," *Journal of Biblical Literature* 122:4 (Winter 2003) 674.

566 Nesse, in *Richard Dawkins*, p. 209.

567 Ibid. p. 210.

CHAPTER 13—Playing God

568 Richard Doerflinger, quoted in Cathy Lynn Grossman, "Roman Catholic Church Updates Code on Reproduction," *USA Today*, 12 December 2008.

569 *Dignitas Personae: On Certain Bioethical Issues*, p. 9. http://www.usccb.org/comm/Dignitaspersonae/Dignitas_Personae.pdf

570 Ibid.

571 Ibid. p. 11.

572 Ibid. p. 13.

573 AP, "Pope Benedict Says Each Embryo an 'Individual,'" Peoria *Journal Star* (28 November 2010), p. A5.

574 Ibid. p. 17.

575 Ibid., italics added.

576 Nick Bostrom, "Human Reproductive Cloning from the Perspective of the Future," (8 March 2005) http://www.nickbostrom.com/views/cloning.html

577 Ibid.

578 Leon Kass, quoted in Cathy Young, "Monkeying Around with the Self," *Reason* (April 2001) http://www.findarticles.com/p/articles/mi_m1568/is_11_32/ai_72344892

579 Young, "Monkeying Around with the Self."

580 Ibid.

581 Ibid.

582 Francis Crick, *The Astonishing Hypothesis*. 1994. Quoted in James W. Haag, "From Cells to Souls—and Beyond: Changing Portraits of Human Nature," Christian Century (12 July 2005) http://www.findarticles.com/p/articles/mi_m1058/is_14_122/ai_n14858635

583 D. Gareth Jones, "A Neurobiological Portrait of the Human Person," in Green, ed., *What About the Soul?* pp. 33-34.

584 Paul Kurtz, "Are Science and Religion Compatible?" *Skeptical Inquirer* (March 2002) http://www.findarticles.com/p/articles/mi_m2843/is_2_26/ai_83585960

585 *Dignitas*, p. 3.

586 Calvin, *The Fate of the Soul.*

587 Hartshorne, *Omnipotence and Other Theological Mistakes*, pp. 100, 101.

588 Ibid. p. 101.

589 Ibid. p. 112.

590 Lee M. Silver, "The Biotechnology Culture Clash," *Science & Theology News* 6:10 (June 2006): 10.

591 Alan G. Padgett, "Padgett Uses Brains to Justify Stem Cell Research," *Science & Technology News* 6:1 (September 2005), p. 5.

592 Ibid. p. 5.

593 Alan G. Padgett, "Presence of Brain Activity is Absolute Criterion," Letter to the Editor, *Science & Theology News* 6:2 (October 2005), p. 6.

594 David Jones, "A Theologians' Brief: On The Place Of The Human Embryo Within The Christian Tradition & The Theological Principles For Evaluating Its Moral Status," *Ethics & Medicine* (Fall 2001) http://www.findarticles.com/p/articles/mi_qa4004/is_200110/ai_n8992376

595 Ibid.

596 Padgett, "Padgett Uses Brains to Justify Stem Cell Research," p. 5.

597 Silver, "The Biotechnology Culture Clash," p. 10.

598 Kenneth Hendrickson, "Truth and Unintended Consequences," *Science & Theology News* 6:10 (June 2006): 26.

599 M. Scott Peck, *Denial of the Soul: Scriptural and Medical Perspectives on Euthanasia and Mortality*. New York: Harmony Books, 1997.

600 Audrey R. Chapman, "Background and Overview," in Audrey R. Chapman, ed., *Perspectives on Genetic Patenting: Religion, Science, and Industry in Dialogue*. Washington, DC: American Association for the Advancement of Science, 1999, p. 11.

601 WCC, quoted in Chapman, "Background and Overview," p. 18.

602 Chapman, "Background and Overview," p. 18f.

603 Ibid. p. 13, 27.

604 Ibid. p. 28, 34f.

605 John H. Evans, "The Uneven Playing Field of the Dialogue on Patenting," in Chapman, p. 59.

606 Ibid. p. 60.

607 Ibid. p. 61.

608 Ibid. p. 64.

609 Baruch A. Brody, "Protecting Human Dignity and the Patenting of Human Genes," in Chapman, p. 112.

610 Dan Eramian, "BIO and the AAAS Genetic Patenting Forum," in Chapman, pp. 54, 55. Eramian is Executive Vice President of BIO, the world's largest biotechnology organization that represents more than 1,200 biotechnology companies, academic institutions, state biotechnology centers, and related organizations. BIO members are involved in the research and development of innovative healthcare, agricultural, industrial and environmental biotechnology products.

611 Brody, p. 115.

612 Ibid. p. 117.

613 Ibid. p. 119.

614 Ted Peters, "DNA and Dignity: A Response to Baruch Brody," in Chapman, p. 127.

615 Carl Sagan and Ann Druyan, "Is It Possible to be Pro-Life and Pro-Choice?" *Parade Magazine*, (22 April 1990), pp. 5, 7.

CHAPTER 14—Is the Church Really Necessary?

616 George Weigel, "A Jesus Beyond Politics," *Newsweek* 149:21 (21 May 2007), p. 49.

617 Daniel C. Dennett, *Breaking the Spell: Religion as a Natural Phenomenon*. New York: Penguin Books, 2006, p. 12.

618 Rachel Zoll, "More Americans Say They Have No Religion," *Peoria Journal-Star* (9 March 2009). See also Jon Meacham, "The End of Christian America," *Newsweek* 153:15 (13 April 2009) pp. 34, 36-38.

619 Dennett, *Breaking the Spell*, p. 18.

620 Ibid. p. 194.

621 Bobby E. Barnhill, "Southern Baptists Don't Align with Other Denominations," Peoria (IL) *Journal Star*, 7 February 2006, p. A4. (Italics added)

622 Paul Knitter, *No Other Name? A Critical Survey of Christian Attitudes toward the World Religions*. Maryknoll, NY: Orbis Books, 1985: p. 185.

623 Alfred North Whitehead, quoted in Brian Henning, "Morality in the Making," *Science & Theology News* 6:10 (June 2006): 32.

624 Paul Kurtz, "Are Science and Religion Compatible?" *Skeptical Inquirer*, March, 2002 http://www.findarticles.com/p/articles/mi_m2843/is_2_26/ai_83585960

625 Ibid.

626 Don Cupitt, "The Radical Christian Worldview."

627 Mary C. Boys, "The Cross: Should a Symbol Betrayed be Reclaimed?" *Cross Currents* 44:1 (Spring 1994):5-31.

628 Ibid.

629 Marc Saperstein, *Moments of Crisis in Jewish-Christian Relations*. Philadelphia: Trinity Press International, 1989, p. 19.

630 Don Cupitt, "The Radical Christian Worldview," *Cross Currents* (Spring-Summer 2000) http://www.findarticles.com/p/articles/mi_m2096/is_2000_Spring-Summer/ai_63300893

631 Alfred Loisy, *The Gospel and the Church*. Trans. Christopher Home. New York: Charles Scribner's Sons, 1904, p. 166.

632 Baigent, *The Jesus Papers*, p. 15.

633 Ibid. p. 13.

634 Ibid. p. 16.

635 Timothy Beal, *The Rise and Fall of the Bible: The Unexpected History of an Accidental Book*. Boston: Houghton Miffin Harcourt, 2011.

636 Sheppard, *Christendom at the Crossroads*, p. 8.

637 Ibid. p. 8.

638 Pedraja, *Teologia*, p. 51.

639 Karl Rahner, quoted in Harries, *God Outside the Box*, p. 71 (italics added).

640 Stephen T. Asma, "Against Transcendentalism: *Monty Python's The Meaning of Life* and Buddhism," in Gary Hardcastle and George A. Reisch, ed., *Monty Python and Philosophy: Nudge Nudge, Think Think!* Chicago: Open Press, 2006, p. 97.

641 Martin Luther King, Jr, "Transformed Nonconformist," in *Strength to Love*. New York: Harper & Row Publishers, 1963, 11.

642 Abraham J. Heschel, *The Prophets*. New York: Harper & Row Publishers, 1962, p. 205.

643 Desmond Tutu, *God Has a Dream: A Vision of Hope for Our Time*. New York: Doubleday, 2004, 23f.

644 Carl Sagan, *The Varieties of Scientific Experience: A Personal View of the Search for God*. New York: Penguin Books, 2006, p. 216, 217.

645 See Katherine Stewart, *The Good News Club: The Christian Right's Stealth Assault on America's Children*. "Public Affairs," Perseus Books, 2012.

CHAPTER 15—Faith in the 21st Century

646 Paul Helm, *Faith with Reason*. Oxford: Oxford University Press, 2000, p. 12.

647 John Locke, *An Essay Concerning Human Understanding*, IV, xvii, 24. http://oregonstate.edu/instruct/phl302/texts/locke/locke1/Book4b.html#Chapter XVII

648 Rosemary Radford Ruether, *Liberation Theology: Human Hope Confronts Christian History and American Power*. New York: Paulist Press, 1972. http://www.questia.com/library/book/liberation-theology-human-hope-confronts-christian-history-and-american-power-by-rosemary-radford-ruether.jsp

649 Karl Rahner, quoted in Harries, *God Outside the Box*, p. 71 (italics added).

650 Reuther, *Liberation Theology*.

651 M. Eugene Boring, "Matthew," *The New Interpreter's Bible*, volume 8. Nashville: Abingdon Press, 1995, p. 196.

652 Toni Vogle Carey, "The Better-Best Fallacy," *Philosophy Now*, 70 (November-December 2008): 19.

653 Ibid. p. 20.

654 Michael Barnes, "Faith and Imagination in Science and Religion," *Theology Today* 40:1 (April 1983), p. 15.

655 Ibid, p. 18.

656 William R. Jones, "Theism and Religious Humanism: The Chasm Narrows," http://www.religion-online.org/showarticle.asp?title=1874

657 John B. Cobb, Jr., *Praying for Jennifer: An Exploration of Intercessory Prayer in Story Form*. Nashville: The Upper Room, 1985.

CHAPTER 16—Conclusions

[658] Davies, *God and the New Physics*, p. 17.

[659] Evalyn Gates, *Einstein's Telescope: The Hunt for Dark Matter and Dark Energy in the Universe*. New York: W.W. Norton & Company, 2009, p. 3.

[660] Ibid. p. 4.

[661] William Tucker, "Complex Questions: The New Science of Spontaneous Order—Complexity Theory," *Reason*, January, 1996 http://www.findarticles.com/p/articles/mi_m1568/is_n8_v27/ai_17779895

[662] Frank M. North, 1903. The lyrics speak of the frenetic bustle of urban life. North wrote this hymn at the request of Caleb T. Winchester of Wesleyan University (New York) for inclusion in the 1905 Methodist Hymnal. It was a hymn celebrated by the Social Gospel Movement and has been included in Methodist and United Methodist hymnals ever since. http://www.cyberhymnal.org/htm/w/h/e/wherecro.htm

[663] Dr. Dow Kirkpatrick was senior pastor of First United Methodist Church in Evanston, Illinois.

BIBLIOGRAPHY

Abe, Masao. *Zen and Western Thought.* Edited by William R. LaFleur. Honolulu: University of Hawaii Press, 1985.

Adler, Jerry. "The New Naysayers," *Newsweek* 148:11 (11 September 2006): 47-49.

Aichele, George. "Fantasy and Myth in the Death of Jesus," *Cross Currents* 44:1 (Spring 1994): 85-97.

Altizer, Thomas. *The Contemporary Jesus.* Albany: State University of New York Press, 1997.

Amazon.com, "Interview with Sam Harris: The Mortal Dangers of Religious Faith," http://www.amazon.com/exec/obidos/tg/feature/-/542154/002-5322908-3699212

Artigas, Mariano. *The Mind of the Universe: Understanding Science and Religion.* Philadelphia: Templeton Foundation Press, 2000.

Aunger, Robert, editor. *Darwinizing Culture: The Status of Memetics as Science.* Oxford: Oxford University Press, 2001.

Bahr, Alfred. "A Physicist's Critique of the Existence of a God," *American Atheist Magazine* 41:4 (Winter 2003) http://goliath.ecnext.com/comsite5/bin/pdinventory.pl?pdlanding=1&referid=2750&item_id=0199-137649&words=Physicists_Critique_Existence

__________. "Of Man and His Soul," *American Atheist Magazine* 43:2 (Spring 2005) http://www.findarticles.com/p/articles/mi_m0OBB/is_2_43/ai_n14935423

Baigent, Michael. *The Jesus Papers: Exposing the Greatest Cover-Up in History.* New York: HarperSanFrancisco, 2006.

Bailey, Ronald and Gillespie, Nick. Interview with Steven Pinker. "Biology vs. The Blank Slate: Evolutionary Psychologist Steven Pinker Deconstructs the Great Myths about How the Mind Works," *Reason* (October 2002).

Bailey, Ronald. "Pulling Our Own String," an interview with Daniel C. Dennett, *Reason* (May 2003) http://www.reason.com/0305/fe.rb.pulling.shtml

Barbour, Ian. *Nature, Human Nature, and God.* Minneapolis: Fortress Press, 2002.

__________. *When Science Meets Religion: Enemies, Strangers, or Partners?* New York: HarperSanFrancisco, 2000.

Barlow, Connie. "The Way of Science—Exploring the Foundations of Humanism," *Humanist* 58:2 (March-April 1998) http://www.findarticles.com/p/articles/mi_m1374/is_n2_v58/ai_20430859

Barrow, John D. "The Great Basilica of Nature," *Science & Theology News* 6:6 (April 2006): 15-16, 19.

Bauer, Susan Wise. *The History of the Ancient World: From the Earliest Accounts to the Fall of Rome.* New York: W.W. Norton & Company, 2007.

__________. *The History of the Medieval World: From the Conversion of Constantine to the First Crusade.* New York: W.W. Norton & Company, 2010.

Behe, Michael J., Review of John Haught's *God After Darwin: A Theology of Evolution. Metaviews* (4 December 1999) http://www.arn.org/docs/behe/mb_godafterdarwinreview.htm

Bensley, D. Alan. "Can Minds Leave Bodies? A Cognitive Science Perspective," *Skeptical Inquirer* 27:4 (July-August 2003) http://www.findarticles.com/p/articles/mi_m2843/is_4_27/ai_104733237

Blackmore, Susan. "The Power of Memes," *Scientific American* 283:4 (October 2000).

__________. *The Meme Machine.* Oxford: Oxford University Press, 1998.

__________. *Waking from the Meme Dream.* Paper presented at The Psychology of Awakening: International Conference on Buddhism, Science and Psychotherapy, November 1996. http://www.memes.org.uk/meme-lab/DART96.HTM

Bodendorfer, Gerhard. "Jewish Voices about Jesus," *Jewish-Christian Relations* http://www.jcrelations.net/en/?item=738

Boteach, Shmuley. "Is It Time for G-D to do Teshuvah?" *Tikkun* (September-October 2002).

Boys, Mary C. "The Cross: Should a Symbol Betrayed be Reclaimed?" *Cross Currents* 44:1 (Spring 1994): 5-31.

Braxton, Donald M. "Certainty and Self-Deception among American Fundamentalism," *Metanexus Anthropos* (9 December 2004) http://www.metanexus.net/metanexus_online/show_article.asp?9195

Brockman, John. Interview with Steven Pinker, "A Biological Understanding of Human Nature: A Talk with Steven Pinker," *Edge* (9 September 2002) http://www.edge.org/3rd_culture/pinker_blank/pinker_blank_index.html

Bromberg, Judith, reviewer. "Is Jesus God: Finding Our Faith," *National Catholic Reporter* 37:36 (10 August 2001) http://www.findarticles.com/p/articles/mi_m1141/is_36_37/ai_77556903

__________. "When Jesus Became God: The Epic Fight over Christ's Divinity in the Last Days of Rome," *National Catholic Reporter* 36:14 (4 February 2000) http://www.findarticles.com/p/articles/mi_m1141/is_14_36/ai_59450119

Brown, Christopher A. "Can Buddhism Save? Finding Resonance in Incommensurability," *Cross Currents* 49:2 (Summer 1999) http://findarticles.com/p/articles/mi_m2096/is_2_49/ai_55106736

Brown, Delwin. "Locating God for the Twenty-first Century," *Quarterly Review* 22:2 (Summer 2002): 113-124.

__________. *Boundaries of our Habitations: Tradition and Theological Construction*. New York: State University of New York Press, 1994.

Bryant, Joseph M. reviewer. "Putting Away Childish Things: The Virgin Birth, the Empty Tomb, and Other Fairy Tales You Don't Need to Believe to Have a Living Faith," *Sociology of Religion* 56:3 (Fall 1995) http://www.findarticles.com/p/articles/mi_m0SOR/is_n3_v56/ai_17612391

Callahan, Sidney. "We're All Original Sinners," *Commonweal* 127:2 (28 January 2000) http://www.findarticles.com/p/articles/mi_m1252/is_2_127/ai_60054355

Calvin, William H. "Competing for Consciousness: How Subconscious Thoughts Cook on the Backburner," (30 April 1998) http://www.edge.org/3rd_culture/calvin/

__________. "Concept Change after Contact. Old Notions Never Die. They Just Incorporate," http://williamcalvin.com/2005/CALVIN%20post-contract%20religion.pdf

__________. "The Creative Explosion," (May 2005) http://williamcalvin.com/2005/CreativeExplosion.htm

__________. "The Fate of the Soul," *Natural History* (June 2004) http://williamcalvin.com/2004/June04NaturalHistory%20download.htm

Chadwick, Henry. "Constantine and the Bishops: The Politics of Intolerance," *English Historical Review*, (April 2001).

Chapman, Audrey R., ed. *Perspectives on Genetic Patenting: Religion, Science, and Industry in Dialogue.* Washington, DC: American Association for the Advancement of Science, 1999.

Clapp, Rodney. *A Peculiar People: The Church as Culture in a Post-Christian Society.* Downers Grove IL: Intervarsity Press, 1993.

Conley, John J. "Proving God," *Cross Currents* 50:4 (Winter 2000) http://www.findarticles.com/p/articles/mi_m2096/is_4_50/ai_70396479

Cronin, Michael. "Babel's Standing Stones: Language, Translation and the Exosomatic," *Crossings: eJournal of Art and Technology* 2:1 (March 2002) http://crossings.tcd.ie/issues/2.1/Cronin/

Crossan, John Dominic. *The Historical Jesus: The Life of a Mediterranean Peasant.* San Francisco: Harper Collins, 1991.

Cupitt, Don. "Religion after the West," speech given to North London SoF Group, (January 2006) http://www.sofn.org.uk/. This was later published in the *Sea of Faith* (March 2006).

__________. "The Radical Christian Worldview," *Cross Currents* (Spring-Summer 2000) http://www.findarticles.com/p/articles/mi_m2096/is_2000_Spring-Summer/ai_63300893

Damasio, Antonio. *Descartes' Error: Emotion, Reason, and the Human Brain.* New York: G. P. Putnam's Sons, 1994.

__________. *The Feeling of What Happens: Body and Emotion in the Making of Consciousness.* New York: Harcourt Brace & Company, 1999.

Davies, Paul. *God and the New Physics.* New York: "A Touchstone Book," Simon & Schuster, Inc., 1983.

__________. *Other Worlds: Space, Superspace, and the Quantum Universe.* New York: "A Touchstone Book," Simon & Schuster, Inc., 1980, 1982.

__________. *Superforce: The Search for a Grand Unified Theory of Nature.* New York: "A Touchstone Book," Simon & Schuster, Inc., 1985.

__________. *The Edge of Infinity: Where the Universe Came from and How It will End.* New York: "A Touchstone Book," Simon & Schuster, Inc., 1981, 1982.

__________. *The Mind of God: The Scientific Basis for a Rational World.* New York: "A Touchstone Book", Simon & Schuster, Inc., 1992.

Dawkins, Richard. "The Future Looks Bright," http://www.edge.org/3rd_culture/bright/bright_index.html

__________. *The God Delusion.* New York: Houghton Mifflin Co, 2006.

__________. *The Selfish Gene.* Oxford: Oxford University Press, 1989.

de Waal, Frans. *Chimpanzee Politic: Power and Sex among Apes*. New York: Harper & Row, 1982.

__________. *Good Natured: The Origins of Right and Wrong in Humans and Other Animals*. Cambridge: Harvard University Press, 1996.

__________. *Our Inner Ape. A Leading Primatologist Explains Why We Are Who We Are*. Riverhead Books, 2005.

Deacon, Terrence. *The Symbolic Species: The Co-Evolution of Language and the Brain*. New York: W. W. Norton, 1997.

Decker, Kevin S. and Eberl, Jason T. eds. *Star Wars and Philosophy: More Powerful Than You Can Possibly Imagine*. New York: Barnes & Noble Inc, 2009.

Del Re, Giuseppe. *The Cosmic Dance: Science Discovers the Mysterious Harmony of the Universe*. Radnor, PA: Templeton Foundation Press, 2000.

Dennett, Daniel C. *Breaking the Spell: Religion as a Natural Phenomenon*. New York: Penquin Books, 2006.

__________. *Darwin's Dangerous Idea: Evolution and the Meanings of Life*. New York: Simon & Schuster, 1995.

__________. *Freedom Evolves*. New York: Viking, 2003.

__________. "Vitalism," http://www.skepdic.com/vitalism.html

Denton, Michael. *Nature's Destiny: How the Laws of Biology Reveal Purpose in the Universe*. New York: Free Press, 1998.

Dietrich, Jeff. "Constantine's Cross Is Still a Pact with the Devil," *National Catholic Reporter* 37:44 (19 October 2001) http://www.findarticles.com/p/articles/mi_m1141/is_44_37/ai_79965508

Doerr, Edd. "Constantine and George II," *Humanist* 61:5 (September 2001) http://findarticles.com/p/articles/mi_m1374/is_5_61/ai_78966519

Donnelly, Matt. "Why Is there Something Rather than Nothing?" *Science & Theology News* 6:7 (March 2006): 18-21.

Drees, Willlem B. "Creation: From Nothing until Now, Part 1," *Metanexus: Views* (17 December 2001).

Duffey, Stephen J. "Blood Spilled in Name of God," *National Catholic Reporter* (10 January 2003).

Dunn, James D. G. "Jesus for Today," *Theology Today* (April 1995) http://www.findarticles.com/p/articles/mi_qa3664/is_199504/ai_n8725673

Dupuis, Jacques. "Religious Plurality and the Christological Debate," *Sedos* (16 Aprile 2005) http://www.sedos.org/

Durham, W. *Coevolution: Genes, Culture, and Human Diversity*. Stanford: Stanford University Press, 1992.

Emile Durkheim "Pragmatism & the Question of Truth," http://www.marxists.org/reference/subject/philosophy/works/fr/durkheim.htm. From his *Pragmatism & Sociology.* Cambridge University Press, 1983

Dyson, George. "Darwin among the Machines: Or, the Origins of [Artificial] Life?" *Edge* (7.8.97) http://www.edge.org/3rd_culture/dyson/dyson_p2.html

Ehrman, Bart D. *Lost Christianities: The Battles for Scripture and the Faiths We Never Knew*. New York: Oxford University Press, 2003.

__________. *Misquoting Jesus: The Story Behind Who Changed the Bible and Why*. New York: HarperSanFrancisco, 2005.

Elenga, Yvon C. "African Christologies: Naming Jesus," *Sedos*, Sabato, (16 Aprile 2005) http://www.sedos.org/

Elliott, John H. "Jesus Was Not an Egalitarian: A Critique of an Anachronistic and Idealist Theory," *Biblical Theology Bulletin* 32:2 (Summer 2002) http://www.findarticles.com/p/articles/mi_m0LAL/is_2_32/ai_94332342

Ellis, George. "On Rationality and Emotion, Faith and Hope," *Metanexus Cosmos*. (21 June 2004) http://www.metanexus.net/metanexus_online/show_article.asp?8916

Falk, Richard. "In Pursuit of the Postmodern," paper presented at the "Toward a Post-Modern World" Conference in Santa Barbara, California (16-20 January 1987).

Farley, Edward. "Fundamentalism: A Theory," *Cross Currents* 55:3 (Fall 2005) http://www.crosscurrents.org/farley2005.htm

Farrell, Michael J. "Ancient Forces Shaped Our Lives," *National Catholic Reporter* 36:29 (19 May 2000) http://www.findarticles.com/p/articles/mi_m1141/is_29_36/ai_62496361

Ferguson, Keith. "Universal Surprises," *Science and Theology News* 6:3 (November 2005): 29.

Feske, Millicent C. "Feminist Theologies and the Possibility of God-Talk," *Quarterly Review* 22:2 (Summer 2002): 138-151.

Feuerbach, Ludwig. *The Essence of Christianity*. Translated by George Eliot. New York: Harper & Row, 1957.

Feynman, Richard P. *What Do You Care What Other People Think?* New York: W.W. Norton. 1988.

Fischer, Kathleen. "An Image of God beyond Violence," *National Catholic Reporter* 36:6 (3 December 1999) http://www.findarticles.com/p/articles/mi_m1141/is_6_36/ai_58170183

Flanagan, Owen. *The Problem of the Soul: Two Visions of Mind and How to Reconcile Them*. New York: Basic Books, 2002.

Ford, Dennis. *The Search for Meaning: A Short History*. Berkley: University of California Press, 2007.

Foucault, Michael. *Power/Knowledge: Selected Interviews and Other Writings*. New York: Pantheon Books, 1977.

Fredriksen, Paula. "Jesus and the Temple, Mark and the War," *SBL Seminar Papers* Atlanta (1990), pp. 293-310.

__________. "What You See Is What You Get: Context And Content In Current Research On The Historical Jesus," *Theology Today* (April 1995) http://www.findarticles.com/p/articles/mi_qa3664/is_199504/ai_n8716213

__________. *From Jesus to Christ: The Origins of the New Testament Images of Jesus*. New Haven: Yale University Press, 1988.

Garvey, John. The Hidden God—All—Powerful and Vanquished," *Commonweal* (7 April 2000).

Garwood, Christine. *Flat Earth: The History of an Infamous Idea*. New York: St. Martin's Press, 2007.

Gates, Evalyn. *Einstein's Telescope: The Hunt for Dark Matter and Dark Energy in the Universe*. New York: W.W. Norton & Company, 2009.

Gazzaniga, Michael S. *Human: The Science Behind What Makes Us Human*. New York: HarperCollins, 2008.

Geering, Lloyd. "How Did Jesus Become God—and Why?" *The Fourth R* 11:5 (September/October 1998) http://www.westarinstitute.org/Periodicals/4R_Articles/Jesus_to_God/jesus_to_god.html

Genoni, Jr., Tom. "Exploring Mind, Memory, and the Psychology of Belief: Part II: Perception, Memory and the Courtroom," *Skeptical Inquirer* (March-April 1995) http://www.csicop.org/si/9503/belief.html

Gensler, Harry. "Treat Others as You Want to be Treated," http://www.jcu.edu/philosophy/gensler/goldrule.htm

Gerhart, Mary and Russell, Allan Melvin. *Metaphoric Process: The Creation of Scientific and Religious Understanding*. Fort Worth, TX: Texas Christian University, 1984.

Gerrish, B.A. "What Do We Mean by Faith in Jesus Christ?" *Christian Century* 116:26 (6 October 1999) http://www.findarticles.com/p/articles/mi_m1058/is_26_116/ai_56249457

Giberson, Karl. "Losing Our Minds," *Science & Theology News* 6:10 (June 2006): 6.

González, Justo L. *Manana: Christian Theology from a Hispanic Perspective.* Nashville: Abingdon Press, 1990.

Gould, Stephen Jay. *Ever since Darwin: Reflections in Natural History*. New York: W.W. Norton & Co., 1979, 1992.

__________. *Rocks of Ages: Science and Religion in the Fullness of Life*. New York: Ballantine, 1999.

Grafen, Alan and Ridley, Mark, eds. *Richard Dawkins: How a Scientist Changed the Way We Think.* Oxford: Oxford University Press, 2006.

Grassie, William. "Biocultural Evolution in the 21st Century—Part One," *Metanexus Techne.* (29 March 2004) http://metanexus.net/metanexus_online/show_article.asp?8779.

__________. "Biocultural Evolution in the 21st Century—Part Two," *Metanexus Techne.* (30 March 2004) http://metanexus.net/metanexus_online/show_article.asp?8786.

Green, Joel B. *What about the Soul? Neuroscience and Christian Anthropology.* Nashville: Abingdon Press, 2004.

Greenfield, Susan. "Making Up Our Minds," *New Statesman* (27 September 1999) http://www.findarticles.com/p/articles/mi_m0FQP/is_128_4456/ai_56749577

Gregersen, Niels Henrik. "The Naturalness of Religious Imagination and the Idea of Revelation," *The Online Journal for Philosophy of Religion* 3 (2003) http://www.arsdisputandi.org/

Grenz, Stanley J. "Christian Spirituality and the Quest for Identity: Toward a Spiritual-Theological Understanding of Life in Christ," *Baptist History and Heritage* (March, 2002) http://www.highbeam.com/doc/1G1-94160844.html

Grevin, Philip. *Spare the Child: The Protestant Roots of Child Abuse.* New York: Knopf, 1991.

Griffin, Carl W. and Paulsen, David L. "Augustine and the Corporeality of God," *Harvard Theological Review* (January 2002).

Griffin, David Ray. *A Process Christology*. Philadelphia: Westminster Press, 1973.

__________. *Two Great Truths: A New Synthesis of Scientific Naturalism and Christian Faith*. Louisville: Westminster John Knox Press, 2004.

Gross, Paul R. "Neo-creationist Tactics Show Troubling Evolution," *Science and Theology News*, 6:2 (October 2005): 5.

Gross, Rita M. "Religious Diversity: Some Implications for Monotheism," *Cross Currents*, 49:3 (Fall 1999) http://www.crosscurrents.org/gross.htm

Gustafson, James M. "Science as Salvation: A Modern Myth and Its Meaning," *Christian Century* (10 March 1993).

Guthrie, Clifton F. "So Human a Book: Pragmatism and Scriptural Authority," *Quarterly Review* 25:3 (Fall 2005): 254-273.

Hall, Douglas John. "Confessing Christ in a Post-Christendom Context," *Ecumenical Review* 52:3 (July 2000) http://findarticles.com/p/articles/mi_m2065/is_3_52/ai_66279081

Hamilton, William. *The Quest for the Post-Historical Jesus.* New York: Continuum Books, 1994.

Hardcastle, Gary, and George A. Reisch, eds. *Monty Python and Philosophy: Nudge Nudge, Think Think!* Chicago: Open Press, 2006.

Hargis, Jeffrey W. *Against the Christians: The Rise of Early Anti-Christian Polemic.* "Patristic Studies," vol. 1; New York: Peter Lang, 1999.

Harries, Richard. *God Outside the Box: Why Spiritual People Object to Christianity.* London: SPCK, 2002.

Harris, Sam. *The End of Faith: Religion, Terror, and the Future of Reason.* New York: W.W. Norton & Company, 2005.

__________. "Q & A with Sam Harris," http://www.samharris.org/press/Q&A-with-Sam-Harris.pdf

Hartshorne, Charles. *Omnipotence and Other Theological Mistakes.* Albany, NY: State University of New York, 1984.

Haught, John F. "Evolution and God's Humility: How Theology Can Embrace Darwin," *Commonweal*, (28 January 2000) http://www.commonwealmagazine.org/article.php3?id_article=470&var_recherche=...Haught

__________. *God after Darwin: A Theology of Evolution.* Boulder, Colorado: Westview Press, 2000.

Hawking, Stephen. *A Brief History of Time: From the Big Bang to Black Holes.* New York: Bantam Books, 1988.

Heaney, Liam F. "The Essence of Language: Metaphorically Speaking," *Contemporary Review* 266 (June 1995) http://www.findarticles.com/p/articles/mi_m2242/is_n1553_v266/ai_17381432

Hefner, Philip. "Created to be Creators," *Metanexus Sophia.* (19 December 2003) http://metanexus.net/metanexus_online/show_article.asp?8664

Heim, S. Mark. "A Faith Worthy of Doubt," *Christian Century*, (29 June 2004).

__________. "Christ Crucified," *Christian Century* 118:8 (7 March 2001) http://www.findarticles.com/p/articles/mi_m1058/is_8_118/ai_72094707

Hemming, Laurence Paul. *Heidegger's Atheism: The Refusal of Theological Voice*. Nortre Dame: University of Notre Dame Press 2002.

Henning, Brian. "Morality in the Making," *Science & Theology News* 6:10 (June 2006): 31-33.

Henry, Patrick. "Images of God in Time and Space," *Theology Today* 61:2 (July 2004): 202-212.

Hick, John. *God and the Universe of Faiths*. London: Macmillan Press, 1975.

__________. *The Myth of God Incarnate*, ed. John Hick, London: SCM Press, 1977, 1993.

Hitchens, Christopher. *God Is Not Great: How Religion Poisons Everything*. New York: Twelve, 2007.

Howell, Nancy R. "A God Adequate for Primate Culture," *Journal of Religion and Society*, 3 (2001) http://moses.creighton.edu/JRS/2001-4a/2001.html

Hutcheon, Pat Duffy. "Beyond the Quest for Certainty—Mind-Matter Duality in Philosophy, Religion and Science," *Humanist*, 61:4 (July 2001) http://www.findarticles.com/p/articles/mi_m1374/is_4_61/ai_76800134

Iacoboni, Marco. *Mirroring People: The New Science of How We Connect with Others*. New York: Farrar, Straus and Giroux, 2008.

Inbody, Tyron. "Methodism and Pragmatism: Promise or Peril?" *Quarterly Review* 25:3 (Fall 2005): 274-291.

Jamison, Peter."Human and Ultimate Consciousness; The Pitfalls of Rationalist Cosmology," *Humanist* 58:4 (July-August 1998) http://www.findarticles.com/p/articles/mi_m1374/is_n4_v58/ai_20979799

Jones, Arthur. "Is Capitalism Compatible With The Golden Rule?" *Human Quest* (March/April 2002) http://www.findarticles.com/p/articles/mi_qa3861/is_200203/ai_n9041005

Jones, David. "A Theologians' Brief: On The Place Of The Human Embryo Within The Christian Tradition & The Theological Principles For Evaluating Its Moral Status," *Ethics & Medicine* (Fall, 2001) http://www.findarticles.com/p/articles/mi_qa4004/is_200110/ai_n8992376

Kaku, Michio. *Physics of the Impossible: A Scientific Exploration into the World of Phasers, Force Fields, Teleportation, and Time Travel*. New York: Doubleday, 2008.

Kaplan, Mordecai M. "When Is Religion Authentic?" *Reconstructionist* 30:11 (2 October 1964), 15-16.

__________. *The Future of the American Jew*. New York: The Macmillan Company, 1948, 1949.

__________. *The Meaning of God in Modern Jewish Religion*. New York: Reconstructionist Press, 1937, 1962.

__________. *The Religion of Ethical Nationhood: Judaism's Contribution to World Peace*. New York: The Macmillan Company, 1970.

Kauffman, Stuart A. *Reinventing the Sacred: A New View of Science, Reason, and Religion*. New York: Basic Books, 2008.

Kaufman, Gordon D. "Re-conceiving God and Humanity in Light of Today's Ecological Consciousness: A Brief Statement," *Cross Currents* 50:1-2 (Spring/Summer 2000) http://www.findarticles.com/p/articles/mi_m2096/is_2000_Spring-Summer/ai_63300896

__________. *Jesus and Creativity*. Minneapolis: Fortress Press, 2006.

Keller, Catherine. "Power Lines," *Theology Today* 52:2 (July 1995): 188-203.

Keller, Julia C. "Taking the Design Out of the Argument over ID," *Science and Theology News* 6:3 (November 2005): 30.

Kensky, Allan. "Moses And Jesus: The Birth of the Savior," *Judaism* 42:1 (Winter 1993) http://www.findarticles.com/p/articles/mi_m0411/is_n1_v42/ai_13796415

Kessler, Seymour. "Soloveitchik and Levinas: Pathways to the Other," *Judaism* 51:4 (Fall 2002) http://findarticles.com/p/articles/mi_m0411/is_4_51/ai_106730955

Kirk, Alan. "'Love Your Enemies,' The Golden Rule, and Ancient Reciprocity: (Luke 6:27-35)," *Journal of Biblical Literature* 122:4 (Winter 2003) 667-686.

Klarreich, Erica. "Generous Players: Game Theory Explores the Golden Rule's Place in Biology," *Science News* 166:4 (24 July 2004) http://www.findarticles.com/p/articles/mi_m1200/is_4_166/ai_n6151880

Knitter, Paul F. "Theocentric Christology," *Theology Today* 40:2 (July 1983): 130-149 http://theologytoday.ptsem.edu/search/index-search.htm

Koch, Andrew. "Interpreting God's Truth: A Postmodern Interpretation of Medieval Epistemology," *International Social Science Review*, (Fall-Winter 2000) http://www.findarticles.com/p/articles/mi_m0IMR/is_2000_Fall-Winter/ai_70378603

Kramer, Marilyn M. "Christology and Patriarchy," *Cross Currents* 48:3 (Fall 1998) http://www.findarticles.com/p/articles/mi_m2096/is_n3_v48/ai_21202895

Kurtz, Paul. "Are Science and Religion Compatible?" *Skeptical Inquirer* 26:2 (March 2002) http://www.findarticles.com/p/articles/mi_m2843/is_2_26/ai_83585960

Lakoff, George. *The Political Mind: Why You Can't Understand 21st Century Politics with an 18th-Century Brain.* New York: Viking, 2008.

Lakoff, George and Johnson, Mark. *Philosophy in the Flesh: The Embodied Mind and Its Challenge to Western Thought*, New York: Basic Books 1999.

Lazzo, Janelle. "Heaven, Self-Respect and the Golden Rule: Diverse Group Contemplates Reasons to be Good," *National Catholic Reporter* 39:7 (13 December 2002) http://www.findarticles.com/p/articles/mi_m1141/is_7_39/ai_95632000

Lester, Gregory W. "Why Bad Beliefs Don't Die," *Skeptical Inquirer* (November 2000) http://www.csicop.org/si/2000-11/beliefs.html

Levinas, Emmanuel. *Alterity and Transcendence*, translated by Michael B. Smith. New York: Columbia University Press, 1999.

__________. *God, Death and Time*, translated by Bettina Bergo. Stanford, CA: Stanford University Press, 2000.

__________. *The Levinas Reader.* Sean Hand, editor. Cambridge MA: Blackwell, 1989.

__________. *Totality and Infinity: An Essay on Exteriority*, translated by Alphonso Lingis. Pittsburgh, PA Duquesne University Press, 1969.

Lindbeck, George A. *The Nature of Doctrine: Religion and Theology in a Postliberal Age.* Philadelphia: Westminster Press, 1984.

Lindsay, Mark R. "History, Holocaust, and Revelation: Beyond the Barthian Limits," *Theology Today* 61:4 (January 2005): 455-470.

Luther, Martin. "The Damned Whore, Reason," http://www.jesuscult.com/Luther_Anti-Reason.htm

Lyotard, Jean-Francois. *The Postmodern Condition: A Report on Knowledge*, translated by Geoff Bennington and Brian Massumi. Minneapolis: University of Minnesota Press, 1984.

Macquarrie, John. "Current Trends in Anglican Christology," *Anglican Theological Review* (Fall 1977) http://www.findarticles.com/p/articles/mi_qa3818/is_199710/ai_n8774191

Maddox, Randy L. *Responsible Grace: John Wesley's Practical Theology.* Nashville, TN: Kingswood Books, 1994.

Madsen, Catherine. "Notes on God's Violence," *Cross Currents* 51:2 (Summer 2001) http://www.findarticles.com/p/articles/mi_m2096/is_2_51/ai_77674976

Malin, Shimon. *Nature Loves to Hide: Quantum Physics and the Nature of Reality, a Western Perspective.* New York: Oxford University Press, 2001.

Marx, Karl. *The Eighteenth Brumaire of Louis Bonaparte* (1852). http://www.marxists.org/archive/marx/works/1852/18th-brumaire/ch01.htm.

Marxsen, Willi. *New Testament Foundations for Christian Ethics.* Minneapolis: Fortress, 1993.

McFague, Sallie. *Models of God: Theology for an Ecological, Nuclear Age.* Philadelphia: Fortress Press, 1987.

Meeks, Wayne A. *The Origins of Christian Morality.* New Haven: Yale, 1994.

David G. Myers, "Do What You Feel, Maybe: The Power and Perils of Relying on Intuition," http://www.incharacter.org/article.php?article=88.

__________. David G. Myers, *Intuition: Its Powers and Perils.* New Haven, CT: Yale University Press, 2002.

Midgley, Mary. *Beast and Man: The Roots of Human Nature.* Ithaca, NY: Cornell University Press, 1978.

__________. *Science as Salvation: A Modern Myth and Its Meaning.* New York: Routledge, 1992.

Miles, Jack. "The Myth of the Suppressing Church: A Comment on Walter Wink's *The Human Being*," *Cross Currents* 53:2 (Summer 2003) http://www.crosscurrents.org/MilestoWinksummer2003.htm

__________. *Christ: A Crisis in the Life of God.* New York: Alfred A. Knopf, 2001.

Miller, James B., ed. *An Evolving Dialogue: Scientific, Historical, Philosophical and Theological Perspectives on Evolution.* Washington, DC: American Association for the Advancement of Science, 1998.

Miller, Kenneth R. *Finding Darwin's God: A Scientist's Search for Common Ground between God and Evolution.* New York: HarperCollins, 2000.

Miller, Patrick D. "A Strange Kind of Monotheism," *Theology Today* 54:3 (October 1997): 293-297.

__________. "Revisiting the God Who Acts," *Theology Today* 54:1 (April 1977): 1-5.

Miller, Robert J. "Did Jesus Fulfill Prophecy? Probing Matthew's Gospel," *The Fourth R* 16:2 (March/April 2003) http://www.westarinstitute.org/Periodicals/4R_Articles/Prophecy/prophecy.html

Moltmann, Jurgen. *Science and Wisdom.* Trans., Margaret Kohl. Minneapolis: Fortress Press, 2003.

Monod, Jacques. *Chance and Necessity: An Essay on the Natural Philosophy of Modern Biology.* New York: Alfred A. Knopf, 1971.

Moore, R. Laurence. *Selling God: American Religion in the Marketplace of Culture.* New York: Oxford University Press, 1994.

Morwood, Michael. *Is Jesus God: Finding Our Faith.* New York: Crossroads, 2001.

Naff, Clay. "A House of Many Mansions, Part One," *Metanexus Sophia* (14 April 2004) http://metanexus.net/metanexus_online/show_article.asp?8806

Nelson, David W. "God as Big Bang: New Way to Comprehend the Divine," *Science and Theology News,* 6:3 (November 2005): 34.

__________. *Judaism, Physics, and God: Searching for Sacred Metaphors in a Post-Einstein World.* Woodstock, VT: Jewish Lights Publishing, 2005.

Neuhaus, Richard John. "Christ and Creation's Longing," *First Things* 78 (December 1997): 20-25. http://www.firstthings.com/ftissues/ft9712/articles/neuhaus.html

Neville, Robert C. "Pragmatism and Theology's Truth," *Quarterly Review* 25:3 (Fall 2005): 241-253.

__________. *Reconstruction of Thinking.* Albany, New York: SUNY Press, 1981.

Nicholas Nicastro, *Circumference: Eratosthenes and the Ancient Quest to Measure the Globe.* New York: St. Martin's Press, 2008.

Nielson, Kai. *Ethics Without God.* Amhurst, NY: Prometheus Books, 1990.

Nissley, Tom. "Where Were You When You Realized the World Is Flat? (Or Have You?): A Conversation with Thomas L. Friedman," http://www.amazon.com/exec/obidos/tg/feature/-/562744/ref=lbrc_inter2/102-6650176-4755342

Nottingham, William J. "Arius: Heresy and Tradition," *Encounter* (Autumn 2003)

O'Donnell, John. "Christianity as Radical Monotheism?" *Aix-en-Provence* (1-6 April 2002).

Oden, Thomas C. "Can We Talk about Heresy?" *Christian Century* (12 April 1995).

Odin, Steve. "A Post Modern View of Aesthetic Symbolism: Shingon Esoteric Buddhism and Whitehead's Theory of Symbolic Reference," paper delivered at the "Toward a Post-Modern World" Conference in Santa Barbara, California (16-20 January 1987).

Ottati, Douglas F. "Which Way Is Up? An Experiment in Christian Theology and Modern Cosmology," *Interpretation*, 59:4 (October 2005): 370-381.

Oxford-Carpenter, Rebecca. "Gender and the Trinity," *Theology Today* 40 (April 1984): 7-25.

Oxley, Greg. "A Materialist Vision of the Afterlife," *UNESCO Courier* (March 1998) http://www.findarticles.com/p/articles/mi_m1310/is_1998_March/ai_20463714

Padgett, Alan G. "Padgett Uses Brains to Justify Stem Cell Research," *Science & Technology News* 6:1 (September 2005): 5.

Padgett, Alan G. "Presence of Brain Activity is Absolute Criterion," Letter to the Editor, *Science & Theology News* 6:2 (October 2005): 6.

Pailin, David A. "On the Significance of the Sovereignty of God," *Theology Today* 53:1 (April 1996): 35-46.

Paine, Thomas. *The Age of Reason: Being an Investigation of True and Fabulous Theology* (1793), http://www.infidels.org/library/historical/thomas_paine/age_of_reason/part1.html#3

Pawlikowski, John T. "Christian Anti-Semitism: Past History, Present Challenges," *Journal of Religion and Society*, 6 (2004) http://moses.creighton.edu/JRS/2004/2004-10.html

Peacocke, Arthur R. *God and the New Biology*. New York: Harper & Row, 1986.

Pedraja, Luis G. "Suffering God: Theodicy in the Twenty-first Century, *Quarterly Review* 22:2 (Summer 2002): 166-178.

__________. *Teologia: An Introduction to Hispanic Theology*. Nashville: Abingdon Press, 2003.

Perelmuter, Hayim Goren. *Siblings: Rabbinic Judaism and Early Christianity at Their Beginnings*. Mahwah, NJ: Paulist Press, 1989.

Perkins, Pheme. "Jesus and Ethics," *Theology Today*, (April 1995) http://www.findarticles.com/p/articles/mi_qa3664/is_199504/ai_n8717852

Perrin, Norman. *The Resurrection According to Matthew, Mark, and Luke*. Philadelphia: Fortress Press, 1977.

Peters, Ted and Hewlett, Martinez. *Evolution from Creation to New Creation: Conflict, Conversation, and Convergence*. Nashville: Abingdon Press, 2003.

Peters, Ted. "How We Believe: The Search for God in an Age of Science," *Christian Century* (15 November 2000).

Pfau, Julie Shoshana and Blumenthal, David R. "The Violence of God: Dialogic Fragments," *Judaism* 51:2 (Summer 2001) http://www.crosscurrents.org/blumenthal0701.htm

Pinker, Steven, *The Blank Slate: The Modern Denial of Human Nature*. New York: Viking, 2002.

Piper, Otto A. "Christology and History," *Theology Today* 19:3 (October 1962): 324-340.

Placher, William C. "The Acts of God: What Do We Mean by Revelation?" *Christian Century* 113:10 (20 March 1996) http://www.findarticles.com/p/articles/mi_m1058/is_n10_v113/ai_18159949

__________. *Unapologetic Theology*. Louisville, KY: Westminster John Knox, 1989.

Plotkin, H. "People Do More than Imitate," *Scientific American* 283:4 (October 2000).

Polkinghorne, John C. "Natural Science, Temporality, and Divine Action," *Theology Today* 55:3 (October 1998): 329-343.

__________. *Belief in God in an Age of Science*. New Haven, CT: Yale University Press, 1998.

__________. *Quarks, Chaos and Christianity*. New York: Crossroad, 1996.

Pollefeyt, Didier. "Christology after Auschwitz: A Catholic Perspective," *Jews of Euro-Asia* # 1 (8) Januari - March 2005 (Tevet - Adar II 5765) http://www.eajc.org/publish_print_e.php?rowid=98

Pope Benedict XVI. *Dignitas Personae: On Certain Bioethical Issues*, p. 9. http://www.usccb.org/comm/Dignitaspersonae/Dignitas_Personae.pdf

Poulshock, Joseph. "Meme Schemes: Problems and Potentials in Memes," http://www.ling.ed.ac.uk/~naphtali/MemeSchemes3.PDF

__________. "Memetics, Language, and Theology," A paper given to the Society for the Study of Theology and Christian Philosophy at Tokyo Christian Institute, 26 June 2001. http://www.ling.ed.ac.uk/~naphtali/MLT.PDF

__________. "Universal Darwinism and the Potential of Memetics," htttp://www.ling.ed.ac.uk/~naphtali/UniversalDarwinism.PDF

Karl Rahner, *Theological Investigations*, 22 volumes. Translated by Cornelius Ernst et al. London: Darton, Longman & Todd, 1965-1991.

Ralls, Mark. "Reclaiming Heaven: What Can We Say about the Afterlife?" *Christian Century* 121:25 (14 December 2004) http://www.findarticles.com/p/articles/mi_m1058/is_25_121/ai_n8702624

Raymo, Chet."Celebrating Creation," *Skeptical Inquirer* 23:4 (July-August 1999) http://www.findarticles.com/p/articles/mi_m2843/is_4_23/ai_55208045

Reilly, John J., reviewer. "Daemonomania," *First Things* 111 (March 2001) 53-56.

Ricoeur, Paul. *Interpretation Theory: Discourse and the Surplus of Meaning*. Fort Worth, TX: Texas Christian University, 1976.

Riley, Gregory J. *The River of God: A New History of Christian Origins*. New York: HarperSanFrancisco, 2003.

Robinson, Charles K. "The Space Age and Christology," *Theology Today* 19:4 (January 1963): 500-509.

Robinson, James M. "Breaking The Cycle," *Christian Century* 122:19 (20 September 2005) http://www.findarticles.com/p/articles/mi_m1058/is_19_122/ai_n15674700

Rock, Andrea. *The Mind at Night: The New Science of How and Why We Dream*. New York: Basic Books, 2005.

Rorty, Richard. "Consequences of Pragmatism," http://www.marxists.org/reference/subject/philosophy/works/us/rorty.htm

Richard Rorty, "Religious Faith, Intellectual Responsibility, and Romance," *American Journal of Theology and Philosophy* (May 1996): 121-140.

Rubinstein, Richard E. *When Jesus Became God: The Epic Fight over Christ's Divinity in the Last Days of Rome*. New York: "A Harvest Book"; Harcourt Brace & Company, 1999.

Russell, Robert John. "Does 'The God Who Acts' Really Act? New Approaches to Divine Action in Light of Science," *Theology Today* 54:1 (April 1997): 43-65.

Sagan, Carl. "The God Hypothesis," *Skeptic* 13:1 (2007): 39-45.

__________. *The Varieties of Scientific Experience: A Personal View of the Search for God*. Edited by Ann Druyan. New York: Penguin Books, 2006.

Sanchez, Julian. "Self Delusions: Does Morality Require a Soul?" *Reason* 35:8 (January 2004) http://www.findarticles.com/p/articles/mi_m1568/is_8_35/ai_111574443

Saperstein, Marc. *Moments of Crisis in Jewish-Christian Relations*. Philadelphia: Trinity Press International, 1989.

Sauter, Gerhard. *The Question of Meaning: A Theological and Philosophical Orientation*. Grand Rapids: Eerdmans, 1995.

Schmitz-Moorman, Karl. *Theology of Creation in an Evolutionary World.* Cleveland, Ohio: Pilgrim Press, 1997.

Schneider, Susan, ed., *Science Fiction and Philosophy: From Time Travel to Superintelligence*. Chichester, West Sussex, UK: Wiley-Blackwell, 2009.

Schneiders, Sandra M. "Theology and Spirituality: Strangers, Rivals, or Partners," *Horizons* 13:2 (1986): 265-267.

Seife, Charles. *Decoding the Universe: How the New Science of Information Is Explaining Everything in the Cosmos, from Our Brains to Black Holes.* New York: Viking, 2006.

Sharpe, Kevin and Bryant, Rebecca. "Providence and the Biology of Purpose," *Cross Currents* 52:3 (Fall 2002) http://findarticles.com/p/articles/mi_m2096/is_3_52/ai_94983822

Sheehan, Thomas. "How Did Easter Originally Happen? A Hypothesis," *The Fourth R* 14:4 (July/August 2001) http://www.westarinstitute.org/Periodicals/4R_Articles/Easter/easter.html

Sheppard, James A. *Christendom at the Crossroads: The Medieval Era.* "The Westminster History of Christian Thought;" Louisville KY: Westminster John Knox Press, 2005.

Shermer, Michael. "A Skeptical Manifesto," *Skeptic* 1:1 (Spring 1992): 15-21. http://www.skeptic.com/01.1.shermer-skep-manifesto.html

__________. "Adam's Maxim and Spinoza's Conjecture," *Scientific American* 298:3 (March 2008): 36-37.

__________. "The Soul Problem," *Psychology Today* 35:6 (November-December 2002) http://www.findarticles.com/p/articles/mi_m1175/is_6_35/ai_92849367

__________. "Why People Believe in God: An Empirical Study on a Deep Question," *Humanist* 59:6 (November 1999) http://www.findarticles.com/p/articles/mi_m1374/is_6_59/ai_57800244

__________. *The Science of Good and Evil: Why People Cheat, Gossip, Care, Share, and Follow the Golden Rule*. New York: Times Books, 2004.

Silver, Lee M. "The Biotechnology Culture Clash," *Science & Theology News* 6:10 (June 2006): 10.

Smith, David Livingstone. *Why We Lie: the Evolutionary Roots of Deception and the Unconscious Mind.* New York: St Martin's Press, 2004.

Snider, Theodore M. *The Continuity of Salvation: A Study of Paul's Letter to the Romans.* Jefferson, NC: McFarland & Company, 1984.

__________. *The Divine Activity: An Approach to Incarnational Theology.* New York: Peter Lang, 1990.

Sobrine, Jon. *Where Is God? Earthquake, Terrorism, Barbarity, and Hope.* Maryknoll, NY: Orbis Press, 2004.

Soskice, Janet Martin. "God of Power and Might," *Theology Today*, 54:1 (April 1997): 19-28.

Spencer, Herbert. "Progress: Its Law and Causes," *The Westminster Review*, 67 (April 1857): pp. 445-447, 451, 454-456, 464-65.

Spong, John Shelby. "Christian Anthropology: Definition of Our Humanity, Or Ancient Pathology?" *Human Quest* (July/August 1999) http://www.findarticles.com/p/articles/mi_qa3861/is_199907/ai_n8853324

__________. "Jesus Did Not Die for Our Sins," *Catholic New Times* 29:12 (July 3, 2005) http://www.findarticles.com/p/articles/mi_m0MKY/is_12_29/ai_n14863640

__________. "Reforming Christology: He Did Not Die For My Sins!" *Human Quest* (November/December 1999) http://www.findarticles.com/p/articles/mi_qa3861/is_199911/ai_n8871743

__________. "Re-Imagining God in a Post-Tsunami World," *Catholic New Times* 29:4 (13 February 2005) http://findarticles.com/p/articles/mi_mOMKY/is_3_29/ai_n11838806

__________. *Why Christianity Must Change or Die.* New York: HarperSanFrancisco, 1998.

Srajek, Martin. "Messianism: Connections between Cohen, Benjamin, and Derrida," *The Postmodern Jewish Philosophy Bitnetwork* (now *The Journal of Textual Reasoning*) 2:2 (February 1993) http://etext.lib.virginia.edu/journals/tr/archive/pmjp/pmjp2_2.html

Stannard, Russell. *Grounds for Reasonable Belief.* Edinburgh: Scottish Academic Press, 1989.

Stanton, Robert. "Forum: The Reality of Reality," *Skeptical Inquirer*, May/June 1999 http://www.csicop.org/si/9905/reality-of-reality.html

Stecher, Carl. "Looking for God in All the Wrong Places," *Humanist* 58:3 (May-June 1998) http://www.findarticles.com/p/articles/mi_m1374/is_n3_v58/ai_20770510

Steffen, Lloyd. "The Dangerous God: A Profile of William Hamilton," *Christian Century*, (27 September 1989): 844 http://www.religion-online.org/showarticle.asp?title=892

Stein, Ross L. "On the Possibility of an Immediate Experience of God," *The Journal of Liberal Religion* 3:2 (Summer 2002) http://www.meadville.edu/stein_3_2.html

Stenger, Victor J. *God: The Failed Hypothesis—How Science Shows that God Does Not Exist*. Amherst NY: Prometheus Books, 2007.

___________. *Quantum Gods: Creation, Chaos, and the Search for Cosmic Consciousness*. New York: Prometheus Books, 2009.

Swatos, William H. Jr. Review of "Acts of Faith: Explaining the Human Side of Religion," *Sociology of Religion* 63:2 (Summer 2002) http://www.findarticles.com/p/articles/mi_m0SOR/is_2_63/ai_89078713

Sweet, Leonard. "'Personal Lord and Savior:' Christology and the Devotional Image," http://www.leonardsweet.com/includes/ShowSweetenedArticles.asp?articleID=92

Taleb, Nassim Nicholas. *The Black Swan: The Impact of the Highly Improbable*. New York: Random House, 2007.

Tanner, Kathryn. "Incarnation, Cross, and Sacrifice: A Feminist-Inspired Reappraisal," *Anglican Theological Review* (Winter 2004) http://www.findarticles.com/p/articles/mi_qa3818/is_200401/ai_n9347121

Taylor, Jay Werbinox. "Attacking the Soul Hypothesis," *American Atheist Magazine* 42:2 (Spring 2004) http://www.findarticles.com/p/articles/mi_m0OBB/is_2_42/ai_n6100434

Templeton, John Marks, ed. *Evidence of Purpose: Scientists Discover the Creator*. New York: Continuum, 1994.

Thomas, Owen C. "Chaos, Complexity, and God: A Review Essay," *Theology Today* (April 1997): 66-76.

Thompson, Ernest. "Problems with Atonement," *Interpretation* 60:4 (October 2006): 484.

Tipler, Frank. "The Omega Point as Eschaton: Answers to Pannenberg's Questions for Scientists," *Zygon*, 24 (1989): 241-242.

Toolan, David S. "Praying in a Post-Einsteinian Universe," *Cross Currents* 46:4 (Winter 1996-97) http://www.crosscurrents.org/toolin.html

Tucker, William. "Complex Questions: The New Science of Spontaneous Order—Complexity Theory," *Reason* 27:8 (January 1996) http://www.findarticles.com/p/articles/mi_m1568/is_n8_v27/ai_17779895

Ulrich, Stephen M. "The Lynching of Nestorius," *Institute for Holy Land Studies* www.metamind.net/nestor.html

Underhill, James W. "Meaning, Language, And Mind: An Interview with Mark Turner," *Style*, 36:4 (Winter 2002) http://www.findarticles.com/p/articles/mi_m2342/is_4_36/ai_98167920

Van Huyssteen, J. Wentzel, reviewer, "God after Darwin: A Theology of Evolution," *Theology Today* 58:1 (April 2001): 138-139.

__________. "Tradition and the Task of Theology," *Theology Today* (July 1998): 213-228.

Van Ness, Peter H. "Introduction: Spirituality and the Secular Quest," in *Spirituality and the Secular Quest*, ed. Peter H. Van Ness, Vol 22 of *World Spirituality: An Encyclopedic History of the Religious Quest* (New York: Crossroad, 1996), 2.

Ward, Graham, ed., *The Blackwell Companion to Postmodern Theology*. Oxford: Blackwell Publishing, 2005.

Ward, Keith. *Rationality Theology and the Creativity of God*. New York: Pilgrim Press, 1982.

Wax, Heather and Shaw, Gerald. "Master of His Universe," *Science & Spirit* 16:1 (January-February 2005): 28-36.

Wax, Heather. "Concerning Hobbits," *Science & Spirit* 16:1 (January-February 2005): 24.

Weiman, Henry Nelson. *The Source of Human Good*. Carbondale, IL: "Arcturus Books;" Southern Illinois University Press, 1946, 1964.

Weinandy, Thomas G. "Does God Suffer?" *The Online Journal for Philosophy of Religion*, Vol. 2 (2002) http://www.arsdisputandi.org/

Welker, Michael. "God's Eternity, God's Temporality, and Trinitarian Theology," *Theology Today*, 55:3 (October 1998): 317-328.

__________. "Who Is Jesus Christ for Us Today?" *Harvard Theological Review* 95:2 (April 2002): 129-146.

Werth, Barry. *Banquet at Delmonico's: Great Minds, the Gilded Age, and the Triumph of Evolution in America*. New York: Random House, 2009.

White, L. Michael. *From Jesus to Christianity: How Four Generations of Visionaries & Storytellers Created the New Testament and Christian Faith*. New York: HarperCollins, Publishers, 2004.

Whitehead, Alfred North. *Process and Reality: An Essay in Cosmology*. New York: Harper & Brothers, 1929, 1960; Macmillan Company, 1978.

Wiesel, Elie. *The Trial of God: (as it was held on February 25, 1649 in Shamgorod)*. New York: Random House, 1979.

Wilbur, Ken, editor. *Quantum Questions.* Boulder: New Science Library, 1984.

Williams, Rowan. *Arius: Heresy and Tradition.* Grand Rapids: William B. Eerdmans Publishing Co., 2002.

Wilson, Edward O. *Consilience: The Unity of Knowledge.* New York: Alfred A. Knopf, 1998.

Wilson, Mike. "Arius Sleeps with the Fishes," *Cross Currents* 51:1 (Spring 2001) http://www.findarticles.com/p/articles/mi_m2096/is_1_51/ai_74992678

Winerman, Lea. "What We Know Without Knowing How," *Monitor on Psychology* 36:3 (March 2005) http://www.apa.org/monitor/mar05/knowing.html

Wolf, Arnold Jacob. "Jesus and the Jews—Personal Narrative," *Judaism* 42:3 (Summer 1993) http://www.findarticles.com/p/articles/mi_m0411/is_n3_v42/ai_14234300

Worthing, Mark William. *God, Creation, and Contemporary Physics.* Minneapolis: Fortress Press, 1996.

Yonker, Nicholas J. *God, Man, and the Planetary Age: Preface for a Theistic Humanism.* Corvallis, OR: Oregon State University Press, 1978.

Young, Cathy. "Monkeying Around with the Self," *Reason* 32:11 (April 2001) http://www.findarticles.com/p/articles/mi_m1568/is_11_32/ai_72344892

Young, Peter A. "Confessions of a Believer in Exile," *Cross Currents* 48:4 (Winter 1998) http://www.findarticles.com/p/articles/mi_m2096/is_4_48/ai_54064306

Zimmer, Carl. *Soul Made Flesh: The Discovery of the Brain—and How It Changed the World.* New York: Free Press, 2004.

Zulik, Margaret D. "Prophecy and Providence: The Anxiety over Prophetic Authority," *The Journal of Communication and Religion* 26:2 (September 2003).